John Philip Newman,
Jan 13"
1900.

THE

WORKS

OF

THE RIGHT HONORABLE

EDMUND BURKE.

THIRD EDITION.

VOL. VII.

BOSTON:
LITTLE, BROWN, AND COMPANY.
1869.

CONTENTS OF VOL. VII.

———•———

FRAGMENTS AND NOTES

OF

SPEECHES.

₊ During the period of Mr. Burke's Parliamentary labors, some alterations in the Acts of Uniformity, and the repeal of the Test and Corporation Acts, were agitated at various times in the House of Commons. It appears from the state of his manuscript papers, that he had designed to publish some of the Speeches which he delivered in those discussions, and with that view had preserved the following Fragments and detached Notes, which are now given to the public with as much order and connection as their imperfect condition renders them capable of receiving. The Speeches on the Middlesex Election, on shortening the Duration of Parliaments, on the Reform of the Representation in Parliament, on the Bill for explaining the Power of Juries in Prosecutions for Libels, and on the Repeal of the Marriage Act, were found in the same imperfect state.

SPEECH

ON

THE ACTS OF UNIFORMITY.

FEBRUARY 6, 1772.

NOTE.

THE following Speech was occasioned by a petition to the
House of Commons from certain clergymen of the Church of
England, and certain of the two professions of Civil Law and
Physic, and others, praying to be relieved from subscription to
the Thirty-Nine Articles, as required by the Acts of Uniformity.
The persons associated for this purpose were distinguished at the
time by the name of " The Feathers Tavern Association," from
the place where their meetings were usually held. Their petition was presented on the 6th of February, 1772 ; and on a
motion that it should be brought up, the same was negatived on
a division, in which Mr. Burke voted in the majority, by 217
against 71.

SPEECH.

M R. SPEAKER,—I should not trouble the House upon this question, if I could at all acquiesce in many of the arguments, or justify the vote I shall give upon several of the reasons which have been urged in favor of it. I should, indeed, be very much concerned, if I were thought to be influenced to that vote by those arguments.

In particular, I do most exceedingly condemn all such arguments as involve any kind of reflection on the personal character of the gentlemen who have brought in a petition so decent in the style of it, and so constitutional in the mode. Besides the unimpeachable integrity and piety of many of the promoters of this petition, which render those aspersions as idle as they are unjust, such a way of treating the subject can have no other effect than to turn the attention of the House from the merits of the petition, the only thing properly before us, and which we are sufficiently competent to decide upon, to the motives of the petitioners, which belong exclusively to the Great Searcher of Hearts.

We all know that those who loll at their ease in high dignities, whether of the Church or of the State, are commonly averse to all reformation. It is hard to persuade them that there can be anything amiss in establishments which by feeling experience they find to be so very comfortable. It is as true, that, from

the same selfish motives, those who are struggling upwards are apt to find everything wrong and out of
order.   These are truths upon one side and on the
other ; and neither on the one side or the other in
argument are they worth a single farthing.   I wish,
therefore, so much had not been said upon these ill-
chosen, and worse than ill-chosen, these very invidious topics.

I wish still more that the dissensions and animosities which had slept for a century had not been just
now most unseasonably revived.   But if we must be
driven, whether we will or not, to recollect these
unhappy transactions, let our memory be complete
and equitable, let us recollect the whole of them together.   If the Dissenters, as an honorable gentleman has described them, have formerly risen from a
" whining, canting, snivelling generation," to be a
body dreadful and ruinous to all our establishments,
let him call to mind the follies, the violences, the
outrages, and persecutions, that conjured up, very
blamably, but very naturally, that same spirit of retal-
iation.   Let him recollect, along with the injuries, the
services which Dissenters have done to our Church
and to our State.   If they have once destroyed, more
than once they have saved them.   This is but common justice, which they and all mankind have a right
to.

There are, Mr. Speaker, besides these prejudices
and animosities, which I would have wholly removed
from the debate, things more regularly and argu-
mentatively urged against the petition, which, however, do not at all appear to me conclusive.

First, two honorable gentlemen, one near me, the
other, I think, on the other side of the House, assert,

that, if you alter her symbols, you destroy the being
of the Church of England. This, for the sake of the
liberty of that Church, I must absolutely deny. The
Church, like every body corporate, may alter her
laws without changing her identity. As an independent church, professing fallibility, she has claimed
a right of acting without the consent of any other;
as a church, she claims, and has always exercised, a
right of reforming whatever appeared amiss in her
doctrine, her discipline, or her rites. She did so,
when she shook off the Papal supremacy in the reign
of Henry the Eighth, which was an act of the body
of the English Church, as well as of the State (I
don't inquire how obtained). She did so, when she
twice changed the Liturgy in the reign of King Edward, when she then established Articles, which were
themselves a variation from former professions. She
did so, when she cut off three articles from her original forty-two, and reduced them to the present thirty-
nine; and she certainly would not lose her corporate identity, nor subvert her fundamental principles,
though she were to leave ten of the thirty-nine which
remain out of any future confession of her faith. She
would limit her corporate powers, on the contrary,
and she would oppose her fundamental principles, if
she were to deny herself the prudential exercise of
such capacity of reformation. This, therefore, can be
no objection to your receiving the petition.

In the next place, Sir, I am clear, that the Act of
Union, reciting and ratifying one Scotch and one English act of Parliament, has not rendered any change
whatsoever in our Church impossible, but by a dissolution of the union between the two kingdoms.

The honorable gentleman who has last touched

upon that point has not gone quite so far as the gentlemen who first insisted upon it. However, as none of them wholly abandon that post, it will not be safe to leave it behind me unattacked. I believe no one will wish their interpretation of that act to be considered as authentic. What shall we think of the wisdom (to say nothing of the competence) of that legislature which should ordain to itself such a fundamental law, at its outset, as to disable itself from executing its own functions, — which should prevent it from making any further laws, however wanted, and that, too, on the most interesting subject that belongs to human society, and where she most frequently wants its interposition, — which should fix those fundamental laws that are forever to prevent it from adapting itself to its opinions, however clear, or to its own necessities, however urgent? Such an act, Mr. Speaker, would forever put the Church out of its own power; it certainly would put it far above the State, and erect it into that species of independency which it has been the great principle of our policy to prevent.

The act never meant, I am sure, any such unnatural restraint on the joint legislature it was then forming. History shows us what it meant, and all that it could mean with any degree of common sense.

In the reign of Charles the First a violent and ill-considered attempt was made unjustly to establish the platform of the government and the rites of the Church of England in Scotland, contrary to the genius and desires of far the majority of that nation. This usurpation excited a most mutinous spirit in that country. It produced that shocking fanatical Covenant (I mean the Covenant of '36) for forcing their ideas of religion on England, and indeed on all mankind. This became the occasion, at length, of other covenants, and of a Scotch army marching into England to fulfil them; and the Parliament of England (for its own purposes) adopted their scheme, took their last covenant, and destroyed the Church of England. The Parliament, in their ordinance of 1643, expressly assign their desire of conforming to the Church of Scotland as a motive for their alteration.

To prevent such violent enterprises on the one side or on the other, since each Church was going to be disarmed of a legislature wholly and peculiarly affected to it, and lest this new uniformity in the State should be urged as a reason and ground of ecclesiastical uniformity, the Act of Union provided that presbytery should continue the Scotch, as episcopacy the English establishment, and that this separate and mutually independent Church-government was to be considered as a part of the Union, without aiming at putting the regulation within each Church out of its own power, without putting both Churches out of the power of the State. It could not mean to forbid us to set anything ecclesiastical in order, but at the expense of tearing up all foundations, and forfeiting the inestimable benefits (for inestimable they are) which we derive from the happy union of the two kingdoms. To suppose otherwise is to suppose that the act intended we could not meddle at all with the Church, but we must as a preliminary destroy the State.

Well, then, Sir, this is, I hope, satisfactory. The Act of Union does not stand in our way. But, Sir, gentlemen think we are not competent to the reformation desired, chiefly from our want of theological learning. If we were the legal assembly . . . .

If ever there was anything to which, from reason, nature, habit, and principle, I am totally averse, it is persecution for conscientious difference in opinion. If these gentlemen complained justly of any compulsion upon them on that article, I would hardly wait for their petitions; as soon as I knew the evil, I would haste to the cure; I would even run before their complaints.

I will not enter into the abstract merits of our Articles and Liturgy. Perhaps there are some things in them which one would wish had not been there. They are not without the marks and characters of human frailty.

But it is not human frailty and imperfection, and even a considerable degree of them, that becomes a ground for your alteration; for by no alteration will you get rid of those errors, however you may delight yourselves in varying to infinity the fashion of them. But the ground for a legislative alteration of a legal establishment is this, and this only, — that you find the inclinations of the majority of the people, concurring with your own sense of the intolerable nature of the abuse, are in favor of a change.

If this be the case in the present instance, certainly you ought to make the alteration that is proposed, to satisfy your own consciences, and to give content to your people. But if you have no evidence of this nature, it ill becomes your gravity, on the petition of a few gentlemen, to listen to anything that tends to shake one of the capital pillars of the state, and alarm the body of your people upon that one ground, in which every hope and fear, every interest, passion, prejudice, everything which can affect the human breast, are all involved together. If you make this a season for religious alterations, depend upon it, you will soon find it a season of religious tumults and religious wars.

These gentlemen complain of hardship. No considerable number shows discontent; but, in order to give satisfaction to any number of respectable men, who come in so decent and constitutional a mode before us, let us examine a little what that hardship is. They want to be preferred clergymen in the Church of England as by law established; but their consciences will not suffer them to conform to the doctrines and practices of that Church: that is, they want to be teachers in a church to which they do not belong; and it is an odd sort of hardship. They want to receive the emoluments appropriated for teaching one set of doctrines, whilst they are teaching another. A church, in any legal sense, is only a certain system of religious doctrines and practices fixed and ascertained by some law, — by the difference of which laws different churches (as different commonwealths) are made in various parts of the world; and the establishment is a tax laid by the same sovereign authority for payment of those who so teach and so practise: for no legislature was ever so absurd as to tax its people to support men for teaching and acting as they please, but by some prescribed rule.

The hardship amounts to this, — that the people of England are not taxed two shillings in the pound to pay them for teaching, as divine truths, their own particular fancies. For the state has so taxed the people; and by way of relieving these gentlemen, it would be a cruel hardship on the people to be compelled to pay, from the sweat of their brow, the most heavy of all taxes to men, to condemn as heretical the doctrines which they repute to be orthodox, and to reprobate as superstitious the practices which they use as pious and holy. If a man leaves by will an establishment for preaching, such as Boyle's Lectures, or for charity sermons, or funeral sermons, shall any one complain of an hardship, because he has an excellent sermon upon matrimony, or on the martyrdom of King Charles, or on the Restoration, which I, the trustee of the establishment, will not pay him for preaching? — S. Jenyns, Origin of Evil. — Such is the hardship which they complain of under the present Church establishment, that they have not the power of taxing the people of England for the maintenance of their private opinions.

The laws of toleration provide for every real grievance that these gentlemen can rationally complain of. Are they hindered from professing their belief of what they think to be truth? If they do not like the Establishment, there are an hundred different modes of Dissent in which they may teach. But even if they are so unfortunately circumstanced that of all that variety none will please them, they have free liberty to assemble a congregation of their own; and if any persons think their fancies (they may be brilliant imaginations) worth paying for, they are at liberty to maintain them as their clergy: nothing hinders it. But if they cannot get an hundred people together who will pay for their reading a liturgy after their form, with what face can they insist upon the nation's conforming to their ideas, for no other visible purpose than the enabling them to receive with a good conscience the tenth part of the produce of your lands?

Therefore, beforehand, the Constitution has thought

proper to take a security that the tax raised on the people shall be applied only to those who profess such doctrines and follow such a mode of worship as the legislature, representing the people, has thought most agreeable to their general sense, — binding, as usual, the minority, not to an assent to the doctrines, but to a payment of the tax.

But how do you ease and relieve? How do you know, that, in making a new door into the Church for these gentlemen, you do not drive ten times their number out of it? Supposing the contents and not-contents strictly equal in numbers and consequence, the possession, to avoid disturbance, ought to carry it. You displease all the clergy of England now actually in office, for the chance of obliging a score or two, perhaps, of gentlemen, who are, or want to be, beneficed clergymen: and do you oblige? Alter your Liturgy, — will it please all even of those who wish an alteration? will they agree in what ought to be altered? And after it is altered to the mind of every one, you are no further advanced than if you had not taken a single step; because a large body of men will then say you ought to have no liturgy at all: and then these men, who now complain so bitterly that they are shut out, will themselves bar the door against thousands of others. Dissent, not satisfied with toleration, is not conscience, but ambition.

You altered the Liturgy for the Directory. This was settled by a set of most learned divines and learned laymen: Selden sat amongst them. Did this please? It was considered upon both sides as a most unchristian imposition. Well, at the Restoration they rejected the Directory, and reformed the Common Prayer, — which, by the way, had been three times reformed before. Were they then contented? Two thousand (or some great number) of clergy resigned their livings in one day rather than read it: and truly, rather than raise that second idol, I should have adhered to the Directory, as I now adhere to the Common Prayer. Nor can you content other men's conscience, real or pretended, by any concessions : follow your own ; seek peace and ensue it. You have no symptoms of discontent in the people to their Establishment. The churches are too small for their congregations. The livings are too few for their candidates. The spirit of religious controversy has slackened by the nature of things : by act you may revive it. I will not enter into the question, how much truth is preferable to peace. Perhaps truth may be far better. But as we have scarcely ever the same certainty in the one that we have in the other, I would, unless the truth were evident indeed, hold fast to peace, which has in her company charity, the highest of the virtues.

This business appears in two points of view : 1st, Whether it is a matter of grievance ; 2nd, Whether it is within our province to redress it with propriety and prudence. Whether it comes properly before us on a petition upon matter of grievance I would not inquire too curiously. I know, technically speaking, that nothing agreeable to law can be considered as a grievance. But an over-attention to the rules of any act does sometimes defeat the ends of it ; and I think it does so in this Parliamentary act, as much at least as in any other. I know many gentlemen think that the very essence of liberty consists in being governed according to law, as if grievances had nothing real and intrinsic ; but I cannot be of that opinion.

Grievances may subsist by law. Nay, I do not know whether any grievance can be considered as intolerable, until it is established and sanctified by law. If the Act of Toleration were not perfect, if there were a complaint of it, I would gladly consent to amend it. But when I heard a complaint of a pressure on religious liberty, to my astonishment I find that there was no complaint whatsoever of the insufficiency of the act of King William, nor any attempt to make it more sufficient. The matter, therefore, does not concern toleration, but establishment; and it is not the rights of private conscience that are in question, but the propriety of the terms which are proposed by law as a title to public emoluments: so that the complaint is not, that there is not toleration of diversity in opinion, but that diversity in opinion is not rewarded by bishoprics, rectories, and collegiate stalls. When gentlemen complain of the subscription as matter of grievance, the complaint arises from confounding private judgment, whose rights are anterior to law, and the qualifications which the law creates for its own magistracies, whether civil or religious. To take away from men their lives, their liberty, or their property, those things for the protection of which society was introduced, is great hardship and intolerable tyranny; but to annex any condition you please to benefits artificially created is the most just, natural, and proper thing in the world. When *e novo* you form an arbitrary benefit, an advantage, preëminence, or emolument, not by Nature, but institution, you order and modify it with all the power of a creator over his creature. Such benefits of institution are royalty, nobility, priesthood, all of which you may limit to birth: you might prescribe even shape and stature. The Jewish priesthood was hereditary. Founders' kinsmen have a preference in the election of fellows in many colleges of our universities: the qualifications at All Souls are, that they should be *optime nati, bene vestiti, mediocriter docti.*

By contending for liberty in the candidate for orders, you take away the liberty of the elector, which is the people, that is, the state. If they can choose, they may assign a reason for their choice; if they can assign a reason, they may do it in writing, and prescribe it as a condition; they may transfer their authority to their representatives, and enable them to exercise the same. In all human institutions, a great part, almost all regulations, are made from the mere necessity of the case, let the theoretical merits of the question be what they will. For nothing happened at the Reformation but what will happen in all such revolutions. When tyranny is extreme, and abuses of government intolerable, men resort to the rights of Nature to shake it off. When they have done so, the very same principle of necessity of human affairs to establish some other authority, which shall preserve the order of this new institution, must be obeyed, until they grow intolerable; and you shall not be suffered to plead original liberty against such an institution. See Holland, Switzerland.

If you will have religion publicly practised and publicly taught, you must have a power to say what that religion will be which you will protect and encourage, and to distinguish it by such marks and characteristics as you in your wisdom shall think fit. As I said before, your determination may be unwise in this as in other matters; but it cannot be unjust, hard, or oppressive, or contrary to the liberty of

any man, or in the least degree exceeding your province. It is, therefore, as a grievance, fairly none at
all, — nothing but what is essential, not only to the
order, but to the liberty, of the whole community.

The petitioners are so sensible of the force of these
arguments, that they do admit of one subscription, —
that is, to the Scripture. I shall not consider how
forcibly this argument militates with their whole
principle against subscription as an usurpation on
the rights of Providence : I content myself with
submitting to the consideration of the House, that,
if that rule were once established, it must have some
authority to enforce the obedience ; because, you well
know, a law without a sanction will be ridiculous.
Somebody must sit in judgment on his conformity ;
he must judge on the charge ; if he judges, he must
ordain execution. These things are necessary consequences one of the other ; and then this judgment
is an equal and a superior violation of private judgment ; the right of private judgment is violated in
a much greater degree than it can be by any previous
subscription. You come round again to subscription,
as the best and easiest method ; men must judge of
his doctrine, and judge definitively : so that either his
test is nugatory, or men must first or last prescribe
his public interpretation of it.

If the Church be, as Mr. Locke defines it, *a voluntary society*, &c., then it is essential to this voluntary
society to exclude from her voluntary society any
member she thinks fit, or to oppose the entrance of
any upon such conditions as she thinks proper. For,
otherwise, it would be a voluntary society acting contrary to her will, which is a contradiction in terms.
And this is Mr. Locke's opinion, the advocate for the

largest scheme of ecclesiastical and civil toleration to
Protestants (for to Papists he allows no toleration at
all).

They dispute only the extent of the subscription;
they therefore tacitly admit the equity of the principle itself. Here they do not resort to the original
rights of Nature, because it is manifest that those
rights give as large a power of controverting every
part of Scripture, or even the authority of the whole,
as they do to the controverting any articles whatsoever. When a man requires you to sign an assent to
Scripture, he requires you to assent to a doctrine as
contrary to your natural understanding, and to your
rights of free inquiry, as those who require your conformity to any one article whatsoever.

The subscription to Scripture is the most astonishing idea I ever heard, and will amount to just nothing at all. Gentlemen so acute have not, that I have
heard, ever thought of answering a plain, obvious
question: What is that Scripture to which they are
content to subscribe? They do not think that a book
becomes of divine authority because it is bound in
blue morocco, and is printed by John Baskett and his
assigns. The Bible is a vast collection of different
treatises: a man who holds the divine authority of
one may consider the other as merely human. What
is his Canon? The Jewish? St. Jerome's? that of
the Thirty-Nine Articles? Luther's? There are some
who reject the Canticles; others, six of the Epistles;
the Apocalypse has been suspected even as heretical,
and was doubted of for many ages, and by many great
men. As these narrow the Canon, others have enlarged it by admitting St. Barnabas's Epistles, the
Apostolic Constitutions, to say nothing of many oth-

er Gospels. Therefore, to ascertain Scripture, you must have one article more; and you must define what that Scripture is which you mean to teach. There are, I believe, very few who, when Scripture is so ascertained, do not see the absolute necessity of knowing what general doctrine a man draws from it, before he is sent down authorized by the state to teach it as pure doctrine, and receive a tenth of the produce of our lands.

The Scripture is no one summary of doctrines regularly digested, in which a man could not mistake his way. It is a most venerable, but most multifarious, collection of the records of the divine economy : a collection of an infinite variety, — of cosmogony, theology, history, prophecy, psalmody, morality, apologue, allegory, legislation, ethics, carried through different books, by different authors, at different ages, for different ends and purposes. It is necessary to sort out what is intended for example, what only as narrative, — what to be understood literally, what figuratively, — where one precept is to be controlled and modified by another, — what is used directly, and what only as an argument *ad hominem*, — what is temporary, and what of perpetual obligation, — what appropriated to one state and to one set of men, and what the general duty of all Christians. If we do not get some security for this, we not only permit, but we actually pay for, all the dangerous fanaticism which can be produced to corrupt our people, and to derange the public worship of the country. We owe the best we can (not infallibility, but prudence) to the subject, — first sound doctrine, then ability to use it.

SPEECH

ON

A BILL FOR THE RELIEF OF PROTESTANT DISSENTERS.

MARCH 17, 1773.

NOTE.

THIS speech is given partly from the manuscript papers of Mr. Burke, and partly from a very imperfect short-hand note taken at the time by a member of the House of Commons. The bill under discussion was opposed by petitions from several congregations calling themselves " Protestant Dissenters," who appear to have been principally composed of the people who are generally known under the denomination of " Methodists," and particularly by a petition from a congregation of that description residing in the town of Chatham.

SPEECH.

I ASSURE you, Sir, that the honorable gentleman who spoke last but one need not be in the least fear that I should make a war of particles upon his opinion, whether the Church of England *should*, *would*, or *ought* to be alarmed. I am very clear that this House has no one reason in the world to think she is alarmed by the bill brought before you. It is something extraordinary that the only symptom of alarm in the Church of England should appear in the petition of some Dissenters, with whom, I believe, very few in this House are yet acquainted, and of whom you know no more than that you are assured by the honorable gentleman that they are not Mahometans. Of the Church we know they are not, by the name that they assume. They are, then, Dissenters. The first symptom of an alarm comes from some Dissenters assembled round the lines of Chatham : these lines become the security of the Church of England! The honorable gentleman, in speaking of the lines of Chatham, tells us that they serve not only for the security of the wooden walls of England, but for the defence of the Church of England. I suspect the wooden walls of England secure the lines of Chatham, rather than the lines of Chatham secure the wooden walls of England.

Sir, the Church of England, if only defended by this miserable petition upon your table, must, I am afraid, upon the principles of true fortification, be soon destroyed. But, fortunately, her walls, bulwarks, and bastions are constructed of other materials than of stubble and straw, — are built up with the strong and stable matter of the gospel of liberty, and founded on a true, constitutional, legal establishment. But, Sir, she has other securities : she has the security of her own doctrines; she has the security of the piety, the sanctity, of her own professors, — their learning is a bulwark to defend her ; she has the security of the two universities, not shook in any single battlement, in any single pinnacle.

But the honorable gentleman has mentioned, indeed, principles which astonish me rather more than ever. The honorable gentleman thinks that the Dissenters enjoy a large share of liberty under a connivance ; and he thinks that the establishing toleration by law is an attack upon Christianity.

The first of these is a contradiction in terms. Liberty under a connivance ! Connivance is a relaxation from slavery, not a definition of liberty. What is connivance, but a state under which all slaves live ? If I was to describe slavery, I would say, with those who *hate* it, it is living under will, not under law ; if as it is stated by its advocates, I would say, that, like earthquakes, like thunder, or other wars the elements make upon mankind, it happens rarely, it occasionally comes now and then upon people, who, upon ordinary occasions, enjoy the same legal government of liberty. Take it under the description of those who would soften those features, the state of slavery and connivance is the same thing. If the liberty enjoyed be a liberty not of toleration, but of connivance, the only question is, whether establishing such by law is an

attack upon Christianity. Toleration an attack upon
Christianity! What, then! are we come to this pass,
to suppose that nothing can support Christianity but
the principles of persecution? Is that, then, the idea
of establishment? Is it, then, the idea of Christianity itself, that it ought to have establishments, that it
ought to have laws against Dissenters, but the breach
of which laws is to be connived at? What a picture
of toleration! what a picture of laws, of establishments! what a picture of religious and civil liberty!
I am persuaded the honorable gentleman does not
see it in this light. But these very terms become
the strongest reasons for my support of tne bill: for I
am persuaded that toleration, so far from being an
attack upon Christianity, becomes the best and surest
support that possibly can be given to it. The Christian religion itself arose without establishment, — it
arose even without toleration; and whilst its own
principles were not tolerated, it conquered all the
powers of darkness, it conquered all the powers of the
world. The moment it began to depart from these
principles, it converted the establishment into tyranny; it subverted its foundations from that very hour.
Zealous as I am for the principle of an establishment,
so just an abhorrence do I conceive against whatever may shake it. I know nothing but the supposed
necessity of persecution that can make an establishment disgusting. I would have toleration a part of
establishment, as a principle favorable to Christianity,
and as a part of Christianity.

All seem agreed that the law, as it stands, inflict-
ing penalties on all religious teachers and on school-
masters who do not sign the Thirty-Nine Articles
of Religion, ought not to be executed. We are all

agreed that *the law is not good :* for that, I presume, is undoubtedly the idea of a law that ought not to be executed. The question, therefore, is, whether in a well-constituted commonwealth, which we desire ours to be thought, and I trust intend that it should be, whether in such a commonwealth it is wise to retain those laws which it is not proper to execute. A penal law not ordinarily put in execution seems to me to be a very absurd and a very dangerous thing. For if its principle be right, if the object of its prohibitions and penalties be a real evil, then you do in effect permit that very evil, which not only the reason of the thing, but your very law, declares ought not to be permitted; and thus it reflects exceedingly on the wisdom, and consequently derogates not a little from the authority, of a legislature who can at once forbid and suffer, and in the same breath promulgate penalty and in-demnity to the same persons and for the very same actions. But if the object of the law be no moral or political evil, then you ought not to hold even a ter-ror to those whom you ought certainly not to punish: for if it is not right to hurt, it is neither right nor wise to menace. Such laws, therefore, as they must be defective either in justice or wisdom or both, so they cannot exist without a considerable degree of danger. Take them which way you will, they are pressed with ugly alternatives.

1st. All penal laws are either upon popular pros-ecution, or on the part of the crown. Now if they may be roused from their sleep, whenever a minister thinks proper, as instruments of oppression, then they put vast bodies of men into a state of slavery and court dependence; since their liberty of conscience and their power of executing their functions depend entirely on his will. I would have no man derive his means of continuing any function, or his being restrained from it, but from the laws only : they should be his only superior and sovereign lords.

2nd. They put statesmen and magistrates into an habit of playing fast and loose with the laws, straining or relaxing them as may best suit their political purposes, — and in that light tend to corrupt the executive power through all its offices.

3rd. If they are taken up on popular actions, their operation in that light also is exceedingly evil. They become the instruments of private malice, private avarice, and not of public regulation ; they nourish the worst of men to the prejudice of the best, punishing tender consciences, and rewarding informers.

Shall we, as the honorable gentleman tells us we may with perfect security, trust to the manners of the age ? I am well pleased with the general manners of the times ; but the desultory execution of penal laws, the thing I condemn, does not depend on the manners of the times. I would, however, have the laws tuned in unison with the manners. Very dissonant are a gentle country and cruel laws ; very dissonant, that your reason is furious, but your passions moderate, and that you are always equitable except in your courts of justice.

I will beg leave to state to the House one argument which has been much relied upon : that the Dissenters are not unanimous upon this business ; that many persons are alarmed ; that it will create a disunion among the Dissenters.

When any Dissenters, or any body of people, come here with a petition, it is not the number of people, but the reasonableness of the request, that should weigh with the House. A body of Dissenters come to this House, and say, "Tolerate us: we desire neither the parochial advantage of tithes, nor dignities, nor the stalls of your cathedrals: no! let the venerable orders of the hierarchy exist with all their advantages." And shall I tell them, "I reject your just and reasonable petition, not because it shakes the Church, but because there are others, while you lie grovelling upon the earth, that will kick and bite you"? Judge which of these descriptions of men comes with a fair request: that which says, "Sir, I desire liberty for my own, because I trespass on no man's conscience," — or the other, which says, "I desire that these men should not be suffered to act according to their consciences, though I am tolerated to act according to mine. But I sign a body of Articles, which is my title to toleration; I sign no more, because more are against my conscience. But I desire that you will not tolerate these men, because they will not go so far as I, though I desire to be tolerated, who will not go as far as you. No, imprison them, if they come within five miles of a corporate town, because they do not believe what I do in point of doctrines." Shall I not say to these men, *Arrangez-vous, canaille?* You, who are not the predominant power, will not give to others the relaxation under which you are yourself suffered to live. I have as high an opinion of the doctrines of the Church as you. I receive them implicitly, or I put my own explanation on them, or take that which seems to me to come best recommended by authority. There are those of the Dissenters who think more rigidly of the doctrine of the Articles relative to Predestination

than others do. They sign the Article relative to
it *ex animo*, and literally. Others allow a latitude of
construction. These two parties are in the Church,
as well as among the Dissenters; yet in the Church
we live quietly under the same roof. I do not see
why, as long as Providence gives us no further light
into this great mystery, we should not leave things
as the Divine Wisdom has left them. But suppose
all these things to me to be clear, (which Providence,
however, seems to have left obscure,) yet, whilst Dissenters claim a toleration in things which, seeming
clear to me, are obscure to them, without entering
into the merit of the Articles, with what face can
these men say, "Tolerate us, but do not tolerate
them"? Toleration is good for all, or it is good for
none.

The discussion this day is not between establishment on one hand and toleration on the other, but
between those who, being tolerated themselves, refuse
toleration to others. That power should be puffed
up with pride, that authority should degenerate into
rigor, if not laudable, is but too natural. But this
proceeding of theirs is much beyond the usual allowance to human weakness: it not only is shocking to
our reason, but it provokes our indignation. *Quid
domini facient, audent cum talia fures?* It is not the
proud prelate thundering in his Commission Court,
but a pack of manumitted slaves, with the lash of the
beadle flagrant on their backs, and their legs still
galled with their fetters, that would drive their
brethren into that prison-house from whence they
have just been permitted to escape. If, instead of
puzzling themselves in the depths of the Divine counsels, they would turn to the mild morality of the

Gospel, they would read their own condemnation: —
" O thou wicked servant, I forgave thee all that debt
because thou desiredst me: shouldest not thou also
have compassion on thy fellow-servant, even as I had
pity on thee ? "

In my opinion, Sir, a magistrate, whenever he goes
to put any restraint upon religious freedom, can only
do it upon this ground, — that the person dissenting
does not dissent from the scruples of ill-informed conscience, but from a party ground of dissension, in
order to raise a faction in the state. We give, with
regard to rites and ceremonies, an indulgence to tender consciences. But if dissent is at all punished in
any country, if at all it can be punished upon any
pretence, it is upon a presumption, not that a man is
supposed to differ conscientiously from the establishment, but that he resists truth for the sake of faction,
— that he abets diversity of opinions in religion to
distract the state, and to destroy the peace of his
country. This is the only plausible, — for there is
no true ground of persecution. As the laws stand,
therefore, let us see how we have thought fit to
act.

If there is any one thing within the competency of
a magistrate with regard to religion, it is this: that
he has a right to direct the exterior ceremonies of
religion ; that, whilst interior religion is within the
jurisdiction of God alone, the external part, bodily
action, is within the province of the chief governor.
Hooker, and all the great lights of the Church, have
constantly argued this to be a part within the province of the civil magistrate. But look at the Act of
Toleration of William and Mary: there you will see
the civil magistrate has not only dispensed with those

things which are more particularly within his province, with those things which faction might be supposed to take up for the sake of making visible and
external divisions and raising a standard of revolt,
but has also from sound politic considerations relaxed
on those points which are confessedly without his
province.

The honorable gentleman, speaking of the heathens, certainly could not mean to recommend anything that is derived from that impure source. But
he has praised the tolerating spirit of the heathens.
Well! but the honorable gentleman will recollect that
heathens, that polytheists, must permit a number of
divinities. It is the very essence of its constitution.
But was it ever heard that polytheism tolerated a dissent from a polytheistic establishment, — the belief
of one God only? Never! never! Sir, they constantly carried on persecution against that doctrine.
I will not give heathens the glory of a doctrine which
I consider the best part of Christianity. The honorable gentleman must recollect the Roman law, that
was clearly against the introduction of any foreign
rites in matters of religion. You have it at large in
Livy, how they persecuted in the first introduction
the rites of Bacchus; and even before Christ, to say
nothing of their subsequent persecutions, they persecuted the Druids and others. Heathenism, therefore,
as in other respects erroneous, was erroneous in point
of persecution. I do not say every heathen who persecuted was therefore an impious man : I only say he
was mistaken, as such a man is now. But, says the
honorable gentleman, they did not persecute Epicureans. No : the Epicureans had no quarrel with their
religious establishment, nor desired any religion for

themselves. It would have been very extraordinary, if irreligious heathens had desired either a religious establishment or toleration. But, says the honorable gentleman, the Epicureans entered, as others, into the temples. They did so; they defied all subscription; they defied all sorts of conformity; there was no subscription to which they were not ready to set their hands, no ceremonies they refused to practise; they made it a principle of their irreligion outwardly to conform to any religion. These atheists eluded all that you could do: so will all freethinkers forever. Then you suffer, or the weakness of your law has suffered, those great dangerous animals to escape notice, whilst you have nets that entangle the poor fluttering silken wings of a tender conscience.

The honorable gentleman insists much upon this circumstance of objection, — namely, the division amongst the Dissenters. Why, Sir, the Dissenters, by the nature of the term, are open to have a division among themselves. They are Dissenters because they differ from the Church of England: not that they agree among themselves. There are Presbyterians, there are Independents,—some that do not agree to infant baptism, others that do not agree to the baptism of adults, or any baptism. All these are, however, tolerated under the acts of King William, and subsequent acts; and their diversity of sentiments with one another did not and could not furnish an argument against their toleration, when their difference with ourselves furnished none.

But, says the honorable gentleman, if you suffer them to go on, they will shake the fundamental principles of Christianity. Let it be considered, that this argument goes as strongly against connivance, which you allow, as against toleration, which you reject. The gentleman sets out with a principle of perfect liberty, or, as he describes it, connivance. But, for fear of dangerous opinions, you leave it in your power to vex a man who has not held any one dangerous opinion whatsoever. If one man is a professed atheist, another man the best Christian, but dissents from two of the Thirty-Nine Articles, I may let escape the atheist, because I know him to be an atheist, because I am, perhaps, so inclined myself, and because I may connive where I think proper; but the conscientious Dissenter, on account of his attachment to that general religion which perhaps I hate, I shall take care to punish, because I may punish when I think proper. Therefore, connivance being an engine of private malice or private favor, not of good government, — an engine which totally fails of suppressing atheism, but oppresses conscience, — I say that principle becomes, not serviceable, but dangerous to Christianity; that it is not toleration, but contrary to it, even contrary to peace; that the penal system to which it belongs is a dangerous principle in the economy either of religion or government.

The honorable gentleman (and in him I comprehend all those who oppose the bill) bestowed in support of their side of the question as much argument as it could bear, and much more of learning and decoration than it deserved. He thinks connivance consistent, but legal toleration inconsistent, with the interests of Christianity. Perhaps I would go as far as that honorable gentleman, if I thought toleration inconsistent with those interests. God forbid! I may be mistaken, but I take toleration to be a part of religion. I do not know which I would sacrifice:

I would keep them both : it is not necessary I should sacrifice either. I do not like the idea of tolerating the doctrines of Epicurus : but nothing in the world propagates them so much as the oppression of the poor, of the honest and candid disciples of the religion we profess in common, — I mean revealed religion ; nothing sooner makes them take a short cut out of the bondage of sectarian vexation into open and direct infidelity than tormenting men for every difference. My opinion is, that, in establishing the Christian religion wherever you find it, curiosity or research is its best security ; and in this way a man is a great deal better justified in saying, Tolerate all kinds of consciences, than in imitating the heathens, whom the honorable gentleman quotes, in tolerating those who have none. I am not over-fond of calling for the secular arm upon these misguided or misguiding men ; but if ever it ought to be raised, it ought surely to be raised against these very men, not against others, whose liberty of religion you make a pretext for proceedings which drive them into the bondage of impiety. What figure do I make in saying, I do not attack the works of these atheistical writers, but I will keep a rod hanging over the conscientious man, their bitterest enemy, because these atheists may take advantage of the liberty of their foes to introduce irreligion ? The best book that ever, perhaps, has been written against these people is that in which the author has collected in a body the whole of the infidel code, and has brought the writers into one body to cut them all off together. This was done by a Dissenter, who never did subscribe the Thirty-Nine Articles, — Dr. Leland. But if, after all this, danger is to be apprehended, if you

are really fearful that Christianity will indirectly suffer by this liberty, you have my free consent: go directly, and by the straight way, and not by a circuit
in which in your road you may destroy your friends;
point your arms against these men who do the mischief you fear promoting; point your arms against
men who, not contented with endeavoring to turn
your eyes from the blaze and effulgence of light by
which life and immortality is so gloriously demonstrated by the Gospel, would even extinguish that
faint glimmering of Nature, that only comfort supplied to ignorant man before this great illumination,
— them who, by attacking even the possibility of
all revelation, arraign all the dispensations of Providence to man. These are the wicked Dissenters you
ought to fear; these are the people against whom
you ought to aim the shaft of the law; these are
the men to whom, arrayed in all the terrors of government, I would say, You shall not degrade us into
brutes! These men, these factious men, as the honorable gentleman properly called them, are the just
objects of vengeance, not the conscientious Dissenter,
— these men, who would take away whatever enno-
bles the rank or consoles the misfortunes of human
nature, by breaking off that connection of observan-
ces, of affections, of hopes and fears, which bind us
to the Divinity, and constitute the glorious and distinguishing prerogative of humanity, that of being a
religious creature: against these I would have the
laws rise in all their majesty of terrors, to fulminate
such vain and impious wretches, and to awe them
into impotence by the only dread they can fear or
believe, to learn that eternal lesson, *Discite justitiam moniti, et non temnere Divos!*

At the same time that I would cut up the very root of atheism, I would respect all conscience, — all conscience that is really such, and which perhaps its very tenderness proves to be sincere. I wish to see the Established Church of England great and powerful; I wish to see her foundations laid low and deep, that she may crush the giant powers of rebellious darkness; I would have her head raised up to that heaven to which she conducts us. I would have her open wide her hospitable gates by a noble and liberal comprehension, but I would have no breaches in her wall; I would have her cherish all those who are within, and pity all those who are without; I would have her a common blessing to the world, an example, if not an instructor, to those who have not the happiness to belong to her; I would have her give a lesson of peace to mankind, that a vexed and wandering generation might be taught to seek for repose and toleration in the maternal bosom of Christian charity, and not in the harlot lap of infidelity and indifference. Nothing has driven people more into that house of seduction than the mutual hatred of Christian congregations. Long may we enjoy our church under a learned and edifying episcopacy! But episcopacy may fail, and religion exist. The most horrid and cruel blow that can be offered to civil society is through atheism. Do not promote diversity; when you have it, bear it; have as many sorts of religion as you find in your country; there is a reasonable worship in them all. The others, the infidels, are outlaws of the constitution, not of this country, but of the human race. They are never, never to be supported, never to be tolerated. Under the systematic attacks of these people, I see some of

the props of good government already begin to fail; I
see propagated principles which will not leave to religion even a toleration. I see myself sinking every
day under the attacks of these wretched people. How
shall I arm myself against them? By uniting all
those in affection, who are united in the belief of
the great principles of the Godhead that made and
sustains the world. They who hold revelation give
double assurance to their country. Even the man
who does not hold revelation, yet who wishes that it
were proved to him, who observes a pious silence with
regard to it, such a man, though not a Christian, is
governed by religious principles. Let him be tolerated in this country. Let it be but a serious religion,
natural or revealed, take what you can get. Cherish,
blow up the slightest spark: one day it may be a
pure and holy flame. By this proceeding you form
an alliance offensive and defensive against those great
ministers of darkness in the world who are endeavoring to shake all the works of God established in
order and beauty.

Perhaps I am carried too far; but it is in the road
into which the honorable gentleman has led me. The
honorable gentleman would have us fight this confederacy of the powers of darkness with the single arm
of the Church of England, — would have us not only
fight against infidelity, but fight at the same time
with all the faith in the world except our own. In
the moment we make a front against the common enemy, we have to combat with all those who are the
natural friends of our cause. Strong as we are, we
are not equal to this. The cause of the Church of
England is included in that of religion, not that of
religion in the Church of England. I will stand up

at all times for the rights of conscience, as it is such, — not for its particular modes against its general principles. One may be right, another mistaken; but if I have more strength than my brother, it shall be employed to support, not to oppress his weakness; if I have more light, it shall be used to guide, not to dazzle him. . . . .

SPEECH

ON A

MOTION MADE IN THE HOUSE OF COMMONS BY THE RIGHT HON. C. J. FOX,

MAY 11, 1792,

FOR LEAVE TO BRING IN

A BILL TO REPEAL AND ALTER CERTAIN ACTS RESPECTING RELIGIOUS OPINIONS,

UPON THE OCCASION OF

A PETITION OF THE UNITARIAN SOCIETY.

SPEECH.

* * * * *

I NEVER govern myself, no rational man ever did govern himself, by abstractions and universals. I do not put abstract ideas wholly out of any question; because I well know that under that name I should dismiss principles, and that without the guide and light of sound, well-understood principles, all reasonings in politics, as in everything else, would be only a confused jumble of particular facts and details, without the means of drawing out any sort of theoretical or practical conclusion. A statesman differs from a professor in an university: the latter has only the general view of society; the former, the statesman, has a number of circumstances to combine with those general ideas, and to take into his consideration. Circumstances are infinite, are infinitely combined, are variable and transient: he who does not take them into consideration is not erroneous, but stark mad; *dat operam ut cum ratione insaniat;* he is metaphysically mad. A statesman, never losing sight of principles, is to be guided by circumstances; and judging contrary to the exigencies of the moment, he may ruin his country forever.

I go on this ground, — that government, representing the society, has a general superintending control over all the actions and over all the publicly propagated doctrines of men, without which it never could provide adequately for all the wants of society : but then it is to use this power with an equitable discretion, the only bond of sovereign authority. For it is not, perhaps, so much by the assumption of unlawful powers as by the unwise or unwarrantable use of those which are most legal, that governments oppose their true end and object : for there is such a thing as tyranny, as well as usurpation. You can hardly state to me a case to which legislature is the most confessedly competent, in which, if the rules of benignity and prudence are not observed, the most mischievous and oppressive things may not be done. So that, after all, it is a moral and virtuous discretion, and not any abstract theory of right, which keeps governments faithful to their ends. Crude, unconnected truths are in the world of practice what falsehoods are in theory. A reasonable, prudent, provident, and moderate coercion may be a means of preventing acts of extreme ferocity and rigor : for by propagating excessive and extravagant doctrines, such extravagant disorders take place as require the most perilous and fierce corrections to oppose them.

It is not morally true that we are bound to establish in every country that form of religion which in *our* minds is most agreeable to truth, and conduces most to the eternal happiness of mankind. In the same manner, it is not true that we are, against the conviction of our own judgment, to establish a system of opinions and practices directly contrary to those ends, only because some majority of the people, told by the head, may prefer it. No conscientious man would willingly establish what he knew to be false and mischievous in religion, or in anything else. No wise man, on the contrary, would tyrannically set up his own sense so as to reprobate that of the great prevailing body of the community, and pay no regard to the established opinions and prejudices of mankind, or refuse to them the means of securing a religious instruction suitable to these prejudices. A great deal depends on the state in which you find men. . . . .

An alliance between Church and State in a Christian commonwealth is, in my opinion, an idle and a fanciful speculation. An alliance is between two things that are in their nature distinct and independent, such as between two sovereign states. But in a Christian commonwealth the Church and the State are one and the same thing, being different integral parts of the same whole. For the Church has been always divided into two parts, the clergy and the laity, — of which the laity is as much an essential integral part, and has as much its duties and privileges, as the clerical member, and in the rule, order, and government of the Church has its share. Religion is so far, in my opinion, from being out of the province or the duty of a Christian magistrate, that it is, and it ought to be, not only his care, but the principal thing in his care ; because it is one of the great bonds of human society, and its object the supreme good, the ultimate end and object of man himself. The magistrate, who is a man, and charged with the concerns of men, and to whom very specially nothing human is remote and indifferent, has a right and a duty to watch over it with an unceasing vigilance, to protect, to promote, to forward it by every rational, just, and prudent means. It is principally his duty to prevent the abuses which grow out of every strong and efficient principle that actuates the human mind.

As religion is one of the bonds of society, he ought not to suffer it to be made the pretext of destroying its peace, order, liberty, and its security. Above all, he ought strictly to look to it, when men begin to form new combinations, to be distinguished by new names, and especially when they mingle a political system with their religious opinions, true or false, plausible or implausible.

It is the interest, and it is the duty, and because it is the interest and the duty, it is the right of government to attend much to opinions; because, as opinions soon combine with passions, even when they do not produce them, they have much influence on actions. Factions are formed upon opinions, which factions become in effect bodies corporate in the state; nay, factions generate opinions, in order to become a centre of union, and to furnish watchwords to parties; and this may make it expedient for government to forbid things in themselves innocent and neutral. I am not fond of defining with precision what the ultimate rights of the sovereign supreme power, in providing for the safety of the commonwealth, may be, or may not extend to. It will signify very little what my notions or what their own notions on the subject may be; because, according to the exigence, they will take, in fact, the steps which seem to them necessary for the preservation of the whole: for as self-preservation in individuals is the first law of Nature, the same will prevail in societies, who will, right or wrong, make that an object paramount to all other rights whatsoever. There are ways and means by which a good man would not even save the commonwealth. . . . . . All things founded on the idea of danger ought in a great degree to be

temporary. All policy is very suspicious that sacrifices any part to the ideal good of the whole. The
object of the state is (as far as may be) the happiness
of the whole. Whatever makes multitudes of men
utterly miserable can never answer that object; indeed, it contradicts it wholly and entirely ; and the
happiness or misery of mankind, estimated by their
feelings and sentiments, and not by any theories of
their rights, is, and ought to be, the standard for the
conduct of legislators towards the people. This naturally and necessarily conducts us to the peculiar
and characteristic situation of a people, and to a
knowledge of their opinions, prejudices, habits, and
all the circumstances that diversify and color life.
The first question a good statesman would ask himself, therefore, would be, How and in what circumstances do you find the society ? and to act upon
them.

To the other laws relating to other sects I have
nothing to say : I only look to the petition which has
given rise to this proceeding. I confine myself to
that, because in my opinion its merits have little or
no relation to that of the other laws which the right
honorable gentleman has with so much ability blended
with it. With the Catholics, with the Presbyterians,
with the Anabaptists, with the Independents, with the
Quakers, I have nothing at all to do. They are in
possession, — a great title in all human affairs. The
tenor and spirit of our laws, whether they were restraining or whether they were relaxing, have hitherto taken another course. The spirit of our laws has
applied their penalty or their relief to the supposed
abuse to be repressed or the grievance to be relieved ;
and the provision for a Catholic and a Quaker has

been totally different, according to his exigence: you did not give a Catholic liberty to be freed from an oath, or a Quaker power of saying mass with impunity. You have done this, because you never have laid it down as an universal proposition, as a maxim, that nothing relative to religion was your concern, but the direct contrary; and therefore you have always examined whether there was a grievance. It has been so at all times: the legislature, whether right or wrong, went no other way to work but by circumstances, times, and necessities. My mind marches the same road; my school is the practice and usage of Parliament.

Old religious factions are volcanoes burnt out; on the lava and ashes and squalid scoriæ of old eruptions grow the peaceful olive, the cheering vine, and the sustaining corn. Such was the first, such the second condition of Vesuvius. But when a new fire bursts out, a face of desolations comes on, not to be rectified in ages. Therefore, when men come before us, and rise up like an exhalation from the ground, they come in a questionable shape, and we must *exorcise* them, and try whether their intents be wicked or charitable, whether they bring airs from heaven or blasts from hell. This is the first time that our records of Parliament have heard, or our experience or history given us an account of any religious congregation or association known by the name which these petitioners have assumed. We are now to see by what people, of what character, and under what temporary circumstances, this business is brought before you. We are to see whether there be any and what mixture of political dogmas and political practices with their religious tenets, of what nature they are, and how far they are at present practically separable from them. This faction (the authors of the petition) are not confined to a *theological* sect, but are also a *political* faction. 1st, As theological, we are to show that they do not aim at the quiet enjoyment of their own liberty, but are *associated* for the express purpose of proselytism. In proof of this first proposition, read their primary association. 2nd, That their purpose of proselytism is to collect a multitude sufficient by force and violence to overturn the Church. In proof of the second proposition, see the letter of Priestley to Mr. Pitt, and extracts from his works. 3rd, That the designs against the Church are concurrent with a design to subvert the State. In proof of the third proposition, read the advertisement of the Unitarian Society for celebrating the 14th of July. 4th, On what *model* they intend to build,— that it is the *French*. In proof of the fourth proposition, read the correspondence of the Revolution Society with the clubs of France, read Priestley's adherence to their opinions. 5th, What the *French* is with regard to religious toleration, and with regard to, 1. Religion,— 2. Civil happiness,— 3. Virtue, order, and real liberty,— 4. Commercial opulence,— 5. National defence. In proof of the fifth proposition, read the representation of the French minister of the Home Department, and the report of the committee upon it.

Formerly, when the superiority of two parties contending for dogmas and an establishment was the question, we knew in such a contest the whole of the evil. We knew, for instance, that Calvinism would prevail according to the Westminster Catechism with regard to *tenets*. We knew that Presbytery would

prevail in *church government*. But we do not know
what opinions would prevail, if the present Dissenters
should become masters. They will not tell us their
present opinions ; and one principle of modern Dissent is, not to discover them. Next, as their religion
is in a continual fluctuation, and is so by principle
and in profession, it is impossible for us to know
what it will be. If religion only related to the individual, and was a question between God and the conscience, it would not be wise, nor in my opinion
equitable, for human authority to step in. But when
religion is embodied into faction, and factions have
objects to pursue, it will and must, more or less, become a question of power between them. If even,
when embodied into congregations, they limited their
principle to their own congregations, and were satisfied themselves to abstain from what they thought
unlawful, it would be cruel, in my opinion, to molest
them in that tenet, and a consequent practice. But
we know that they not only entertain these opinions,
but entertain them with a zeal for propagating them
by force, and employing the power of law and place
to destroy establishments, if ever they should come
to power sufficient to effect their purpose : that is, in
other words, they declare they would persecute the
heads of our Church ; and the question is, whether
you should keep them within the bounds of toleration, or subject yourself to their persecution.

A bad and very censurable practice it is to warp
doubtful and ambiguous expressions to a perverted
sense, which makes the charge not the crime of others, but the construction of your own malice ; nor is
it allowed to draw conclusions from allowed premises, which those who lay down the premises utterly

deny, and disown as their conclusions. For this, though it may possibly be good logic, cannot by any possibility whatsoever be a fair or charitable representation of any man or any set of men. It may show the erroneous nature of principles, but it argues nothing as to dispositions and intentions. Far be such a mode from me! A mean and unworthy jealousy it would be to do anything upon the mere speculative apprehension of what men will do. But let us pass by *our* opinions concerning the danger of the Church. What do the gentlemen themselves think of that danger? They from whom the danger is apprehended, what do they declare to be their own designs? What do they conceive to be their own forces? And what do they proclaim to be their means? Their designs they declare to be to destroy the Established Church, and not to set up a new one of their own. See Priestley. If they should find the State stick to the Church, the question is, whether they love the constitution in *State* so well as that they would not destroy the constitution of the State in order to destroy that of the Church. Most certainly they do not.

The foundations on which obedience to governments is founded are not to be constantly discussed. That we are here supposes the discussion already made and the dispute settled. We must assume the rights of what represents the public to control the individual, to make his will and his acts to submit to their will, until some intolerable grievance shall make us know that it does not answer its end, and will submit neither to reformation nor restraint. Otherwise we should dispute all the points of morality, before we can punish a murderer, robber, and adulterer;

we should analyze all society. Dangers by being despised grow great ; so they do by absurd provision against them. *Stulti est dixisse, Non putáram.* Whether an early discovery of evil designs, an early declaration, and an early precaution against them be more wise than to stifle all inquiry about them, for fear they should declare themselves more early than otherwise they would, and therefore precipitate the evil, — all this depends on the reality of the danger. Is it only an unbookish jealousy, as Shakspeare calls it ? It is a question of fact. Does a design against the Constitution of this country exist ? If it does, and if it is carried on with increasing vigor and activity by a restless faction, and if it receives countenance by the most ardent and enthusiastic applauses of its object in the great council of this kingdom, by men of the first parts which this kingdom produces, perhaps by the first it has ever produced, can I think that there is no danger ? If there be danger, must there be no precaution at all against it ? If you ask whether I think the danger urgent and immediate, I answer, Thank God, I do not. The body of the people is yet sound, the Constitution is in their hearts, while wicked men are endeavoring to put another into their heads. But if I see the very same beginnings which have commonly ended in great calamities, I ought to act as if they might produce the very same effects. Early and provident fear is the mother of safety ; because in that state of things the mind is firm and collected, and the judgment unembarrassed. But when the fear and the evil feared come on together, and press at once upon us, deliberation itself is ruinous, which saves upon all other occasions ; because, when perils are instant, it delays decision :

the man is in a flutter, and in a hurry, and his judgment is gone, — as the judgment of the deposed King
of France and his ministers was gone, if the latter
did not premeditately betray him. He was just come
from his usual amusement of hunting, when the head
of the column of treason and assassination was arrived at his house. Let not the king, let not the
Prince of Wales, be surprised in this manner. Let
not both Houses of Parliament be led in triumph
along with him, and have law dictated to them by
the Constitutional, the Revolution, and the Unitarian
Societies. These insect reptiles, whilst they go on
only caballing and toasting, only fill us with disgust;
if they get above their natural size, and increase the
quantity whilst they keep the quality of their venom,
they become objects of the greatest terror. A spider
in his natural size is only a spider, ugly and loath-
some ; and his flimsy net is only fit for catching flies.
But, good God! suppose a spider as large as an ox,
and that he spread cables about us, all the wilds of
Africa would not produce anything so dreadful : —

> Quale portentum neque militaris
> Daunia in latis alit esculetis,
> Nec Jubæ tellus generat, leonum
> Arida nutrix.

Think of them who dare menace in the way they
do in their present state, what would they do, if they
had power commensurate to their malice ? God forbid I ever should have a despotic master ! — but if
I must, my choice is made. I will have Louis the
Sixteenth rather than Monsieur Bailly, or Brissot, or
Chabot, — rather George the Third, or George the
Fourth, than Dr. Priestley, or Dr. Kippis, — persons
who would not load a tyrannous power by the poi-

soned taunts of a vulgar, low-bred insolence. I hope
we have still spirit enough to keep us from the one
or the other. The contumelies of tyranny are the
worst parts of it.

But if the danger be existing in reality, and silently maturing itself to our destruction, what! is it not
better to take *treason* unprepared than that *treason*
should come by surprise upon us and take us unprepared? If we must have a conflict, let us have
it with all our forces fresh about us, with our government in full function and full strength, our troops
uncorrupted, our revenues in the legal hands, our
arsenals filled and possessed by government, — and
not wait till the conspirators met to commemorate
the 14th of July shall seize on the Tower of London
and the magazines it contains, murder the governor,
and the mayor of London, seize upon the king's person, drive out the House of Lords, occupy your gal-
lery, and thence, as from an high tribunal, dictate to
you. The degree of danger is not only from the
circumstances which threaten, but from the value
of the objects which are threatened. A small danger menacing an inestimable object is of more importance than the greatest perils which regard one
that is indifferent to us. The whole question of the
danger depends upon facts. The first fact is, whether those who sway in France at present confine themselves to the regulation of their internal affairs, — or
whether upon system they nourish cabals in all other
countries, to extend their power by producing revolutions similar to their own. 2. The next is, whether
we have any cabals formed or forming within these
kingdoms, to coöperate with them for the destruction
of our Constitution. On the solution of these two

questions, joined with our opinion of the value of
the object to be affected by their machinations, the
justness of our alarm and the necessity of our vigilance must depend.   Every private conspiracy, every
open attack upon the laws, is dangerous.   One robbery is an alarm to all property ; else I am sure we
exceed measure in our punishment.   As robberies increase in number and audacity, the alarm increases.
These wretches are at war with us upon principle.
They hold this government to be an usurpation.
See the language of the Department.

The whole question is on the *reality* of the danger.
Is it such a danger as would justify that fear *qui ca-
dere potest in hominem constantem et non metuentem ?*
This is the fear which the principles of jurisprudence
declare to be a lawful and justifiable fear.   When
a man threatens my life openly and publicly, I may
demand from him securities of the peace.   When
every act of a man's life manifests such a design
stronger than by words, even though he does not
make such a declaration, I am justified in being on
my guard.   They are of opinion that they are already one fifth of the kingdom.   If so, their force
is naturally not contemptible.   To say that in all
contests the decision will of course be in favor of
the greater number is by no means true in fact.
For, first, the greater number is generally composed
of men of sluggish tempers, slow to act, and unwilling to attempt, and, by being in possession, are so
disposed to peace that they are unwilling to take
early and vigorous measures for their defence, and
they are almost always caught unprepared : —

Nec coïere pares : alter vergentibus annis
In senium, longoque togæ tranquillior usu,

Dedidicit jam pace ducem ; . . .
Nec reparare novas vires, multumque priori
Credere fortunæ : stat magni nominis umbra.*

A smaller number, more expedite, awakened, active,
vigorous, and courageous, who make amends for
what they want in weight by their superabundance
of velocity, will create an acting power of the greatest possible strength.   When men are furiously and
fanatically fond of an object, they will prefer it, as
is well known, to their own peace, to their own property, and to their own lives: and can there be a
doubt, in such a case, that they would prefer it to
the peace of their country ?   Is it to be doubted, that,
if they have not strength enough at home, they will
call in foreign force to aid them ?

Would you deny them *what is reasonable*, for fear
they should ?   Certainly not.   It would be barbarous
to pretend to look into the minds of men.   I would
go further : it would not be just even to trace consequences from principles which, though evident to
me, were denied by them.   Let them disband as a
faction, and let them act as individuals, and when
I see them with no other views than to enjoy their
own conscience in peace, I, for one, shall most cheer-
fully vote for their relief.

A tender conscience, of all things, ought to be ten-
derly handled ; for if you do not, you injure not only
the conscience, but the whole moral frame and constitution is injured, recurring at times to remorse,
and seeking refuge only in making the conscience callous.   But the conscience of faction, — the conscience
of sedition, — the conscience of conspiracy, war, and
confusion . . . . .

* Lucan, I. 129 to 135.

Whether anything be proper to be denied, which is right in itself, because it may lead to the demand of others which it is improper to grant? Abstractedly speaking, there can be no doubt that this question ought to be decided in the negative. But as no moral questions are ever abstract questions, this, before I judge upon any abstract proposition, must be embodied in circumstances; for, since things are right or wrong, morally speaking, only by their relation and connection with other things, this very question of what it is politically right to grant depends upon this relation to its effects. It is the direct office of wisdom to look to the consequences of the acts we do: if it be not this, it is worth nothing, it is out of place and of function, and a downright fool is as capable of government as Charles Fox. A man desires a sword: why should he be refused? A sword is a means of defence, and defence is the natural right of man, — nay, the first of all his rights, and which comprehends them all. But if I know that the sword desired is to be employed to cut my own throat, common sense, and my own self-defence, dictate to me to keep out of his hands this natural right of the sword. But whether this denial be wise or foolish, just or unjust, prudent or cowardly, depends entirely on the state of the man's means. A man may have very ill dispositions, and yet be so very weak as to make all precaution foolish. See whether this be the case of these Dissenters, as to their designs, as to their means, numbers, activity, zeal, foreign assistance.

The first question to be decided, when we talk of the Church's being in danger from any particular measure, is, whether the danger to the Church is a public evil: for to those who think that the national

Church Establishment is itself a national grievance, to desire them to forward or to resist any measure, upon account of its conducing to the safety of the Church or averting its danger, would be to the last degree absurd. If you have reason to think thus of it, take the reformation instantly into your own hands, whilst you are yet cool, and can do it in measure and proportion, and not under the influence of election tests and popular fury. But here I assume that by far the greater number of those who compose the House are of opinion that this national Church Establishment is a great national benefit, a great public blessing, and that its existence or its non-existence of course is a thing by no means indifferent to the public welfare: then to them its danger or its safety must enter deeply into every question which has a relation to it. It is not because ungrounded alarms have been given that there never can exist a real danger: perhaps the worst effect of an ungrounded alarm is to make people insensible to the approach of a real peril. Quakerism is strict, methodical, in its nature highly aristocratical, and so regular that it has brought the whole community to the condition of one family; but it does not actually interfere with the government. The principle of your petitioners is no passive conscientious dissent, on account of an over-scrupulous habit of mind: the dissent on their part is fundamental, goes to the very root; and it is at issue not upon this rite or that ceremony, on this or that school opinion, but upon this one question of an Establishment, as unchristian, unlawful, contrary to the Gospel and to natural right, Popish and idolatrous. These are the principles violently and fanatically held and pursued, — taught to their children, who are sworn at the altar like Hannibal. The war is with the Establishment itself, — no quarter, no compromise. As a party, they are infinitely mischievous : see the declarations of Priestley and Price, — declarations, you will say, of *hot* men. Likely enough : but who are the *cool* men who have disclaimed them ? Not one, — no, not one. Which of them has ever told you that they do not mean to *destroy the Church*, if ever it should be in their power ? Which of them has told you that this would not be the first and favorite use of any power they should get ? Not one, — no, not one. Declarations of hot men ! The danger is thence, that they are under the *conduct* of hot men : *falsos in amore odia non fingere.*

They say they are well affected to the State, and mean only to destroy the Church. If this be the utmost of their meaning, you must first consider whether you wish your Church Establishment to be destroyed. If you do, you had much better do it now in temper, in a grave, moderate, and parliamentary way. But if you think otherwise, and that you think it to be an invaluable blessing, a way fully sufficient to nourish a manly, rational, solid, and at the same time humble piety, — if you find it well fitted to the frame and pattern of your civil constitution, — if you find it a barrier against fanaticism, infidelity, and atheism, —if you find that it furnishes support to the human mind in the afflictions and distresses of the world, consolation in sickness, pain, poverty, and death, — if it dignifies our nature with the hope of immortality, leaves inquiry free, whilst it preserves an authority to teach, where authority only can teach, *communia altaria, œque ac patriam, diligite, colite, fovete.*

In the discussion of this subject which took place in the year 1790, Mr. Burke declared his intention, in case the motion for repealing the Test Acts had been agreed to, of proposing to substitute the following test in the room of what was intended to be repealed: —

'I, *A. B.*, do, in the presence of God, sincerely profess and believe that a religious establishment in this state is not contrary to the law of God, or disagreeable to the law of Nature, or to the true principles of the Christian religion, or that it is noxious to the community; and I do sincerely promise and engage, before God, that I never will, by any conspiracy, contrivance, or political device whatever, attempt, or abet others in any attempt, to subvert the constitution of the Church of England, as the same is now by law established, and that I will not employ any power or influence which I may derive from any office corporate, or any other office which I hold or shall hold under his Majesty, his heirs and successors, to destroy and subvert the same, or to cause members to be elected into any corporation or into Parliament, give my vote in the election of any member or members of Parliament, or into any office, for or on account of their attachment to any other or different religious opinions or establishments, or with any hope that they may promote the same to the prejudice of the Established Church, but will dutifully and peaceably content myself with my private liberty of conscience, as the same is allowed by law. So help me God."

SPEECH

ON

THE MOTION MADE IN THE HOUSE OF COMMONS,

FEBRUARY 7, 1771,

RELATIVE TO

THE MIDDLESEX ELECTION.

NOTE.

The motion supported in the following Speech, which was for leave to bring in a bill to ascertain the rights of the electors in respect to the eligibility of persons to serve in Parliament, was rejected by a majority of 167 against 103.

SPEECH.

IN every complicated constitution (and every free constitution is complicated) cases will arise when the several orders of the state will clash with one another, and disputes will arise about the limits of their several rights and privileges. It may be almost impossible to reconcile them. . . . .

Carry the principle on by which you expelled Mr. Wilkes, there is not a man in the House, hardly a man in the nation, who may not be disqualified. That this House should have no power of expulsion is an hard saying: that this House should have a general discretionary power of disqualification is a dangerous saying. That the people should not choose their own representative is a saying that shakes the Constitution: that this House should name the representative is a saying which, followed by practice, subverts the Constitution. They have the right of electing; you have a right of expelling: they of choosing; you of judging, and only of judging, of the choice. What bounds shall be set to the freedom of that choice? Their right is prior to ours: we all originate there. They are the mortal enemies of the House of Commons who would persuade them to think or to act as if they were a self-originated magistracy, independent of the people, and unconnected with their opinions and feelings. Under a

pretence of exalting the dignity, they undermine the
very foundations of this House. When the question
is asked *here*, What disturbs the people? whence all
this clamor? we apply to the Treasury bench, and
they tell us it is from the efforts of libellers, and the
wickedness of the people: a worn-out ministerial pretence. If abroad the people are deceived by popular,
within we are deluded by ministerial cant.

The question amounts to this: Whether you mean
to be a legal tribunal, or an arbitrary and despotic
assembly? I see and I feel the delicacy and difficulty of the ground upon which we stand in this question. I could wish, indeed, that they who advise the
crown had not left Parliament in this very ungrace-
ful distress, in which they can neither retract with
dignity nor persist with justice. Another Parliament
might have satisfied the people without lowering
themselves. But our situation is not in our own
choice: our conduct in that situation is all that is in
our own option. The substance of the question is, to
put bounds to your own power by the rules and principles of law. This is, I am sensible, a difficult thing
to the corrupt, grasping, and ambitious part of human
nature. But the very difficulty argues and enforces
the necessity of it. First, because the greater the
power, the more dangerous the abuse. Since the
Revolution, at least, the power of the nation has all
flowed with a full tide into the House of Commons.
Secondly, because the House of Commons, as it is
the most powerful, is the most corruptible part of the
whole Constitution. Our public wounds cannot be
concealed; to be cured, they must be laid open. The
public does think we are a corrupt body. In our
legislative capacity, we are, in most instances, es-

teemed a very wise body; in our judicial, we have
no credit, no character at all.   Our judgments stink
in the nostrils of the people.   They think us to be
not only without virtue, but without shame.   Therefore the greatness of our power, and the great and
just opinion of our corruptibility and our corruption,
render it necessary to fix some bound, to plant some
landmark, which we are never to exceed.   This is
what the bill proposes.

First, on this head, I lay it down as a fundamental rule in the law and Constitution of this
country, that this House has not by itself alone a
legislative authority in any case whatsoever.   I know
that the contrary was the doctrine of the usurping
House of Commons, which threw down the fences
and bulwarks of law, which annihilated first the
lords, then the crown, then its constituents.   But
the first thing that was done on the restoration of
the Constitution was to settle this point.   Secondly, I
lay it down as a rule, that the power of occasional
incapacitation, on discretionary grounds, is a legislative power.   In order to establish this principle, if
it should not be sufficiently proved by being stated,
tell me what are the criteria, the characteristics, by
which you distinguish between a legislative and a juridical act.   It will be necessary to state, shortly, the
difference between a legislative and a juridical act.

A legislative act has no reference to any rule but
these two, — original justice, and discretionary application.   Therefore it can give rights, — rights where
no rights existed before; and it can take away rights
where they were before established.   For the law,
which binds all others, does not and cannot bind
the law-maker: he, and he alone, is above the law.

But a judge, a person exercising a judicial capacity, is neither to apply to original justice nor to a discretionary application of it. He goes to justice and discretion only at second hand, and through the medium of some superiors. He is to work neither upon his opinion of the one nor of the other, but upon a fixed rule, of which he has not the making, but singly and solely the *application* to the case.

The power assumed by the House neither is nor can be judicial power exercised according to known law. The properties of law are, first, that it should be known; secondly, that it should be fixed, and not occasional. First, this power cannot be according to the first property of law; because no man does or can know it, nor do you yourselves know upon what grounds you will vote the incapacity of any man. No man in Westminster Hall, or in any court upon earth, will say that is law, upon which, if a man going to his counsel should say to him, "What is my tenure in law of this estate?" he would answer, "Truly, Sir, I know not; the court has no rule but its own discretion; they will determine." It is not a fixed law; because you profess you vary it according to the occasion, exercise it according to your discretion, no man can call for it as a right. It is argued, that the incapacity is not originally voted, but a consequence of a power of expulsion. But if you expel, not upon legal, but upon arbitrary, that is, upon discretionary grounds, and the incapacity is *ex vi termini* and inclusively comprehended in the expulsion, is not the incapacity voted in the expulsion? Are they not convertible terms? And if incapacity is voted to be inherent in expulsion, if expulsion be arbitrary, incapacity is arbitrary also. I have therefore shown that the power of incapacitation is a legislative power; I have shown that legislative power does not belong to the House of Commons; and therefore it follows that the House of Commons has not a power of incapacitation.

I know not the origin of the House of Commons, but am very sure that it did not create itself; the electors were prior to the elected, whose rights originated either from the people at large, or from some other form of legislature, which never could intend for the chosen a power of superseding the choosers.

If you have not a power of declaring an incapacity simply by the mere act of declaring it, it is evident to the most ordinary reason you cannot have a right of expulsion, inferring, or rather including, an incapacity. For as the law, when it gives any direct right, gives also as necessary incidents all the means of acquiring the possession of that right, so, where it does not give a right directly, it refuses all the means by which such a right may by any mediums be exercised, or in effect be indirectly acquired. Else it is very obvious that the intention of the law in refusing that right might be entirely frustrated, and the whole power of the legislature baffled. If there be no certain, invariable rule of eligibility, it were better to get simplicity, if certainty is not to be had, and to resolve all the franchises of the subject into this one short proposition, — the will and pleasure of the House of Commons.

The argument drawn from the courts of law applying the principles of law to new cases as they emerge is altogether frivolous, inapplicable, and arises from a total ignorance of the bounds between civil and criminal jurisdiction, and of the separate maxims that govern these two provinces of law, that are eternally separate. Undoubtedly the courts of law, where a new case comes before them, as they do every hour, then, that there may be no defect in justice, call in similar principles, and the example of the nearest determination, and do everything to draw the law to as near a conformity to general equity and right reason as they can bring it with its being a fixed principle. *Boni judicis est ampliare justitiam*, — that is, to make open and liberal justice. But in criminal matters this parity of reason and these analogies ever have been and ever ought to be shunned.

Whatever is incident to a court of judicature is necessary to the House of Commons as judging in elections. But a power of making incapacities is not necessary to a court of judicature : therefore a power of making incapacities is not necessary to the House of Commons.

Incapacity, declared by whatever authority, stands upon two principles : first, an incapacity arising from the supposed incongruity of two duties in the commonwealth ; secondly, an incapacity arising from unfitness by infirmity of nature or the criminality of conduct. As to the first class of incapacities, they have no *hardship* annexed to them. The persons so incapacitated are paid by one dignity for what they abandon in another, and for the most part the situation arises from their own choice. But as to the second, arising from an unfitness not fixed by Nature, but superinduced by some positive acts, or arising from honorable motives, such as an occasional personal disability, of all things it ought to be defined by the fixed rule of law, what Lord Coke calls the golden metwand of the law, and not by the

crooked cord of discretion. Whatever is general is
better borne. We take our common lot with men of
the same description. But to be selected and marked
out by a particular brand of unworthiness among our
fellow-citizens is a lot of all others the hardest to
be borne, and consequently is of all others that act
which ought only to be trusted to the legislature, as
not only *legislative* in its nature, but of all parts of
legislature the most odious. The question is over,
if this is shown not to be a legislative act.

But what is very usual and natural is, to corrupt
judicature into legislature. On this point it is proper to inquire whether a court of judicature which decides without appeal has it as a necessary incident of
such judicature, that whatever it decides is *de jure*
law. Nobody will, I hope, assert this; because the
direct consequence would be the entire extinction
of the difference between true and false judgments.
For if the judgment makes the law, and not the law
directs the judgment, it is impossible there should be
such a thing as an illegal judgment given.

But instead of standing upon this ground, they
introduce another question wholly foreign to it:
Whether it ought not to be submitted to as if it were
law? And then the question is, — By the Constitution of this country, what degree of submission is due
to the authoritative acts of a limited power? This
question of submission, determine it how you please,
has nothing to do in this discussion and in this
House. Here it is not, how long the people are
bound to tolerate the illegality of our judgments, but
whether we have a right to substitute our occasional
opinion in the place of law, so as to deprive the citizen of his franchise. . . . .

SPEECH

ON

A BILL FOR SHORTENING THE DURATION OF PARLIAMENTS.

MAY 8, 1780.

SPEECH.

IT is always to be lamented, when men are driven to search into the foundations of the commonwealth. It is certainly necessary to resort to the theory of your government, whenever you propose any alteration in the frame of it, — whether that alteration means the revival of some former antiquated and forsaken constitution of state, or the introduction of some new improvement in the commonwealth. The object of our deliberation is, to promote the good purposes for which elections have been instituted, and to prevent their inconveniences. If we thought frequent elections attended with no inconvenience, or with but a trifling inconvenience, the strong overruling principle of the Constitution would sweep us like a torrent towards them. But your remedy is to be suited to your disease, your present disease, and to your whole disease. That man thinks much too highly, and therefore he thinks weakly and delusively, of any contrivance of human wisdom, who believes that it can make any sort of approach to perfection. There is not, there never was, a principle of government under heaven, that does not, in the very pursuit of the good it proposes, naturally and inevitably lead into some inconvenience which makes it absolutely necessary to counterwork and weaken the application of that first principle itself, and to abandon something of the extent of the advantage you proposed by it, in order to prevent also the inconveniences which have arisen from the instrument of all the good you had in view.

To govern according to the sense and agreeably to the interests of the people is a great and glorious object of government. This object cannot be obtained but through the medium of popular election; and popular election is a mighty evil. It is such and so great an evil, that, though there are few nations whose monarchs were not originally elective, very few are now elected. They are the distempers of elections that have destroyed all free states. To cure these distempers is difficult, if not impossible; the only thing, therefore, left to save the commonwealth is, to prevent their return too frequently. The objects in view are, to have Parliaments as frequent as they can be without distracting them in the prosecution of public business: on one hand, to secure their dependence upon the people; on the other, to give them that quiet in their minds and that ease in their fortunes as to enable them to perform the most arduous and most painful duty in the world with spirit, with efficiency, with independency, and with experience, as real public counsellors, not as the canvassers at a perpetual election. It is wise to compass as many good ends as possibly you can, and, seeing there are inconveniences on both sides, with benefits on both, to give up a part of the benefit to soften the inconvenience. The perfect cure is impracticable; because the disorder is dear to those from whom alone the cure can possibly be derived. The utmost to be done is to palliate, to mitigate, to respite, to put off the evil day of the Constitution to its latest possible hour, — and may it be a very late one!

This bill, I fear, would precipitate one of two consequences, — I know not which most likely, or which most dangerous: either that the crown, by its constant, stated power, influence, and revenue, would wear out all opposition in elections, or that a violent and furious popular spirit would arise. I must see, to satisfy me, the remedies; I must see, from their operation in the cure of the old evil, and in the cure of those new evils which are inseparable from all remedies, how they balance each other, and what is the total result. The excellence of mathematics and metaphysics is, to have but one thing before you; but he forms the best judgment in all moral disquisitions who has the greatest number and variety of considerations in one view before him, and can take them in with the best possible consideration of the middle results of all.

We of the opposition, who are not friends to the bill, give this pledge at least of our integrity and sincerity to the people, — that in our situation of systematic opposition to the present ministers, in which all our hope of rendering it effectual depends upon popular interest and favor, we will not flatter them by a surrender of our uninfluenced judgment and opinion; we give a security, that, if ever we should be in another situation, no flattery to any other sort of power and influence would induce us to act against the true interests of the people.

All are agreed that Parliaments should not be perpetual; the only question is, What is the most convenient time for their duration? — on which there are three opinions. We are agreed, too, that the term ought not to be chosen most likely in its operation to spread corruption, and to augment the already overgrown influence of the crown. On these principles I mean to debate the question. It is easy to pretend a zeal for liberty. Those who think themselves not likely to be incumbered with the performance of their promises, either from their known inability or total indifference about the performance, never fail to entertain the most lofty ideas. They are certainly the most specious; and they cost them neither reflection to frame, nor pains to modify, nor management to support. The task is of another nature to those who mean to promise nothing that it is not in their intention, or may possibly be in their power to perform, — to those who are bound and principled no more to delude the understandings than to violate the liberty of their fellow-subjects. Faithful watchmen we ought to be over the rights and privileges of the people. But our duty, if we are qualified for it as we ought, is to give them information, and not to receive it from them: we are not to go to school to them, to learn the principles of law and government. In doing so, we should not dutifully serve, but we should basely and scandalously betray the people, who are not capable of this service by nature, nor in any instance called to it by the Constitution. I reverentially look up to the opinion of the people, and with an awe that is almost superstitious. I should be ashamed to show my face before them, if I changed my ground as they cried up or cried down men or things or opinions, — if I wavered and shifted about with every change, and joined in it or opposed as best answered any low interest or passion, — if I held them up hopes which I knew I never intended, or promised what I well knew I could not perform.   Of all these things they are perfect sovereign judges without appeal; but as to the detail of particular measures, or to any general schemes of policy, they have neither enough of spec-ulation in the closet nor of experience in business to decide upon it.   They can well see whether we are tools of a court or their honest servants.   Of that they can well judge, — and I wish that they always exercised their judgment; but of the particular mer-its of a measure I have other standards. . . . .

That the frequency of elections proposed by this bill has a tendency to increase the power and consid-eration of the electors, not lessen corruptibility, I do most readily allow: so far it is desirable.   This is what it has: I will tell you now what it has not. 1st. It has no sort of tendency to increase their in-tegrity and public spirit, unless an increase of power has an operation upon voters in elections, that it has in no other situation in the world, and upon no other part of mankind.   2nd. This bill has no tendency to limit the quantity of influence in the crown, to ren-der its operation more difficult, or to counteract that operation which it cannot prevent in any way what-soever.   It has its full weight, its full range, and its uncontrolled operation on the electors exactly as it had before.   3rd. Nor, thirdly, does it abate the in-terest or inclination of ministers to apply that influ-ence to the electors: on the contrary, it renders it much more necessary to them, if they seek to have a majority in Parliament, to increase the means of that influence, and redouble their diligence, and to sharpen dexterity in the application.   The whole ef-fect of the bill is, therefore, the removing the appli-

cation of some part of the influence from the elected
to the electors, and further to strengthen and extend
a court interest already great and powerful in boroughs : here to fix their magazines and places of
arms, and thus to make them the principal, not the
secondary, theatre of their manœuvres for securing
a determined majority in Parliament.

I believe nobody will deny that the electors are
corruptible. They are men, — it is saying nothing
worse of them ; many of them are but ill informed
in their minds, many feeble in their circumstances,
easily overreached, easily seduced. If they are many,
the wages of corruption are the lower ; and would to
God it were not rather a contemptible and hypocriti-
cal adulation than a charitable sentiment, to say that
there is already no debauchery, no corruption, no
bribery, no perjury, no blind fury and interested faction among the electors in many parts of this kingdom ! — nor is it surprising, or at all blamable, in
that class of private men, when they see their neighbors aggrandized, and themselves poor and virtuous
without that *éclat* or dignity which attends men in
higher situations.

But admit it were true that the great mass of the
electors were too vast an object for court influence to
grasp or extend to, and that in despair they must
abandon it; he must be very ignorant of the state
of every popular interest, who does not know that in
all the corporations, all the open boroughs, indeed in
every district of the kingdom, there is some leading
man, some agitator, some wealthy merchant or considerable manufacturer, some active attorney, some
popular preacher, some money-lender, &c., &c., who
is followed by the whole flock. This is the style of
all free countries.

Multum in Fabiâ valet hic, valet ille Velinâ;
Cuilibet hic fasces dabit, eripietque curule.

These spirits, each of which informs and governs his
own little orb, are neither so many, nor so little powerful, nor so incorruptible, but that a minister may,
as he does frequently, find means of gaining them,
and through them all their followers. To establish,
therefore, a very general influence among electors
will no more be found an impracticable project than
to gain an undue influence over members of Parliament. Therefore I am apprehensive that this bill,
though it shifts the place of the disorder, does by no
means relieve the Constitution. I went through almost every contested election in the beginning of this
Parliament, and acted as a manager in very many of
them; by which, though as at a school of pretty severe
and rugged discipline, I came to have some degree
of instruction concerning the means by which Parliamentary interests are in general procured and supported.

Theory, I know, would suppose that every general
election is to the representative a day of judgment,
in which he appears before his constituents to account
for the use of the talent with which they intrusted
him, and for the improvement he has made of it for
the public advantage. It would be so, if every corruptible representative were to find an enlightened
and incorruptible constituent. But the practice and
knowledge of the world will not suffer us to be ignorant that the Constitution on paper is one thing, and
in fact and experience is another. We must know
that the candidate, instead of trusting at his election
to the testimony of his behavior in Parliament, must
bring the testimony of a large sum of money, the ca-

pacity of liberal expense in entertainments, the power of serving and obliging the rulers of corporations, of winning over the popular leaders of political clubs, associations, and neighborhoods. It is ten thousand times more necessary to show himself a man of power than a man of integrity, in almost all the elections with which I have been acquainted. Elections, therefore, become a matter of heavy expense ; and if contests are frequent, to many they will become a matter of an expense totally ruinous, which no fortunes can bear, but least of all the landed fortunes, incumbered as they often, indeed as they mostly are, with debts, with portions, with jointures, and tied up in the hands of the possessor by the limitations of settlement. It is a material, it is in my opinion a lasting consideration, in all the questions concerning election. Let no one think the charges of elections a trivial matter.

The charge, therefore, of elections ought never to be lost sight of in a question concerning their frequency ; because the grand object you seek is independence. Independence of mind will ever be more or less influenced by independence of fortune; and if every three years the exhausting sluices of entertainments, drinkings, open houses, to say nothing of bribery, are to be periodically drawn up and renewed, — if government favors, for which now, in some shape or other, the whole race of men are candidates, are to be called for upon every occasion, I see that private fortunes will be washed away, and every, even to the least, trace of independence borne down by the torrent. I do not seriously think this Constitution, even to the wrecks of it, could survive five triennial elections. If you are to fight the battle,

you must put on the armor of the ministry, you must
call in the public to the aid of private money. The
expense of the last election has been computed (and
I am persuaded that it has not been overrated) at
1,500,000*l.*, — three shillings in the pound more in
[than ?] the land-tax. About the close of the last Parliament and the beginning of this, several agents for
boroughs went about, and I remember well that it was
in every one of their mouths, " Sir, your election will
cost you three thousand pounds, if you are independent ; but if the ministry supports you, it may be done
for two, and perhaps for less." And, indeed, the thing
spoke itself. Where a living was to be got for one, a
commission in the army for another, a lift in the navy
for a third, and custom-house offices scattered about
without measure or number, who doubts but money
may be saved? The Treasury may even add money :
but, indeed, it is superfluous. A gentleman of two
thousand a year, who meets another of the same fortune, fights with equal arms ; but if to one of the
candidates you add a thousand a year in places for
himself, and a power of giving away as much among
others, one must, or there is no truth in arithmetical
demonstration, ruin his adversary, if he is to meet
him and to fight with him every third year. It will
be said I do not allow for the operation of character :
but I do ; and I know it will have its weight in most
elections, — perhaps it may be decisive in some ; but
there are few in which it will prevent great expenses.

The destruction of independent fortunes will be
the consequence on the part of the candidate. What
will be the consequence of triennial corruption, triennial drunkenness, triennial idleness, triennial lawsuits,
litigations, prosecutions, triennial frenzy, — of society

dissolved, industry interrupted, ruined, — of those personal hatreds that will never be suffered to soften, those animosities and feuds which will be rendered immortal, those quarrels which are never to be appeased, — morals vitiated and gangrened to the vitals ? I think no stable and useful advantages were ever made by the money got at elections by the voter, but all he gets is doubly lost to the public : it is money given to diminish the general stock of the community, which is in the industry of the subject. I am sure that it is a good while before he or his family settle again to their business. Their heads will never cool; the temptations of elections will be forever glittering before their eyes. They will all grow politicians; every one, quitting his business, will choose to enrich himself by his vote. They will all take the gauging-rod; new places will be made for them; they will run to the custom-house quay; their looms and ploughs will be deserted.

So was Rome destroyed by the disorders of contin- ual elections, though those of Rome were sober disor- ders. They had nothing but faction, bribery, bread, and stage-plays, to debauch them : we have the in- flammation of liquor superadded, a fury hotter than any of them. There the contest was only between citizen and citizen : here you have the contests of am- bitious citizens of one side supported by the crown to oppose to the efforts (let it be so) of private and un- supported ambition on the other. Yet Rome was de- stroyed by the frequency and charge of elections, and the monstrous expense of an unremitted courtship to the people. I think, therefore, the independent can- didate and elector may each be destroyed by it, the whole body of the community be an infinite sufferer, and a vicious ministry the only gainer.

Gentlemen, I know, feel the weight of this argument; they agree, that this would be the consequence of more frequent elections, if things were to continue as they are. But they think the greatness and frequency of the evil would itself be a remedy for it, — that, sitting but for a short time, the member would not find it worth while to make such vast expenses, while the fear of their constituents will hold them the more effectually to their duty.

To this I answer, that experience is full against them. This is no new thing ; we have had triennial Parliaments ; at no period of time were seats more eagerly contested. The expenses of elections ran higher, taking the state of all charges, than they do now. The expense of entertainments was such, that an act, equally severe and ineffectual, was made against it ; every monument of the time bears witness of the expense, and most of the acts against corruption in elections were then made ; all the writers talked of it and lamented it. Will any one think that a corporation will be contented with a bowl of punch or a piece of beef the less, because elections are every three, instead of every seven years ? Will they change their wine for ale, because they are to get more ale three years hence ? Don't think it. Will they make fewer demands for the advantages of patronage in favors and offices, because their member is brought more under their power ? We have not only our own historical experience in England upon this subject, but we have the experience coexisting with us in Ireland, where, since their Parliament has been shortened, the expense of elections has been so far from being lowered, that it has been very near doubled. Formerly they sat for the king's life ; the

ordinary charge of a seat in Parliament was then
fifteen hundred pounds. They now sit eight years,
four sessions ; it is now twenty-five hundred pounds,
and upwards. The spirit of *emulation* has also been
extremely increased, and all who are acquainted with
the tone of that country have no doubt that the spirit is still growing, that new candidates will take the
field, that the contests will be more violent, and the
expenses of elections larger than ever.

It never can be otherwise. A seat in this House,
for good purposes, for bad purposes, for no purposes
at all, (except the mere consideration derived from
being concerned in the public counsels,) will ever be
a first-rate object of ambition in England. Ambition is no exact calculator. Avarice itself does not
calculate strictly, when it games. One thing is certain, — that in this political game the great lottery
of power is that into which men will purchase with
millions of chances against them. In Turkey, where
the place, where the fortune, where the head itself
are so insecure that scarcely any have died in their
beds for ages, so that the bowstring is the natural
death of bashaws, yet in no country is power and
distinction (precarious enough, God knows, in all)
sought for with such boundless avidity, — as if the
value of place was enhanced by the danger and inse-
curity of its tenure. Nothing will ever make a seat
in this House not an object of desire to numbers by
any means or at any charge, but the depriving it of
all power and all dignity. This would do it. This
is the true and only nostrum for that purpose. But
an House of Commons without power and without
dignity, either in itself or in its members, is no
House of Commons for the purposes of this Constitution.

But they will be afraid to act ill, if they know that the day of their account is always near. I wish it were true; but it is not: here again we have experience, and experience is against us. The distemper of this age is a poverty of spirit and of genius: it is trifling, it is futile, worse than ignorant, superficially taught, with the politics and morals of girls at a boarding-school rather than of men and statesmen: but it is not yet desperately wicked, or so scandalously venal as in former times. Did not a triennial Parliament give up the national dignity, approve the peace of Utrecht, and almost give up everything else, in taking every step to defeat the Protestant succession? Was not the Constitution saved by those who had no election at all to go to, the Lords, because the court applied to electors, and by various means carried them from their true interests, so that the Tory ministry had a majority without an application to a single member? Now as to the conduct of the members, it was then far from pure and independent. Bribery was infinitely more flagrant. A predecessor of yours, Mr. Speaker, put the question of his own expulsion for bribery. Sir William Musgrave was a wise man, a grave man, an independent man, a man of good fortune and good family; however, he carried on, while in opposition, a traffic, a shameful traffic, with the ministry. Bishop Burnet knew of six thousand pounds which he had received at one payment. I believe the payment of sums in hard money, plain, naked bribery, is rare amongst us. It was then far from uncommon.

A triennial was near ruining, a septennial Parliament saved your Constitution; nor, perhaps, have you ever known a more flourishing period, for the union of national prosperity, dignity, and liberty, than the sixty years you have passed under that constitution of Parliament.

The shortness of time in which they are to reap the profits of iniquity is far from checking the avidity of corrupt men ; it renders them infinitely more ravenous. They rush violently and precipitately on their object ; they lose all regard to decorum. The moments of profits are precious ; never are men so wicked as during a general mortality. It was so in the great plague at Athens, every symptom of which (and this its worse symptom amongst the rest) is so finely related by a great historian of antiquity. It was so in the plague of London in 1665. It appears in soldiers, sailors, &c. Whoever would contrive to render the life of man much shorter than it is would, I am satisfied, find the surest receipt for increasing the wickedness of our nature.

Thus, in my opinion, the shortness of a triennial sitting would have the following ill effects : It would make the member more shamelessly and shockingly corrupt ; it would increase his dependence on those who could best support him at his election ; it would wrack and tear to pieces the fortunes of those who stood upon their own fortunes and their private interest ; it would make the electors infinitely more venal ; and it would make the whole body of the people, who are, whether they have votes or not, concerned in elections, more lawless, more idle, more debauched ; it would utterly destroy the sobriety, the industry, the integrity, the simplicity of all the people, and undermine, I am much afraid, the deepest and best-laid foundations of the commonwealth.

Those who have spoken and written upon this sub

ject without doors do not so much deny the probable existence of these inconveniences in their measure as they trust for their prevention to remedies
of various sorts which they propose. First, a place
bill. But if this will not do, as they fear it will not,
then, they say, We will have a rotation, and a certain number of you shall be rendered incapable of
being elected for ten years. Then for the electors,
they shall ballot. The members of Parliament also
shall decide by ballot. A fifth project is the change
of the present legal representation of the kingdom.
On all this I shall observe, that it will be very unsuitable to your wisdom to adopt the project of a
bill to which there are objections insuperable by anything in the bill itself, upon the hope that those objections may be removed by subsequent projects,
every one of which is full of difficulties of its own,
and which are all of them very essential alterations
in the Constitution. This seems very irregular and
unusual. If anything should make this a very doubtful measure, what can make it more so than that
in the opinion of its advocates it would aggravate
all our old inconveniences in such a manner as to
require a total alteration in the Constitution of the
kingdom? If the remedies are proper in triennial,
they will not be less so in septennial elections. Let
us try them first, — see how the House relishes them,
— see how they will operate in the nation, — and
then, having felt your way, and prepared against
these inconveniences . . . .

The honorable gentleman sees that I respect the
principle upon which he goes, as well as his intentions and his abilities. He will believe that I do not
differ from him wantonly and on trivial grounds.

He is very sure that it was not his embracing one way which determined me to take the other. *I* have not in newspapers, to derogate from his fair fame with the nation, printed the first rude sketch of his bill with ungenerous and invidious comments. *I* have not, in conversations industriously circulated about the town, and talked on the benches of this House, attributed his conduct to motives low and unworthy, and as groundless as they are injurious. *I* do not affect to be frightened with this proposition, as if some hideous spectre had started from hell, which was to be sent back again by every form of exorcism and every kind of incantation. *I* invoke no Acheron to overwhelm him in the whirlpools of its muddy gulf. *I* do not tell the respectable mover and seconder, by a perversion of their sense and expressions, that their proposition halts between the ridiculous and the dangerous. *I* am not one of those who start up, three at a time, and fall upon and strike at him with so much eagerness that our daggers hack one another in his sides. My honorable friend has not brought down a spirited imp of chivalry to win the first achievement and blazon of arms on his milk-white shield in a field listed against him, — nor brought out the generous offspring of lions, and said to them, — "Not against that side of the forest! beware of that! — here is the prey, where you are to fasten your paws!" — and seasoning his unpractised jaws with blood, tell him, — "This is the milk for which you are to thirst hereafter!" *We* furnish at his expense no holiday, — nor suspend hell, that a crafty Ixion may have rest from his wheel, — nor give the common adversary (if he be a common adversary) reason to say, — "I would

have put in my word to oppose, but the eagerness of
your allies in your social war was such that I could
not break in upon you." I hope he sees and feels,
and that every member sees and feels along with
him, the difference between amicable dissent and
civil discord.

have part in my work to oppose, but the eagerness of
your allies in your social war was such that I could
not break in upon you." I hope he sees and feels,
and that every member sees and feels along with
him, the difference between amicable, dissent, and
civil discord.

SPEECH

ON A

MOTION MADE IN THE HOUSE OF COMMONS,

MAY 7, 1782,

FOR

A COMMITTEE TO INQUIRE INTO THE STATE
OF THE REPRESENTATION OF THE
COMMONS IN PARLIAMENT.

SPEECH.

MR. SPEAKER, — We have now discovered, at the close of the eighteenth century, that the Constitution of England, which for a series of ages had been the proud distinction of this country, always the admiration and sometimes the envy of the wise and learned in every other nation, — we have discovered that this boasted Constitution, in the most boasted part of it, is a gross imposition upon the understanding of mankind, an insult to their feelings, and acting by contrivances destructive to the best and most valuable interests of the people. Our political architects have taken a survey of the fabric of the British Constitution. It is singular that they report nothing against the crown, nothing against the lords: but in the House of Commons everything is unsound; it is ruinous in every part; it is infested by the dry rot, and ready to tumble about our ears without their immediate help. You know by the faults they find what are their ideas of the alteration. As all government stands upon opinion, they know that the way utterly to destroy it is to remove that opinion, to take away all reverence, all confidence from it; and then, at the first blast of public discontent and popular tumult, it tumbles to the ground.

In considering this question, they who oppose it oppose it on different grounds. One is in the nature of a previous question: that some alterations may be expedient, but that this is not the time for making them. The other is, that no essential alterations are at all wanting, and that neither *now* nor at *any* time is it prudent or safe to be meddling with the fundamental principles and ancient tried usages of our Constitution, — that our representation is as nearly perfect as the necessary imperfection of human affairs and of human creatures will suffer it to be, — and that it is a subject of prudent and honest use and thankful enjoyment, and not of captious criticism and rash experiment.

On the other side there are two parties, who proceed on two grounds, in my opinion, as they state them, utterly irreconcilable. The one is juridical, the other political. The one is in the nature of a claim of right, on the supposed rights of man as man : this party desire the decision of a suit. The other ground, as far as I can divine what it directly means, is, that the representation is not so politically framed as to answer the theory of its institution. As to the claim of *right*, the meanest petitioner, the most gross and ignorant, is as good as the best : in some respects his claim is more favorable, on account of his ignorance; his weakness, his poverty, and distress only add to his titles; he sues *in forma pauperis;* he ought to be a favorite of the court. But when the *other* ground is taken, when the question is political, when a new constitution is to be made on a sound theory of government, then the presumptuous pride of didactic ignorance is to be excluded from the counsel in this high and arduous matter, which often bids defiance to the experience of the wisest. The first claims a personal representation ; the latter rejects it with scorn and fervor. The language of the first

party is plain and intelligible ; they who plead an absolute right cannot be satisfied with anything short
of personal representation, because all *natural* rights
must be the rights of individuals, as by *nature* there
is no such thing as politic or corporate personality :
all these ideas are mere fictions of law, they are creatures of voluntary institution ; men as men are in
dividuals, and nothing else. They, therefore, who
reject the principle of natural and personal representation are essentially and eternally at variance
with those who claim it. As to the first sort of reformers, it is ridiculous to talk to them of the Brit
ish Constitution upon any or upon all of its bases :
for they lay it down, that every man ought to govern himself, and that, where he cannot go, himself,
he must send his representative ; that all other government is usurpation, and is so far from having a
claim to our obedience, it is not only our right, but
our duty, to resist it. Nine tenths of the reformers
argue thus, — that is, on the natural right.

It is impossible not to make some reflection on
the nature of this claim, or avoid a comparison between the extent of the principle and the present
object of the demand. If this claim be founded, it
is clear to what it goes. The House of Commons,
in that light, undoubtedly, is no representative of
the people, as a collection of individuals. Nobody
pretends it, nobody can justify such an assertion.
When you come to examine into this claim of right,
founded on the right of self-government in each
individual, you find the thing demanded infinitely
short of the principle of the demand. What! *one
third* only of the legislature, and of the government
no share at all ? What sort of treaty of partition

is this for those who have an inherent right to the
whole? Give them all they ask, and your grant is
still a cheat: for how comes only a third to be their
younger-children's fortune in this settlement? How
came they neither to have the choice of kings, or
lords, or judges, or generals, or admirals, or bishops,
or priests, or ministers, or justices of peace? Why,
what have you to answer in favor of the prior rights
of the crown and peerage but this: Our Constitution is a prescriptive constitution; it is a constitution whose sole authority is, that it has existed
time out of mind? It is settled in these *two* portions against one, legislatively, — and in the whole
of the judicature, the whole of the federal capacity,
of the executive, the prudential, and the financial
administration, in one alone. Nor was your House
of Lords and the prerogatives of the crown settled
on any adjudication in favor of natural rights: for
they could never be so partitioned. Your king, your
lords, your judges, your juries, grand and little, all
are prescriptive; and what proves it is the disputes,
not yet concluded, and never near becoming so, when
any of them first originated. Prescription is the
most solid of all titles, not only to property, but,
which is to secure that property, to government.
They harmonize with each other, and give mutual
aid to one another. It is accompanied with another
ground of authority in the constitution of the human mind, presumption. It is a presumption in
favor of any settled scheme of government against
any untried project, that a nation has long existed
and flourished under it. It is a better presumption
even of the *choice* of a nation, — far better than any
sudden and temporary arrangement by actual elec-

tion. Because a nation is not an idea only of local
extent and individual momentary aggregation, but it
is an idea of continuity which extends in time as well
as in numbers and in space. And this is a choice
not of one day or one set of people, not a tumultuary and giddy choice; it is a deliberate election of
ages and of generations; it is a constitution made
by what is ten thousand times better than choice;
it is made by the peculiar circumstances, occasions,
tempers, dispositions, and moral, civil, and social
habitudes of the people, which disclose themselves
only in a long space of time. It is a vestment which
accommodates itself to the body. Nor is prescription of government formed upon blind, unmeaning
prejudices. For man is a most unwise and a most
wise being. The individual is foolish; the multitude, for the moment, is foolish, when they act without deliberation; but the species is wise, and, when
time is given to it, as a species, it almost always
acts right.

The reason for the crown as it is, for the lords
as they are, is my reason for the commons as they
are, the electors as they are. Now if the crown, and
the lords, and the judicatures are all prescriptive,
so is the House of Commons of the very same origin,
and of no other. We and our electors have their
powers and privileges both made and circumscribed
by prescription, as much to the full as the other
parts; and as such we have always claimed them,
and on no other title. The House of Commons is
a legislative body corporate by prescription, not made
upon any given theory, but existing prescriptively,
—just like the rest. This prescription has made
it essentially what it is, an aggregate collection of

three parts, knights, citizens, burgesses. The question is, whether this has been always so, since the House of Commons has taken its present shape and circumstances, and has been an essential operative part of the Constitution, — which, I take it, it has been for at least five hundred years.

This I resolve to myself in the affirmative: and then another question arises: — Whether this House stands firm upon its ancient foundations, and is not, by time and accidents, so declined from its perpendicular as to want the hand of the wise and experienced architects of the day to set it upright again, and to prop and buttress it up for duration; — whether it continues true to the principles upon which it has hitherto stood; — whether this be *de facto* the constitution of the House of Commons, as it has been since the time that the House of Commons has without dispute become a necessary and an efficient part of the British Constitution. To ask whether a thing which has always been the same stands to its usual principle seems to me to be perfectly absurd : for how do you know the principles, but from the construction? and if that remains the same, the principles remain the same. It is true that to say your Constitution is what it has been is no sufficient defence for those who say it is a bad constitution. It is an answer to those who say that it is a degenerate constitution. To those who say it is a bad one, I answer, Look to its effects. In all moral machinery, the moral results are its test.

On what grounds do we go to restore our Constitution to what it has been at some given period, or to reform and reconstruct it upon principles more conformable to a sound theory of government ? A prescriptive government, such as ours, never was the work of any legislator, never was made upon any foregone theory. It seems to me a preposterous way of reasoning, and a perfect confusion of ideas, to take the theories which learned and speculative men have made from that government, and then, supposing it made on those theories which were made from it, to accuse the government as not corresponding with them. I do not vilify theory and speculation: no, because that would be to vilify reason itself. *Neque decipitur ratio, neque decipit unquam.* No, — whenever I speak against theory, I mean always a weak, erroneous, fallacious, unfounded, or imperfect theory; and one of the ways of discovering that it is a false theory is by comparing it with practice. This is the true touchstone of all theories which regard man and the affairs of men, — Does it suit his nature in general? — does it suit his nature as modified by his habits?

The more frequently this affair is discussed, the stronger the case appears to the sense and the feelings of mankind. I have no more doubt than I entertain of my existence, that this very thing, which is stated as an horrible thing, is the means of the preservation of our Constitution whilst it lasts, — of curing it of many of the disorders which, attending every species of institution, would attend the principle of an exact local representation, or a representation on the principle of numbers. If you reject personal representation, you are pushed upon expedience; and then what they wish us to do is, to prefer their speculations on that subject to the happy experience of this country, of a growing liberty and a growing prosperity for five hundred years. Whatever respect I have

for their talents, this, for one, I will not do. Then
what is the standard of expedience ? Expedience is
that which is good for the community, and good for
every individual in it. Now this expedience is the *desideratum*, to be sought either without the experience
of means or with that experience. If without, as
in case of the fabrication of a new commonwealth,
I will hear the learned arguing what promises to
be expedient; but if we are to judge of a commonwealth actually existing, the first thing I inquire is,
What has been *found* expedient or inexpedient?
And I will not take their *promise* rather than the
performance of the Constitution.

. . . . But no, this was not the cause of the discontents. I went through most of the northern
parts, — the Yorkshire election was then raging;
the year before, through most of the western counties, — Bath, Bristol, Gloucester : not one word, either in the towns or country, on the subject of representation ; much on the receipt tax, something on
Mr. Fox's ambition ; much greater apprehension of
danger from thence than from want of representation. One would think that the ballast of the ship
was shifted with us, and that our Constitution had
the gunwale under water. But can you fairly and
distinctly point out what one evil or grievance has
happened which you can refer to the representative not following the opinion of his constituents ?
What one symptom do we find of this inequality ?
But it is not an arithmetical inequality with which
we ought to trouble ourselves. If there be a moral,
a political equality, this is the *desideratum* in our
Constitution, and in every constitution in the world.
Moral inequality is as between places and between

classes. Now, I ask, what advantage do you find
that the places which abound in representation possess over others in which it is more scanty, in security for freedom, in security for justice, or in any one
of those means of procuring temporal prosperity and
eternal happiness, the ends for which society was
formed? Are the local interests of Cornwall and
Wiltshire, for instance, their roads, canals, their prisons, their police, better than Yorkshire, Warwick-
shire, or Staffordshire? Warwick has members: is
Warwick or Stafford more opulent, happy, or free
than Newcastle, or than Birmingham? Is Wiltshire
the pampered favorite, whilst Yorkshire, like the
child of the bondwoman, is turned out to the desert?
This is like the unhappy persons who live, if they can
be said to live, in the statical chair, — who are ever
feeling their pulse, and who do not judge of health
by the aptitude of the body to perform its functions,
but by their ideas of what ought to be the true balance between the several secretions. Is a committee
of Cornwall, &c., thronged, and the others deserted?
No. You have an equal representation, because you
have men equally interested in the prosperity of the
whole, who are involved in the general interest and
the general sympathy; and, perhaps, these places
furnishing a superfluity of public agents and administrators, (whether in strictness they are representatives
or not I do not mean to inquire, but they are agents
and administrators,) they will stand clearer of local
interests, passions, prejudices, and cabals than the
others, and therefore preserve the balance of the
parts, and with a more general view and a more
steady hand than the rest. . . . . .

In every political proposal we must not leave out

of the question the political views and object of the
proposer; and these we discover, not by what he
says, but by the principles he lays down. "I mean,"
says he, "a moderate and temperate reform: that is,
I mean to do as little good as possible." If the Constitution be what you represent it, and there be no
danger in the change, you do wrong not to make the
reform commensurate to the abuse. Fine reformer,
indeed! generous donor! What is the cause of this
parsimony of the liberty which you dole out to the
people? Why all this limitation in giving blessings
and benefits to mankind? You admit that there is
an extreme in liberty, which may be infinitely noxious to those who are to receive it, and which in the
end will leave them no liberty at all. I think so, too.
They know it, and they feel it. The question is,
then, What is the standard of that extreme? What
that gentleman, and the associations, or some parts
of their phalanxes, think proper? Then our liberties
are in their pleasure; it depends on their arbitrary
will how far I shall be free. I will have none of that
freedom. If, therefore, the standard of moderation
be sought for, I will seek for it. Where? Not in
their fancies, nor in my own: I will seek for it where
I know it is to be found, — in the Constitution I actually enjoy. Here it says to an encroaching prerogative, — "Your sceptre has its length; you cannot
add an hair to your head, or a gem to your crown,
but what an eternal law has given to it." Here it
says to an overweening peerage, — "Your pride finds
banks that it cannot overflow": here to a tumultu-
ous and giddy people, — "There is a bound to the
raging of the sea." Our Constitution is like our
island, which uses and restrains its subject sea; in

vain the waves roar. In that Constitution, I know, and exultingly I feel, both that I am free, and that I am not free dangerously to myself or to others. I know that no power on earth, acting as I ought to do, can touch my life, my liberty, or my property. I have that inward and dignified consciousness of my own security and independence, which constitutes, and is the only thing which does constitute, the proud and comfortable sentiment of freedom in the human breast. I know, too, and I bless God for, my safe mediocrity: I know, that, if I possessed all the talents of the gentlemen on the side of the House I sit, and on the other, I cannot, by royal favor, or by popular delusion, or by oligarchical cabal, elevate myself above a certain very limited point, so as to endanger my own fall, or the ruin of my country. I know there is an order that keeps things fast in their place: it is made to us, and we are made to it. Why not ask another wife, other children, another body, another mind?

The great object of most of these reformers is, to prepare the destruction of the Constitution, by disgracing and discrediting the House of Commons. For they think, (prudently, in my opinion,) that, if they can persuade the nation that the House of Commons is so constituted as not to secure the public liberty, not to have a proper connection with the public interests, so constituted as not either actually or virtually to be the representative of the people, it will be easy to prove that a government composed of a monarchy, an oligarchy chosen by the crown, and such a House of Commons, whatever good can be in such a system, can by no means be a system of free government.

The Constitution of England is never to have a quietus; it is to be continually vilified, attacked, reproached, resisted; instead of being the hope and sure anchor in all storms, instead of being the means of redress to all grievances, itself is the grand grievance of the nation, our shame instead of our glory. If the only specific plan proposed, individual personal representation, is directly rejected by the person who is looked on as the great support of this business, then the only way of considering it is a question of convenience. An honorable gentleman prefers the individual to the present. He therefore himself sees no middle term whatsoever, and therefore prefers, of what he sees, the individual : this is the only thing distinct and sensible that has been advocated. He has, then, a scheme, which is the individual representation, — he is not at a loss, not inconsistent, — which scheme the other right honorable gentleman reprobates. Now what does this go to, but to lead directly to anarchy? For to discredit the only government which he either possesses or can project, what is this but to destroy all government? and this is anarchy. My right honorable friend, in supporting this motion, disgraces his friends and justifies his enemies in order to blacken the Constitution of his country, even of that House of Commons which supported him. There is a difference between a moral or political exposure of a public evil relative to the administration of government, whether in men or systems, and a declaration of defects, real or supposed, in the fundamental constitution of your country. The first may be cured in the individual by the motives of religion, virtue, honor, fear, shame, or interest. Men may be made to abandon also false

.systems, by exposing their absurdity or mischievous tendency to their own better thoughts, or to the contempt or indignation of the public; and after all, if they should exist, and exist uncorrected, they only disgrace individuals as fugitive opinions. But it is quite otherwise with the frame and constitution of the state: if that is disgraced, patriotism is destroyed in its very source. No man has ever willingly obeyed, much less was desirous of defending with his blood, a mischievous and absurd scheme of government. Our first, our dearest, most comprehensive relation, our country, is gone.

It suggests melancholy reflections, in consequence of the strange course we have long held, that we are now no longer quarrelling about the character, or about the conduct of men, or the tenor of measures, but we are grown out of humor with the English Constitution itself: this is become the object of the animosity of Englishmen. This Constitution in former days used to be the admiration and the envy of the world: it was the pattern for politicians, the theme of the eloquent, the meditation of the philosopher, in every part of the world. As to Englishmen, it was their pride, their consolation. By it they lived, for it they were ready to die. Its defects, if it had any, were partly covered by partiality, and partly borne by prudence. Now all its excellencies are forgot, its faults are now forcibly dragged into day, exaggerated by every artifice of representation. It is despised and rejected of men, and every device and invention of ingenuity or idleness set up in opposition or in preference to it. It is to this humor, and it is to the measures growing out of it, that I set myself (I hope not alone) in the most determined opposition. Never

before did we at any time in this country meet upon
the theory of our frame of government, to sit in judgment on the Constitution of our country, to call it as
a delinquent before us, and to accuse it of every defect and every vice, — to see whether it, an object of
our veneration, even our adoration, did or did not ac-
cord with a preconceived scheme in the minds of certain gentlemen. Cast your eyes on the journals of
Parliament. It is for fear of losing the inestimable
treasure we have that I do not venture to game it
out of my hands for the vain hope of improving it.
I look with filial reverence on the Constitution of my
country, and never will cut it in pieces, and put it
into the kettle of any magician, in order to boil it,
with the puddle of their compounds, into youth and
vigor. On the contrary, I will drive away such pretenders; I will nurse its venerable age, and with le-
nient arts extend a parent's breath.

SPEECH

A MOTION, MADE BY THE RIGHT HON. WILLIAM DOWDESWELL,

MARCH 7, 1771,

FOR LEAVE TO BRING IN

A BILL FOR EXPLAINING THE POWERS OF JURIES IN PROSECUTIONS FOR LIBELS.

TOGETHER WITH

A LETTER IN VINDICATION OF THAT MEASURE,

AND

A COPY OF THE PROPOSED BILL.

SPEECH.

I HAVE always understood that a superintendence over the doctrines as well as the proceedings of the courts of justice was a principal object of the constitution of this House, — that you were to watch at once over the lawyer and the law, — that there should be an orthodox faith, as well as proper works: and I have always looked with a degree of reverence and admiration on this mode of superintendence. For, being totally disengaged from the detail of juridical practice, we come something perhaps the better qualified, and certainly much the better disposed, to assert the genuine principle of the laws, in which we can, as a body, have no other than an enlarged and a public interest. We have no common cause of a professional attachment or professional emulations to bias our minds; we have no foregone opinions which from obstinacy and false point of honor we think ourselves at all events obliged to support. So that, with our own minds perfectly disengaged from the exercise, we may superintend the execution of the national justice, which from this circumstance is better secured to the people than in any other country under heaven it can be. As our situation puts us in a proper condition, our power enables us to execute this trust. We may, when we see cause of complaint, administer a remedy: it is in our choice by an address to remove an improper judge, by impeachment before the peers to pursue to destruction a corrupt judge, or by bill to assert, to explain, to enforce, or to reform the law, just as the occasion and necessity of the case shall guide us. We stand in a situation very honorable to ourselves and very useful to our country, if we do not abuse or abandon the trust that is placed in us.

The question now before you is upon the power of juries in prosecuting for libels. There are four opinions: — 1. That the doctrine as held by the courts is proper and constitutional, and therefore should not be altered; 2. That it is neither proper nor constitutional, but that it will be rendered worse by your interference; 3. That it is wrong, but that the only remedy is a bill of retrospect; 4. The opinion of those who bring in the bill, that the thing is wrong, but that it is enough to direct the judgment of the court in future.

The bill brought in is for the purpose of asserting and securing a great object in the juridical constitution of this kingdom, which, from a long series of practices and opinions in our judges, has *in one point*, and in one very essential point, deviated from the true principle.

It is the very ancient privilege of the people of England, that they shall be tried, except in the known exceptions, not by judges appointed by the crown, but by their own fellow-subjects, the peers of that county court at which they owe their suit and service; and out of this principle the trial by juries has grown. This principle has not, that I can find, been contested in any case by any authority whatsoever; but there is one case in which, without directly contesting the principle, the whole substance, energy, and virtue of the privilege is taken out of it, — that is, in the case of a trial by indictment or information for a libel. The doctrine in that case, laid down by several judges, amounts to this: that the jury have no competence, where a libel is alleged, except to find the gross corporeal facts of the writing and the publication, together with the identity of the things and persons to which it refers; but that the intent and the tendency of the work, in which intent and tendency the whole criminality consists, is the sole and exclusive province of the judge. Thus having reduced the jury to the cognizance of facts not in themselves presumptively criminal, but actions neutral and indifferent, the whole matter in which the subject has any concern or interest is taken out of the hands of the jury: and if the jury take more upon themselves, what they so take is contrary to their duty ; it is no *moral*, but a merely *natural* power, — the same by which they may do any other improper act, the same by which they may even prejudice themselves with regard to any other part of the issue before them. Such is the matter, as it now stands in possession of your highest criminal courts, handed down to them from very respectable legal ancestors. If this can once be established in this case, the application in principle to other cases will be easy, and the practice will run upon a descent, until the progress of an encroaching jurisdiction (for it is in its nature to encroach, when once it has passed its limits) coming to confine the juries, case after case, to the corporeal fact, and to that alone, and excluding the intention of mind, the only source of merit and demerit, of reward or punishment, juries become a dead letter in the Constitution.

For which reason it is high time to take this matter into the consideration of Parliament : and for
that purpose it will be necessary to examine, first,
whether there is anything in the peculiar nature of
this crime that makes it necessary to exclude the jury
from considering the intention in it, more than in
others.   So far from it, that I take it to be much less
so from the analogy of other criminal cases, where
no such restraint is ordinarily put upon them.   The
act of homicide is *primâ facie* criminal; the intention is afterwards to appear, for the jury to acquit or
condemn.   In burglary do they insist that the jury
have nothing to do but to find the taking of goods,
and that, if they do, they must necessarily find the
party guilty, and leave the rest to the judge, and that
they have nothing to do with the word *felonicè* in the
indictment ?

The next point is, to consider it as a question of
constitutional policy : that is, whether the decision
of the question of libel ought to be left to the judges
as a presumption of law, rather than to the jury as
matter of popular judgment, — as the malice in the
case of murder, the felony in the case of stealing.
If the intent and tendency are not matters within the
province of popular judgment, but legal and technical conclusions formed upon general principles of
law, let us see what they are.   Certainly they are
most unfavorable, indeed totally adverse, to the Constitution of this country.

Here we must have recourse to analogies ; for we
cannot argue on ruled cases one way or the other.
See the history.   The old books, deficient in general
in crown cases, furnish us with little on this head.
As to the crime, in the very early Saxon law I see an

offence of this species, called folk-leasing, made a
capital offence, but no very precise definition of the
crime, and no trial at all. See the statute of 3rd
Edward I. cap. 34. The law of libels could not have
arrived at a very early period in this country. It is
no wonder that we find no vestige of any constitution
from authority, or of any deductions from legal science, in our old books and records, upon that subject.
The statute of *Scandalum Magnatum* is the oldest that
I know, and this goes but a little way in this sort of
learning. Libelling is not the crime of an illiterate
people. When they were thought no mean clerks
who could read and write, when he who could read
and write was presumptively a person in holy orders,
libels could not be general or dangerous; and scandals merely *oral* could *spread* little and must *perish*
soon. It is writing, it is printing more emphatically,
that imps calumny with those eagle-wings on which,
as the poet says, "immortal slanders fly." By the
press they spread, they last, they leave the sting in
the wound. Printing was not known in England
much earlier than the reign of Henry the Seventh,
and in the third year of that reign the court of Star-
Chamber was established. The press and its enemy
are nearly coeval. As no positive law against libels
existed, they fell under the indefinite class of misdemeanors. For the trial of misdemeanors that court
was instituted. Their tendency to produce riots and
disorders was a main part of the charge, and was laid
in order to give the court jurisdiction chiefly against
libels. The offence was new. Learning of their
own upon the subject they had none; and they were
obliged to resort to the only emporium where it was
to be had, the Roman law. After the Star-Chamber

was abolished in the 10th of Charles I., its authority
indeed ceased, but its maxims subsisted and survived
it. The spirit of the Star-Chamber has transmigrated
and lived again ; and Westminster Hall was obliged
to borrow from the Star-Chamber, for the same reasons as the Star-Chamber had borrowed from the
Roman Forum, because they had no law, statute, or
tradition of their own. Thus the Roman law took
possession of our courts, — I mean its doctrine, not
its sanctions : the severity of capital punishment was
omitted, all the rest remained. The grounds of these
laws are just and equitable. Undoubtedly the good
fame of every man ought to be under the protection
of the laws, as well as his life and liberty and property. Good fame is an outwork that defends them all
and renders them all valuable. The law forbids you
to revenge ; when it ties up the hands of some, it
ought to restrain the tongues of others. The good
fame of government is the same ; it ought not to be
traduced. This is necessary in all government ; and
if opinion be support, what takes away this destroys
that support : but the liberty of the press is necessary
to this government.

The wisdom, however, of government is of more
importance than the laws. I should study the temper
of the people, before I ventured on actions of this
kind. I would consider the whole of the prosecution
of a libel of such importance as Junius, as one piece,
as one consistent plan of operations : and I would
contrive it so, that, if I were defeated, I should not
be disgraced, — that even my victory should not be
more ignominious than my defeat ; I would so man-
age, that the lowest in the predicament of guilt
should not be the only one in punishment. I would

not inform against the mere vender of a collection of pamphlets. I would not put him to trial first, if I could possibly avoid it. I would rather stand the consequences of my first error than carry it to a judgment that must disgrace my prosecution or the court. We ought to examine these things in a manner which becomes ourselves, and becomes the object of the inquiry, — not to examine into the most important consideration which can come before us with minds heated with prejudice and filled with passions, with vain popular opinions and humors, and, when we propose to examine into the justice of others, to be unjust ourselves.

An inquiry is wished, as the most effectual way of putting an end to the clamors and libels which are the disorder and disgrace of the times. For people remain quiet, they sleep secure, when they imagine that the vigilant eye of a censorial magistrate watches over all the proceedings of judicature, and that the sacred fire of an eternal constitutional jealousy, which is the guardian of liberty, law, and justice, is alive night and day, and burning in this House. But when the magistrate gives up his office and his duty, the people assume it, and they inquire too much and too irreverently, because they think their representatives do not inquire at all.

We have in a libel, 1st, the writing; 2nd, the communication, called by the lawyers the publication; 3rd, the application to persons and facts; 4th, the intent and tendency; 5th, the matter, — diminution of fame. The law presumptions on all these are in the communication. No intent can make a defamatory publication good, nothing can make it have a good tendency; truth is not pleadable. Taken *jurid-*

ically, the foundation of these law presumptions is not unjust; taken *constitutionally*, they are ruinous, and tend to the total suppression of all publication. If juries are confined to the fact, no writing which censures, however justly or however temperately, the conduct of administration, can be unpunished. Therefore, if the intent and tendency be left to the judge, as legal conclusions growing from the fact, you may depend upon it you can have no public discussion of a public measure ; which is a point which even those who are most offended with the licentiousness of the press (and it is very exorbitant, very provoking) will hardly contend for.

So far as to the first opinion, — that the doctrine is right, and needs no alteration. 2nd. The next is, that it is wrong, but that we are not in a condition to help it. I admit it is true that there are cases of a nature so delicate and complicated that an act of Parliament on the subject may become a matter of great difficulty. It sometimes cannot define with exactness, because the subject-matter will not bear an exact definition. It may seem to *take away* everything which it does not positively *establish*, and this might be inconvenient; or it may seem, *vice versâ*, to *establish* everything which it does not *expressly take away*. It may be more advisable to leave such matters to the enlightened discretion of a judge, awed by a censorial House of Commons. But then it rests upon those who object to a legislative interposition to prove these inconveniences in the particular case before them. For it would be a most dangerous, as it is a most idle and most groundless conceit, to assume as a general principle, that the rights and liberties of the subject are impaired by the care and attention of the legislature to secure them. If so, very ill would the purchase of Magna Charta have merited the deluge of blood which was shed in order to have the body of English privileges defined by a positive written law. This charter, the inestimable monument of English freedom, so long the boast and glory of this nation, would have been at once an instrument of our servitude and a monument of our folly, if this principle were true. The thirty-four confirmations would have been only so many repetitions of their absurdity, so many new links in the chain, and so many invalidations of their right.

You cannot open your statute-book without seeing positive provisions relative to every right of the sub-ject. This business of juries is the subject of not fewer than a dozen. To suppose that juries are something innate in the Constitution of Great Brit-ain, that they have jumped, like Minerva, out of the head of Jove in complete armor, is a weak fancy, sup-ported neither by precedent nor by reason. What-ever is most ancient and venerable in our Constitu-tion, royal prerogative, privileges of Parliament, rights of elections, authority of courts, juries, must have been modelled according to the occasion. I spare your pa-tience, and I pay a compliment to your understand-ing, in not attempting to prove that anything so elaborate and artificial as a jury was not the work of *chance*, but a matter of institution, brought to its present state by the joint efforts of legislative author-ity and juridical prudence. It need not be ashamed of being (what in many parts of it, at least, it is) the offspring of an act of Parliament, unless it is a shame for our laws to be the results of our legislature. Juries, which sensitively shrink from the rude touch of Parliamentary remedy, have been the subject of not fewer than, I think, forty-three acts of Parliament, in which they have been changed with all the authority of a creator over its creature, from Magna Charta to the great alterations which were made in the 29th of George II.

To talk of this matter in any other way is to turn a rational principle into an idle and vulgar superstition, — like the antiquary, Dr. Woodward, who trembled to have his shield scoured, for fear it should be discovered to be no better than an old pot-lid. This species of tenderness to a jury puts me in mind of a gentleman of good condition, who had been reduced to great poverty and distress : application was made to some rich fellows in his neighborhood to give him some assistance ; but they begged to be excused, for fear of affronting a person of his high birth ; and so the poor gentleman was left to starve, out of pure respect to the antiquity of his family. From this principle has arisen an opinion, that I find current amongst gentlemen, that this distemper ought to be left to cure itself : — that the judges, having been well exposed, and something terrified on account of these clamors, will entirely change, if not very much relax from their rigor ; — if the present race should not change, that the chances of succession may put other more constitutional judges in their place ; — lastly, if neither should happen, yet that the spirit of an English jury will always be sufficient for the vindication of its own rights, and will not suffer itself to be overborne by the bench. I confess that I totally dissent from all these opinions. These suppositions

become the strongest reasons with me to evince the
necessity of some clear and positive settlement of
this question of contested jurisdiction. If judges
are so full of levity, so full of timidity, if they are
influenced by such mean and unworthy passions that
a popular clamor is sufficient to shake the resolution
they build upon the solid basis of a legal principle, I would endeavor to fix that mercury by a
positive law. If to please an administration the
judges can go one way to-day, and to please the
crowd they can go another to-morrow, if they will
oscillate backward and forward between power and
popularity, it is high time to fix the law in such a
manner as to resemble, as it ought, the great Author of all law, in whom there is no variableness
nor shadow of turning.

As to their succession I have just the same opinion.
I would not leave it to the chances of promotion, or
to the characters of lawyers, what the law of the land,
what the rights of juries, or what the liberty of the
press should be. My law should not depend upon
the fluctuation of the closet or the complexion of
men. Whether a black-haired man or a fair-haired
man presided in the Court of King's Bench, I would
have the law the same; the same, whether he was
born *in domo regnatrice* and sucked from his infancy
the milk of courts, or was nurtured in the rugged
discipline of a popular opposition. This law of court
cabal and of party, this *mens quædam nullo perturbata
affectu*, this law of complexion, ought not to be en-
dured for a moment in a country whose being depends upon the certainty, clearness, and stability of
institutions.

Now I come to the last substitute for the proposed

bill, — the spirit of juries operating their own jurisdiction. This I confess I think the worst of all, for
the same reasons on which I objected to the others,
— and for other weighty reasons besides, which are
separate and distinct. First, because juries, being
taken at random out of a mass of men infinitely
large, must be of characters as various as the body
they arise from is large in its extent. If the judges
differ in their complexions, much more will a jury.
A timid jury will give way to an awful judge deliver-
ing oracularly the law, and charging them on their
oaths, and putting it home to their consciences to beware of judging, where the law had given them no
competence. We know that they will do so, they
have done so in an hundred instances. A respectable member of your own House, no vulgar man,
tells you, that, on the authority of a judge, he found a
man guilty in whom at the same time he could find
no guilt. But supposing them full of knowledge and
full of manly confidence in themselves, how will their
knowledge or their confidence inform or inspirit others ? They give no reason for their verdict, they can
but condemn or acquit ; and no man can tell the motives on which they have acquitted or condemned.
So that this hope of the power of juries to assert
their own jurisdiction must be a principle blind, as
being without reason, and as changeable as the complexion of men and the temper of the times.

But, after all, is it fit that this dishonorable contention between the court and juries should subsist any
longer ? On what principle is it that a jury [juror?]
refuses to be directed by the court as to his *competence?* Whether a libel or no libel be a question
of law or of fact may be doubtful; but a question

of jurisdiction and competence is certainly a question of law: on this the court ought undoubtedly to judge, and to judge solely and exclusively. If they judge wrong from excusable error, you ought to correct it, as to-day it is proposed, by an explanatory bill, — or if by corruption, by bill of *penalties* declaratory, and by punishment. What does a juror say to a judge, when he refuses his opinion upon a question of judicature ? " You are so corrupt, that I should consider myself a partaker of your crime, were I to be guided by your opinion " ; or, " You are so grossly ignorant, that I, fresh from my hounds, from my plough, my counter, or my loom, am fit to direct you in your own profession." This is an unfitting, it is a dangerous state of things. The spirit of any sort of men is not a fit *rule* for deciding on the bounds of their jurisdiction : first, because it is different in different men, and even different in the same at different times, and can never become the proper directing line of law ; next, because it is not reason, but feeling, and, when once it is irritated, it is not apt to confine itself within its proper limits. If it becomes not difference in opinion upon law, but a trial of spirit between parties, our courts of law are no longer the temple of justice, but the amphitheatre for gladiators. No, — God forbid ! Juries ought to take their law from the bench only ; but it is *our* business that they should hear nothing from the bench but what is agreeable to the principles of the Constitution. The jury are to hear the judge : the judge is to hear the law, where it speaks plain ; where it does not, he is to hear the legislature. As I do not think these opinions of the judges to be agreeable to those principles, I wish

to take the only method in which they can or ought
to be corrected, — by bill.

Next, my opinion is, that it ought to be rather by a
bill for removing controversies than by a bill in the
state of manifest and express declaration and in
words *de præterito*. I do this upon reasons of equity
and constitutional policy. I do not want to censure
the present judges. I think them to be excused for
their error. Ignorance is no excuse for a judge; it is
changing the nature of his crime; it is not absolving.
It must be such error as a wise and conscientious
judge may possibly fall into, and must arise from one
or both these causes: — 1. A plausible principle of
law; 2. The precedents of respectable authorities,
and in good times. In the first, the principle of law,
that the judge is to decide on law, the jury to decide
on fact, is an ancient and venerable principle and
maxim of the law; and if supported in this application by precedents of good times and of good men, the
judge, if wrong, ought to be corrected, — he ought
not to be reproved or to be disgraced, or the authority or respect to your tribunals to be impaired. In
cases in which declaratory bills have been made,
where by violence and corruption some fundamental
part of the Constitution has been struck at, where
they would damn the principle, censure the persons,
and annul the acts, — but where the law has been
by the accident of human frailty depraved or in a
particular instance misunderstood, where you neither
mean to rescind the acts nor to censure the persons,
in such cases you have taken the explanatory mode,
and, without condemning what is done, you direct
the future judgment of the court.

All bills for the reformation of the law must be

according to the subject-matter, the circumstances,
and the occasion, and are of four kinds: — 1. Either
the law is totally wanting, and then a new enacting
statute must be made to supply that want; or, 2.
it is *defective*, then a new law must be made to
enforce it; 3. or it is opposed by power or fraud,
and then an act must be made to declare it; 4. or it
is rendered doubtful and controverted, and then a
law must be made to explain it. These must be
applied according to the exigence of the case: one is
just as good as another of them. Miserable indeed
would be the resources, poor and unfurnished the
stores and magazines of legislation, if we were bound
up to a little narrow form, and not able to frame our
acts of Parliament according to every disposition of
our own minds and to every possible emergency of
the commonwealth, — to make them declaratory, enforcing, explanatory, repealing, just in what mode or
in what degree we please.

Those who think that the judges living and dead
are to be condemned, that your tribunals of justice
are to be dishonored, that their acts and judgments
on this business are to be rescinded, — they will
undoubtedly vote against this bill, and for another
sort.

I am not of the opinion of those gentlemen who
are against disturbing the public repose: I like a
clamor, whenever there is an abuse. The fire-bell at
midnight disturbs your sleep, but it keeps you from
being burned in your bed. The hue-and-cry alarms
the county, but it preserves all the property of the
province. All these clamors aim at *redress*. But a
clamor made merely for the purpose of rendering
the people discontented with their situation, without

an endeavor to give them a practical remedy, is indeed one of the worst acts of sedition.

I have read and heard much upon the conduct of our courts in the business of libels. I was extremely willing to enter into, and very free to act as facts should turn out on that inquiry, aiming constantly at remedy as the end of all clamor, all debate, all writing, and all inquiry; for which reason I did embrace, and do now with joy, this method of giving quiet to the courts, jurisdiction to juries, liberty to the press, and satisfaction to the people. I thank my friends for what they have done; I hope the public will one day reap the benefit of their pious and judicious endeavors. They have now sown the seed; I hope they will live to see the flourishing harvest. Their bill is sown in weakness; it will, I trust, be reaped in power. And then, however, we shall have reason to apply to them what my Lord Coke says was an aphorism continually in the mouth of a great sage of the law, — "Blessed be not the complaining tongue, but *blessed be the amending hand.*"

LETTER

ON

MR. DOWDESWELL'S BILL FOR EXPLAINING THE POW—ERS OF JURIES IN PROSECUTIONS FOR LIBELS.*

A N improper and injurious account of the bill
brought into the House of Commons by Mr.
Dowdeswell has lately appeared in one of the public
papers. I am not at all surprised at it, as I am not
a stranger to the views and politics of those who have
caused it to be inserted.

Mr. Dowdeswell did not *bring in an enacting bill to
give to juries*, as the account expresses it, *a power to
try law and fact in matter of libel.* Mr. Dowdeswell
brought in a bill to put an end to those doubts and
controversies upon that subject which have unhappily
distracted our courts, to the great detriment of the
public, and to the great dishonor of the national
justice.

That it is the province of the jury, in informations
and indictments for libels, to try nothing more than
the fact of the composing and of the publishing aver-
ments and innuendoes is a doctrine held at present by
all the judges of the King's Bench, probably by most
of the judges of the kingdom. The same doctrine

* The manuscript from which this Letter is taken is in Mr.
Burke's own handwriting, but it does not appear to whom it was
addressed, nor is there any date affixed to it. It has been thought
proper to insert it here, as being connected with the subject of the
foregoing Speech.

has been held pretty uniformly since the Revolution; and it prevails more or less with the jury, according to the degree of respect with which they are disposed to receive the opinions of the bench.

This doctrine, which, when it prevails, tends to annihilate the benefit of trial by jury, and when it is rejected by juries, tends to weaken and disgrace the authority of the judge, is not a doctrine proper for an English judicature. For the sake both of judge and jury, the controversy ought to be quieted, and the law ought to be settled in a manner clear, definitive, and constitutional, by the only authority competent to it, the authority of the legislature.

Mr. Dowdeswell's bill was brought in for that purpose. It *gives* to the jury no *new* powers; but, after reciting the doubts and controversies, (which nobody denies actually to subsist,) and after stating, that, if juries are not reputed competent to try the whole matter, the benefit of trial by jury will be of none or imperfect effect, it enacts, not that the jury *shall* have the *power*, but that they shall be *held and reputed in law and right competent* to try the whole matter laid in the information. The bill is directing to the judges concerning the opinion in law which they are known to hold upon this subject, — and does not in the least imply that the jury were to derive a new right and power from that bill, if it should have passed into an act of Parliament. The implication is directly the contrary, and is as strongly conveyed as it is possible for those to do who state a doubt and controversy without charging with criminality those persons who so doubted and so controverted.

Such a style is frequent in acts of this nature, and is that only which is suited to the occasion. An in-

sidious use has been made of the words *enact* and
declare, as if they were formal and operative words
of force to distinguish different species of laws producing different effects. Nothing is more groundless; and I am persuaded no lawyer will stand to
such an assertion. The gentlemen who say that a
bill ought to have been brought in upon the principle
and in the style of the Petition of Right and Declaration of Right ought to consider how far the circumstances are the same in the two cases, and how far
they are prepared to go the whole lengths of the reason of those remarkable laws. Mr. Dowdeswell and
his friends are of opinion that the circumstances are
not the same, and that therefore the bill ought not
to be the same.

It has been always disagreeable to the persons who
compose that connection to engage wantonly in a
paper war, especially with gentlemen for whom they
have an esteem, and who seem to agree with them
in the great grounds of their public conduct; but
they can never consent to purchase any assistance
from any persons by the forfeiture of their own reputation. They respect public opinion; and therefore,
whenever they shall be called upon, they are ready
to meet their adversaries, as soon as they please,
before the tribunal of the public, and there to justify the constitutional nature and tendency, the propriety, the prudence, and the policy of their bill.
They are equally ready to explain and to justify all
their proceedings in the conduct of it, — equally
ready to defend their resolution to make it one object (if ever they should have the power) in a plan
of public reformation.

Your correspondent ought to have been satisfied

with the assistance which his friends have lent to administration in defeating that bill. He ought not to make a feeble endeavor (I dare say, much to the displeasure of those friends) to disgrace the gentleman who brought it in. A measure proposed by Mr. Dowdeswell, seconded by Sir George Savile, and supported by their friends, will stand fair with the public, even though it should have been opposed by that list of names (respectable names, I admit) which have been printed with so much parade and ostentation in your papers.

It is not true that Mr. Burke spoke in praise of Lord Mansfield. If he had found anything in Lord Mansfield praiseworthy, I fancy he is not disposed to make an apology to anybody for doing justice. Your correspondent's reason for asserting it is visible enough; and it is altogether in the strain of other misrepresentations. That gentlemen spoke decently of the judges, and he did no more; most of the gentlemen who debated, on both sides, held the same language; and nobody will think their zeal the less warm, or the less effectual, because it is not attended with scurrility and virulence.

·　　·　　·　　·

LIBEL BILL.

WHEREAS doubts and controversies have aris-
en at various times concerning the right of
jurors to try the whole matter laid in indictments
and informations for seditious and other libels; and
whereas trial by juries would be of none or imperfect effect, if the jurors were not held to be competent to try the whole matter aforesaid: for settling
and clearing such doubts and controversies, and for
securing to the subject the effectual and complete
benefit of trial by juries in such indictments and
informations,

Be it enacted, &c., That jurors duly impanelled
and sworn to try the issue between the king and the
defendant upon any indictment or information for a
seditious libel, or a libel under any other denomination or description, shall be held and reputed competent, to all intents and purposes, in law and in
right, to try every part of the matter laid or charged
in said indictment or information, comprehending
the criminal intention of the defendant, and the
evil tendency of the libel charged, as well as the
mere fact of the publication thereof, and the application by innuendo of blanks, initial letters, pictures,
and other devices; any opinion, question, ambiguity,
or doubt to the contrary notwithstanding.

SPEECH

ON

A BILL FOR THE REPEAL OF THE MARRIAGE ACT.

JUNE 15, 1781.

SPEECH.

THIS act [*the Marriage Act*] stands upon *two* principles: one, that the power of marrying without consent of parents should not take place till twenty-one years of age; the other, that all marriages should be *public*.

The proposition of the honorable mover goes to the first; and undoubtedly his motives are fair and honorable; and even in that measure by which he would take away paternal power, he is influenced to it by filial piety; and he is led into it by a natural, and to him inevitable, but real mistake, — that the ordinary race of mankind advance as fast towards maturity of judgment and understanding as he does.

The question is not now, whether the law ought to acknowledge and protect such a state of life as minority, nor whether the continuance which is fixed for that state be not improperly prolonged in the law of England. Neither of these in general are questioned. The only question is, whether matrimony is to be taken out of the general rule, and whether the minors of both sexes, without the consent of their parents, ought to have a capacity of contracting the matrimonial, whilst they have not the capacity of contracting any other engagement. Now it appears to me very clear that they ought not. It is a great mistake to think that mere *animal* propagation is the sole end of matrimony. Matrimony is instituted not only for the propagation of men, but for their nutrition, their education, their establishment, and for the answering of all the purposes of a rational and moral being ; and it is not the duty of the community to consider alone of how many, but how useful citizens it shall be composed.

It is most certain that men are well qualified for. propagation long before they are sufficiently qualified even by bodily strength, much less by mental prudence, and by acquired skill in trades and professions, for the maintenance of a family. Therefore to enable and authorize any man to introduce citizens into the commonwealth, before a rational security can be given that he may provide for them and educate them as citizens ought to be provided for and educated, is totally incongruous with the whole order of society. Nay, it is fundamentally unjust; for a man that breeds a family without competent means of maintenance incumbers other men with his children, and disables them so far from maintaining their own. The improvident marriage of one man becomes a tax upon the orderly and regular marriage of all the rest. Therefore those laws are wisely constituted that give a man the use of all his faculties at one time, that they may be mutually subservient, aiding and assisting to each other : that the time of his completing his bodily strength, the time of mental discretion, the time of his having learned his trade, and the time at which he has the disposition of his fortune, should be likewise the time in which he is permitted to introduce citizens into the state, and to charge the community with their maintenance. To give a man a family during his apprenticeship, whilst his very labor belongs to another, — to give him a family,

when you do not give him a fortune to maintain it,
— to give him a family before he can contract any
one of those engagements without which no business
can be carried on, would be to burden the state with
families without any security for their maintenance.
When parents themselves marry their children, they
become in some sort security to prevent the ill consequences. You have this security in parental consent; the state takes its security in the knowledge of
human nature. Parents ordinarily consider little the
passion of their children and their present gratification. Don't fear the power of a father: it is kind to
passion to give it time to cool. But their censures
sometimes make me smile, — sometimes, for I am
very infirm, make me angry: *sœpe bilem, sœpe jocum
movent.*

It gives me pain to differ on this occasion from
many, if not most, of those whom I honor and esteem.
To suffer the grave animadversion and censorial re-
buke of the honorable gentleman who made the motion, of him whose good-nature and good sense the
House look upon with a particular partiality, whose
approbation would have been one of the highest ob
jects of my ambition, — this hurts me. It is said the
Marriage Act is aristocratic. I am accused, I am
told abroad, of being a man of aristocratic principles.
If by aristocracy they mean the peers, I have no vulgar admiration, nor any vulgar antipathy towards
them; I hold their order in cold and decent respect.
I hold them to be of an absolute necessity in the Constitution; but I think they are only good when kept
within their proper bounds. I trust, whenever there
has been a dispute between these Houses, the part I
have taken has not been equivocal. If by the aris-

tocracy (which, indeed, comes nearer to the point)
they mean an adherence to the rich and powerful
against the poor and weak, this would, indeed, be a
very extraordinary part. I have incurred the odium
of gentlemen in this House for not paying sufficient
regard to men of ample property. When, indeed,
the smallest rights of the poorest people in the kingdom are in question, I would set my face against any
act of pride and power countenanced by the highest
that are in it; and if it should come to the last
extremity, and to a contest of blood, — God forbid!
God forbid! — my part is taken: I would take my
fate with the poor and low and feeble. But if these
people came to turn their liberty into a cloak for
maliciousness, and to seek a privilege of exemption,
not from power, but from the rules of morality and
virtuous discipline, then I would join my hand to
make them feel the force which a few united in a
good cause have over a multitude of the profligate
and ferocious.

I wish the nature of the ground of repeal were
considered with a little attention. It is said the act
tends to accumulate, to keep up the power of great
families, and to add wealth to wealth. It may be
that it does so. It is impossible that any principle of
law or government useful to the community should
be established without an advantage to those who
have the greatest stake in the country. Even some
vices arise from it. The same laws which secure
property encourage avarice; and the fences made
about honest acquisition are the strong bars which
secure the hoards of the miser. The dignities of
magistracy are encouragements to ambition, with all
the black train of villanies which attend that wicked

passion. But still we must have laws to secure property, and still we must have ranks and distinctions and magistracy in the state, notwithstanding their manifest tendency to encourage avarice and ambition.

By affirming the parental authority throughout the state, parents in high rank will generally aim at, and will sometimes have the means, too, of preserving their minor children from any but wealthy or splendid matches. But this authority preserves from a thousand misfortunes which embitter every part of every man's domestic life, and tear to pieces the dearest ties in human society.

I am no peer, nor like to be, — but am in middle life, in the mass of citizens; yet I should feel for a son who married a prostituted woman, or a daughter who married a dishonorable and prostituted man, as much as any peer in the realm.

You are afraid of the avaricious principle of fathers. But observe that the avaricious principle is here mitigated very considerably. It is avarice by proxy; it is avarice not working by itself or for itself, but through the medium of parental affection, meaning to procure good to its offspring. But the contest is not between love and avarice.

While you would guard against the possible operation of this species of benevolent avarice, the avarice of the father, you let loose another species of avarice, — that of the fortune-hunter, unmitigated, unqualified. To show the motives, who has heard of a man running away with a woman not worth sixpence? Do not call this by the name of the sweet and best passion, — love. It is robbery, — not a jot better than any other.

Would you suffer the sworn enemy of his family,

his life, and his honor, possibly the shame and scandal and blot of human society, to debauch from his care and protection the dearest pledge that he has on earth, the sole comfort of his declining years, almost in infantine imbecility, — and with it to carry into the hands of his enemy, and the disgrace of Nature, the dear-earned substance of a careful and laborious life? Think of the daughter of an honest, virtuous parent allied to vice and infamy. Think of the hopeful son tied for life by the meretricious arts of the refuse of mercenary and promiscuous lewdness. Have mercy on the youth of both sexes; protect them from their ignorance and inexperience; protect one part of life by the wisdom of another; protect them by the wisdom of laws and the care of Nature.

SPEECH

ON A

MOTION MADE IN THE HOUSE OF COMMONS,

FEBRUARY 17, 1772,

FOR LEAVE TO BRING IN

A BILL TO QUIET THE POSSESSIONS OF THE SUBJECT AGAINST DORMANT CLAIMS OF THE CHURCH.

SPEECH.

IF I considered this bill as an attack upon the Church, brought in for the purpose of impoverishing and weakening the clergy, I should be one of the foremost in an early and vigorous opposition to it.

I admit, the same reasons do not press for limiting the claims of the Church that existed for limiting the crown, by that wisest of all laws which has secured the property, the peace, and the freedom of this country from the most dangerous mode of attack which could be made upon them all.

I am very sensible of the propriety of maintaining that venerable body with decency, — and with more than mere decency. I would maintain it according to the ranks wisely established in it, with that sober and temperate splendor that is suitable to a sacred character invested with high dignity.

There ought to be a symmetry between all the parts and orders of a state. A *poor* clergy in an *opulent* nation can have little correspondence with the body it is to instruct, and it is a disgrace to the public sentiments of religion. Such irreligious frugality is even bad economy, as the little that is given is entirely thrown away. Such an impoverished and degraded clergy in quiet times could never execute their duty, and in time of disorder would infinitely aggravate the public confusions.

That the property of the Church is a favored and

privileged property I readily admit. It is made with great wisdom; since a perpetual body, with a perpetual duty, ought to have a perpetual provision.

The question is not, the property of the Church, or its security. The question is, whether you will render the principle of prescription a principle of the law of this land, and incorporate it with the whole of your jurisprudence, — whether, having given it first against the laity, then against the crown, you will now extend it to the Church.

The acts which were made, giving limitation against the laity, were not acts against the property of those who might be precluded by limitations. The act of quiet against the crown was not against the interests of the crown, but against a power of vexation.

If the principle of prescription be not a constitution of positive law, but a principle of natural equity, then to hold it out against any man is not doing him injustice.

That *tithes* are due of common right is readily granted; and if this principle had been kept in its original straitness, it might, indeed, be supposed that to plead an exemption was to plead a long-continued *fraud*, and that no man could *be deceived* in such a title, — as the moment he bought land, he must know that he bought land tithed : prescription could not aid him, for prescription can only attach on a supposed *bonâ fide* possession. But the fact is, that the principle has been broken in upon.

Here it is necessary to distinguish two sorts of property.

1. Land carries no *mark* on it to distinguish it as ecclesiastical, as tithes do, which are a *charge* on land ; therefore, though it had been made *inalienable*,

it ought perhaps to be subject to limitation. It might *bonâ fide* be held.

But, first, it was not originally inalienable, no, not by the Canon Law, until the restraining act of the 11th [1st?] of Elizabeth. But the great revolution of the dissolution of monasteries, by the 31st Hen., ch. 13, has so mixed and confounded ecclesiastical with lay property, that a man may by every rule of good faith be possessed of it. The statute of Queen Elizabeth, ann. 1, ch. 1, [?] gave away the bishop's lands. So far as to *lands*.

As to *tithes*, they are not things in their own nature subject to be barred by prescription upon the general principle. But tithes and Church lands, by the statutes of Henry VIII. and the 11th [1st?] Eliz., have become objects *in commercio :* for by coming to the crown they became grantable in that way to the subject, and a great part of the Church lands passed through the crown to the people.

By passing to the king, tithes became property to a mixed party ; by passing from the king, they became absolutely *lay* property : the partition-wall was broken down, and tithes and Church possession became no longer synonymous terms. No [A?] man, therefore, might become a fair purchaser of tithes, and of exemption from tithes.

By the statute of Elizabeth, the lands took the same course, (I will not inquire by what justice, good policy, and decency,) but they passed into lay lands, became the object of purchases for valuable consideration, and of marriage settlements.

Now, if tithes might come to a layman, land in the hands of a layman might be also tithe-free. So that there was an object which a layman might become seized of equitably and *bonâ fide;* there was something on which a prescription might attach, the end of which is, to secure the natural well-meaning ignorance of men, and to secure property by the best of all principles, continuance.

I have therefore shown that a layman may be equitably seized of Church lands, — 2. of tithes, — 3. of exemption from tithes; and you will not contend that there should be no prescription. Will you say that the alienations made before the 11th of Elizabeth shall not stand good?

I do not mean anything against the Church, her dignities, her honors, her privileges, or her possessions. I should wish even to enlarge them all: not that the Church of England is incompetently endowed. This is to take nothing from her but the power of making herself odious. If she be secure herself, she can have no objection to the security of others. For I hope she is secure from lay-bigotry and anti-priestcraft, for certainly such things there are. I heartily wish to see the Church secure in such possessions as will not only enable her ministers to preach the Gospel with ease, but of such a kind as will enable them to preach it with its full effect, so that the pastor shall not have the inauspicious appearance of a tax-gatherer, — such a maintenance as is compatible with the civil prosperity and improvement of their country.

HINTS

FOR

AN ESSAY ON THE DRAMA.

NOTE.

THESE Hints appear to have been first thoughts, which were probably intended to be amplified and connected, and so worked up into a regular dissertation. No date appears of the time when they were written, but it was probably before the year 1765.

HINTS

FOR AN ESSAY ON THE DRAMA.

IT is generally observed that no species of writing is so difficult as the dramatic. It must, indeed, appear so, were we to consider it upon one side only. It is a dialogue, or species of composition which in itself requires all the mastery of a complete writer with grace and spirit to support. We may add, that it must have a fable, too, which necessarily requires invention, one of the rarest qualities of the human mind. It would surprise us, if we were to examine the thing critically, how few good original stories there are in the world. The most celebrated borrow from each other, and are content with some new turn, some corrective, addition, or embellishment. Many of the most celebrated writers in that way can claim no other merit. I do not think La Fontaine has one original story. And if we pursue him to those who were his originals, the Italian writers of tales and novels, we shall find most even of them drawing from antiquity, or borrowing from the Eastern world, or adopting and decorating the little popular stories they found current and tradionary in their country. Sometimes they laid the foundation of their tale in real fact. Even after all their borrowing from so many funds, they are still far from opulent. How few stories has Boccace which are tolerable, and how much fewer are there which you would desire to read twice! But this general difficulty is greatly increased, when we come to the drama. Here a fable is essential, — a fable which is to be conducted with rapidity, clearness, consistency, and surprise, without any, or certainly with very little, aid from narrative. This is the reason that generally nothing is more dull in telling than the plot of a play. It is seldom or never a good story in itself; and in this particular, some of the greatest writers, both in ancient and modern theatres, have failed in the most miserable manner. It is well a play has still so many requisites to complete it, that, though the writer should not succeed in these particulars, and therefore should be so far from perfection, there are still enough left in which he may please, at less expense of labor to himself, and perhaps, too, with more real advantage to his auditory. It is, indeed, very difficult happily to excite the passions and draw the characters of men; but our nature leads us more directly to such paintings than to the invention of a story. We are imitative animals; and we are more naturally led to imitate the exertions of character and passion than to observe and describe a series of events, and to discover those relations and dependencies in them which will please. Nothing can be more rare than this quality. Herein, as I believe, consists the difference between the inventive and the descriptive genius. By the inventive genius I mean the creator of agreeable facts and incidents; by the descriptive, the delineator of characters, manners, and passions. Imitation calls us to this; we are in some cases almost forced to it, and it is comparatively easy. More

observe the characters of men than the order of
things : to the one we are formed by Nature, and
by that sympathy from which we are so strongly led
to take a part in the passions and manners of our
fellow-men ; the other is, as it were, foreign and ex-
trinsical.   Neither, indeed, can anything be done,
even in this, without invention ; but it is obvious
that this invention is of a kind altogether different
from the former.   However, though the more sublime genius and the greatest art are required for
the former, yet the latter, as it is more common
and more easy, so it is more useful, and adminis-
ters more directly to the great business of life.

If the drama requires such a combination of talents, the most common of which is very rarely to
be found and difficult to be exerted, it is not surprising, at a time when almost all kinds of poetry
are cultivated with little success, to find that we
have done no great matters in this.   Many causes
may be assigned for our present weakness in that
oldest and most excellent branch of philosophy, poetical learning, and particularly in what regards the
theatre.   I shall here only consider what appears
to me to be one of these causes : I mean the wrong
notion of the art itself, which begins to grow fashionable, especially among people of an elegant turn
of mind with a weak understanding ; and these are
they that form the great body of the idle part of
every polite and civilized nation.   The prevailing
system of that class of mankind is indolence.   This
gives them an aversion to all strong movements.
It infuses a delicacy of sentiment, which, when it
is real, and accompanied with a justness of thought,
is an amiable quality, and favorable to the fine arts ;

but when it comes to make the whole of the character, it injures things more excellent than those which it improves, and degenerates into a false refinement, which diffuses a languor and breathes a frivolous air over everything which it can influence. . . . .

Having differed in my opinion about dramatic composition, and particularly in regard to comedy, with a gentleman for whose character and talents I have a very high respect, I thought myself obliged, on account of that difference, to a new and more exact examination of the grounds upon which I had formed my opinions. I thought it would be impossible to come to any clear and definite idea on this subject, without remounting to the natural passions or dispositions of men, which first gave rise to this species of writing; for from these alone its nature, its limits, and its true character can be determined.

There are but four general principles which can move men to interest themselves in the characters of others, and they may be classed under the heads of good and ill opinion : on the side of the first may be classed admiration and love, hatred and contempt on the other. And these have accordingly divided poetry into two very different kinds, — the panegyrical, and the satirical ; under one of which heads all genuine poetry falls (for I do not reckon the didactic as poetry, in the strictness of speech).

Without question, the subject of all poetry was originally direct and personal. Fictitious character is a refinement, and comparatively modern ; for abstraction is in its nature slow, and always follows the progress of philosophy. Men had always friends and enemies before they knew the exact nature of vice

and virtue ; they naturally, and with their best powers of eloquence, whether in prose or verse, magni-
fied and set off the one, vilified and traduced the
other.

The first species of composition in either way was
probably some general, indefinite topic of praise or
blame, expressed in a song or hymn, which is the
most common and simple kind of panegyric and satire. But as nothing tended to set their hero or
subject in a more forcible light than some story to
their advantage or prejudice, they soon introduced
a narrative, and thus improved the composition into
a greater variety of pleasure to the hearer, and to a
more forcible instrument of honor or disgrace to the
subject.

It is natural with men, when they relate any action with any degree of warmth, to represent the
parties to it talking as the occasion requires ; and
this produces that mixed species of poetry, composed
of narrative and dialogue, which is very universal
in all languages, and of which Homer is the noblest
example in any. This mixed kind of poetry seems
also to be most perfect, as it takes in a variety
of situations, circumstances, reflections, and descriptions, which must be rejected on a more limited
plan.

It must be equally obvious, that men, in relating
a story in a forcible manner, do very frequently
mimic the looks, gesture, and voice of the person
concerned, and for the time, as it were, put themselves into his place. This gave the hint to the
drama, or acting ; and observing the powerful effect
of this in public exhibitions . . . .

But the drama, the most artificial and complicated

of all the poetical machines, was not yet brought to perfection; and like those animals which change their state, some parts of the old narrative still adhered. It still had a chorus, it still had a prologue to explain the design; and the perfect drama, an automaton supported and moved without any foreign help, was formed late and gradually. Nay, there are still several parts of the world in which it is not, and probably never may be, formed. The Chinese drama.

The drama, being at length formed, naturally adhered to the first division of poetry, the satirical and panegyrical, which made tragedy and comedy.

Men, in praising, naturally applaud the dead. Tragedy celebrated the dead.

Great men are never sufficiently shown but in struggles. Tragedy turned, therefore, on melancholy and affecting subjects, — a sort of threnodia, — its passions, therefore, admiration, terror, and pity.

Comedy was satirical. Satire is best on the living.

It was soon found that the best way to depress an hated character was to turn it into ridicule; and therefore the greater vices, which in the beginning were lashed, gave place to the *contemptible*. Its passion, therefore, became ridicule.

Every writing must have its characteristic passion. What is that of comedy, if not ridicule?

Comedy, therefore, is a satirical poem, representing an action carried on by dialogue, to excite laughter by describing ludicrous characters. See Aristotle.

Therefore, to preserve this definition, the ridicule must be either in the action or characters, or both.

An action may be ludicrous, independent of the

characters, by the ludicrous situations and accidents which may happen to the characters.

But the action is not so important as the characters. We see this every day upon the stage.

What are the characters fit for comedy?

It appears that no part of human life which may be subject to ridicule is exempted from comedy; for wherever men run into the absurd, whether high or low, they may be the subject of satire, and consequently of comedy. Indeed, some characters, as kings, are exempted through decency; others might be too insignificant. Some are of opinion that persons in better life are so polished that their true characters and the real bent of their humor cannot appear. For my own part, I cannot give entire credit to this remark. For, in the first place, I believe that good-breeding is not so universal or strong in any part of life as to overrule the real characters and strong passions of such men as would be proper objects of the drama. Secondly, it is not the ordinary, commonplace discourse of assemblies that is to be represented in comedy. The parties are to be put in situations in which their passions are roused, and their real characters called forth; and if their situations are judiciously adapted to the characters, there is no doubt but they will appear in all their force, choose what situation of life you please. Let the politest man alive game, and feel at loss; let this be his character; and his politeness will never hide it, nay, it will put it forward with greater violence, and make a more forcible contrast.*

But genteel comedy puts these characters, not in their passionate, but in their genteel light; makes

* Sic in MS.

elegant cold conversation, and virtuous personages.*
Such sort of pictures disagreeable.

Virtue and politeness not proper for comedy; for
they have too much or no movement.

They are not good in tragedy, much less here.

The greater virtues, fortitude, justice, and the like,
too serious and sublime.

It is not every story, every character, every incident, but those only which answer their end. — Painting of artificial things not good; a thing being useful does not therefore make it most pleasing in
picture. — Natural manners, good and bad. — Sentiment. In common affairs and common life, virtuous sentiments are not even the character of virtuous men; we cannot bear these sentiments, but when
they are pressed out, as it were, by great exigencies,
and a certain contention which is above the general
style of comedy. . . . .

The first character of propriety the lawsuit possesses in an eminent degree. The plot of the play is
an iniquitous suit; there can be no fitter persons to
be concerned in the active part of it than low, necessitous lawyers of bad character, and profligates of
desperate fortune. On the other hand, in the passive part, if an honest and virtuous man had been
made the object of their designs, or a weak man of
good intentions, every successful step they should
take against him ought rather to fill the audience
with horror than pleasure and mirth; and if in the
conclusion their plots should be baffled, even this
would come too late to prevent that ill impression.
But in the lawsuit this is admirably avoided: for the
character chosen is a rich, avaricious usurer: the

* Sic in MS.

pecuniary distresses of such a person can never be looked upon with horror; and if he should be even handled unjustly, we always wait his delivery with patience.

Now with regard to the display of the character, which is the essential part of the plot, nothing can be more finely imagined than to draw a miser in law. If you draw him inclined to love and marriage, you depart from the height of his character in some measure, as Molière has done. Expenses of this kind he may easily avoid. If you draw him in law, to advance brings expense, to draw back brings expense; and the character is tortured and brought out at every moment.

A sort of notion has prevailed that a comedy might subsist without humor. It is an idle disquisition, whether a story in private life, represented in dialogues, may not be carried on with some degree of merit without humor. It may unquestionably; but what shines chiefly in comedy, the painting the manners of life, must be in a great measure wanting. A character which has nothing extravagant, wrong, or singular in it can affect but very little: and this is what makes Aristotle draw the great line of distinction between tragedy and comedy. Ἐν αὐτῇ δὲ τῇ διαφορᾷ καὶ ἡ τραγῳδία, &c. Arist. Poet. Ch. II.

•   •   •   •   •   •

There is not a more absurd mistake than that whatever may not unnaturally happen in an action is of course to be admitted into every painting of it. In Nature, the great and the little, the serious and the ludicrous, things the most disproportionate the one to the other, are frequently huddled together in much confusion. And what then? It is the

business of Art first to choose some determinate
end and purpose, and then to select those parts of
Nature, and those only, which conduce to that end,
avoiding with most religious exactness the intermixture of anything which would contradict it. Else
the whole idea of propriety, that is, the only distinction between the just and chimerical in the arts,
would be utterly lost. An hero eats, drinks, and
sleeps, like other men ; but to introduce such scenes
on the stage, because they are natural, would be ridiculous. And why? Because they have nothing
to do with the end for which the play is written.
The design of a piece might be utterly destroyed by
the most natural incidents in the world. Boileau
has somewhere criticized with what surely is a very
just severity on Ariosto, for introducing a ludicrous
tale from his host to one of the principal persons
of his poem, though the story has great merit in
its way. Indeed, that famous piece is so monstrous
and extravagant in all its parts that one is not
particularly shocked with this indecorum. But, as
Boileau has observed, if Virgil had introduced
Æneas listening to a bawdy story from his host,
what an episode had this formed in that divine
poem! Suppose, instead of Æneas, he had represented the impious Mezentius as entertaining himself in that manner; such a thing would not have
been without probability, but it would have clashed
with the very first principles of taste, and, I would
say, of common sense.

I have heard of a celebrated picture of the Last
Supper, — and if I do not mistake, it is said to be the
work of some of the Flemish masters : in this picture
all the personages are drawn in a manner suitable

to the solemnity of the occasion ; but the painter has filled the void under the table with a dog gnawing bones. Who does not see the possibility of such an incident, and, at the same time, the absurdity of introducing it on such an occasion ? Innumerable such cases might be stated. It is not the incompatibility or agreeableness of incidents, characters, or sentiments with the probable in fact, but with propriety in design, that admits or excludes them from a place in any composition. We may as well urge that stones, sand, clay, and metals lie in a certain manner in the earth, as a reason for building with these materials and in that manner, as for writing according to the accidental disposition of characters in Nature. I have, I am afraid, been longer than it might seem necessary in refuting such a notion ; but such authority can only be opposed by a good deal of reason.

We are not to forget that a play is, or ought to be, a very short composition ; that, if one passion or disposition is to be wrought up with tolerable success, I believe it is as much as can in any reason be expected. If there be scenes of distress and scenes of humor, they must either be in a double or single plot. If there be a double plot, there are in fact two. If they be in checkered scenes of serious and comic, you are obliged continually to break both the thread of the story and the continuity of the passion, — if in the same scene, as Mrs. V. seems to recommend, it is needless to observe how absurd the mixture must be, and how little adapted to answer the genuine end of any passion. It is odd to observe the progress of bad taste : for this mixed passion being universally proscribed in the regions of tragedy, it has taken refuge and shelter in comedy, where it seems firmly estab lished, though no reason can be assigned why we may not laugh in the one as well as weep in the other. The true reason of this mixture is to be sought for in the manners which are prevalent amongst a people. It has become very fashionable to affect delicacy, tenderness of heart, and fine feeling, and to shun all imputation of rusticity. Much mirth is very foreign to this character; they have introduced, therefore, a sort of neutral writing.

Now as to characters, they have dealt in them as in the passions. There are none but lords and footmen. One objection to characters in high life is, that almost all wants, and a thousand happy circumstances arising from them, being removed from it, their whole mode of life is too artificial, and not so fit for painting; and the contrary opinion has arisen from a mistake, that whatever has merit in the reality necessarily must have it in the representation. I have observed that persons, and especially women, in lower life, and of no breeding, are fond of such representations. It seems like introducing them into good company, and the honor compensates the dulness of the entertainment.

Fashionable manners being fluctuating is another reason for not choosing them. — Sensible comedy, — talking sense a dull thing — . . . .

AN ESSAY

ABRIDGMENT OF THE ENGLISH HISTORY.

IN THREE BOOKS.

ABRIDGMENT OF ENGLISH HISTORY.

———•———

BOOK I.

CHAPTER I.

CAUSES OF THE CONNECTION BETWEEN THE ROMANS AND
BRITONS. — CÆSAR'S TWO INVASIONS OF BRITAIN.

IN order to obtain a clear notion of the state of
Europe before the universal prevalence of the
Roman power, the whole region is to be divided into
two principal parts, which we shall call Northern and
Southern Europe. The northern part is everywhere
separated from the southern by immense and continued chains of mountains. From Greece it is
divided by Mount Hæmus; from Spain by the Pyrenees; from Italy by the Alps. This division is not
made by an arbitrary or casual distribution of countries. The limits are marked out by Nature, and in
these early ages were yet further distinguished by a
considerable difference in the manners and usages
of the nations they divided.

If we turn our eyes to the northward of these
boundaries, a vast mass of solid continent lies before us, stretched out from the remotest shore of
Tartary quite to the Atlantic Ocean. A line drawn
through this extent, from east to west, would pass
over the greatest body of unbroken land that is any-
where known upon the globe. This tract, in a course

of some degrees to the northward, is not interrupted by any sea; neither are the mountains so disposed as to form any considerable obstacle to hostile incur sions. Originally it was all inhabited but by one sort of people, known by one common denomination of Scythians. As the several tribes of this comprehensive name lay in many parts greatly exposed, and as by their situation and customs they were much inclined to attack, and by both ill qualified for defence, throughout the whole of that immense region there was for many ages a perpetual flux and reflux of barbarous nations. None of their commonwealths continued long enough established on any particular spot to settle and to subside into a regular order, one tribe continually overpowering or thrusting out another. But as these were only the mixtures of Scythians with Scythians, the triumphs of barbarians over barbarians, there were revolutions in empire, but none in manners. The Northern Europe, until some parts of it were subdued by the progress of the Roman arms, remained almost equally covered with all the ruggedness of primitive barbarism.

The southern part was differently circumstanced. Divided, as we have said, from the northern by great mountains, it is further divided within itself by considerable seas. Spain, Greece, and Italy are peninsulas. By these advantages of situation the inhabitants were preserved from those great and sudden revolutions to which the Northern world had been always liable; and being confined within a space comparatively narrow, they were restrained from wandering into a pastoral and unsettled life. It was upon one side only that they could be invaded by land. Whoever made an attempt on any other part must necessarily have arrived in ships of some magnitude, and must therefore have in a degree been cultivated, if not by the liberal, at least by the mechanic arts.   In fact, the principal colonies which we find these countries to have received were sent from Phœnicia, or the Lesser Asia, or Egypt, the great fountains of the ancient civility and learning.   And they became more or less, earlier or later, polished, as they were situated nearer to or further from these celebrated sources.   Though I am satisfied, from a comparison of the Celtic tongues with the Greek and Roman, that the original inhabitants of Italy and Greece were of the same race with the people of Northern Europe, yet it is certain they profited so much by their guarded situation, by the mildness of their climate favorable to humanity, and by the foreign infusions, that they came greatly to excel the Northern nations in every respect, and particularly in the art and discipline of war.   For, not being so strong in their bodies, partly from the temperature of their climate, partly from a degree of softness induced by a more cultivated life, they applied themselves to remove the few inconveniences of a settled society by the advantages which it affords in art, disposition, and obedience; and as they consisted of many small states, their people were well exercised in arms, and sharpened against each other by continual war.

Such was the situation of Greece and Italy from a very remote period.   The Gauls and other Northern nations, envious of their wealth, and despising the effeminacy of their manners, often invaded them with numerous, though ill-formed armies.   But their greatest and most frequent attempts were against Italy, their connection with which country alone we shall here consider. In the course of these wars, the superiority of the Roman discipline over the Gallic ferocity was at length demonstrated. The Gauls, notwithstanding the numbers with which their irruptions were made, and the impetuous courage by which that nation was distinguished, had no permanent success. They were altogether unskilful either in improving their victories or repairing their defeats. But the Romans, being governed by a most wise order of men, perfected by a traditionary experience in the policy of conquest, drew some advantage from every turn of fortune, and, victorious or vanquished, persisted in one uniform and comprehensive plan of breaking to pieces everything which endangered their safety or obstructed their greatness. For, after having more than once expelled the Northern invaders out of Italy, they pursued them over the Alps; and carrying the war into the country of their enemy, under several able generals, and at last under Caius Cæsar, they reduced all the Gauls from the Mediterranean Sea to the Rhine and the Ocean. During the progress of this decisive war, some of the maritime nations of Gaul had recourse for assistance to the neighboring island of Britain. From thence they received considerable succors; by which means this island first came to be known with any exactness by the Romans, and first drew upon it the attention of that victorious people.

Though Cæsar had reduced Gaul, he perceived clearly that a great deal was still wanting to make his conquest secure and lasting. That extensive country, inhabited by a multitude of populous and fierce nations, had been rather overrun than conquered. The Gauls were not yet broken to the yoke, which

they bore with murmuring and discontent. The ruins
of their own strength were still considerable ; and they
had hopes that the Germans, famous for their invincible courage and their ardent love of liberty, would
be at hand powerfully to second any endeavors for
the recovery of their freedom ; they trusted that the
Britons, of their own blood, allied in manners and religion, and whose help they had lately experienced,
would not then be wanting to the same cause. Cæsar
was not ignorant of these dispositions.   He therefore
judged, that, if he could confine the attention of the
Germans and Britons to their own defence, so that
the Gauls, on which side soever they turned, should
meet nothing but the Roman arms, they must soon
be deprived of all hope, and compelled to seek their
safety in an entire submission.

These were the public reasons which made the
invasion of Britain and Germany an undertaking, at
that particular time, not unworthy a wise and able
general. But these enterprises, though reasonable
in themselves, were only subservient to purposes of
more importance, and which he had more at heart.
Whatever measures he thought proper to pursue on
the side of Germany, or on that of Britain, it was
towards Rome that he always looked, and to the fur-
therance of his interest there that all his motions
were really directed.   That republic had receded
from many of those maxims by which her freedom
had been hitherto preserved under the weight of so
vast an empire.   Rome now contained many citizens
of immense wealth, eloquence, and ability.   Particular men were more considered than the republic ; and
the fortune and genius of the Roman people, which
formerly had been thought equal to everything, came

now to be less relied upon than the abilities of a few popular men. The war with the Gauls, as the old and most dangerous enemy of Rome, was of the last importance ; and Cæsar had the address to obtain the conduct of it for a term of years, contrary to one of the most established principles of their government. But this war was finished before that term was expired, and before the designs which he entertained against the liberty of his country were fully ripened. It was therefore necessary to find some pretext for keeping his army on foot ; it was necessary to employ them in some enterprise that might at once raise his character, keep his interest alive at Rome, endear him to his troops, and by that means weaken the ties which held them to their country.

From this motive, colored by reasons plausible and fit to be avowed, he resolved in one and the same year, and even when that was almost expired, upon two expeditions, the objects of which lay at a great distance from each other, and were as yet untouched by the Roman arms. And first he resolved to pass the Rhine, and penetrate into Germany.

Cæsar spent but twenty-eight days in his German expedition. In ten he built his admirable bridge across the Rhine ; in eighteen he performed all he proposed by entering that country. When the Germans saw the barrier of their river so easily overcome, and Nature herself, as it were, submitted to the yoke, they were struck with astonishment, and never after ventured to oppose the Romans in the field. The most obnoxious of the German countries were ravaged, the strong awed, the weak taken into protection. Thus an alliance being formed, always the first step of the Roman policy, and not only a pre-

tence, but a means, being thereby acquired of entering the country upon any future occasion, he
marched back through Gaul to execute a design of
much the same nature and extent in Britain.

The inhabitants of that island, who were divided
into a great number of petty nations, under a very
coarse and disorderly frame of government, did not
find it easy to plan any effectual measures for their
defence. In order, however, to gain time in
this exigency, they sent ambassadors to Cæ- B. C. 55.
sar with terms of submission. Cæsar could not col-
orably reject their offers. But as their submission
rather clashed than coincided with his real designs,
he still persisted in his resolution of passing over into
Britain ; and accordingly embarked with the infantry
of two legions at the port of Itium.* His landing was
obstinately disputed by the natives, and brought on a
very hot and doubtful engagement. But the superi-
or dispositions of so accomplished a commander, the
resources of the Roman discipline, and the effect of
the military engines on the unpractised minds of a
barbarous people prevailed at length over the best resistance which could be made by rude numbers and
mere bravery. The place where the Romans first
entered this island was somewhere near Deal, and
the time fifty-five years before the birth of Christ.

The Britons, who defended their country with so
much resolution in the engagement, immediately after it lost all their spirit. They had laid no regular plan for their defence. Upon their first failure
they seemed to have no resources left. On the slightest loss they betook themselves to treaty and submission ; upon the least appearance in their favor

* Some think this port to be Witsand, others Boulogne.

they were as ready to resume their arms, without
any regard to their former engagements: a conduct
which demonstrates that our British ancestors had
no regular polity with a standing coercive power.
The ambassadors which they sent to Cæsar laid all
the blame of a war carried on by great armies upon
the rashness of their young men, and they declared
that the ruling people had no share in these hostilities. This is exactly the excuse which the savages
of America, who have no regular government, make
at this day upon the like occasions; but it would be
a strange apology from one of the modern states of
Europe that had employed armies against another.
Cæsar reprimanded them for the inconstancy of their
behavior, and ordered them to bring hostages to secure their fidelity, together with provisions for his
army. But whilst the Britons were engaged in the
treaty, and on that account had free access to the
Roman camp, they easily observed that the army of
the invaders was neither numerous nor well provided; and having about the same time received intelligence that the Roman fleet had suffered in a storm,
they again changed their measures, and came to a
resolution of renewing the war. Some prosperous
actions against the Roman foraging parties inspired
them with great confidence. They were betrayed by
their success into a general action in the open field.
Here the disciplined troops obtained an easy and
complete victory; and the Britons were taught the
error of their conduct at the expense of a terrible
slaughter.

Twice defeated, they had recourse once more to
submission. Cæsar, who found the winter approaching, provisions scarce, and his fleet not fit to contend

with that rough and tempestuous sea in a winter voyage, hearkened to their proposals, exacting double the number of the former hostages. He then set sail with his whole army.

In this first expedition into Britain, Cæsar did not make, nor indeed could he expect, any considerable advantage. He acquired a knowledge of the sea-coast, and of the country contiguous to it; and he became acquainted with the force, the manner of fighting, and the military character of the people. To compass these purposes he did not think a part of the summer ill-bestowed. But early in the next he prepared to make a more effective use of the experience he had gained. He embarked again at the same port, but with a more numerous army. The Britons, on their part, had prepared more regularly for their defence in this than the former year. Several of those states which were nearest and most exposed to the danger had, during Cæsar's absence, combined for their common safety, and chosen Cassibelan, a chief of power and reputation, for the leader of their union. They seemed resolved to dispute the landing of the Romans with their former intrepidity. But when they beheld the sea covered, as far as the eye could reach, with the multitude of the enemy's ships, (for they were eight hundred sail,) they despaired of defending the coast, they retired into the woods and fastnesses, and Cæsar landed his army without opposition.

The Britons now saw the necessity of altering their former method of war. They no longer, therefore, opposed the Romans in the open field; they formed frequent ambuscades; they divided themselves into light flying parties, and continually harassed the enemy on his march. This plan, though in their circumstances the most judicious, was attended with no great success. Cæsar forced some of their strongest intrenchments, and then carried the war directly into the territories of Cassibelan.

The only fordable passage which he could find over the Thames was defended by a row of palisadoes which lined the opposite bank; another row of sharpened stakes stood under water along the middle of the stream. Some remains of these works long subsisted, and were to be discerned in the river * down almost to the present times. The Britons had made the best of the situation; but the Romans plunged into the water, tore away the stakes and palisadoes, and obtained a complete victory. The capital, or rather chief fastness, of Cassibelan was then taken, with a number of cattle, the wealth of this barbarous city. After these misfortunes the Britons were no longer in a condition to act with effect. Their ill-success in the field soon dissolved the ill-cemented union of their councils. They split into factions, and some of them chose the common enemy for their protector, insomuch that, after some feeble and desultory efforts, most of the tribes to the southward of the Thames submitted themselves to the conqueror. Cassibelan, worsted in so many encounters, and deserted by his allies, was driven at length to sue for peace. A tribute was imposed; and as the summer began to wear away, Cæsar, having finished the war to his satisfaction, embarked for Gaul.

The whole of Cæsar's conduct in these two campaigns sufficiently demonstrates that he had no intention of making an absolute conquest of any part of

* Coway Stakes, near Kingston-on-Thames.

Britain. Is it to be believed, that, if he had formed
such a design, he would have left Britain without an
army, without a legion, without a single cohort, to secure his conquest, and that he should sit down contented with an empty glory and the tribute of an indigent people, without any proper means of securing
a continuance of that small acquisition ? This is not
credible. But his conduct here, as well as in Germany, discovers his purpose in both expeditions : for
by them he confirmed the Roman dominion in Gaul,
he gained time to mature his designs, and he afforded
his party in Rome an opportunity of promoting his
interest and exaggerating his exploits, which they
did in such a manner as to draw from the Senate
a decree for a very remarkable acknowledgment of
his services in a supplication or thanksgiving of
twenty days. This attempt, not being pursued, stands
single, and has little or no connection with the subsequent events.

Therefore I shall in this place, where the narrative
will be the least broken, insert from the best authorities which are left, and the best conjectures which in
so obscure a matter I am able to form, some account
of the first peopling of this island, the manners of its
inhabitants, their art of war, their religious and civil
discipline. These are matters not only worthy of
attention as containing a very remarkable piece of
antiquity, but as not wholly unnecessary towards
comprehending the great change made in all these
points, when the Roman conquest came afterwards
to be completed.

CHAPTER II.

SOME ACCOUNT OF THE ANCIENT INHABITANTS OF BRITAIN.

THAT Britain was first peopled from Gaul we are assured by the best proofs, — proximity of situation, and resemblance in language and manners. Of the time in which this event happened we must be contented to remain in ignorance, for we have no monuments. But we may conclude that it was a very ancient settlement, since the Carthaginians found this island inhabited when they traded hither for tin, — as the Phœnicians, whose tracks they followed in this commerce, are said to have done long before them. It is true, that, when we consider the short interval between the universal deluge and that period, and compare it with the first settlement of men at such a distance from this corner of the world, it may seem not easy to reconcile such a claim to antiquity with the only authentic account we have of the origin and progress of mankind, — especially as in those early ages the whole face of Nature was extremely rude and uncultivated, when the links of commerce, even in the countries first settled, were few and weak, navigation imperfect, geography unknown, and the hardships of travelling excessive. But the spirit of migration, of which we have now only some faint ideas, was then strong and universal, and it fully compensated all these disadvantages. Many writers, indeed, imagine that these migrations, so common in the primitive times, were caused by the prodigious increase of people beyond what their several territories could maintain. But this opinion, far from being

supported, is rather contradicted by the general appearance of things in that early time, when in every
country vast tracts of land were suffered to lie almost
useless in morasses and forests.   Nor is it, indeed,
more countenanced by the ancient modes of life, no
way favorable to population.   I apprehend that these
first settled countries, so far from being overstocked
with inhabitants, were rather thinly peopled, and that
the same causes which occasioned that thinness occasioned also those frequent migrations which make so
large a part of the first history of almost all nations.
For in these ages men subsisted chiefly by pasturage
or hunting.   These are occupations which spread the
people without multiplying them in proportion ; they
teach them an extensive knowledge of the country ;
they carry them frequently and far from their homes,
and weaken those ties which might attach them to
any particular habitation.

It was in a great degree from this manner of life
that mankind became scattered in the earliest times
over the whole globe.   But their peaceful occupations
did not contribute so much to that end as their wars,
which were not the less frequent and violent because
the people were few, and the interests for which they
contended of but small importance.   Ancient history
has furnished us with many instances of whole nations,
expelled by invasion, falling in upon others, which
they have entirely overwhelmed, — more irresistible
in their defeat and ruin than in their fullest prosperity.   The rights of war were then exercised with great
inhumanity.   A cruel death, or a servitude scarcely
less cruel, was the certain fate of all conquered people ; the terror of which hurried men from habitations to which they were but little attached, to seek

security and repose under any climate that, however
in other respects undesirable, might afford them refuge from the fury of their enemies. Thus the bleak
and barren regions of the North, not being peopled
by choice, were peopled as early, in all probability, as
many of the milder and more inviting climates of the
Southern world; and thus, by a wonderful disposition of the Divine Providence, a life of hunting,
which does not contribute to increase, and war,
which is the great instrument in the destruction of
men, were the two principal causes of their being
spread so early and so universally over the whole
earth. From what is very commonly known of the
state of North America, it need not be said how often
and to what distance several of the nations on that
continent are used to migrate, who, though thinly
scattered, occupy an immense extent of country. Nor
are the causes of it less obvious, — their hunting life,
and their inhuman wars.

Such migrations, sometimes by choice, more frequently from necessity, were common in the ancient
world. Frequent necessities introduced a fashion
which subsisted after the original causes. For how
could it happen, but from some universally estab
lished public prejudice, which always overrules and
stifles the private sense of men, that a whole nation
should deliberately think it a wise measure to quit
their country in a body, that they might obtain in a
foreign land a settlement which must wholly depend
upon the chance of war? Yet this resolution was
taken and actually pursued by the entire nation of
the Helvetii, as it is minutely related by Cæsar. The
method of reasoning which led them to it must appear to us at this day utterly inconceivable. They

were far from being compelled to this extraordinary
migration by any want of subsistence at home; for it
appears that they raised, without difficulty, as much
corn in one year as supported them for two; they
could not complain of the barrenness of such a soil.

This spirit of migration, which grew out of the ancient manners and necessities, and sometimes operated like a blind instinct, such as actuates birds of
passage, is very sufficient to account for the early
habitation of the remotest parts of the earth, and in
some sort also justifies that claim which has been so
fondly made by almost all nations to great antiquity.

Gaul, from whence Britain was originally peopled,
consisted of three nations: the Belgæ, towards the
north; the Celtæ, in the middle countries; and the
Aquitani, to the south. Britain appears to have received its people only from the two former. From
the Celtæ were derived the most ancient tribes of the
Britons, of which the most considerable were called
Brigantes. The Belgæ, who did not even settle in
Gaul until after Britain had been peopled by colonies
from the former, forcibly drove the Brigantes into
the inland countries, and possessed the greatest part
of the coast, especially to the south and west. These
latter, as they entered the island in a more improved
age, brought with them the knowledge and practice
of agriculture, which, however, only prevailed in
their own countries. The Brigantes still continued
their ancient way of life by pasturage and hunting.
In this respect alone they differed: so that what
we shall say, in treating of their manners, is equally
applicable to both. And though the Britons were
further divided into an innumerable multitude of
lesser tribes and nations, yet all being the branches

of these two stocks, it is not to our purpose to consider them more minutely.

Britain was in the time of Julius Cæsar what it is at this day, in climate and natural advantages, temperate and reasonably fertile. But destitute of all those improvements which in a succession of ages it has received from ingenuity, from commerce, from riches and luxury, it then wore a very rough and savage appearance. The country, forest or marsh ; the habitations, cottages ; the cities, hiding-places in woods; the people naked, or only covered with skins; their sole employment, pasturage and hunting. They painted their bodies for ornament or terror, by a custom general amongst all savage nations, who, being passionately fond of show and finery, and having no object but their naked bodies on which to exercise this disposition, have in all times painted or cut their skins, according to their ideas of ornament. They shaved the beard on the chin ; that on the upper lip was suffered to remain, and grow to an extraordinary length, to favor the martial appearance, in which they placed their glory. They were in their natural temper not unlike the Gauls, impatient, fiery, inconstant, ostentatious, boastful, fond of novelty, — and like all barbarians, fierce, treacherous, and cruel. Their arms were short javelins, small shields of a slight texture, and great cutting swords with a blunt point, after the Gaulish fashion.

Their chiefs went to battle in chariots, not unartfully contrived nor unskilfully managed. I cannot help thinking it something extraordinary, and not easily to be accounted for, that the Britons should have been so expert in the fabric of those chariots, when they seem utterly ignorant in all other mechanic

arts : but thus it is delivered to us. They had also
horse, though of no great reputation, in their armies.
Their foot was without heavy armor ; it was no firm
body, nor instructed to preserve their ranks, to make
their evolutions, or to obey their commanders ; but
in tolerating hardships, in dexterity of forming ambuscades, (the art military of savages,) they are said
to have excelled. A natural ferocity and an impetuous onset stood them in the place of discipline.

It is very difficult, at this distance of time, and
with so little information, to discern clearly what
sort of civil government prevailed among the ancient
Britons. In all very uncultivated countries, as society is not close nor intricate, nor property very valuable, liberty subsists with few restraints. The natural equality of mankind appears and is asserted, and
therefore there are but obscure lines of any form of
government. In every society of this sort the natural connections are the same as in others, though the
political ties are weak. Among such barbarians,
therefore, though there is little authority in the magistrate, there is often great power lodged, or rather
left, in the father : for, as among the Gauls, so among
the Britons, he had the power of life and death in his
own family, over his children and his servants.

But among freemen and heads of families, causes
of all sorts seem to have been decided by the Druids :
they summoned and dissolved all the public assemblies ; they alone had the power of capital punishments, and indeed seem to have had the sole execution and interpretation of whatever laws subsisted
among this people. In this respect the Celtic nations did not greatly differ from others, except that
we view them in an earlier stage of society. Justice

was in all countries originally administered by the priesthood: nor, indeed, could laws in their first feeble state have either authority or sanction, so as to compel men to relinquish their natural independence, had they not appeared to come down to them enforced by beings of more than human power. The first openings of civility have been everywhere made by religion. Amongst the Romans, the custody and interpretation of the laws continued solely in the college of the pontiffs for above a century.*

The time in which the Druid priesthood was instituted is unknown. It probably rose, like other institutions of that kind, from low and obscure beginnings, and acquired from time, and the labors of able men, a form by which it extended itself so far, and attained at length so mighty an influence over the minds of a fierce and otherwise ungovernable people. Of the place where it arose there is somewhat less doubt: Cæsar mentions it as the common opinion that this institution began in Britain, that there it always remained in the highest perfection, and that from thence it diffused itself into Gaul. I own I find it not easy to assign any tolerable cause why an order of so much authority and a discipline so exact should have passed from the more barbarous people to the more civilized, from the younger to the older, from the colony to the mother country: but it is not wonderful that the early extinction of this order, and that general contempt in which the Romans held all the barbarous nations, should have left these matters obscure and full of difficulty.

The Druids were kept entirely distinct from the body of the people; and they were exempted from all

* Digest. Lib. I. Tit. ii. De Origine et Progressu Juris, § 6.

the inferior and burdensome offices of society, that
they might be at leisure to attend the important
duties of their own charge. They were chosen out
of the best families, and from the young men of the
most promising talents : a regulation which placed
and preserved them in a respectable light with the
world. None were admitted into this order but after
a long and laborious novitiate, which made the character venerable in their own eyes by the time and
difficulty of attaining it. They were much devoted
to solitude, and thereby acquired that abstracted and
thoughtful air which is so imposing upon the vulgar ;
and when they appeared in public, it was seldom,
and only on some great occasion, — in the sacrifices
of the gods, or on the seat of judgment. They prescribed medicine ; they formed the youth ; they paid
the last honors to the dead ; they foretold events ;
they exercised themselves in magic. They were at
once the priests, lawgivers, and physicians of their nation, and consequently concentred in themselves all
that respect that men have diffusively for those who
heal their diseases, protect their property, or reconcile them to the Divinity. What contributed not a
little to the stability and power of this order was the
extent of its foundation, and the regularity and proportion of its structure. It took in both sexes ; and
the female Druids were in no less esteem for their
knowledge and sanctity than the males. It was divided into several subordinate ranks and classes ; and
they all depended upon a chief or Arch-Druid, who
was elected to his place with great authority and pre-
eminence for life. They were further armed with
a power of interdicting from their sacrifices, or ex-
communicating, any obnoxious persons. This inter-

diction, so similar to that used by the ancient Athe-
nians, and to that since practised among Christians,
was followed by an exclusion from all the benefits of
civil community; and it was accordingly the most
dreaded of all punishments. This ample authority
was in general usefully exerted; by the interposition
of the Druids differences were composed, and wars
ended; and the minds of the fierce Northern people,
being reconciled to each other under the influence of
religion, united with signal effect against their common enemies.

There was a class of the Druids whom they called
Bards, who delivered in songs (their only history)
the exploits of their heroes, and who composed those
verses which contained the secrets of Druidical discipline, their principles of natural and moral philosophy, their astronomy, and the mystical rites of their
religion. These verses in all probability bore a near
resemblance to the Golden Verses of Pythagoras, —
to those of Phocylides, Orpheus, and other remnants
of the most ancient Greek poets. The Druids, even
in Gaul, where they were not altogether ignorant of
the use of letters, in order to preserve their knowledge in greater respect, committed none of their pre-
cepts to writing. The proficiency of their pupils was
estimated principally by the number of technical
verses which they retained in their memory: a circumstance that shows this discipline rather calculated to preserve with accuracy a few plain maxims
of traditionary science than to improve and extend
it. And this is not the sole circumstance which
leads us to believe that among them learning had
advanced no further than its infancy.

The scholars of the Druids, like those of Pythagoras, were carefully enjoined a long and religious silence : for, if barbarians come to acquire any knowledge, it is rather by instruction than examination; they must therefore be silent. Pythagoras, in the rude times of Greece, required silence in his disciples; but Socrates, in the meridian of the Athenian refinement, spoke less than his scholars : everything was disputed in the Academy.

The Druids are said to be very expert in astronomy, in geography, and in all parts of mathematical knowledge ; and authors speak in a very exaggerated strain of their excellence in these, and in many other sciences. Some elemental knowledge I suppose they had ; but I can scarcely be persuaded that their learning was either deep or extensive. In all countries where Druidism was professed, the youth were generally instructed by that order ; and yet was there little either in the manners of the people, in their way of life, or their works of art, that demonstrates profound science or particularly mathematical skill. Britain, where their discipline was in its highest perfection, and which was therefore resorted to by the people of Gaul as an oracle in Druidical questions, was more barbarous in all other respects than Gaul itself, or than any other country then known in Europe. Those piles of rude magnificence, Stonehenge and Abury, are in vain produced in proof of their mathematical abilities. These vast structures have nothing which can be admired, but the greatness of the work ; and they are not the only instances of the great things which the mere labor of many hands united, and persevering in their purpose, may accomplish with very little help from mechanics. This may be evinced by the immense buildings and the low state of the sciences among the original Peruvians.

The Druids were eminent above all the philosophic lawgivers of antiquity for their care in impressing the doctrine of the soul's immortality on the minds of their people, as an operative and leading principle. This doctrine was inculcated on the scheme of Transmigration, which some imagine them to have derived from Pythagoras. But it is by no means necessary to resort to any particular teacher for an opinion which owes its birth to the weak struggles of unenlightened reason, and to mistakes natural to the human mind. The idea of the soul's immortality is indeed ancient, universal, and in a manner inherent in our nature; but it is not easy for a rude people to conceive any other mode of existence than one similar to what they had experienced in life, nor any other world as the scene of such an existence but this we inhabit, beyond the bounds of which the mind extends itself with great difficulty. Admiration, indeed, was able to exalt to heaven a few selected heroes: it did not seem absurd that those who in their mortal state had distinguished themselves as superior and overruling spirits should after death ascend to that sphere which influences and governs everything below, or that the proper abode of beings at once so illustrious and permanent should be in that part of Nature in which they had always observed the greatest splendor and the least mutation. But on ordinary occasions it was natural some should imagine that the dead retired into a remote country, separated from the living by seas or mountains. It was natural that some should follow their imagination with

a simplicity still purer, and pursue the souls of men
no further than the sepulchres in which their bodies
had been deposited;* whilst others of deeper pene-
tration, observing that bodies worn out by age or
destroyed by accident still afforded the materials
for generating new ones, concluded likewise that a
soul being dislodged did not wholly perish, but was
destined, by a similar revolution in Nature, to act
again, and to animate some other body. This last
principle gave rise to the doctrine of Transmigration : but we must not presume of course, that, where
it prevailed, it necessarily excluded the other opinions; for it is not remote from the usual procedure
of the human mind, blending in obscure matters
imagination and reasoning together, to unite ideas
the most inconsistent. When Homer represents the
ghosts of his heroes appearing at the sacrifices of
Ulysses, he supposes them endued with life, sensa-
tion, and a capacity of moving; but he has joined
to these powers of living existence uncomeliness,
want of strength, want of distinction, the characteristics of a dead carcass. This is what the mind
is apt to do : it is very apt to confound the ideas
of the surviving soul and the dead body. The
vulgar have always and still do confound these very
irreconcilable ideas. They lay the scene of appa-
ritions in churchyards; they habit the ghost in a
shroud ; and it appears in all the ghastly paleness
of a corpse. A contradiction of this kind has given
rise to a doubt whether the Druids did in reality
hold the doctrine of Transmigration. There is posi- •
tive testimony that they did hold it; there is also
testimony as positive that they buried or burned

* Cic. Tusc. Quest. Lib. I.

with the dead utensils, arms, slaves, and whatever might be judged useful to them, as if they were to be removed into a separate state. They might have held both these opinions ; and we ought not to be surprised to find error inconsistent.

The objects of the Druid worship were many. In this respect they did not differ from other heathens : but it must be owned that in general their ideas of divine matters were more exalted than those of the Greeks and Romans, and that they did not fall into an idolatry so coarse and vulgar. That their gods should be represented under a human form they thought derogatory to beings uncreated and imperishable. To confine what can endure no limits within walls and roofs they judged absurd and impious. In these particulars there was something refined and suitable enough to a just idea of the Divinity. But the rest was not equal. Some notions they had, like the greatest part of mankind, of a Being eternal and infinite ; but they also, like the greatest part of mankind, paid their worship to inferior objects, from the nature of ignorance and superstition always tending downwards.

The first and chief objects of their worship were the elements, — and of the elements, fire, as the most pure, active, penetrating, and what gives life and energy to all the rest. Among fires, the preference was given to the sun, as the most glorious visible being, and the fountain of all life. Next they venerated the moon and the planets. After fire, water was held in reverence. This, when pure, and ritually prepared, was supposed to wash away all sins, and to qualify the priest to approach the altar of the gods with more acceptable prayers : washing with water being a type natural enough of inward cleansing and purity of mind. They also worshipped fountains and lakes and rivers.

Oaks were regarded by this sect with a' particular veneration, as, by their greatness, their shade, their stability, and duration, not ill representing the perfections of the Deity. From the great reverence in which they held this tree, it is thought their name of Druids is derived: the word Deru, in the Celtic language, signifying an oak. But their reverence was not wholly confined to this tree. All forests were held sacred; and many particular plants were respected, as endued with a particular holiness. No plant was more revered than the mistletoe, especially if it grew on the oak, — not only because it is rarely found upon that tree, but because the oak was among the Druids peculiarly sacred. Towards the end of the year they searched for this plant, and when it was found great rejoicing ensued; it was approached with reverence; it was cut with a golden hook; it was not suffered to fall to the ground, but received with great care and solemnity upon a white garment.

In ancient times, and in all countries, the profession of physic was annexed to the priesthood. Men imagined that all their diseases were inflicted by the immediate displeasure of the Deity, and therefore concluded that the remedy would most probably proceed from those who were particularly employed in his service. Whatever, for the same reason, was found of efficacy to avert or cure distempers was considered as partaking somewhat of the Divinity. Medicine was always joined with magic: no remedy was administered without mysterious ceremony and incantation. The use of plants and herbs, both in medici-

nal and magical practices, was early and general.
The mistletoe, pointed out by its very peculiar appearance and manner of growth, must have struck
powerfully on the imaginations of a superstitious
people. Its virtues may have been soon discovered.
It has been fully proved, against the opinion of
Celsus, that internal remedies were of very early
use.* Yet if it had not, the practice of the present
savage nations supports the probability of that opinion. By some modern authors the mistletoe is said
to be of signal service in the cure of certain convulsive distempers, which, by their suddenness, their violence, and their unaccountable symptoms, have been
ever considered as supernatural. The epilepsy was
by the Romans for that reason called *morbus sacer;*
and all other nations have regarded it in the same
light. The Druids also looked upon vervain, and
some other plants, as holy, and probably for a similar reason.

The other objects of the Druid worship were chiefly serpents, in the animal world, and rude heaps of
stone, or great pillars without polish or sculpture, in
the inanimate. The serpent, by his dangerous qualities, is not ill adapted to inspire terror, — by his annual renewals, to raise admiration, — by his make,
easily susceptible of many figures, to serve for a variety of symbols, — and by all, to be an object of religious observance : accordingly, no object of idolatry
has been more universal.† And this is so natural,

---

* See this point in the Divine Legation of Moses.

† Παρὰ παντὶ νομιζομένων παρ' ὑμῖν θεῶν ὄφις σύμβολον μέγα καὶ
μυστήριον ἀναγράφεται. — Justin Martyr, in Stillingfleet's Origines
Sacræ.

that serpent-veneration seems to be rising again even in the bosom of Mahometanism.*

The great stones, it has been supposed, were originally monuments of illustrious men, or the memorials of considerable actions, — or they were landmarks for deciding the bounds of fixed property. In time the memory of the persons or facts which these stones were erected to perpetuate wore away; but the reverence which custom, and probably certain periodical ceremonies, had preserved for those places was not so soon obliterated. The monuments themselves then came to be venerated, — and not the less because the reason for venerating them was no longer known. The landmark was in those times held sacred on account of its great uses, and easily passed into an object of worship. Hence the god Terminus amongst the Romans. This religious observance towards rude stones is one of the most ancient and universal of all customs. Traces of it are to be found in almost all, and especially in these Northern nations; and to this day, in Lapland, where heathenism is not yet entirely extirpated, their chief divinity, which they call *Storjunkare*, is nothing more than a rude stone.†

Some writers among the moderns, because the Druids ordinarily made no use of images in their worship, have given into an opinion that their religion was founded on the unity of the Godhead. But this is no just consequence. The spirituality of the idea, admitting their idea to have been spiritual, does not infer the unity of the object. All the ancient authors who speak of this order agree, that, besides those great and more distinguishing ob-

* Norden's Travels.
† Scheffer's Lapland, p. 92, the translation.

jects of their worship already mentioned, they had gods answerable to those adored by the Romans. And we know that the Northern nations, who over-ran the Roman Empire, had in fact a great plurality of gods, whose attributes, though not their names, bore a close analogy to the idols of the Southern world.

The Druids performed the highest act of religion by sacrifice, agreeably to the custom of all other nations. They not only offered up beasts, but even human victims: a barbarity almost universal in the heathen world, but exercised more uniformly, and with circumstances of peculiar cruelty, amongst those nations where the religion of the Druids prevailed. They held that the life of a man was the only atone-ment for the life of a man. They frequently inclosed a number of wretches, some captives, some criminals, and, when these were wanting, even innocent victims, in a gigantic statue of wicker-work, to which they set fire, and invoked their deities amidst the horrid cries and shrieks of the sufferers, and the shouts of those who assisted at this tremendous rite.

There were none among the ancients more eminent for all the arts of divination than the Druids. Many of the superstitious practices in use to this day among the country people for discovering their future for-tune seem to be remains of Druidism. Futurity is the great concern of mankind. Whilst the wise and learned look back upon experience and history, and reason from things past about events to come, it is natural for the rude and ignorant, who have the same desires without the same reasonable means of satisfaction, to inquire into the secrets of futu-rity, and to govern their conduct by omens, dreams, and prodigies. The Druids, as well as the Etruscan and Roman priesthood, attended with diligence the flight of birds, the pecking of chickens, and the entrails of their animal sacrifices. It was obvious that no contemptible prognostics of the weather were to be taken from certain motions and appearances in birds and beasts.* A people who lived mostly in the open air must have been well skilled in these observations. And as changes in the weather influenced much the fortune of their huntings or their harvests, which were all their fortunes, it was easy to apply the same prognostics to every event by a transition very natural and common ; and thus probably arose the science of auspices, which formerly guided the deliberations of councils and the motions of armies, though now they only serve, and scarcely serve, to amuse the vulgar.

The Druid temple is represented to have been nothing more than a consecrated wood. The ancients speak of no other. But monuments remain which show that the Druids were not in this respect wholly confined to groves. They had also a species of building which in all probability was destined to religious use. This sort of structure was, indeed, without walls or roof. It was a colonnade, generally circular, of huge, rude stones, sometimes single, sometimes double, sometimes with, often without, an architrave. These open temples were not in all respects peculiar to the Northern nations. Those of the Greeks, which were dedicated to the celestial gods, ought in strictness to have had no roof, and were thence called *hypœthra.*†

* Cic. de Divinatione, Lib. I.
† Decor. . . . . perficitur statione, ... cum Jovi Fulguri, et

Many of these monuments remain in the British islands, curious for their antiquity, or astonishing for the greatness of the work :. enormous masses of rock, so poised as to be set in motion with the slightest touch, yet not to be pushed from their place by a very great power; vast altars, peculiar and mystical in their structure, thrones, basins, heaps or cairns; and a variety of other works, displaying a wild industry, and a strange mixture of ingenuity and rudeness. But they are all worthy of attention, — not only as such monuments often clear up the darkness and supply the defects of history, but as they lay open a noble field of speculation for those who study the changes which have happened in the manners, opinions, and sciences of men, and who think them as worthy of regard as the fortune of wars and the revolutions of kingdoms.

The short account which I have here given does not contain the whole of what is handed down to us by ancient writers, or discovered by modern research, concerning this remarkable order. But I have selected those which appear to me the most striking features, and such as throw the strongest light on the genius and true character of the Druidical institution. In some respects it was undoubtedly very singular ; it stood out more from the body of the people than the priesthood of other nations; and their knowledge and policy appeared the more striking by being contrasted with the great simplicity and rudeness of the people over whom they presided. But, notwithstanding some peculiar appearances and

Cœlo, et Soli, et Lunæ ædificia sub divo hypæthraque constituentur. Horum enim deorum et species et effectus in aperto mundo atque lucenti præsentes videmus. — Vitruv. de Architect. p. 6. de Laet. Antwerp.

practices, it is impossible not to perceive a great conformity between this and the ancient orders which
have been established for the purposes of religion in
almost all countries. For, to say nothing of the resemblance which many have traced between this and
the Jewish priesthood, the Persian Magi, and the In-
dian Brahmans, it did not so greatly differ from the
Roman priesthood, either in the original objects or
in the general mode of worship, or in the constitution
of their hierarchy. In the original institution neither
of these nations had the use of images; the rules of
the Salian as well as Druid discipline were delivered
in verse; both orders were under an elective head;
and both were for a long time the lawyers of their
country. So that, when the order of Druids was
suppressed by the Emperors, it was rather from a
dread of an influence incompatible with the Roman
government than from any dislike of their religious
opinions.

CHAPTER III.

THE REDUCTION OF BRITAIN BY THE ROMANS.

THE death of Cæsar, and the civil wars which ensued, afforded foreign nations some respite from the
Roman ambition. Augustus, having restored peace
to mankind, seems to have made it a settled maxim
of his reign not to extend the Empire. He found
himself at the head of a new monarchy; and he was
more solicitous to confirm it by the institutions of
sound policy than to extend the bounds of its dominion. In consequence of this plan Britain was neglected.

Tiberius came a regular successor to an established government. But his politics were dictated rather by his character than his situation. He was a lawful prince, and he acted on the maxims of an usurper. Having made it a rule never to remove far from the capital, and jealous of every reputation which seemed too great for the measure of a subject, he neither undertook any enterprise of moment in his own person nor cared to commit the conduct of it to another. There was little in a British triumph that could affect a temper like that of Tiberius.

His successor, Caligula, was not influenced by this, nor indeed by any regular system; for, having undertaken an expedition to Britain without any determinate view, he abandoned it on the point of execution without reason. And adding ridicule to his disgrace, his soldiers returned to Rome loaded with shells. These spoils he displayed as the ornaments of a triumph which he celebrated over the Ocean, — if in all these particulars we may trust to the historians of that time, who relate things almost incredible of the folly of their masters and the patience of the Roman people.

But the Roman people, however degenerate, still retained much of their martial spirit; and as the Emperors held their power almost entirely by the affection of the soldiery, they found themselves often obliged to such enterprises as might prove them no improper heads of a military constitution. An expedition to Britain was well adapted to answer all the purposes of this ostentatious policy. The country was remote and little known, so that every exploit there, as if achieved in another world, appeared at Rome with double pomp and lustre; whilst the sea,

which divided Britain from the continent, prevented
a failure in that island from being followed by any
consequences alarming to the body of the Empire.
A pretext was not wanting to this war. The maritime Britons, while the terror of the Roman arms
remained fresh upon their minds, continued regularly to pay the tribute imposed by Cæsar. But the
generation which experienced that war having passed
away, that which succeeded felt the burden, but
knew from rumor only the superiority which had
imposed it ; and being very ignorant, as of all things
else, so of the true extent of the Roman power, they
were not afraid to provoke it by discontinuing the
payment of the tribute.

This gave occasion to the Emperor Clau-
dius, ninety-seven years after the first expe-   A. D. 43.
dition of Cæsar, to invade Britain in person, and with
a great army. But he, having rather surveyed than
conducted the war, left in a short time the management of it to his legate, Plautius, who subdued without much difficulty those countries which lay to the
southward of the Thames, the best cultivated and most
accessible parts of the island. But the inhabitants of
the rough inland countries, the people called Cattivel-
launi, made a more strenuous opposition. They were
under the command of Caractacus, a chief of great
and just renown amongst all the British nations.
This leader wisely adjusted his conduct of the war to
the circumstances of his savage subjects and his rude
country. Plautius obtained no decisive advantages
over him. He opposed Ostorius Scapula, who succeeded that general, with the same bravery, but with
unequal success ; for he was, after various turns of
fortune, obliged to abandon his dominions, which Ostorius at length subdued and disarmed.

This bulwark of the British freedom being over-turned, Ostorius was not afraid to enlarge his plan. Not content with disarming the enemies of Rome, he proceeded to the same extremities with those nations who had been always quiet, and who, under the name of an alliance, lay ripening for subjection. This fierce people, who looked upon their arms as their only valuable possessions, refused to submit to terms as severe as the most absolute conquest could impose. They unanimously entered into a league against the Romans. But their confederacy was either not sufficiently strong or fortunate to resist so able a commander, and only afforded him an opportunity, from a more comprehensive victory, to extend the Roman province a considerable way to the northern and western parts of the island. The frontiers of this acquisition, which extended along the rivers Severn and Nen, he secured by a chain of forts and stations; the inland parts he quieted by the settlement of colonies of his veteran troops at Maldon and Verulam: and such was the beginning of those establishments which afterwards became so numerous in Britain. This commander was the first who traced in this island a plan of settlement and civil policy to concur with his military operations. For, after he had settled these colonies, considering with what difficulty any and especially an uncivilized people are broke into submission to a foreign government, he imposed it on some of the most powerful of the British nations in a more indirect manner. He placed them under kings of their own race; and whilst he paid this compliment to their pride, he secured their obedience by the interested fidelity of a prince who knew, that, as he

owed the beginning, so he depended for the duration of his authority wholly upon their favor. Such
was the dignity and extent of the Roman policy,
that they could number even royalty itself amongst
their instruments of servitude.

Ostorius did not confine himself within the boundaries of these rivers. He observed that the Silures,
inhabitants of South Wales, one of the most martial
tribes in Britain, were yet unhurt and almost untouched by the war. He could expect to make no
progress to the northward, whilst an enemy of such
importance hung upon his rear, — especially as they
were now commanded by Caractacus, who preserved
the spirit of a prince, though he had lost his dominions, and fled from nation to nation, wherever
he could find a banner erected against the Romans.
His character obtained him reception and command.

Though the Silures, thus headed, did everything
that became their martial reputation, both in the
choice and defence of their posts, the Romans, by
their discipline and the weight and excellence of
their arms, prevailed over the naked bravery of this
gallant people, and defeated them in a great
battle. Caractacus was soon after betrayed
into their hands, and conveyed to Rome. The merit
of the prisoner was the sole ornament of a triumph
celebrated over an indigent people headed by a gallant chief. The Romans crowded eagerly to behold
the man who, with inferior forces, and in an obscure
corner of the world, had so many years stood up
against the weight of their empire.

As the arts of adulation improved in proportion
as the real grandeur of Rome declined, this advantage was compared to the greatest conquests in the

A. D. 51.

most flourishing times of the Republic: and so far as regarded the personal merit of Caractacus, it could not be too highly rated. Being brought before the emperor, he behaved with such manly fortitude, and spoke of his former actions and his present condition with so much plain sense and unaffected dignity, that he moved the compassion of the emperor, who remitted much of that severity which the Romans formerly exercised upon their captives. Rome was now a monarchy, and that fierce republican spirit was abated which had neither feeling nor respect for the character of unfortunate sovereigns.

The Silures were not reduced by the loss of Caractacus, and the great defeat they had suffered. They resisted every measure of force or artifice that could be employed against them, with the most generous obstinacy: a resolution in which they were confirmed by some imprudent words of the legate, threatening to extirpate, or, what appeared to them scarcely less dreadful, to transplant their nation. Their natural bravery thus hardened into despair, and inhabiting a country very difficult of access, they presented an impenetrable barrier to the progress of that commander; insomuch that, wasted with continual cares, and with the mortification to find the end of his affairs so little answerable to the splendor of their beginning, Ostorius died of grief, and left all things in confusion.

The legates who succeeded to his charge did little more for about sixty years than secure the frontiers of the Roman province. But in the beginning of Nero's reign the command in Britain was devolved on Suetonius Paulinus, a soldier of merit and experience, who, when he came to view the theatre of his future operations, and had well considered the nature of the country, discerned evidently that the war must of necessity be protracted to a great length, if he should be obliged to penetrate into every fastness to which the enemy retired, and to combat their flying parties one by one. He therefore resolved to make such a blow at the head as must of course disable all the inferior members.

The island then called Mona, now Anglesey, at that time was the principal residence of the Druids. Here their councils were held, and their commands from hence were dispersed among all the British nations. Paulinus proposed, in reducing this their favorite and sacred seat, to destroy, or at least greatly to weaken, the body of the Druids, and thereby to extinguish the great actuating principle of all the Celtic people, and that which was alone capable of communicating order and energy to their operations.

Whilst the Roman troops were passing that strait which divides this island from the continent of Britain, they halted on a sudden, — not checked by the resistance of the enemy, but suspended by a spectacle of an unusual and altogether surprising nature. On every side of the British army were seen bands of Druids in their most sacred habits surrounding the troops, lifting their hands to heaven, devoting to death their enemies, and animating their disciples to religious frenzy by the uncouth ceremonies of a savage ritual, and the horrid mysteries of a superstition familiar with blood. The female Druids also moved about in a troubled order, their hair dishevelled, their garments torn, torches in their hands, and, with an horror increased by the perverted softness

of their sex, howled out the same curses and incanta-
tions with greater clamor.*   Astonished at this sight,
the Romans for some time neither advanced nor returned the darts of the enemy.   But at length, rousing from their trance, and animating each other with
the shame of yielding to the impotence of female and
fanatical fury, they found the resistance by no means
proportioned to the horror and solemnity of the preparations.   These overstrained efforts had, as frequently happens, exhausted the spirits of the men, and stifled that ardor they were intended to kindle.   The
Britons were defeated ; and Paulinus, pretending to
detest the barbarity of their superstition, in reality
from the cruelty of his own nature, and that he might
cut off the occasion of future disturbances, exercised
the most unjustifiable severities on this unfortunate
people.   He burned the Druids in their own fires ;
and that no retreat might be afforded to that order,
their consecrated woods were everywhere destroyed.
Whilst he was occupied in this service, a general rebellion broke out, which his severity to the Druids
served rather to inflame than allay.

From the manners of the republic a custom had
been ingrafted into the monarchy of Rome altogether
unsuitable to that mode of government.   In the time

* There is a curious instance of a ceremony not unlike this in a
fragment of an ancient Runic history, which it may not be disagreeable to compare with this part of the British manners. "Ne vero
regem ex improviso adoriretur Ulafus, admoto sacculo suo, eundem
quatere cœpit, carmen simul magicum obmurmurans, hac verborum
formula : Duriter increpetur cum tonitru ; stringant Cyclopia tela ; in-
jiciant manum Parcæ ; . . . . acriter excipient monticolæ genii plu-
rimi, atque gigantes . . . . contundent ; quatient ; procellæ . . . . ,
disrumpent lapides navigium ejus . . . ." — Hickesii Thesaur. Vol.
II. p. 140.

of the Commonwealth, those who lived in a dependent and cliental relation on the great men used frequently to show marks of their acknowledgment by
considerable bequests at their death. But when all
the scattered powers of that state became united in
the emperor, these legacies followed the general current, and flowed in upon the common patron. In
the will of every considerable person he inherited
with the children and relations, and such devises
formed no inconsiderable part of his revenue: a
monstrous practice, which let an absolute sovereign
into all the private concerns of his subjects, and
which, by giving the prince a prospect of one day
sharing in all the great estates, whenever he was
urged by avarice or necessity, naturally pointed out
a resource by an anticipation always in his power.
This practice extended into the provinces. A king
of the Iceni * had devised a considerable part of his
substance to the emperor. But the Roman procurator, not satisfied with entering into his master's portion, seized upon the rest, — and pursuing his injustice to the most horrible outrages, publicly scourged
Boadicea, queen to the deceased prince, and violated
his daughters. These cruelties, aggravated by the
shame and scorn that attended them, — the general
severity of the government, — the taxes, (new to a
barbarous people,) laid on without discretion, extorted without mercy, and, even when respited, made
utterly ruinous by exorbitant usury, — the further
mischiefs they had to dread, when more completely
reduced, — all these, with the absence of the legate
and the army on a remote expedition, provoked all
the tribes of the Britons, provincials, allies, enemies,

* Inhabitants of Norfolk and Suffolk.

to a general insurrection. The command of this confederacy was conferred on Boadicea, as the first in rank, and resentment of injuries. They began by cutting off a Roman legion; then they fell upon the colonies of Camelodunum and Verulam, and with a barbarous fury butchered the Romans and their adherents to the number of seventy thousand.

An end had been now put to the Roman power in this island, if Paulinus, with unexampled vigor and prudence, had not conducted his army through the midst of the enemy's country from Anglesey to London. There uniting the soldiers that remained dispersed in different garrisons, he formed an army of ten thousand men, and marched to attack the enemy in the height of their success and security. The army of the Britons is said to have amounted to two hundred and thirty thousand; but it was ill composed, and without choice or order, — women, boys, old men, priests, — full of presumption, tumult, and confusion. Boadicea was at their head, — a woman of masculine spirit, but precipitant, and without any military knowledge.

The event was such as might have been expected. Paulinus, having chosen a situation favorable to the smallness of his numbers, and encouraged his troops not to dread a multitude whose weight was dangerous only to themselves, piercing into the midst of that disorderly crowd, after a blind and furious resistance, obtained a complete victory. Eighty thousand Britons fell in this battle.

A. D. 61.   Paulinus improved the terror this slaughter had produced by the unparalleled severities which he exercised. This method would probably have succeeded to subdue, but at the same time

to depopulate the nation, if such loud complaints
had not been made at Rome of the legate's cruelty
as procured his recall.

Three successive legates carried on the affairs of
Britain during the latter part of Nero's reign, and
during the troubles occasioned by the disputed succession. But they were all of an inactive character.
The victory obtained by Paulinus had disabled the
Britons from any new attempt. Content, therefore,
with recovering the Roman province, these generals
compounded, as it were, with the enemy for the rest
of the island. They caressed the troops; they indulged them in their licentiousness; and not being
of a character to repress the seditions that continually arose, they submitted to preserve their ease and
some shadow of authority by sacrificing the most material parts of it. And thus they continued, soldiers
and commanders, by a sort of compact, in a common
neglect of all duty on the frontiers of the Empire, in
the face of a bold and incensed enemy.

But when Vespasian arrived to the head
of affairs, he caused the vigor of his govern-   A. D. 69.
ment to be felt in Britain, as he had done in all the
other parts of the Empire. He was not afraid to receive great services. His legates, Cerealis and Fron-
tinus, reduced the Silures and Brigantes, — one the
most warlike, the other the most numerous people
in the island. But its final reduction and
perfect settlement were reserved for Julius   A. D. 71.
Agricola, a man by whom it was a happiness for the
Britons to be conquered. He was endued with all
those bold and popular virtues which would have
given him the first place in the times of the free
Republic; and he joined to them all that reserve

and moderation which enabled him to fill great offices with safety, and made him a good subject under a jealous despotism.

Though the summer was almost spent when he arrived in Britain, knowing how much the vigor and success of the first stroke influences all subsequent measures, he entered immediately into action. After reducing some tribes, Mona became the principal object of his attention. The cruel ravages of Paulinus had not entirely effaced the idea of sanctity which the Britons by a long course of hereditary reverence had annexed to that island: it became once more a place of consideration by the return of the Druids. Here Agricola observed a conduct very different from that of his predecessor, Paulinus: the island, when he had reduced it, was treated with great lenity. Agricola was a man of humanity and virtue: he pitied the condition and respected the prejudices of the conquered. This behavior facilitated the progress of his arms, insomuch that in less than two campaigns all the British nations comprehended in what we now call England yielded themselves to the Roman government, as soon as they found that peace was no longer to be considered as a dubious blessing. Agricola carefully secured the obedience of the conquered people by building forts and stations in the most important and commanding places. Having taken these precautions for securing his rear, he advanced northwards, and, penetrating into Caledonia as far as the river Tay, he there built a *prætentura*, or line of forts, between the two friths, which are in that place no more than twenty miles asunder. The enemy, says Tacitus, was removed as it were into another island. And this line Agricola seems to have destined as the boundary of the Empire. For though in the following year he carried his arms further, and, as it is thought, to the foot of the Grampian Mountains, and there defeated a confederate army of the Caledonians, headed by Galgacus, one of their most famous chiefs, yet he built no fort to the northward of this line : a measure which he never omitted, when he intended to preserve his conquests. The expedition of that summer was probably designed only to disable the Caledonians from attempting anything against this barrier. But he left them their mountains, their arms, and their liberty : a policy, perhaps, not altogether worthy of so able a commander. He might the more easily have completed the conquest of the whole island by means of the fleet which he equipped to coöperate with his land forces in that expedition. This fleet sailed quite round Britain, which had not been before, by any certain proof, A. D. 84. known to be an island : a circumnavigation, in that immature state of naval skill, of little less fame than a voyage round the globe in the present age.

In the interval between his campaigns Agricola was employed in the great labors of peace. He knew that the general must be perfected by the legislator, and that the conquest is neither permanent nor honorable which is only an introduction to tyranny. His first care was the regulation of his household, which under former legates had been always full of faction and intrigue, lay heavy on the province, and was as difficult to govern. He never suffered his private partialities to intrude into the conduct of public business, nor in appointing to employments did he permit solicitation to supply the place of merit, wisely sensible that a proper choice of officers is almost the

whole of government. He eased the tribute of the
province, not so much by reducing it in quantity as
by cutting off all those vexatious practices which attended the levying of it, far more grievous than the
imposition itself. Every step in securing the subjection of the conquered country was attended with the
utmost care in providing for its peace and internal order. Agricola reconciled the Britons to the Roman
government by reconciling them to the Roman manners. He moulded that fierce nation by degrees to
soft and social customs, leading them imperceptibly
into a fondness for baths, for gardens, for grand
houses, and all the commodious elegancies of a cultivated life. He diffused a grace and dignity over this
new luxury by the introduction of literature. He
invited instructors in all the arts and sciences from
Rome ; and he sent the principal youth of Britain to
that city to be educated at his own expense. In
short, he subdued the Britons by civilizing them,
and made them exchange a savage liberty for a polite and easy subjection. His conduct is the most
perfect model for those employed in the unhappy,
but sometimes necessary task, of subduing a rude
and free people.

Thus was Britain, after a struggle of fifty-four
years, entirely bent under the yoke, and moulded
into the Roman Empire. How so stubborn an opposition could have been so long maintained against
the greatest power on earth by a people ill armed,
worse united, without revenues, without discipline,
has justly been deemed an object of wonder. Authors are generally contented with attributing it to
the extraordinary bravery of the ancient Britons.
But certainly the Britons fought with armies as

brave as the world ever saw, with superior discipline, and more plentiful resources.

To account for this opposition, we must have recourse to the general character of the Roman politics
at this time.   War, during this period, was carried
on upon principles very different from those that
actuated the Republic.   Then one uniform spirit animated one body through whole ages.   With whatever
state they were engaged, the war was so prosecuted
as if the republic could not subsist, unless that particular enemy were totally destroyed.   But when the
Roman dominion had arrived to as great an extent
as could well be managed, and that the ruling power
had more to fear from disaffection to the government
than from enmity to the Empire, with regard to foreign affairs common rules and a moderate policy took
place.   War became no more than a sort of exercise
for the Roman forces.*   Even whilst they were declaring war they looked towards an accommodation,
and were satisfied with reasonable terms when they
concluded it.   Their politics were more like those
of the present powers of Europe, where kingdoms
seek rather to spread their influence than to extend
their dominion, to awe and weaken rather than to
destroy.   Under unactive and jealous princes the
Roman legates seldom dared to push the advantages
they had gained far enough to produce a dangerous
reputation.†   They wisely stopped, when they came
to the verge of popularity.   And these emperors fearing as much from the generals as their generals from

---

* Rem Romanam huc satietate gloriæ provectam, ut externis quoque gentibus quietem velit. — Tacit. Annal. XII. 11.

† Nam duces, ubi impetrando triumphalium insigni sufficere res
suas crediderant, hostem omittebant. — Tacit. Annal. IV. 23.

them, such frequent changes were made in the command that the war was never systematically carried on. Besides, the change of emperors (and their reigns were not long) almost always brought on a change of measures; and the councils even of the same reign were continually fluctuating, as opposite court factions happened to prevail. Add to this, that during the commotions which followed the death of Nero the contest for the purple turned the eyes of the world from every other object. All persons of consequence interested themselves in the success of some of the contending parties; and the legates in Britain, suspended in expectation of the issue of such mighty quarrels, remained unactive till it could be determined for what master they were to conquer.

On the side of the Roman government these seem to have been some of the causes which so long protracted the fate of Britain. Others arose from the nature of the country itself, and from the manners of its inhabitants. The country was then extremely woody and full of morasses. There were originally no roads. The motion of armies was therefore difficult, and communication in many cases impracticable. There were no cities, no towns, no places of cantonment for soldiers; so that the Roman forces were obliged to come into the field late and to leave it early in the season. They had no means to awe the enemy, and to prevent their machinations during the winter. Every campaign they had nearly the same work to begin. When a civilized nation suffers some great defeat, and loses some place critically situated, such is the mutual dependence of the several parts by commerce, and by the orders of a well-regulated community, that the whole is easily secured. A long-continued state of war is unnatural to such a nation. They abound with artisans, with traders, and a number of settled and unwarlike people, who are less disturbed in their ordinary course by submitting to almost any power than in a long opposition ; and as this character diffuses itself through the whole nation, they find it impossible to carry on a war, when they are deprived of the usual resources. But in a country like ancient Britain there are as many soldiers as inhabitants. They unite and disperse with ease. They require no pay nor formal subsistence ; and the hardships of an irregular war are not very remote from their ordinary course of life. Victories are easily obtained over such a rude people, but they are rarely decisive ; and the final conquest becomes a work of time and patience. All that can be done is to facilitate communication by roads, and to secure the principal avenues and the most remarkable posts on the navigable rivers by forts and stations. To conquer the people, you must subdue the nature of the country. The Romans at length effected this ; but until this was done, they never were able to make a perfect conquest.

I shall now add something concerning the government the Romans settled here, and of those methods which they used to preserve the conquered people under an entire subjection. Those nations who had either passively permitted or had been instrumental in the conquest of their fellow-Britons were dignified with the title of allies, and thereby preserved their possessions, laws, and magistrates : they were subject to no kind of charge or tribute. But as their league was not equal, and that they were under the protection of a superior power, they were entirely divested of the right of war and peace; and in many cases an appeal lay to Rome in consequence of their subordinate and dependent situation. This was the lightest species of subjection; and it was generally no more than a step preparatory to a stricter government.

The condition of those towns and communities called *municipia,* by their being more closely united to the greater state, seemed to partake a degree less of independence. They were adopted citizens of Rome; but whatever was detracted from their ancient liberty was compensated by a more or less complete possession of the privileges which constituted a Roman city, according to the merits which had procured their adoption. These cities were models of Rome in little; their courts and magistrates were the same; and though they were at liberty to retain their old laws, and to make new at their pleasure, they commonly conformed to those of Rome. The *municipia* were not subject to tribute.

When a whole people had resisted the Roman power with great obstinacy, had displayed a readiness to revolt upon every occasion, and had frequently broken their faith, they were reduced into what the Romans called the form of a province: that is, they lost their laws, their liberties, their magistrates; they forfeited the greatest part of their lands; and they paid a heavy tribute for what they were permitted to retain.

In these provinces the supreme government was in the prætor sent by the senate, who commanded the army, and in his own person exercised the judicial power. Where the sphere of his government was large, he deputed his legates to that employment, who

judged according to the standing laws of the republic, aided by those occasional declarations of law
called the prætorial edicts. The care of the revenue was in the quæstor. He was appointed to that
office in Rome; but when he acted in a judicial capacity, it was always by commission from the prætor
of the province.* Between these magistrates and
all others who had any share in the provincial government the Roman manners had established a kind
of sacred relation, as inviolable as that of blood.†
All the officers were taught to look up to the prætor
as their father, and to regard each other as brethren:
a firm and useful bond of concord in a virtuous administration; a dangerous and oppressive combina
tion in a bad one. But, like all the Roman institutions, it operated strongly towards its principal purpose, the security of dominion, which is by nothing
so much exposed as the factions and competitions
of the officers, when the governing party itself gives
the first example of disobedience.

On the overthrow of the Commonwealth, a remarkable revolution ensued in the power and the
subordination of these magistrates. For, as the
prince came alone to possess all that was by a
proper title either imperial or prætorial authority,
the ancient prætors dwindled into his legates, by
which the splendor and importance of that dignity
were much diminished. The business of the quæstor at this time seems to have been transferred to
the emperor's procurator. The whole of the public
revenue became part of the fisc, and was considered
as the private estate of the prince. But the old office

* Sigonii de Antiquo Jure Provinciarum, Lib. 1 and 2.
† Cic. in Verrem, 1.

under this new appellation rose in proportion as the
prætorship had declined. For the procurator seems
to have drawn to himself the cognizance of all civil,
while capital cases alone were reserved for the judgment of the legate.* And though his power was
at first restrained within narrow bounds, and all his
judgments were subject to a review and reversal by
the prætor and the senate, he gradually grew into
independence of both, and was at length by Claudius
invested with a jurisdiction absolutely uncontrollable. Two causes, I imagine, joined to produce this
change : first, the sword was in the hands of the legate ; the policy of the emperors, in order to balance
this dangerous authority, thought too much weight
could not be thrown into the scale of the procurator : secondly, as the government was now entirely despotical, a connection between the inferior
officers of the empire and the senate† was found
to shock the reason of that absolute mode of government, which extends the sovereign power in all
its fulness to every officer in his own district, and
renders him accountable to his master alone for the
abuse of it.

The veteran soldiers were always thought entitled
to a settlement in the country which had been subdued by their valor. The whole legion, with the
tribunes, the centurions, and all the subordinate officers, were seated on an allotted portion of the conquered lands, which were distributed among them

* Duobus insuper inserviendum tyrannis ; quorum legatus in san-
guinem, procurator in bona sæviret. — Tacit. Annal. XII. 60.

† Ne vim principatus resolveret cuncta ad senatum vocando, eam
conditionem esse imperandi, ut non aliter ratio constet, quam si uni
reddatur. — Tacit. Annal. I. 6.

according to their rank. These colonies were disposed throughout the conquered country, so as to sustain each other, to surround the possessions that were left to the conquered, to mix with the *municipia* or free towns, and to overawe the allies. Rome extended herself by her colonies into every part of her empire, and was everywhere present. I speak here only of the military colonies, because no other, I imagine, were ever settled in Britain.

There were few countries of any considerable extent in which all these different modes of government and different shades and gradations of servitude did not exist together. There were allies, *municipia*, provinces, and colonies in this island, as elsewhere; and those dissimilar parts, far from being discordant, united to make a firm and compact body, the motion of any member of which could only serve to confirm and establish the whole; and when time was given to this structure to coalesce and settle, it was found impossible to break any part of it from the Empire.

By degrees the several parts blended and softened into one another. And as the remembrance of enmity, on the one hand, wore away by time, so, on the other, the privileges of the Roman citizens at length became less valuable. When nothing throughout so vast an extent of the globe was of consideration but a single man, there was no reason to make any distinction amongst his subjects. Claudius first gave the full rights of the city to all the Gauls. Under Antoninus Rome opened her gates still wider. All the subjects of the Empire were made partakers of the same common rights. The provincials flocked in; even slaves were no sooner enfranchised than they were advanced to the highest posts; and the plan of comprehension, which had overturned the republic, strengthened the monarchy.

Before the partitions were thus broken down, in order to support the Empire, and to prevent commotions, they had a custom of sending spies into all the provinces, where, if they discovered any provincial laying himself out for popularity, they were sure of finding means, for they scrupled none, to repress him. It was not only the prætor, with his train of lictors and apparitors, the rods and the axes, and all the insolent parade of a conqueror's jurisdiction; every private Roman seemed a kind of magistrate: they took cognizance of all their words and actions, and hourly reminded them of that jealous and stern authority, so vigilant to discover and so severe to punish the slightest deviations from obedience.

As they had framed the action *de pecuniis repetundis* against the avarice and rapacity of the provincial governors, they made at length a law [*] which, one may say, was against their virtues. For they prohibited them from receiving addresses of thanks on their administration, or any other public mark of acknowledgment, lest they should come to think that their merit or demerit consisted in the good or ill opinion of the people over whom they ruled. They dreaded either a relaxation of government, or a dangerous influence in the legate, from the exertion of an humanity too popular.

These are some of the civil and political methods by which the Romans held their dominion over conquered nations; but even in peace they kept up a great military establishment. They looked upon the interior country to be sufficiently secured by the

---

[*] Tacit. Annal. XV. 21, 22.

colonies ; their forces were therefore generally quartered on the frontiers.   There they had their *sta-
tiva*, or stations, which were strong intrenched camps,
many of them fitted even for a winter residence.
The communication between these camps, the colonies, and the municipal towns was formed by great
roads, which they called military ways.   The two
principal of these ran in almost straight lines, the
whole length of England, from north to south.   Two
others intersected them from east to west.   The remains show them to have been in their perfection
noble works, in all respects worthy the Roman military prudence and the majesty of the Empire.   The
Anglo-Saxons called them streets.*   Of all the Roman works, they respected and kept up these alone.
They regarded them with a sort of sacred reverence,
granting them a peculiar protection and great immunities.   Those who travelled on them were privileged from arrests in all civil suits.

As the general character of the Roman government was hard and austere, it was particularly so
in what regarded the revenue.   This revenue was
either fixed or occasional.   The fixed consisted, first,
of an annual tax on persons and lands, but in what
proportion to the fortunes of the one or the value
of the other I have not been able to ascertain.   Next
was the imposition called *decuma*, which consisted
of a tenth, and often a greater portion of the corn
of the province, which was generally delivered in
kind.   Of all other products a fifth was paid.   After
this tenth had been exacted on the corn, they were
obliged to sell another tenth, or a more considerable

---

* The four roads they called Watling Street, Ikenild Street, Ermin
Street, and the Fosseway.

part, to the prætor, at a price estimated by himself. Even what remained was still subject to be bought up in the same manner, and at the pleasure of the same magistrate, who, independent of these taxes and purchases, received for the use of his household a large portion of the corn of the province. The most valuable of the pasture grounds were also reserved to the public, and a considerable revenue was thence derived, which they called *scriptura*. The state made a monopoly of almost the whole produce of the land, which paid several taxes, and was further enhanced by passing through several hands before it came to popular consumption.

The third great branch of the Roman revenue was the *portorium*, which did not differ from those impositions which we now call customs and duties of export and import.

This was the ordinary revenue; besides which there were occasional impositions for shipping, for military stores and provisions, and for defraying the expense of the prætor and his legates on the various circuits they made for the administration of the province. This last charge became frequently a means of great oppression, and several ways were from time to time attempted, but with little effect, to confine it within reasonable bounds.* Amongst the extraordinary impositions must be reckoned the obligation they laid on the provincials to labor at the public works, after the manner of what the French call the *corvée*, and we term statute-labor.

As the provinces, burdened by the ordinary charges, were often in no condition of levying these occasional taxes, they were obliged to borrow at interest. In-

* Cod. Lib. XII. Tit. lxii.

terest was then to communities at the same exorbitant rate as to individuals.   No province was free
from a most onerous public debt; and that debt was
far from operating like the same engagement contracted in modern states, by which, as the creditor
is thrown into the power of the debtor, they often
add considerably to their strength, and to the number and attachment of their dependants.   The prince
in this latter case borrows from a subject or from
a stranger.   The one becomes more the subject, and
the other less a stranger.   But in the Roman provinces the subject borrowed from his master, and he
thereby doubled his slavery.   The overgrown favorites and wealthy nobility of Rome advanced money
to the provincials; and they were in a condition both
to prescribe the terms of the loan and to enforce the
payment.   The provinces groaned at once under all
the severity of public imposition and the rapaciousness of private usury.   They were overrun by pub-
licans, farmers of the taxes, agents, confiscators,
usurers, bankers, those numerous and insatiable
bodies which always flourish in a burdened and
complicated revenue.   In a word, the taxes in the
Roman Empire were so heavy, and in many respects
so injudiciously laid on, that they have been not improperly considered as one cause of its decay and
ruin.   The Roman government, to the very last,
carried something of the spirit of conquest in it;
and this system of taxes seems rather calculated for
the utter impoverishment of nations, in whom a long
subjection had not worn away the remembrance of
enmity, than for the support of a just commonwealth.

CHAPTER IV.

THE FALL OF THE ROMAN POWER IN BRITAIN.

AFTER the period which we have just closed, no mention is made of the affairs of Britain until the reign of Adrian. At that time was wrought the first remarkable change in the exterior policy of Rome. Although some of the emperors contented themselves with those limits which they found at their accession, none before this prince had actually contracted the bounds of the Empire: for, being more perfectly acquainted with all the countries that composed it than any of his predecessors, what was strong and what weak, and having formed to himself a plan wholly defensive, he purposely abandoned several large tracts of territory, that he might render what remained more solid and compact.

A. D. 117.

This plan particularly affected Britain. All the conquests of Agricola to the northward of the Tyne were relinquished, and a strong rampart was built from the mouth of that river, on the east, to Solway Frith, on the Irish Sea, a length of about eighty miles. But in the reign of his successor, Antoninus Pius, other reasonings prevailed, and other measures were pursued. The legate who then commanded in Britain, concluding that the Caledonians would construe the defensive policy of Adrian into fear, that they would naturally grow more numerous in a larger territory, and more haughty when they saw it abandoned to them, the frontier was again advanced to Agricola's second line, which extended between the Friths of Forth and Clyde, and the stations which had been estab-

A. D. 121.

A. D. 140.

lished by that general were connected with a continued wall.

From this time those walls become the principal object in the British history. The Caledonians, or (as they are called) the Picts, made very frequent and sometimes successful attempts upon this barrier, taking advantage more particularly of every change in government, whilst the soldiery throughout the Empire were more intent upon the choice of a master than the motions of an enemy. In this dubious state of unquiet peace and unprosecuted war the province continued until Severus came to the purple, who, finding that Britain had grown into one of the most considerable provinces of A. D. 207. the Empire, and was at the same time in a dangerous situation, resolved to visit that island in person, and to provide for its security. He led a vast army into the wilds of Caledonia, and A. D. 208. was the first of the Romans who penetrated to the most northern boundary of this island. The natives, defeated in some engagements, and wholly unable to resist so great and determined a power, were obliged to submit to such a peace as the emperor thought proper to impose. Contenting himself with a submission, always cheaply won from a barbarous people, and never long regarded, Severus made no sort of military establishment in that country. On the contrary, he abandoned the advanced work which had been raised in the A. D. 209. reign of Antoninus, and, limiting himself by the plan of Adrian, he either built a new wall near the former, or he added to the work of that emperor such considerable improvements and repairs that it has since been called the Wall of Severus.

Severus with great labor and charge terrified the Caledonians; but he did not subdue them. He neglected those easy and assured means of subjection which the nature of that part of Britain affords to a power master of the sea, by the bays, friths, and lakes with which it is everywhere pierced, and in some places almost cut through. A few garrisons at the necks of land, and a fleet to connect them and to awe the coast, must at any time have been sufficient irrecoverably to subdue that part of Britain. This was a neglect in Agricola occasioned probably by a limited command; and it was not rectified by boundless authority in Severus. The Caledonians again resumed their arms, and renewed their ravages on the Roman frontier. Severus died before he could take any new measures; and from his death there is an almost total silence concerning the affairs of Britain until the division of the Empire.

Had the unwieldy mass of that overgrown dominion been effectively divided, and divided into large portions, each forming a state, separate and absolutely independent, the scheme had been far more perfect. Though the Empire had perished, these states might have subsisted; and they might have made a far better opposition to the inroads of the barbarians even than the whole united; since each nation would have its own strength solely employed in resisting its own particular enemies. For, notwithstanding the resources which might have been expected from the entireness of so great a body, it is clear from history that the Romans were never able to employ with effect and at the same time above two armies, and that on the whole they were very unequal to the defence of a frontier of many thousand miles in circuit.

But the scheme which was pursued, the scheme of joint emperors, holding by a common title, each governing his proper territory, but not wholly without authority in the other portions, this formed a species of government of which it is hard to conceive any just idea. It was a government in continual fluctuation from one to many, and from many again to a single hand. Each state did not subsist long enough independent to fall into those orders and connected classes of men that are necessary to a regular commonwealth; nor had they time to grow into those virtuous partialities from which nations derive the first principle of their stability.

The events which follow sufficiently illustrate these reflections, and will show the reason of introducing them in this place, with regard to the Empire in general, and to Britain more particularly.

In the division which Diocletian first made of the Roman territory, the western provinces, in which Britain was included, fell to Maximian. It was during his reign that Britain, by an extraordinary revolution, was for some time entirely separated from the body of the Empire. Carausius, a man of obscure birth, and a barbarian, (for now not only the army, but the senate, was filled with foreigners,) had obtained the government of Boulogne. He was also intrusted with the command of a fleet stationed in that part to oppose the Saxon pirates, who then began cruelly to infest the northwest parts of Gaul and the opposite shore of Britain. But Carausius made use of the power with which he had been intrusted, not so much to suppress the pirates as to aggrandize himself. He even permitted their depredations, that he might intercept them on their return, and enrich himself with the retaken plunder. By such methods he acquired immense wealth, which he distributed with so politic a bounty among the seamen of his fleet and the legions in Britain that by degrees he disposed both the one and the other to a revolt in his favor.

As there were then no settled principles either of succession or election in the Empire, and all depended on the uncertain faith of the army, Carausius made his attempt, perhaps, with the less guilt, and found the less difficulty in prevailing upon the provincial Britons to submit to a sovereignty which seemed to reflect a sort of dignity on themselves. In this island he established the seat of his new dominion; but he kept up and augmented his fleet, by which he preserved his communication with his old government, and commanded the intermediate seas. He entered into a close alliance with the A. D. 286. Saxons and Frisians, by which he at once preserved his own island from their depredations and rendered his maritime power irresistible. He humbled the Picts by several defeats; he repaired the frontier wall, and supplied it with good garrisons. He made several roads equal to the works of the greatest emperors. He cut canals, with vast labor and expense, through all the low eastern parts of Britain, at the same time draining those fenny countries, and promoting communication and commerce. On these canals he built several cities. Whilst he thus labored to promote the internal A. D. 290. strength and happiness of his kingdom, he contended with so much success against his former masters that they were at length obliged not only to relinquish their right to his acquisition, but to admit him to a participation of the imperial titles. He reigned after this for seven years prosperously and with great glory, because he wisely set bounds to his ambition, and contented himself with the possession of a great country, detached from the rest of the world, and therefore easily defended. Had he lived long enough, and pursued this plan with consistency, Britain, in all probability, might then have become, and might have afterwards been, an independent and powerful kingdom, instructed in the Roman arts, and freed from their dominion. But the same distemper of the state which had raised Carausius to power did not suffer him long to enjoy it. The Roman soldiery at that time was wholly destitute of military principle. That religious regard to their oath, the great bond of ancient discipline, had been long worn out; and the want of it was not supplied by that punctilio of honor and loyalty which is the support of modern armies. Carausius was assassinated, and succeeded in his kingdom by Allectus, the captain of his guards. But the murderer, who did not possess abilities to support the power he had acquired by his crimes, was in a short time defeated, and in his turn put to death, by Constantius Chlorus. In about three years from the death of Carausius, Britain, after a short experiment of independency, was again united to the body of the Empire.

A. D. 293.

Constantius, after he came to the purple, chose this island for his residence. Many authors affirm that his wife Helena was a Briton. It is more certain that his son Constantine the Great was born here, and enabled to succeed his father principally by the helps which he derived from Britain.

A. D. 304.

A. D. 306.

Under the reign of this great prince there was an almost total revolution in the internal policy of the Empire. This was the third remarkable change in the Roman government since the dissolution of the Commonwealth. The first was that by which Antoninus had taken away the distinctions of the *municipium*, province, and colony, communicating to every part of the Empire those privileges which had formerly distinguished a citizen of Rome. Thus the whole government was cast into a more uniform and simple frame, and every mark of conquest was finally effaced. The second alteration was the division of the Empire by Diocletian. The third was the change made in the great offices of the state, and the revolution in religion, under Constantine.

The *præfecti prætorio*, who, like the commanders of the janizaries of the Porte, by their ambition and turbulence had kept the government in continual ferment, were reduced by the happiest art imaginable. Their number, only two originally, was increased to four, by which their power was balanced and broken. Their authority was not lessened, but its nature was totally changed : for it became from that time a dignity and office merely civil. The whole Empire was divided into four departments under these four officers. The subordinate districts were governed by their *vicarii ;* and Britain, accordingly, was under a vicar, subject to the *præfectus prætorio* of Gaul. The military was divided nearly in the same manner ; and it was placed under officers also of a new creation, the *magistri militiæ*. Immediately under these were the *duces*, and under those the *comites*, dukes and counts, titles unknown in the time of the Republic or in the higher Empire ; but afterwards they ex-

:ended beyond the Roman territory, and having been
:onferred by the Northern nations upon their leaders,
they subsist to this day, and contribute to the dignity
of the modern courts of Europe.

But Constantine made a much greater change with
regard to religion by the establishment of Christianity.   At what time the Gospel was first preached in
this island I believe it impossible to ascertain, as it
came in gradually, and without, or rather contrary
to, public authority.   It was most probably first introduced among the legionary soldiers; for we find
St. Alban, the first British martyr, to have been of
that body.   As it was introduced privately, so its
growth was for a long time insensible; but it shot
up at length with great vigor, and spread itself wide-
ly, at first under the favor of Constantius and the
protection of Helena, and at length under the establishment of Constantine.   From this time it is to be
considered as the ruling religion; though heathenism
subsisted long after, and at last expired imperceptibly, and with as little noise as Christianity had been
at first introduced.

In this state, with regard to the civil, military, and
religious establishment, Britain remained without any
change, and at intervals in a tolerable state of repose,
until the reign of Valentinian.   Then it was attacked
all at once with incredible fury and success, and as it
were in concert, by a number of barbarous
nations.   The principal of these were the A. D. 364.
Scots, a people of ancient settlement in Ireland, and
who had thence been transplanted into the northern
part of Britain, which afterwards derived its name
from that colony.   The Scots of both nations united
with the Picts to fall upon the Roman province.   To

these were added the piratical Saxons, who issued
from the mouths of the Rhine. For some years they
met but slight resistance, and made a most miserable
havoc, until the famous Count Theodosius was sent to
the relief of Britain, — who, by an admirable conduct
in war, and as vigorous application to the cure of domestic disorders, for a time freed the country from its
enemies and oppressors, and having driven the Picts
and Scots into the barren extremity of the island, he
shut and barred them in with a new wall, advanced
as far as the remotest of the former, and, what had
hitherto been imprudently neglected, he erected the
intermediate space into a Roman province,
A.D. 368.   and a regular government, under the name
of Valentia. But this was only a momentary relief.
The Empire was perishing by the vices of its constitution.

Each province was then possessed by the inconsiderate ambition of appointing a head to the whole ; although, when the end was obtained, the victorious
province always returned to its ancient insignificance,
and was lost in the common slavery. A great army
of Britons followed the fortune of Maximus, whom
they had raised to the imperial titles, into Gaul.
They were there defeated ; and from their
A.D. 388.   defeat, as it is said, arose a new people.
They are supposed to have settled in Armorica,
which was then, like many other parts of the sickly Empire, become a mere desert; and that country, from this accident, has been since called Bretagne.

The Roman province thus weakened afforded opportunity and encouragement to the barbarians again
to invade and ravage it. Stilicho, indeed, during the

minority of Honorius, obtained some advantages over them, which procured a short intermission of their hostilities. But as the Empire on the continent was now attacked on all sides, and staggered under the innumerable shocks which it received, that minister ventured to recall the Roman forces from Britain, in order to sustain those parts which he judged of more importance and in greater danger.

On the intelligence of this desertion, their barbarous enemies break in upon the Britons, and are no longer resisted. Their ancient protection withdrawn, the people became stupefied with terror and despair. They petition the emperor for succor in the most moving terms. The emperor, protesting his weakness, commits them to their own defence, absolves them from their allegiance, and confers on them a freedom which they have no longer the sense to value nor the virtue to defend. The princes whom after this desertion they raised and deposed with a stupid inconstancy were styled Emperors. So hard it is to change ideas to which men have been long accustomed, especially in government, that the Britons had no notion of a sovereign who was not to be emperor, nor of an emperor who was not to be master of the Western world. This single idea ruined Britain. Constantine, a native of this island, one of those shadows of imperial majesty, no sooner found himself established at home than, fatally for himself and his country, he turned his eyes towards the continent. Thither he carried the flower of the British youth, — all who were any ways eminent for birth, for courage, for their skill in the military or mechanic arts ; but his success was not equal to his hopes or his forces. The remains of his routed army

A. D. 411.

joined their countrymen in Armorica, and a baffled attempt upon the Empire a second time recruited Gaul and exhausted Britain.

The Scots and Picts, attentive to every advantage, rushed with redoubled violence into this vacuity. The Britons, who could find no protection but in slavery, again implore the assistance of their former masters. At that time Aëtius commanded the imperial forces in Gaul, and with the virtue and military skill of the ancient Romans supported the Empire, tottering with age and weakness. Though he was then hard pressed by the vast armies of Attila, which like a deluge had overspread Gaul, he afforded them a small and temporary succor. This detachment of Romans repelled the Scots ; they repaired the walls ; and animating the Britons by their example and instructions to maintain their freedom, they departed. But the Scots easily perceived and took advantage of their departure. Whilst they ravaged the country, the Britons renewed their supplications to Aëtius. They once more obtained a reinforcement, which again reëstablished their affairs. They were, however, given to understand that this was to be their last relief. The Roman auxiliaries were recalled, and the Britons abandoned to their own fortune forever.

A.D. 432.   When the Romans deserted this island, they left a country, with regard to the arts of war or government, in a manner barbarous, but destitute of that spirit or those advantages with which sometimes a state of barbarism is attended. They carried out of each province its proper and natural strength, and supplied it by that of some other, which had no connection with the country. The troops raised in Britain often served in Egypt ; and those which

were employed for the protection of this island were
sometimes from Batavia or Germany, sometimes from
provinces far to the east. Whenever the strangers
were withdrawn, as they were very easily, the province was left in the hands of men wholly unpractised in war. After a peaceable possession of more
than three hundred years, the Britons derived but
very few benefits from their subjection to the conquerors and civilizers of mankind. Neither does
it appear that the Roman people were at any time
extremely numerous in this island, or had spread
themselves, their manners, or their language as ex-
tensively in Britain as they had done in the other
parts of their Empire. The Welsh and the Anglo-
Saxon languages retain much less of Latin than the
French, the Spanish, or the Italian. The Romans
subdued Britain at a later period, at a time when Italy herself was not sufficiently populous to supply so
remote a province : she was rather supplied from her
provinces. The military colonies, though in some
respects they were admirably fitted for their purposes, had, however, one essential defect : the lands
granted to the soldiers did not pass to their posterity ;
so that the Roman people must have multiplied poorly in this island, when their increase principally depended on a succession of superannuated soldiers.
From this defect the colonies were continually ·falling
to decay. They had also in many respects degenerat-
ed from their primitive institution.* We must add,

* Neque conjugiis suscipiendis neque alendis liberis sueti, orbas
sine posteris domos relinquebant. Non enim, ut olim, universæ le-
giones deducebantur cum tribunis et centurionibus et suis cujusque
ordinis militibus, ut consensu et caritate rempublicam efficerent, sed
ignoti inter se, diversis manipulis, sine rectore, sine affectibus mutuis,

that in the decline of the Empire a great part of the troops in Britain were barbarians, Batavians or Germans. Thus, at the close of this period, this unhappy country, desolated of its inhabitants, abandoned by its masters, stripped of its artisans, and deprived of all its spirit, was in a condition the most wretched and forlorn.

quasi ex alio genere mortalium repente in unum collecti, numerus magis quam colonia. — Tacit. Annal. XIV. 27.

BOOK II.

CHAPTER I.

A FTER having been so long subject to a A. D. 447.
foreign dominion, there was among the
Britons no royal family, no respected order in the
state, none of those titles to government, confirmed
by opinion and long use, more efficacious than the
wisest schemes for the settlement of the nation.
Mere personal merit was then the only pretence to
power. But this circumstance only added to the
misfortunes of a people who had no orderly method
of election, and little experience of merit in any of
the candidates. During this anarchy, whilst they
suffered the most dreadful calamities from the fury
of barbarous nations which invaded them, they fell
into that disregard of religion, and those loose, disorderly manners, which are sometimes the consequence of desperate and hardened wretchedness, as
well as the common distempers of ease and prosperity.

At length, after frequent elections and deposings,
rather wearied out by their own inconstancy than
fixed by the merit of their choice, they suffered Vortigern to reign over them. This leader had made
some figure in the conduct of their wars and factions.
But he was no sooner settled on the throne than he

showed himself rather like a prince born of an exhausted stock of royalty in the decline of empire than
one of those bold and active spirits whose manly talents obtain them the first place in their country, and
stamp upon it that character of vigor essential to the
prosperity of a new commonwealth.   However, the
mere settlement, in spite of the ill administration of
government, procured the Britons some internal repose, and some temporary advantages over their enemies, the Picts.   But having been long habituated
to defeats, neither relying on their king nor on themselves, and fatigued with the obstinate attacks of
an enemy whom they sometimes checked, but could
never remove, in one of their national assemblies it
was resolved to call in the mercenary aid of the Saxons, a powerful nation of Germany, which had been
long by their piratical incursions terrible not only to
them, but to all the adjacent countries.   This resolution has been generally condemned.   It has been
said, that they seem to have through mere cowardice
distrusted a strength not yet worn down, and a fortune sufficiently prosperous.   But as it was taken by
general counsel and consent, we must believe that
the necessity of such a step was felt, though the
event was dubious.   The event, indeed, might be
dubious : in a state radically weak, every measure
vigorous enough for its protection must endanger
its existence.

There is an unquestioned tradition among the
Northern nations of Europe, importing that all that
part of the world had suffered a great and general
revolution by a migration from Asiatic Tartary of a
people whom they call Asers.   These everywhere expelled or subdued the ancient inhabitants of the Cel-

tic and Cimbric original. The leader of this Asiatic army was called Odin or Wodin: first their general, afterwards their tutelar deity. The time of this great change is lost in the imperfection of traditionary history, and the attempts to supply it by fable. It is, however, certain that the Saxon nation believed themselves the descendants of those conquerors: and they had as good a title to that descent as any other of the Northern tribes; for they used the same language which then was and is still spoken, with small variation of the dialects, in all the countries which extend from the polar circle to the Danube. This people most probably derived their name, as well as their origin, from the Sacæ, a nation of the Asiatic Scythia. At the time of which we write they had seated themselves in the Cimbric Chersonesus, or Jutland, in the countries of Holstein and Sleswick, and thence extended along the Elbe and Weser to the coast of the German Ocean, as far as the mouths of the Rhine. In that tract they lived in a sort of loose military commonwealth of the ordinary German model, under several leaders, the most eminent of whom was Hengist, descended from Odin, the great conductor of the Asiatic colonies. It was to this chief that the Britons applied themselves. They invited him by a promise of ample pay for his troops, a large share of their common plunder, and the Isle of Thanet for a settlement.

The army which came over under Hengist did not exceed fifteen hundred men. The opinion which the Britons had entertained of the Saxon prowess was well founded; for they had the principal share in a decisive victory which was obtained over the Picts soon after their arrival, a victory which forever freed the Britons from all terror of the Picts and Scots, but in the same moment exposed them to an enemy no less dangerous.

Hengist and his Saxons, who had obtained by the free vote of the Britons that introduction into this island they had so long in vain attempted by arms, saw that by being necessary they were superior to their allies. They discovered the character of the king; they were eye-witnesses of the internal weakness and distraction of the kingdom. This state of Britain was represented with so much effect to the Saxons in Germany, that another and much greater embarkation followed the first; new bodies daily crowded in. As soon as the Saxons began to be sensible of their strength, they found it their interest to be discontented; they complained of breaches of a contract, which they construed according to their own designs; and then fell rudely upon their unprepared and feeble allies, who, as they had not been able to resist the Picts and Scóts, were still less in a condition to oppose that force by which they had been protected against those enemies, when turned unexpectedly upon themselves. Hengist, with very little opposition, subdued the province of Kent, and there laid the foundation of the first Saxon kingdom. Every battle the Britons fought only prepared them for a new defeat, by weakening their strength and displaying the inferiority of their courage. Vortigern, instead of a steady and regular resistance, opposed a mixture of timid war and unable negotiation. In one of their meetings, wherein the business, according to the German mode, was carried on amidst feasting and riot, Vortigern was struck with the beauty of a Saxon virgin, a kinswoman of Hen-

gist, and entirely under his influence. Having mar-.
ried her, he delivered himself over to her counsels.

His people, harassed by their enemies, betrayed by their prince, and indignant at the   A. D. 452.
feeble tyranny that oppressed them, deposed him, and
set his son Vortimer in his place. But the change
of the king proved no remedy for the exhausted state
of the nation and the constitutional infirmity of the
government. For even if the Britons could have
supported themselves against the superior abilities
and efforts of Hengist, it might have added to their
honor, but would have contributed little to their
safety. The news of his success had roused all
Saxony. Five great bodies of that adventurous
people, under different and independent commanders, very nearly at the same time broke in upon as
many different parts of the island. They came no
longer as pirates, but as invaders. Whilst the Britons contended with one body of their fierce enemies,
another gained ground, and filled with slaughter and
desolation the whole country from sea to sea. A
devouring war, a dreadful famine, a plague, the most
wasteful of any recorded in our history, united to
consummate the ruin of Britain. The ecclesiastical
writers of that age, confounded at the view of those
complicated calamities, saw nothing but the arm of
God stretched out for the punishment of a sinful
and disobedient nation. And truly, when we set
before us in one point of view the condition of almost all the parts which had lately composed the
Western Empire, — of Britain, of Gaul, of Italy, of
Spain, of Africa, — at once overwhelmed by a re-
sistless inundation of most cruel barbarians, whose
inhuman method of war made but a small part of

the miseries with which these nations were afflicted,
we are almost driven out of the circle of political
inquiry: we are in a manner compelled to acknowledge the hand of God in those immense revolutions
by which at certain periods He so signally asserts
His supreme dominion, and brings about that great
system of change which is perhaps as necessary to
the moral as it is found to be in the natural world.

But whatever was the condition of the other parts
of Europe, it is generally agreed that the state of
Britain was the worst of all. Some writers have
asserted, that, except those who took refuge in the
mountains of Wales and in Cornwall, or fled into
Armorica, the British race was in a manner destroyed. What is extraordinary, we find England
in a very tolerable state of population in less than
two centuries after the first invasion of the Saxons;
and it is hard to imagine either the transplantation
or the increase of that single people to have been
in so short a time sufficient for the settlement of
so great an extent of country. Others speak of
the Britons, not as extirpated, but as reduced to a
state of slavery; and here these writers fix the origin
of personal and predial servitude in England.

I shall lay fairly before the reader all I have
been able to discover concerning the existence or
condition of this unhappy people. That they were
much more broken and reduced than any other nation which had fallen under the German power I
think may be inferred from two considerations.
First, that in all other parts of Europe the ancient
language subsisted after the conquest, and at length
incorporated with that of the conquerors; whereas
in England the Saxon language received little or

no tincture from the Welsh; and it seems, even among the lowest people, to have continued a dialect of pure Teutonic to the time in which it was itself blended with the Norman. Secondly, that on the continent the Christian religion, after the Northern irruptions, not only remained, but flourished. It was very early and universally adopted by the ruling people. In England it was so entirely extinguished, that, when Augustin undertook his mission, it does not appear that among all the Saxons there was a single person professing Christianity.

The sudden extinction of the ancient religion and language appears sufficient to show that Britain must have suffered more than any of the neighboring nations on the continent. But it must not be concealed that there are likewise proofs that the British race, though much diminished, was not wholly extirpated, and that those who remained were not, merely as Britons, reduced to servitude. For they are mentioned as existing in some of the earlier Saxon laws. In these laws they are A. D. 500. allowed a compensation on the footing of the meaner kind of English; and they are even permitted, as well as the English, to emerge out of that low rank into a more liberal condition. This is degradation, but not slavery.* The affairs of that whole period are, however, covered with an obscurity not to be dissipated. The Britons had little leisure or ability to write a just account of a war by which they were ruined; and the Anglo-Saxons who succeeded them, attentive only to arms, were, until their conversion, ignorant of the use of letters.

It is on this darkened theatre that some old writers

* Leges Inæ, 32, De Cambrico Homine Agrum possidente. — Id. 54.

have introduced those characters and actions which have afforded such ample matter to poets and so much perplexity to historians. This is the fabulous and heroic age of our nation. After the natural and just representations of the Roman scene, the stage is again crowded with enchanters, giants, and all the extravagant images of the wildest and most remote antiquity. No personage makes so conspicuous a figure in these stories as King Arthur: a prince whether of British or Roman origin, whether born on this island or in America, is uncertain; but it appears that he opposed the Saxons with remarkable virtue and no small degree of success, which has rendered him and his exploits so large an argument of romance that both are almost disclaimed by history. Light scarce begins to dawn until the introduction of Christianity, which, bringing with it the use of letters and the arts of civil life, affords at once a juster account of things and facts that are more worthy of relation: nor is there, indeed, any revolution so remarkable in the English story.

The bishops of Rome had for some time meditated the conversion of the Anglo-Saxons. Pope Gregory, who is surnamed the Great, affected that pious design with an uncommon zeal; and he at length found a circumstance highly favorable to it in the marriage of a daughter of Charibert, a king of the Franks, to the reigning monarch of Kent. This opportunity induced Pope Gregory to commission Augustin, a monk of Rheims, and a man of distinguished piety, to undertake this arduous enterprise.

A. D. 600.   It was in the year of Christ 600, and 150 years after the coming of the first Saxon colonies into England, that Ethelbert, king of Kent, received intelligence of the arrival in his dominions of a number of men in a foreign garb, practising several strange and unusual ceremonies, who desired to be conducted to the king's presence, declaring that they had things to communicate to him and to his people of the utmost importance to their eternal welfare. This was Augustin, with forty of the associates of his mission, who now landed in the Isle of Thanet, the same place by which the Saxons had before entered, when they extirpated Christianity.

The king heard them in the open air, in order to defeat,* upon a principle of Druidical superstition, the effects of their enchantments. Augustin spoke by a Frankish interpreter. The Franks and Saxons were of the same origin, and used at that time the same language. He was favorably received; and a place in the city of Canterbury, the capital of Kent, was allotted for the residence of him and his companions. They entered Canterbury in procession, preceded by two persons who bore a silver cross and the figure of Christ painted on a board, singing, as they went, litanies to avert the wrath of God from that city and people.

The king was among their first converts. The principal of his nobility, as usual, followed that example, moved, as it is related, by many signal miracles, but undoubtedly by the extraordinary zeal of the missionaries, and the pious austerity of their lives. The new religion, by the protection of so respected a prince, who held under his dominion or influence all the countries to the southward of the Humber, spread itself with great rapidity. Paganism, after a faint resistance, everywhere gave way.

* " Veteri usus augurio," says Henry of Huntingdon, p. 321.

And, indeed, the chief difficulties which Christianity
had to encounter did not arise so much from the
struggles of opposite religious prejudices as from the
gross and licentious manners of a barbarous people.
One of the Saxon princes expelled the Christians
from his territory because the priest refused to give
him some of that white bread which he saw distributed to his congregation.

It is probable that the order of Druids either did
not at all subsist amongst the Anglo-Saxons, or that
at this time it had declined not a little from its ancient authority and reputation; else it is not easy to
conceive how they admitted so readily a new system,
which at one stroke cut off from their character its
whole importance. We even find some chiefs of the
Pagan priesthood amongst the foremost in submitting to the new doctrine. On the first preaching of
the Gospel in Northumberland, the heathen pontiff
of that territory immediately mounted a horse, which
to those of his order was unlawful, and, breaking into
the sacred inclosure, hewed to pieces the idol he had
so long served.*

If the order of the Druids did not subsist amongst
the Saxons, yet the chief objects of their religion appear to have been derived from that fountain. They,
indeed, worshipped several idols under various forms
of men and beasts; and those gods to whom they
dedicated the days of the week bore in their attributes, and in the particular days that were consecrated to them, though not in their names, a near resemblance to the divinities of ancient Rome. But still
the great and capital objects of their worship were
taken from Druidism, — trees, stones, the elements,

* Bede, Hist. Eccl. Lib. II. c. 13.

and the heavenly bodies.* These were their principal devotions, laid the strongest hold upon their minds, and resisted the progress of the Christian religion with the greatest obstinacy : for we find these superstitions forbidden amongst the latest Saxon laws. A worship which stands in need of the memorial of images or books to support it may perish when these are destroyed ; but when a superstition is established upon those great objects of Nature which continually solicit the senses, it is extremely difficult to turn the mind from things that in themselves are striking, and that are always present. Amongst the objects of this class must be reckoned the goddess Eostre, who, from the etymology of the name, as well as from the season sacred to her, was probably that beautiful planet which the Greeks and Romans worshipped under the names of Lucifer and Venus. It is from this goddess that in England the paschal festival has been called Easter.† To these they joined the reverence of various subordinate genii, or demons, fairies, and goblins, — fantastical ideas, which, in a state of uninstructed Nature, grow spontaneously out of the wild fancies or fears of men. Thus, they worshipped a sort of goddess, whom they called Mara, formed from those frightful appearances that oppress men in their sleep ; and the name is still retained among us.‡

As to the manners of the Anglo-Saxons, they were such as might be expected in a rude people, — fierce, and of a gross simplicity. Their clothes were short.

---

* Deos gentiles, et solem vel lunam, ignem vel fluvium, torrentem vel saxa, vel alicujus generis arborum ligna. — L. Cnut. 5. — Superstitiosus ille conventus, qui Frithgear dicitur, circa lapidem, arborem, fontem. — Leg. Presb. Northumb.

† Spelman's Glossary, Tit. eod.   ‡ The night-mare.

As all barbarians are much taken with exterior form, and the advantages and distinctions which are conferred by Nature, the Saxons set an high value on comeliness of person, and studied much to improve it. It is remarkable that a law of King Ina orders the care and education of foundlings to be regulated by their beauty.* They cherished their hair to a great length, and were extremely proud and jealous of this natural ornament. Some of their great men were distinguished by an appellative taken from the length of their hair.† To pull the hair was punishable; ‡ and forcibly to cut or injure it was considered in the same criminal light with cutting off the nose or thrusting out the eyes. In the same design of barbarous ornament, their faces were generally painted and scarred. They were so fond of chains and bracelets that they have given a surname to some of their kings from their generosity in bestowing such marks of favor.§

Few things discover the state of the arts amongst people more certainly than the presents that are made to them by foreigners. The Pope, on his first mission into Northumberland, sent to the queen of that country some stuffs with ornaments of gold, an ivory comb inlaid with the same metal, and a silver mirror. A queen's want of such female ornaments and utensils shows that the arts were at this time little cultivated amongst the Saxons. These are the sort of presents commonly sent to a barbarous people.

---

* L. Inæ, 26.

† Oslacus . . . . promissâ cæsarie heros. — Chron. Saxon. 123.

‡ L. Ælfred. 31.   L. Cnut. apud Brompt. 27.

§ Eadgarus nobilibus torquium largitor. — Chron. Sax. 123. Bed. Hist. Eccl. Lib. IV. c. 29.

Thus ignorant in sciences and arts, and unpractised in trade or manufacture, military exercises,
war, and the preparation for war, was their employment, hunting their pleasure. They dwelt in
cottages of wicker-work plastered with clay and
thatched with rushes, where they sat with their
families, their officers and domestics, round a fire
made in the middle of the house. In this manner
their greatest princes lived amidst the ruins of Roman
magnificence. But the introduction of Christianity,
which, under whatever form, always confers such
inestimable benefits on mankind, soon made a sensible change in these rude and fierce manners.

It is by no means impossible, that, for an end so
worthy, Providence on some occasions might directly
have interposed. The books which contain the history of this time and change are little else than a narrative of miracles, — frequently, however, with such
apparent marks of weakness or design that they afford little encouragement to insist on them. They
were then received with a blind credulity : they have
been since rejected with as undistinguishing a disregard. But as it is not in my design nor inclination,
nor indeed in my power, either to establish or refute
these stories, it is sufficient to observe, that the reality
or opinion of such miracles was the principal cause of
the early acceptance and rapid progress of Christianity in this island. Other causes undoubtedly concurred ; and it will be more to our purpose to consider some of the human and politic ways by which
religion was advanced in this nation, and those more
particularly by which the monastic institution, then
interwoven with Christianity, and making an equal
progress with it, attained to so high a pitch of prop-

erty and power, so as, in a time extremely short, to form a kind of order, and that not the least considerable, in the state.

CHAPTER II.

The marriage of Ethelbert to a Christian princess was, we have seen, a means of introducing Christianity into his dominions. The same influence contributed to extend it in the other kingdoms of the Heptarchy, the sovereigns of which were generally converted by their wives. Among the ancient nations of Germany, the female sex was possessed not only of its natural and common ascendant, but it was believed peculiarly sacred,[*] and favored with more frequent revelations of the Divine will; women were therefore heard with an uncommon attention in all deliberations, and particularly in those that regarded religion. The Pagan superstition of the North furnished, in this instance, a principle which contributed to its own destruction.

In the change of religion, care was taken to render the transition from falsehood to truth as little violent as possible. Though the first proselytes were kings, it does not appear that there was any persecution. It was a precept of Pope Gregory, under whose auspices this mission was conducted, that the heathen temples should not be destroyed, especially

---

[*] Inesse quinetiam sanctum aliquid et providum putant; nec aut consilia earum aspernantur aut responsa negligunt. — Tacit. de Mor. Ger. c. 8.

where they were well built, — but that, first removing the idols, they should be consecrated anew by
holier rites and to better purposes,*. in order that
the prejudices of the people might not be too rudely
shocked by a declared profanation of what they had
so long held sacred, and that, everywhere beholding
the same places to which they had formerly resorted
for religious comfort, they might be gradually reconciled to the new doctrines and ceremonies which
were there introduced; and as the sacrifices used
in the Pagan worship were always attended with
feasting, and consequently were highly grateful to
the multitude, the Pope ordered that oxen should
as usual be slaughtered near the church, and the
people indulged in their ancient festivity.† Whatever popular customs of heathenism were found to
be absolutely not incompatible with Christianity were
retained; and some of them were continued to a
very late period. Deer were at a certain season
brought into St. Paul's church in London, and laid
on the altar; ‡ and this custom subsisted until the
Reformation. The names of some of the Church
festivals were, with a similar design, taken from those
of the heathen which had been celebrated at the
same time of the year. Nothing could have been
more prudent than these regulations: they were,
indeed, formed from a perfect understanding of human nature.

Whilst the inferior people were thus insensibly led
into a better order, the example and countenance
of the great completed the work. For the Saxon
kings and ruling men embraced religion with so

* Bed. Hist. Eccl. Lib. I. c. 30.   † Id. c. eod.
‡ Dugdale's History of St. Paul's.

signal, and in their rank so unusual a zeal, that in many instances they even sacrificed to its advancement the prime objects of their ambition. Wulfhere, king of the West Saxons, bestowed the Isle of Wight on the king of Sussex, to persuade him to embrace Christianity.* This zeal operated in the same manner in favor of their instructors. The greatest kings and conquerors frequently resigned their crowns and shut themselves up in monasteries. When kings became monks, a high lustre was reflected upon the monastic state, and great credit accrued to the power of their doctrine, which was able to produce such extraordinary effects upon persons over whom religion has commonly the slightest influence.

The zeal of the missionaries was also much assisted by their superiority in the arts of civil life. At their first preaching in Sussex, that country was reduced to the greatest distress from a drought, which had continued for three years. The barbarous inhabitants, destitute of any means to alleviate the famine, in an epidemic transport of despair frequently united forty and fifty in a body, and, joining their hands, precipitated themselves from the cliffs, and were either drowned or dashed to pieces on the rocks. Though a maritime people, they knew not how to fish; and this ignorance probably arose from a remnant of Druidical superstition, which had forbidden the use of that sort of diet. In this calamity, Bishop Wilfrid, their first preacher, collecting nets, at the head of his attendants, plunged into the sea; and having opened this great resource of food, he reconciled the desperate people to life, and their minds to the spiritual care of those who had shown

* Bed. Hist. Eccl. Lib. IV. c. 13.

themselves so attentive to their temporal preservation.*

The same regard to the welfare of the people
appeared in all their actions. The Christian kings
sometimes made donations to the Church of lands
conquered from their heathen enemies. The clergy
immediately baptized and manumitted their new vassals. Thus they endeared to all sorts of men doctrines and teachers which could mitigate the rigorous
law of conquest; and they rejoiced to see religion and
liberty advancing with an equal progress. Nor were
the monks in this time in anything more worthy of
praise than in their zeal for personal freedom. In
the canon wherein they provided against the alienation of their lands, among other charitable exceptions
to this restraint they particularize the purchase of liberty.† In their transactions with the great the same
point was always strenuously labored. When they
imposed penance, they were remarkably indulgent to
persons of that rank; but they always made them
purchase the remission of corporal austerity by acts
of beneficence. They urged their powerful penitents
to the enfranchisement of their own slaves, and to the
redemption of those which belonged to others; they
directed them to the repair of highways, and to the
construction of churches, bridges, and other works
of general utility.‡ They extracted the fruits of virtue even from crimes; and whenever a great man
expiated his private offences, he provided in the same

---

* Bed. Hist. Eccl. Lib. IV. c. 13.   † Spelm. Concil. p. 329.

‡ Instauret etiam Dei ecclesiam; . . . . et instauret vias publicas
pontibus super aquas profundas et super cænosas vias; . . . . manu-
mittat servos suos proprios, et redimat ab aliis hominibus servos suos
ad libertatem. — L. Eccl. Edgari, 14.

act for the public happiness. The monasteries were then the only bodies corporate in the kingdom; and if any persons were desirous to perpetuate their charity by a fund for the relief of the sick or indigent, there was no other way than to confide this trust to some monastery. The monks were the sole channel through which the bounty of the rich could pass in any continued stream to the poor; and the people turned their eyes towards them in all their distresses.

We must observe, that the monks of that time, especially those from Ireland,* who had a considerable share in the conversion of all the northern parts, did not show that rapacious desire of riches which long disgraced and finally ruined their successors. Not only did they not seek, but seemed even to shun such donations. This prevented that alarm which might have arisen from an early and declared avarice. At this time the most fervent and holy anchorites retired to places the furthest that could be found from human concourse and help, to the most desolate and barren situations, which even from their horror seemed particularly adapted to men who had renounced the world. Many persons followed them in order to partake of their instructions and prayers, or to form themselves upon their example. An opinion of their miracles after their death drew still greater numbers. Establishments were gradually made. The monastic life was frugal, and the government moderate. These causes drew a constant concourse. Sanctified deserts assumed a new face; the marshes

---

* Aidanus, Finan, Colmannus miræ sanctitatis fuerunt et parsimoniæ. . . . . Adeo autem sacerdotes erant illius temporis ab avaritia immunes, ut nec territoria nisi coacti acciperent. — Hen. Huntingd. Lib. III. p. 333. Bed. Hist. Eccl. Lib. III. c. 26.

were drained, and the lands cultivated. And as this revolution seemed rather the effect of the holiness of the place than of any natural causes, it increased their credit; and every improvement drew with it a new donation. In this manner the great abbeys of Croyland and Glastonbury, and many others, from the most obscure beginnings, were advanced to a degree of wealth and splendor little less than royal.

In these rude ages government was not yet fixed upon solid principles, and everything was full of tumult and distraction. As the monasteries were better secured from violence by their character than any other places by laws, several great men, and even sovereign princes, were obliged to take refuge in convents; who, when, by a more happy revolution in their fortunes, they were reinstated in their former dignities, thought they could never make a sufficient return for the safety they had enjoyed under the sacred hospitality of these roofs. Not content to enrich them with ample possessions, that others also might partake of the protection they had experienced, they formally erected into an asylum those monasteries, and their adjacent territory. So that all thronged to that refuge who were rendered unquiet by their crimes, their misfortunes, or the severity of their lords; and content to live under a government to which their minds were subject, they raised the importance of their masters by their numbers, their labor, and, above all, by an inviolable attachment.

The monastery was always the place of sepulture for the greatest lords and kings. This added to the other causes of reverence a sort of sanctity, which, in universal opinion, always attends the repositories of the dead: and they acquired also thereby a more particular protection against the great and powerful; for who would violate the tomb of his ancestors or his own? It was not an unnatural weakness to think that some advantage might be derived from lying in holy places and amongst holy persons : and this superstition was fomented with the greatest industry and art. The monks of Glastonbury spread a notion that it was almost impossible any person should be damned whose body lay in their cemetery. This must be considered as coming in aid of the amplest of their resources, prayer for the dead.

But there was no part of their policy, of whatever nature, that procured to them a greater or juster credit than their cultivation of learning and useful arts : for, if the monks contributed to the fall of science in the Roman Empire, it is certain that the introduction of learning and civility into this Northern world is entirely owing to their labors. It is true that they cultivated letters only in a secondary way, and as subsidiary to religion. But the scheme of Christianity is such that it almost necessitates an attention to many kinds of learning. For the Scripture is by no means an irrelative system of moral and divine truths; but it stands connected with so many histories, and with the laws, opinions, and manners of so many various sorts of people, and in such different times, that it is altogether impossible to arrive to any tolerable knowledge of it without having recourse to much exterior inquiry : for which reason the progress of this religion has always been marked by that of letters. There were two other circumstances at this time that contributed no less to the revival of learning. The sacred writings had not been translated into any vernacular language, and even the ordinary service of the Church was still continued in the Latin tongue; all, therefore, who formed themselves for the ministry, and hoped to make any figure in it, were in a manner driven to the study of the writers of polite antiquity, in order to qualify themselves for their most ordinary functions. By this means a practice liable in itself to great objections had a considerable share in preserving the wrecks of literature, and was one means of conveying down to our times those inestimable monuments which otherwise, in the tumult of barbarous confusion on one hand, and untaught piety on the other, must inevitably have perished. The second circumstance, the pilgrimages of that age, if considered in itself, was as liable to objection as the former; but it proved of equal advantage to the cause of literature. A principal object of these pious journeys was Rome, which contained all the little that was left in the Western world of ancient learning and taste. The other great object of those pilgrimages was Jerusalem: this led them into the Grecian Empire, which still subsisted in the East with great majesty and power. Here the Greeks had not only not discontinued the ancient studies, but they added to the stock of arts many inventions of curiosity and convenience that were unknown to antiquity. When, afterwards, the Saracens prevailed in that part of the world, the pilgrims had also by the same means an opportunity of profiting from the improvements of that laborious people; and however little the majority of these pious travellers might have had such objects in their view, something useful must unavoidably have stuck to them; a few certainly saw with more discernment, and rendered their travels serviceable to their coun

try by importing other things besides miracles and
legends. Thus a communication was opened between this remote island and countries of which it
otherwise could then scarcely have heard mention
made; and pilgrimages thus preserved that intercourse amongst mankind which is now formed by
politics, commerce, and learned curiosity.

It is not wholly unworthy of observation, that
Providence, which strongly appears to have intended the continual intermixture of mankind, never
leaves the human mind destitute of a principle to
effect it. This purpose is sometimes carried on by
a sort of migratory instinct, sometimes by the spirit
of conquest; at one time avarice drives men from
their homes, at another they are actuated by a thirst
of knowledge; where none of these causes can operate, the sanctity of particular places attracts men
from the most distant quarters. It was this motive
which sent thousands in those ages to Jerusalem
and Rome, and now, in a full tide, impels half the
world annually to Mecca.

By those voyages the seeds of various kinds of
knowledge and improvement were at different times
imported into England. They were cultivated in
the leisure and retirement of monasteries; otherwise they could not have been cultivated at all:
for it was altogether necessary to draw certain men
from the general rude and fierce society, and wholly
to set a bar between them and the barbarous life of
the rest of the world, in order to fit them for study
and the cultivation of arts and science. Accordingly,
we find everywhere in the first institutions for the
propagation of knowledge amongst any people, that
those who followed it were set apart and secluded
from the mass of the community.

The great ecclesiastical chair of this kingdom, for near a century, was filled by foreigners. They were nominated by the Popes, who were in that age just or politic enough to appoint persons of a merit in some degree adequate to that important charge. Through this series of foreign and learned prelates, continual accessions were made to the originally slender stock of English literature. The greatest and most valuable of these accessions was made in the time and by the care of Theodorus, the seventh Archbishop of Canterbury. He was a Greek by birth, a man of a high ambitious spirit, and of a mind more liberal and talents better cultivated than generally fell to the lot of the Western prelates. He first introduced the study of his native language into this island. He brought with him a number of valuable books in many faculties, and amongst them a magnificent copy of the works of Homer, the most ancient and best of poets, and the best chosen to inspire a people just initiated into letters with an ardent love and with a true taste for the sciences. Under his influence a school was formed at Canterbury; and thus the other great fountain of knowledge, the Greek tongue, was opened in England in the year of our Lord 669.

A. D. 669.

The southern parts of England received their improvements directly through the channel of Rome. The kingdom of Northumberland, as soon as it was converted, began to contend with the southern provinces in an emulation of piety and learning. The ecclesiastics then [there?] also kept up and profited by their intercourse with Rome; but they found their principal resources of knowledge from another and a more extraordinary quarter. The island of Hii, or

Columbkill,* is a small and barren rock in the Western Ocean. But in those days it was high in reputation as the site of a monastery which had acquired great renown for the rigor of its studies and the severity of its ascetic discipline. Its authority was extended over all the northern parts of Britain and Ireland ; and the monks of Hii even exercised episcopal jurisdiction over all those regions. They had a considerable share both in the religious and literate institution of the Northumbrians. Another island, of still less importance, in the mouth of the Tees [Tweed ?], and called Lindisfarne, was about this time sanctified by the austerities of an hermit called Cuthbert. It soon became also a very celebrated monastery. It was, from a dread of the ravages of pirates, removed first to the adjacent part of the continent, and on the same account finally to Durham. The heads of this monastery omitted nothing which could contribute to the glory of their founder and to the dignity of their house, which became, in a very short time, by their assiduous endeavors, the most considerable school perhaps in Europe.

The great and justest boast of this monastery is the Venerable Beda, who was educated and spent his whole life there. An account of his writings is an account of the English learning in that age, taken in its most advantageous view. Many of his works remain, and he wrote both in prose and verse, and upon all sorts of subjects. His theology forms the most considerable part of his writings. He wrote comments upon almost the whole Scripture, and several homilies on the principal festivals of the Church. Both the comments and sermons are generally allegorical in the construction of the text, and simply

* Icolmkill, or Iona.

moral in the application. In these discourses several things seem strained and fanciful; but herein he followed entirely the manner of the earlier fathers, from whom the greatest part of his divinity is not so much imitated as extracted. The systematic and logical method, which seems to have been first introduced into theology by John of Damascus, and which after wards was known by the name of School Divinity, was not then in use, at least in the Western Church, though soon after it made an amazing progress. In this scheme the allegorical gave way to the literal explication, the imagination had less scope, and the affections were less touched. But it prevailed by an appearance more solid and philosophical, by an order more scientific, and by a readiness of application either for the solution or the exciting of doubts and difficulties.

They also cultivated in this monastery the study of natural philosophy and astronomy. There remain of Beda one entire book and some scattered essays on these subjects. This book, *De Rerum Natura*, is concise and methodical, and contains no very contemptible abstract of the physics which were taught in the decline of the Roman Empire. It was somewhat unfortunate that the infancy of English learning was supported by the dotage of the Roman, and that even the spring-head from whence they drew their instructions was itself corrupted. However, the works of the great masters of the ancient science still remained; but in natural philosophy the worst was the most fashionable. The Epicurean physics, the most approaching to rational, had long lost all credit by being made the support of an impious theology and a loose morality. The fine visions of Plato fell into some discredit by the abuse which heretics had made of them; and the writings of Aristotle seem to have been then the only ones much regarded, even in natural philosophy, in which branch of science alone they are unworthy of him. Beda entirely follows his system. The appearances of Nature are explained by matter and form, and by the four vulgar elements, acted upon by the four supposed qualities of hot, dry, moist, and cold. His astronomy is on the common system of the ancients, sufficient for the few purposes to which they applied it, but otherwise imperfect and grossly erroneous. He makes the moon larger than the earth; though a reflection on the nature of eclipses, which he understood, might have satisfied him of the contrary. But he had so much to copy that he had little time to examine. These speculations, however erroneous, were still useful; for, though men err in assigning the causes of natural operations, the works of Nature are by this means brought under their consideration, which cannot be done without enlarging the mind. The science may be false or frivolous; the improvement will be real. It may here be remarked, that soon afterwards the monks began to apply themselves to astronomy and chronology, from the disputes, which were carried on with so much heat and so little effect, concerning the proper time of celebrating Easter; and the English owed the cultivation of these noble sciences to one of the most trivial controversies of ecclesiastic discipline.

Beda did not confine his attention to those superior sciences. He treated of music, and of rhetoric, of grammar, and the art of versification, and of arithmetic, both by letters and on the fingers; and his

work on this last subject is the only one in which
that piece of antique curiosity has been preserved to
us. All these are short pieces; some of them are in
the catechetical method, and seem designed for the
immediate use of the pupils in his monastery, in order to furnish them with some leading ideas in the
rudiments of these arts, then newly introduced into
his country. He likewise made, and probably for the
same purpose, a very ample and valuable collection
of short philosophical, political, and moral maxims,
from Aristotle, Plato, Seneca, and other sages of
heathen antiquity. He made a separate book of
shining commonplaces and remarkable passages extracted from the works of Cicero, of whom he was
a great admirer, though he seems to have been not
an happy or diligent imitator in his style. From a
view of these pieces we may form an idea of what
stock in the science the English at that time possessed, and what advances they had made. That
work of Beda which is the best known and most
esteemed is the Ecclesiastical History of the English nation. Disgraced by a want of choice and
frequently by a confused ill disposition of his matter, and blemished with a degree of credulity next
to infantine, it is still a valuable, and for the time
a surprising performance. The book opens with a
description of this island which would not have disgraced a classical author; and he has prefixed to
it a chronological abridgment of sacred and profane
history connected, from the beginning of the world,
which, though not critically adapted to his main design, is of far more intrinsic value, and indeed dis-
plays a vast fund of historical erudition. On the
whole, though this father of the English learning

seems to have been but a genius of the middle class, neither elevated nor subtile, and one who wrote in a low style, simple, but not elegant, yet, when we reflect upon the time in which he lived, the place in which he spent his whole life, within the walls of a monastery, in so remote and wild a country, it is impossible to refuse him the praise of an incredible industry and a generous thirst of knowledge.

That a nation who not fifty years before had but just begun to emerge from a barbarism so perfect that they were unfurnished even with an alphabet should in so short a time have established so flourishing a seminary of learning, and have produced so eminent a teacher, is a circumstance which I imagine no other nation besides England can boast.

Hitherto we have spoken only of their Latin and Greek literature. They cultivated also their native language, which, according to the opinions of the most adequate judges, was deficient neither in energy nor beauty, and was possessed of such an happy flexibility as to be capable of expressing with grace and effect every new technical idea introduced either by theology or science. They were fond of poetry; they sung at all their feasts; and it was counted extremely disgraceful not to be able to take a part in these performances, even when they challenged each other to a sudden exertion of the poetic spirit. Cœdmon, afterwards one of the most eminent of their poets, was disgraced in this manner into an exertion of a latent genius. He was desired in his turn to sing, but, being ignorant and full of natural sensibility, retired in confusion from the company, and by instant and strenuous application soon became a distinguished proficient in the art.

CHAPTER III.

SERIES OF ANGLO-SAXON KINGS FROM ETHELBERT TO
ALFRED: WITH THE INVASION OF THE DANES.

THE Christian religion, having once taken root in
Kent, spread itself with great rapidity throughout
all the other Saxon kingdoms in England. The
manners of the Saxons underwent a notable alteration by this change in their religion: their ferocity was much abated; they became more mild and
sociable; and their laws began to partake of the
softness of their manners, everywhere recommend-
ing mercy and a tenderness for Christian blood.
There never was any people who embraced religion
with a more fervent zeal than the Anglo-Saxons,
nor with more simplicity of spirit. Their history
for a long time shows us a remarkable conflict between their dispositions and their principles. This
conflict produced no medium, because they were
absolutely contrary, and both operated with almost
equal violence. Great crimes and extravagant pen-
ances, rapine and an entire resignation of worldly
goods, rapes and vows of perpetual chastity, succeeded each other in the same persons. There
was nothing which the violence of their passions
could not induce them to commit; nothing to which
they did not submit to atone for their offences, when
reflection gave an opportunity to repent. But by
degrees the sanctions of religion began to prepon-
derate; and as the monks at this time attracted all
the religious veneration, religion everywhere began
to relish of the cloister: an inactive spirit, and a
spirit of scruples prevailed; they dreaded to put

the greatest criminal to death; they scrupled to engage in any worldly functions. A king of the Saxons dreaded that God would call him to an account for the time which he spent in his temporal affairs and had stolen from prayer. It was frequent for kings to go on pilgrimages to Rome or to Jerusalem, on foot, and under circumstances of great hardship. Several kings resigned their crowns to devote themselves to religious contemplation in monasteries, — more at that time and in this nation than in all other nations and in all times. This, as it introduced great mildness into the tempers of the people, made them less warlike, and consequently prepared the way to their forming one body under Egbert, and for the other changes which followed.

The kingdom of Wessex, by the wisdom and courage of King Ina, the greatest legislator and politician of those times, had swallowed up Cornwall, for a while a refuge for some of the old Britons, together with the little kingdom of the South Saxons. By this augmentation it stretched from the Land's End to the borders of Kent, the Thames flowing on the north, the ocean washing it on the south. By their situation the people of Wessex naturally came to engross the little trade which then fed the revenues of England ; and their minds were somewhat opened by a foreign communication, by which they became more civilized and better acquainted with the arts of war and of government. Such was the condition of A. D. 799. the kingdom of Wessex, when Egbert was called to the throne of his ancestors. The civil commotions which for some time prevailed had driven this prince early in life into an useful banishment. He was honorably received at the court of

Charlemagne, where he had an opportunity of study-
ing government in the best school, and of forming
himself after the most perfect model. Whilst Charlemagne was reducing the continent of Europe into one
empire, Egbert reduced England into one kingdom.
The state of his own dominions, perfectly united under him, with the other advantages which we have
just mentioned, and the state of the neighboring Saxon governments, made this reduction less difficult.
Besides Wessex, there were but two kingdoms of consideration in England, — Mercia and Northumberland.
They were powerful enough in the advantages of Nature, but reduced to great weakness by their divisions. As there is nothing of more moment to any
country than to settle the succession of its government on clear and invariable principles, the Saxon
monarchies, which were supported by no such principles, were continually tottering. The right of government sometimes was considered as in the eldest
son, sometimes in all; sometimes the will of the deceased prince disposed of the crown, sometimes a
popular election bestowed it. The consequence of
this was the frequent division and frequent reunion
of the same territory, which were productive of infinite mischief; many various principles of succession
gave titles to some, pretensions to more; and plots,
cabals, and crimes could not be wanting to all the
pretenders. Thus was Mercia torn to pieces; and
the kingdom of Northumberland, assaulted on one
side by the Scots, and ravaged on the other by the
Danish incursions, could not recover from a long an
archy into which its intestine divisions had plunged
it. Egbert knew how to make advantage of these
divisions : fomenting them by his policy at first, and

quelling them afterwards by his sword, he reduced these two kingdoms under his government. The same power which conquered Mercia and Northumberland made the reduction of Kent and Essex easy, — the people on all hands the more readily submitting, because there was no change made in their laws, manners, or the form of their government.

Egbert, A. D. 827.   Egbert, when he had brought all England under his dominion, made the Welsh tributary, and carried his arms with success into Scotland, assumed the title of Monarch of all Britain.* The southern part of the island was now for the first time authentically known by the name of England, and by every appearance promised to have arrived at the fortunate moment for forming a permanent and splendid monarchy. But Egbert had not reigned seven years in peace, when the Danes, who had before showed themselves in some scattered parties, and

A. D. 832.   made some inconsiderable descents, entered the kingdom in a formidable body. This people came from the same place whence the English themselves were derived, and they differed from them in little else than that they still retained their original barbarity and heathenism. These, assisted by the Norwegians, and other people of Scandinavia, were the last torrent of the Northern ravagers which overflowed Europe. What is remarkable, they attacked England and France when these two kingdoms were in the height of their grandeur, — France under Charlemagne, England united by Egbert. The good fortune of Egbert met its first check from these people, who defeated his forces with great slaughter near Charmouth in Dorsetshire. It generally hap-

* No Saxon monarch until Athelstan.

pens that a new nation, with a new method of making war, succeeds against a people only exercised in
arms by their own civil dissensions. Besides, England, newly united, was not without those jealousies
and that disaffection which give such great advantage to an invader. But the vigilance and courage of Egbert repaired this defeat; he repulsed the
Danes; and died soon after at Winchester, full of
years and glory.

He left a great, but an endangered suc- Ethelwolf,
cession, to his son Ethelwolf, who was a mild A. D. 838.
and virtuous prince, full of a timid piety, which utterly disqualifies for government; and he began to
govern at a time when the greatest capacity was
wanted. The Danes pour in upon every side; the
king rouses from his lethargy; battles are fought
with various success, which it were useless and tedious to recount. The event seems to have been,
that in some corners of the kingdom the Danes
gained a few inconsiderable settlements; the rest of
the kingdom, after being terribly ravaged, was left
a little time to recover, in order to be plundered
anew. But the weak prince took no advantage of
this time to concert a regular plan of defence, or
to rouse a proper spirit in his people. Yielding
himself wholly to speculative devotion, he entirely
neglected his affairs, and, to complete the ruin of
his kingdom, abandoned it, in such critical circumstances, to make a pilgrimage to Rome. At Rome
he behaved in the manner that suited his little genius, in making charitable foundations, and in extending the Rome-scot or Peter-pence, which the
folly of some princes of the Heptarchy had granted
for their particular dominions, over the whole king-

dom. His shameful desertion of his country raised
so general a discontent, that in his absence his own
son, with the principal of his nobility and bishops,
conspired against him. At his return, he found,
however, that several still adhered to him; but here,
too, incapable of acting with vigor, he agreed to an
accommodation, which placed the crown on the head
of his rebellious son, and only left to himself a sphere
of government as narrow as his genius, — the district of Kent, whither he retired to enjoy an inglorious privacy with a wife whom he had married in
France.

Ethelred,   On his death, his son Ethelred still held
A. D. 866.   the crown, which he had preoccupied by
his rebellion, and which he polluted with a new
stain. He married his father's widow. The confused history of these times furnishes no clear account either of the successions of the kings or of
their actions. During the reign of this prince and
his successors Ethelbert and Ethelred, the people in
several parts of England seem to have withdrawn
from the kingdom of Wessex, and to have revived
their former independency. This, added to the weakness of the government, made way for new swarms
of Danes, who burst in upon this ill-governed and
divided people, ravaging the whole country in a
terrible manner, but principally directing their fury
against every monument of civility or piety. They
had now formed a regular establishment in Northumberland, and gained a very considerable footing in
Mercia and East Anglia; they hovered over every
part of the kingdom with their fleets; and being established in many places in the heart of the coun
try, nothing seemed able to resist them.

CHAPTER IV.

REIGN OF KING ALFRED.

It was in the midst of these distractions that Alfred succeeded to a sceptre which A. D. 871. was threatened every moment to be wrenched from his hands. He was then only twenty-two years of age, but exercised from his infancy in troubles and in wars that formed and displayed his virtue. Some of its best provinces were torn from his kingdom, which was shrunk to the ancient bounds of Wessex; and what remained was weakened by dissension, by a long war, by a raging pestilence, and surrounded by enemies whose numbers seemed inexhaustible, and whose fury was equally increased by victories or defeats. All these difficulties served only to increase the vigor of his mind. He took the field without delay; but he was defeated with considerable loss. This ominous defeat displayed more fully the greatness of his courage and capacity, which found in desperate hopes and a ruined kingdom such powerful resources. In a short time after he was in a condition to be respected: but he was not led away by the ambition of a young warrior. He neglected no measures to procure peace for his country, which wanted a respite from the calamities which had long oppressed it. A peace was concluded for Wessex. Then the Danes turned their faces once more towards Mercia and East Anglia. They had before stripped the inhabitants of all their movable substance, and now they proceeded without resistance to seize upon their lands. Their success encouraged new swarms of Danes to crowd over, who, finding all the northern parts of England possessed by their friends, rushed into Wessex. They were adventurers under different and independent leaders; and a peace little regarded by the particular party that made it had no influence at all upon the others.

A. D. 875.

Alfred opposed this shock with so much firmness that the barbarians had recourse to a stratagem: they pretended to treat; but taking advantage of the truce, they routed a body of the West Saxon cavalry that were off their guard, mounted their horses, and, crossing the country with amazing celerity, surprised the city of Exeter. This was an acquisition of infinite advantage to their affairs, as it secured them a port in the midst of Wessex.

Alfred, mortified at this series of misfortunes, perceived clearly that nothing could dislodge the Danes, or redress their continual incursions, but a powerful fleet which might intercept them at sea. The want of this, principally, gave rise to the success of that people. They used suddenly to land and ravage a part of the country; when a force opposed them, they retired to their ships, and passed to some other part, which in a like manner they ravaged, and then retired as before, until the country, entirely harassed, pillaged, and wasted by these incursions, was no longer able to resist them. Then they ventured safely to enter a desolated and disheartened country, and to establish themselves in it. These considerations made Alfred resolve upon equipping a fleet. In this enterprise nothing but difficulties presented themselves: his revenue was scanty, and his subjects altogether unskilled in maritime affairs, either as to the construction or the navigation of ships. He did not therefore despair. With great promises attending a little money, he engaged in his service a number of Frisian seamen, neighbors to the Danes, and pirates, as they were. He brought, by the same means, ship-wrights from the continent. He was himself present to everything; and having performed the part of a king in drawing together supplies of every kind, he descended with no less dignity into the artist, — improving on the construction, inventing new machines, and supplying by the greatness of his genius the defects and imperfections of the arts in that rude period. By his indefatigable application the first English navy was in a very short time in readiness to put to sea. At that time the Danish fleet of one hundred and twenty-five ships stood with full sail for Exeter; they met; but, with an omen prosperous to the new naval power, the Danish fleet was entirely vanquished and dispersed. This success drew on the surrendry of Exeter, and a peace, which Alfred much wanted to put the affairs of his kingdom in order.

This peace, however, did not last long. As the Danes were continually pouring into some part of England, they found most parts already in Danish hands; so that all these parties naturally directed their course to the only English kingdom. All the Danes conspired to put them in possession of it, and bursting unexpectedly with the united force of their whole body upon Wessex, Alfred was entirely overwhelmed, and obliged to drive before the storm of his fortune. He fled in disguise into a fastness in the Isle of Athelney, where he remained four A. D. 876. months in the lowest state of indigence, supported by an heroic humility, and that spirit of piety which neither adverse fortune nor prosperity could overcome. It is much to be lamented that a character

so formed to interest all men, involved in reverses of
fortune that make the most agreeable and useful part
of history, should be only celebrated by pens so little
suitable to the dignity of the subject.   These revolutions are so little prepared, that we neither can perceive distinctly the causes which sunk him nor those
which again raised him to power.   A few naked facts
are all our stock.   From these we see Alfred, assisted
by the casual success of one of his nobles, issuing
from his retreat; he heads a powerful army once
more, defeats the Danes, drives them out of Wessex, follows his blow, expels them from Mercia, sub-
dues them in Northumberland, and makes them tributary in East Anglia; and thus established by a
number of victories in a full peace, he is presented
to us in that character which makes him venerable
to posterity.   It is a refreshment, in the midst of
such a gloomy waste of barbarism and desolation,
to fall upon so fair and cultivated a spot.

A. D. 880.
When Alfred had once more reunited the
kingdoms of his ancestors, he found the
whole face of things in the most desperate condition : there was no observance of law and order;
religion had no force ; there was no honest industry; the most squalid poverty and the grossest ignorance had overspread the whole kingdom.   Alfred
at once enterprised the cure of all these evils.   To

A. D. 896.
remedy the disorders in the government, he
revived, improved, and digested all the Saxon institutions, insomuch that he is generally honored as the founder of our laws and Constitution.*

* Historians, copying after one another, and examining little,
have attributed to this monarch the institution of juries, an institution which certainly did never prevail amongst the Saxons.   They

The shire he divided into hundreds, the hundreds into tithings; every freeman was obliged to be entered into some tithing, the members of which were mutually bound for each other, for the preservation of the peace, and the avoiding theft and rapine. For securing the liberty of the subject, he introduced the method of giving bail, the most certain fence against the abuses of power. It has been observed that the reigns of weak princes are times favorable to liberty; but the wisest and bravest of all the English princes is the father of their freedom. This great man was even jealous of the privileges of his subjects; and as his whole life was spent in protecting them, his last will breathes the same spirit, declaring that he had left his people as free as their own thoughts. He not only collected with great care a complete body of laws, but he wrote comments on them for the instruction of his judges, who were in general, by the misfor-

have likewise attributed to him the distribution of England into shires, hundreds, and tithings, and of appointing officers over these divisions. But it is very obvious that the shires were never settled upon any regular plan, nor are they the result of any single design. But these reports, however ill imagined, are a strong proof of the high veneration in which this excellent prince has always been held; as it has been thought that the attributing these regulations to him would endear them to the nation. He probably settled them in such an order, and made such reformations in his government, that some of the institutions themselves which he improved have been attributed to him: and, indeed, there was one work of his which serves to furnish us with a higher idea of the political capacity of that great man than any of these fictions. He made a general survey and register of all the property in the kingdom, who held it, and what it was distinctly: a vast work for an age of ignorance and time of confusion, which has been neglected in more civilized nations and settled times. It was called the Roll of Winton, and served as a model of a work of the same kind made by William the Conqueror.

tune of the time, ignorant. And if he took care to correct their ignorance, he was rigorous towards their corruption. He inquired strictly into their conduct, he heard appeals in person ; he held his Wittena-gemotes, or Parliaments, frequently ; and kept every part of his government in health and vigor.

Nor was he less solicitous for the defence than he had shown himself for the regulation of his kingdom. He nourished with particular care the new naval strength which he had established ; he built forts and castles in the most important posts ; he settled bea-cons to spread an alarm on the arrival of an enemy ; and ordered his militia in such a manner that there was always a great power in readiness to march, well appointed and well disciplined. But that a suitable revenue might not be wanting for the support of his fleets and fortifications, he gave great encouragement to trade, which, by the piracies on the coasts, and the rapine and injustice exercised by the people within, had long become a stranger to this island.

In the midst of these various and important cares, he gave a peculiar attention to learning, which by the rage of the late wars had been entirely extin-guished in his kingdom. " Very few there were " (says this monarch) " on this side the Humber that understood their ordinary prayers, or that were able to translate any Latin book into English, — so few, that I do not remember even one qualified to the southward of the Thames when I began my reign." To cure this deplorable ignorance, he was indefatiga-ble in his endeavors to bring into England men of learning in all branches from every part of Europe, and unbounded in his liberality to them. He enact-ed by a law that every person possessed of two hides

of land should send their children to school until sixteen. Wisely considering where to put a stop to his
love even of the liberal arts, which are only suited to
a liberal condition, he enterprised yet a greater design than that of forming the growing generation, —
to instruct even the grown: enjoining all his earldor-
men and sheriffs immediately to apply themselves to
learning. or to quit their offices. To facilitate these
great purposes, he made a regular foundation of an
university, which with great reason is believed to
have been at Oxford. Whatever trouble he took to
extend the benefits of learning amongst his subjects,
he showed the example himself, and applied to the
cultivation of his mind with unparalleled diligence
and success. He could neither read nor write at
twelve years old; but he improved his time in such a
manner that he became one of the most knowing men
of his age, in geometry, in philosophy, in architec
ture, and in music. He applied himself to the improvement of his native language; he translated several valuable works from Latin; and wrote a vast
number of poems in the Saxon tongue with a wonderful facility and happiness. He not only excelled in
the theory of the arts and sciences, but possessed a
great mechanical genius for the executive part; he
improved the manner of ship-building, introduced a
more beautiful and commodious architecture, and
even taught his countrymen the art of making bricks,
— most of the buildings having been of wood before
his time. In a word, he comprehended in the greatness of his mind the whole of government and all its
parts at once, and, what is most difficult to human
frailty, was at the same time sublime and minute.

Religion, which in Alfred's father was so prejudicial to affairs, without being in him at all inferior in its zeal and fervor, was of a more enlarged and noble kind; far from being a prejudice to his government, it seems to have been the principle that supported him in so many fatigues, and fed like an abundant source his civil and military virtues. To his religious exercises and studies he devoted a full third part of his time. It is pleasant to trace a genius even in its smallest exertions, — in measuring and allotting his time for the variety of business he was engaged in. According to his severe and methodical custom, he had a sort of wax candles made of different colors in different proportions, according to the time he allotted to each particular affair; as he carried these about with him wherever he went, to make them burn evenly he invented horn lanterns. One cannot help being amazed that a prince, who lived in such turbulent times, who commanded personally in fifty-four pitched battles, who had so disordered a province to regulate, who was not only a legislator, but a judge, and who was continually superintending his armies, his navies, the traffic of his kingdom, his revenues, and the conduct of all his officers, could have bestowed so much of his time on religious exercises and speculative knowledge; but the exertion of all his faculties and virtues seemed to have given a mutual strength to all of them. Thus all historians speak of this prince, whose whole history was one panegyric; and whatever dark spots of human frailty may have adhered to such a character, they are entirely hid in the splendor of his many shining qualities and grand virtues, that throw a glory over the obscure period in which he lived, and which is for no other reason worthy of our knowledge.

The latter part of his reign was molested with new and formidable attempts from the Danes: but they no longer found the country in its former condition; their fleets were attacked; and those that landed found a strong and regular opposition. There were now fortresses which restrained their ravages, and armies well appointed to oppose them in the field; they were defeated in a pitched battle; and after several desperate marches from one part of the country to the other, everywhere harassed and hunted, they were glad to return with A. D. 897. half their number, and to leave Alfred in quiet to accomplish the great things he had projected. This prince reigned twenty-seven years, and died at last of a disorder in his bowels, which had afflicted him, without interrupting his designs or souring his temper, during the greatest part of his life.

CHAPTER V.

SUCCESSION OF KINGS FROM ALFRED TO HAROLD.

HIS son Edward succeeded. Though of less learning than his father, he equalled Edward, A. D. 900. him in his political virtues. He made war with success on the Welsh, the Scots, and the Danes, and left his kingdom strongly fortified, and exercised, not weakened, with the enterprises of a vigorous reign. Because his son Edmund was under age, the crown was set on the head of his illegitimate offspring, Athelstan. His, like the reigns of all the princes of this time, was molested Athelstan, A. D. 925. by the continual incursions of the Danes; and notbing but a succession of men of spirit, capacity, and love of their country, which providentially happened at this time, could ward off the ruin of the kingdom. Such Athelstan was; and such was his brother Ed-

Edmund,
A. D. 942.

mund, who reigned five years with great reputation, but was at length, by an obscure ruffian, assassinated in his own palace. Edred, his

Edred,
A. D. 947.

brother, succeeded to the late monarchy: though he had left two sons, Edwin and Edgar, both were passed by on account of their minority. But on this prince's death, which happened after a troublesome reign of ten years, valiantly

Edwin,
A. D. 957.

supported against continual inroads of the Danes, the crown devolved on Edwin; of whom little can be said, because his reign was short, and he was so embroiled with his clergy that we can take his character only from the monks, who in such a case are suspicious authority.

Edgar,
A. D. 959.

Edgar, the second son of King Edmund, came young to the throne; but he had the happiness to have his youth formed and his kingdom ruled by men of experience, virtue, and authority. The celebrated Dunstan was his first minister, and had a mighty influence over all his actions. This prelate had been educated abroad, and had seen the world to advantage. As he had great power at court by the superior wisdom of his counsels, so by the sanctity of his life he had great credit with the people, which gave a firmness to the government of his master, whose private character was in many respects extremely exceptionable. It was in his reign, and chiefly by the means of his minister, Dunstan, that the monks, who had long prevailed in the opinion of the generality of the people, gave a total overthrow to their rivals, the secular clergy. The secular clergy were at this time for the most part married, and were therefore too near the common modes of mankind to draw a great deal of their respect; their character was supported by a very small portion of learning, and their lives were not such as people wish to see in the clergy. But the monks were unmarried, austere in their lives, regular in their duties, possessed of the learning of the times, well united under a proper subordination, full of art, and implacable towards their enemies. These circumstances, concurring with the dispositions of the king and the designs of Dunstan, prevailed so far that it was agreed in a council convened for that purpose to expel the secular clergy from their livings, and to supply their places with monks, throughout the kingdom. Although the partisans of the secular priests were not a few, nor of the lowest class, yet they were unable to withstand the current of the popular desire, strengthened by the authority of a potent and respected monarch. However, there was a seed of discontent sown on this occasion, which grew up afterwards to the mutual destruction of all the parties. During the whole reign of Edgar, as he had secured the most popular part of the clergy, and with them the people, in his interests, there was no internal disturbance; there was no foreign war, because this prince was always ready for war. But he principally owed his security to the care he took of his naval power, which was much greater and better regulated than that of any English monarch before him. He had three fleets always equipped, one of which annually sailed round the island. Thus the Danes, the Scots, the Irish, and the Welsh were kept in awe. He assumed the title of King of all Albion. His court was magnificent, and much frequented by strangers. His revenues were in excellent order, and no prince of his time supported the royal character with more dignity.

Edgar had two wives, Elfleda and Elfrida. By the first he had a son called Edward ; the second bore him one called Ethelred. On Edgar's death, Ed-
Edward,
A. D. 975. ward, in the usual order of succession, was called to the throne ; but Elfrida caballed in favor of her son, and finding it impossible to set him up in the life of his brother, she murdered him with her own hands in her castle of Corfe, whither he had retired to refresh himself, wearied with hunt-
Ethelred,
A. D. 979. ing. Ethelred, who by the crimes of his mother ascended a throne sprinkled with his brother's blood, had a part to act which exceeded the capacity that could be expected in one of his youth and inexperience. The partisans of the secular clergy, who were kept down by the vigor of Edgar's government, thought this a fit time to renew their pretensions. The monks defended themselves in their possession ; there was no moderation on either side, and the whole nation joined in these parties. The murder of Edward threw an odious stain on the king, though he was wholly innocent of that crime. There was a general discontent, and every corner was full of murmurs and cabals. In this state of the kingdom, it was equally dangerous to exert the fulness of the sovereign authority or to suffer it to relax. The temper of the king was most inclined to the latter method, which is of all things the worst. A weak government, too easy, suffers

evils to grow which often make the most rigorous and illegal proceedings necessary. Through an extreme lenity it is on some occasions tyrannical. This was the condition of Ethelred's nobility, who, by being permitted everything, were never contented.

Thus all the principal men held a sort of factious and independent authority; they despised the king, they oppressed the people, and they hated one another. The Danes, in every part of England but Wessex as numerous as the English themselves, and in many parts more numerous, were ready to take advantage of these disorders, and waited with impatience some new attempt from abroad, that they might rise in favor of the invaders. They were not long without such an occasion; the Danes pour in almost upon every part at once, and distract the defence which the weak prince was preparing to make.

In those days of wretchedness and ignorance, when all the maritime parts of Europe were attacked by these formidable enemies at once, they never thought of entering into any alliance against them; they equally neglected the other obvious method to prevent their incursions, which was, to carry the war into the invaders' country.

What aggravated these calamities, the no- A. D. 987. bility, mostly disaffected to the king, and entertaining very little regard to their country, made, some of them, a weak and cowardly opposition to the enemy; some actually betrayed their trust; some even were found who undertook the trade of piracy themselves. It was in this condition, that Edric, Duke of Mercia, a man of some ability, but light, inconstant, and utterly devoid of all principle, proposed to buy a peace from the Danes. The gen-

eral weakness and consternation disposed the king
and people to take this pernicious advice. At first

A. D. 991.

10,000*l.* was given to the Danes, who retired with this money and the rest of their
plunder. The English were now, for the first time,
taxed to supply this payment. The imposition was
called Danegelt, not more burdensome in the thing
than scandalous in the name. The scheme of pur-
chasing peace not only gave rise to many internal
hardships, but, whilst it weakened the kingdom, it
inspired such a desire of invading it to the enemy,
that Sweyn, King of Denmark, came in person soon
after with a prodigious fleet and army. The English,
having once found the method of diverting the storm
by an inglorious bargain, could not bear to think of
any other way of resistance. A greater sum, 48,000*l.*,
was now paid, which the Danes accepted with pleasure, as they could by this means exhaust their enemies and enrich themselves with little danger or
trouble. With very short intermissions they still returned, continually increasing in their demands. In
a few years they extorted upwards of 160,000*l.* from
the English, besides an annual tribute of 48,000*l.*
The country was wholly exhausted both of money
and spirit. The Danes in England, under the protection of the foreign Danes, committed a thousand
insolencies; and so infatuated with stupidity and
baseness were the English at this time, that they
employed hardly any other soldiers for their defence.

A. D. 1002.

In this state of shame and misery, their
sufferings suggested to them a design rather
desperate than brave. They resolved on a massacre
of the Danes. Some authors say, that in one night
the whole race was cut off. Many, probably all the

military men, were so destroyed.   But this massacre, injudicious as it was cruel, was certainly not universal ; nor did it serve any other or better end than to exasperate those of the same nation abroad, who the next year landed in England with a powerful army to revenge it, and committed outrages even beyond the usual tenor of the Danish cruelty.   There was in England no money left to purchase a peace, nor courage to wage a successful war ; and the King of Denmark, Sweyn, a prince of capacity, at the head of a large body of brave and enterprising men, soon mastered the whole kingdom, except London.   Ethelred, abandoned by fortune and his subjects, was forced to fly into Normandy.

A. D. 1003.

As there was no good order in the English affairs, though continually alarmed, they were always surprised ; they were only roused to arms by the cruelty of the enemy, and they were only formed into a body by being driven from their homes : so that they never made a resistance until they seemed to be entirely conquered.   This may serve to account for the frequent sudden reductions of the island, and the frequent renewals of their fortune when it seemed the most desperate.   Sweyn, in the midst of his victories, dies, and, though succeeded by his son Canute, who inherited his father's resolution, their affairs were thrown into some disorder by this accident. The English were encouraged by it.   Ethelred was recalled, and the Danes retired out of the kingdom ; but it was only to return the next year with a greater and better appointed force.   Nothing seemed able to oppose them.   The king dies.   A great part of the land was surrendered, without resistance, to Canute.   Edmund, the eldest son of Ethelred, supported,

Edmund
Ironside,
A. D. 1016. however, the declining hopes of the English for some time; in three months he fought three victorious battles; he attempted a fourth, but lost it by the base desertion of Edric, the principal author of all these troubles. It is common with the conquered side to attribute all their misfortunes to the treachery of their own party. They choose to be thought subdued by the treachery of their friends rather than the superior bravery of their enemies. All the old historians talk in this strain; and it must be acknowledged that all adherents to a declining party have many temptations to infidelity. .

Edmund, defeated, but not discouraged, retreated to the Severn, where he recruited his forces. Canute followed at his heels. And now the two armies were drawn up which were to decide the fate of England, when it was proposed to determine the war by a single combat between the two kings. Neither was unwilling; the Isle of Alney in the Severn was chosen for the lists. Edmund had the advantage by the greatness of his strength, Canute by his address; for when Edmund had so far prevailed as to disarm him, he proposed a parley, in which he persuaded Edmund to a peace, and to a division of the kingdom. Their armies accepted the agreement, and both kings departed in a seeming friendship. But Edmund died soon after, with a probable suspicion of being murdered by the instruments of his associate in the empire.

The Danish
race.
Canute. Canute, on this event, assembled the states of the kingdom, by whom he was acknowledged King of all England. He was a prince truly great; for, having acquired the kingdom by his valor, he maintained and improved it

by his justice and clemency. Choosing rather to rule by the inclination of his subjects than the right of conquest, he dismissed his Danish army, and committed his safety to the laws. He reëstablished the order and tranquillity which so long a series of bloody wars had banished. He revived the ancient statutes of the Saxon princes, and governed through his whole reign with such steadiness and moderation that the English were much happier under this foreign prince than they had been under their natural kings. Canute, though the beginning of his life was stained with those marks of violence and injustice which attend conquest, was remarkable in his latter end for his piety. According to the mode of that time, he made a pilgrimage to Rome, with a view to expiate the crimes which paved his way to the throne; but he made a good use of this peregrination, and returned full of the observations he had made in the country through which he passed, which he turned to the benefit of his extensive dominions. They comprehended England, Denmark, Norway, and many of the countries which lie upon the Baltic. Those he left, established in peace and security, to his children. The fate of his Northern possessions is not of this place. England fell to his son Harold, though not without much competition in favor of the sons of Edmund Ironside, while some contended for the right of the sons of Ethelred, Alfred and Edward. Harold inherited none of the virtues of Canute; he banished his mother Emma, murdered his half-brother Alfred, and died without issue after a short reign, full of violence, weakness, and cruelty. His brother Hardicanute, who suc- Harold I., A. D. 1035.

Hardica-nute, A. D. 1039.

ceeded him, resembled him in his character; he
committed new cruelties and injustices in revenging
those which his brother had committed, and he died
after a yet shorter reign. The Danish power, es
tablished with so much blood, expired of itself; and
The Saxon line restored.   Edward, the only surviving son of Ethelred,
then an exile in Normandy, was called to
the throne by the unanimous voice of the kingdom.

Edward the Confessor, A. D. 1041.   This prince was educated in a monastery,
where he learned piety, continence, and hu-
mility, but nothing of the art of government. He
was innocent and artless, but his views were narrow,
and his genius contemptible. The character of such
a prince is not, therefore, what influences the government, any further than as it puts it in the hands of
others. When he came to the throne, Godwin, Earl
of Kent, was the most popular man in England; he
possessed a very great estate, an enterprising disposition, and an eloquence beyond the age he lived in;
he was arrogant, imperious, assuming, and of a conscience which never put itself in the way of his interest. He had a considerable share in restoring
Edward to the throne of his ancestors; and by this
merit, joined to his popularity, he for some time directed everything according to his pleasure. He intended to fortify his interest by giving in marriage to
the king his daughter, a lady of great beauty, great
virtue, and an education beyond her sex. Godwin
had, however, powerful rivals in the king's favor.
This monarch, who possessed many of the private
virtues, had a grateful remembrance of his favorable reception in Normandy; he caressed the people
of that country, and promoted several to the first
places, ecclesiastical and civil, in his kingdom. This

begot an uneasiness in all the English; but Earl Godwin was particularly offended. The Normans, on the other hand, accused Godwin of a design on the crown, the justice of which imputation the whole tenor of his conduct evinced sufficiently. But as his cabals began to break into action before they were in perfect ripeness for it, the Norman party prevailed, and Godwin was banished. This man was not only very popular at home by his generosity and address, but he found means to engage even foreigners in his interests. Baldwin, Earl of Flanders, gave him a very kind reception. By his assistance Godwin fitted out a fleet, hired a competent force, sailed to England, and having near Sandwich deceived the king's navy, he presented himself at London before he was expected. The king made ready as great a force as the time would admit to oppose him. The galleys of Edward and Godwin met on the Thames; but such was the general favor to God-win, such the popularity of his cause, that the king's men threw down their arms, and refused to fight against their countrymen in favor of strangers. Edward was obliged to treat with his own subjects, and in consequence of this treaty to dismiss the Normans, whom he believed to be the best attached to his interests. Godwin used the power to which he was restored to gratify his personal revenge, showing no mercy to his enemies. Some of his sons behaved in the most tyrannical manner. The great lords of the kingdom envied and hated a greatness which annihilated the royal authority, eclipsed them, and oppressed the people; but Godwin's death soon after quieted for a while their mur- A. D. 1053. murs. The king, who had the least share in the transactions of his own reign, and who was of a temper not to perceive his own insignificance, begun in his old age to think of a successor. He had no children: for some weak reasons of religion or personal dislike, he had never cohabited with his wife. He sent for his nephew Edward, the son of Edmund Ironside, out of Hungary, where he had taken refuge; but he died soon after he came to England, leaving a son called Edgar Atheling. The king himself, irresolute in so momentous an affair, died without making any settlement. His reign was properly that of his great men, or rather of their factions. All of it that was his own was good. He was careful of the privileges of his subjects, and took care to have a body of the Saxon laws, very favorable to them, digested and enforced. He remitted the heavy imposition called Danegelt, amounting to 40,000*l.* a year, which had been constantly collected after the occasion had ceased; he even repaid to his subjects what he found in the treasury at his accession. In short, there is little in his life that can call his title to sanctity in question, though he can never be reckoned among the great kings.

A. D. 1066.

CHAPTER VI.

HAROLD II. — INVASION OF THE NORMANS. — ACCOUNT OF THAT PEOPLE, AND OF THE STATE OF ENGLAND AT THE TIME OF THE INVASION.

Harold II., A. D. 1066. THOUGH Edgar Atheling had the best title to the succession, yet Harold, the son of Earl Godwin, on account of the credit of his father,

and his own great qualities, which supported and
extended the interest of his family, was by the general voice set upon the throne. The right of Edgar,
young, and discovering no great capacity, gave him
little disturbance in comparison of the violence of his
own brother Tosti, whom for his infamous oppression
he had found himself obliged to banish. This man,
who was a tyrant at home and a traitor abroad, insulted the maritime parts with a piratical fleet, whilst
he incited all the neighboring princes to fall upon his
country. Harold Harfager, King of Norway, after
the conquest of the Orkneys, with a powerful navy
hung over the coasts of England. But nothing troubled Harold so much as the pretensions and the formidable preparation of William, Duke of Normandy,
one of the most able, ambitious, and enterprising men
of that age. We have mentioned the partiality of
King Edward to the Normans, and the hatred he
bore to Godwin and his family. The Duke of Normandy, to whom Edward had personal obligations,
had taken a tour into England, and neglected no
means to improve these dispositions to his own advantage. It is said that he then received the fullest
assurances of being appointed to the succession, and
that Harold himself had been sent soon after into
Normandy to settle whatever related to it. This is
an obscure transaction, and would, if it could be
cleared up, convey but little instruction. So that
whether we believe or not that William had engaged Harold by a solemn oath to secure him the
kingdom, we know that he afterwards set up a will
of King Edward in his favor, which, however, he
never produced, and probably never had to produce.
In these delicate circumstances Harold was not want-

ing to himself. By the most equitable laws and the most popular behavior he sought to secure the affections of his subjects; and he succeeded so well, that when he marched against the King of Norway, who had invaded his kingdom and taken York, without difficulty he raised a numerous army of gallant men, zealous for his cause and their country. He obtained a signal and decisive victory over the Norwegians. The King Harfager, and the traitor Tosti, who had joined him, were slain in the battle, and the Norwegians were forced to evacuate the country. Harold had, however, but little time to enjoy the fruits of his victory.

Scarce had the Norwegians departed, when William, Duke of Normandy, landed in the southern part of the kingdom with an army of sixty thousand chosen men, and struck a general terror through all the nation, which was well acquainted with the character of the commander and the courage and discipline of his troops.

The Normans were the posterity of those Danes who had so long and so cruelly harassed the British islands and the shore of the adjoining continent. In the days of King Alfred, a body of these adventurers, under their leader, Rollo, made an attempt upon England; but so well did they find every spot defended by the vigilance and bravery of that great monarch that they were compelled to retire. Beaten from these shores, the stream of their impetuosity bore towards the northern parts of France, which had been reduced to the most deplorable condition by their former ravages. Charles the Simple then sat on the throne of that kingdom; unable to resist this torrent of barbarians, he was obliged to yield to it;

he agreed to give up to Rollo the large and fertile
province of Neustria, to hold of him as his feudatory.
This province, from the new inhabitants, was called
Normandy. Five princes succeeded Rollo, who maintained with great bravery and cultivated with equal
wisdom his conquests. The ancient ferocity of this
people was a little softened by their settlement; but
the bravery which had made the Danes so formidable
was not extinguished in the Normans, nor the spirit
of enterprise. Not long before this period, a private
gentleman of Normandy, by his personal bravery, had
acquired the kingdom of Naples. Several others followed his fortunes, who added Sicily to it. From
one end of Europe to the other the Norman name
was known, respected, and feared. Robert, the sixth
Duke of Normandy, to expiate some crime which lay
heavy upon his conscience, resolved, according to the
ideas of that time, upon a pilgrimage to Jerusalem.
It was in vain that his nobility, whom he had assembled to notify this resolution to them, represented to
him the miserable state to which his country would
be reduced, abandoned by its prince, and uncertain
of a legal successor. The Duke was not to be moved
from his resolution, which appeared but the more
meritorious from the difficulties which attended it.
He presented to the states William, then an infant,
born of an obscure woman, whom, notwithstanding,
he doubted not to be his son; him he appointed to
succeed; him he recommended to their virtue and
loyalty; and then, solemnly resigning the government in his favor, he departed on the pilgrimage,
from whence he never returned. The states, hesi-
tating some time between the mischiefs that attend
the allowing an illegitimate succession and those

which might arise from admitting foreign pretensions, thought the former the least prejudicial, and accordingly swore allegiance to William. But this oath was not sufficient to establish a right so doubtful. The Dukes of Burgundy and Brittany, as well as several Norman noblemen, had specious titles. The endeavors of all these disquieted the reign of the young prince with perpetual troubles. In these troubles he was formed early in life to vigilance, activity, secrecy, and a conquest over all those passions, whether bad or good, which obstruct the way to greatness. He had to contend with all the neighboring princes, with the seditions of a turbulent and unfaithful nobility, and the treacherous protection of his feudal lord, the King of France. All of these in their turns, sometimes all of these together, distressed him. But with the most unparalleled good fortune and conduct he overcame all opposition, and triumphed over every enemy, raising his power and reputation above that of all his ancestors, as much as he was exalted by his bravery above the princes of his own time.

Such was the prince who, on a pretended claim from the will of King Edward, supported by the common and popular pretence of punishing offenders and redressing grievances, landed at Pevensey in Sussex, to contest the crown with Harold. Harold had no sooner advice of his landing than he advanced to meet him with all possible diligence; but there did not appear in his army, upon this occasion, the same unanimity and satisfaction which animated it on its march against the Norwegians. An ill-timed economy in Harold, which made him refuse to his soldiers the plunder of the Norwegian camp, had created a general discontent. Several deserted; and the soldiers who remained followed heavily a leader under whom there was no hope of plunder, the greatest incitement of the soldiery. Notwithstanding this ill disposition, Harold still urged forward, and by forced marches advanced within seven miles of the enemy. The Norman, on his landing, is said to have sent away his ships, that his army might have no way of safety but in conquest; yet had he fortified his camp, and taken every prudent precaution, that so considerable an enterprise should not be reduced to a single effort of despair. When the armies, charged with the decision of so mighty a contest, had approached each other, Harold paused awhile. A great deal depended on his conduct at this critical time. The most experienced in the council of war, who knew the condition of their troops, were of opinion that the engagement ought to be deferred, — that the country ought to be wasted, — that, as the winter approached, the Normans would in all probability be obliged to retire of themselves, — that, if this should not happen, the Norman army was without resources, whilst the English would be every day considerably augmented, and might attack their enemy at a time and manner which might make their success certain. To all these reasons nothing was opposed but a false point of honor and a mistaken courage in Harold, who urged his fate, and resolved on an engagement. The Norman, as soon as he perceived that the English were determined on a battle, left his camp to post himself in an advantageous situation, in which his whole army remained the night which preceded the action.

This night was spent in a manner which prognosticated the event of the following day. On the part of

the Normans it was spent in prayer, and in a cool
and steady preparation for the engagement; on the
side of the English, in riot and a vain confidence
that neglected all the necessary preparations. The
two armies met in the morning; from seven to five
the battle was fought with equal vigor, until at last
the Norman army pretending to break in confusion,
a stratagem to which they had been regularly formed,
the English, elated with success, suffered that firm
order in which their security consisted to dissipate,
which when William observed, he gave the signal to
his men to regain their former disposition, and fall
upon the English, broken and dispersed. Harold in
this emergency did everything which became him,
everything possible to collect his troops and to renew the engagement; but whilst he flew from place
to place, and in all places restored the battle, an
arrow pierced his brain, and he died a king, in a
manner worthy of a warrior. The English immediately fled ; the rout was total, and the slaughter
prodigious.

The consternation which this defeat and the death
of Harold produced over the kingdom was more fatal
than the defeat itself. If William had marched directly to London, all contest had probably been at an
end ; but he judged it more prudent to secure the
sea-coast, to make way for reinforcements, distrusting
his fortune in his success more than he had done in
his first attempts. He marched to Dover, where the
effect of his victory was such that the strong castle
there surrendered without resistance. Had this fortress made any tolerable defence, the English would
have had leisure to rouse from their consternation,
and plan some rational method for continuing the

war; but now the conqueror was on full march to London, whilst the English were debating concerning the measures they should take, and doubtful in what manner they should fill the vacant throne. However, in this emergency it was necessary to take some resolution. The party of Edgar Atheling prevailed, and he was owned king by the city of London, which even at this time was exceedingly powerful, and by the greatest part of the nobility then present. But his reign was of a short duration. William advanced by hasty marches, and, as he approached, the perplexity of the English redoubled: they had done nothing for the defence of the city; they had no reliance on their new king; they suspected one another; there was no authority, no order, no counsel; a confused and ill-sorted assembly of unwarlike people, of priests, burghers, and nobles confounded with them in the general panic, struck down by the consternation of the late defeat, and trembling under the bolts of the Papal excommunication, were unable to plan any method of defence: insomuch that, when he had passed the Thames and drew near to London, the clergy, the citizens, and the greater part of the nobles, who had so lately set the crown on the head of Edgar, went out to meet him; they submitted to him, and having brought him in triumph to Westminster, he was there solemnly crowned King of England. The whole nation followed the example of London; and one battle gave England to the Normans, which had cost the Romans, the Saxons, and Danes so much time and blood to acquire.

At first view it is very difficult to conceive how this could have happened to a powerful nation, in

which it does not appear that the conqueror had one
partisan. It stands a single event in history, unless,
perhaps, we may compare it with the reduction of
Ireland, some time after, by Henry the Second. An
attentive consideration of the state of the kingdom at
that critical time may, perhaps, in some measure, lay
open to us the cause of this extraordinary revolution.

The nobility of England, in which its strength consisted, was much decayed. Wars and confiscations,
but above all the custom of gavelkind, had reduced
that body very low. At the same time some few
families had been raised to a degree of power unknown in the ancient Saxon times, and dangerous
in all. Large possessions, and a larger authority,
were annexed to the offices of the Saxon magistrates, whom they called Aldermen. This authority,
in their long and bloody wars with the Danes, it was
found necessary to increase, and often to increase
beyond the ancient limits. Aldermen were created
for life; they were then frequently made hereditary;
some were vested with a power over others; and at
this period we begin to hear of dukes who governed
over several shires, and had many aldermen subject
to them. These officers found means to turn the
royal bounty into an instrument of becoming independent of its authority. Too great to obey, and too
little to protect, they were a dead weight upon the
country. They began to cast an eye on the crown,
and distracted the nation by cabals to compass their
designs. At the same time they nourished the most
terrible feuds amongst themselves. The feeble government of Edward established these abuses. He
could find no method of humbling one subject
grown too great, but by aggrandizing in the same

excessive degree some others. Thus, he endeavored to balance the power of Earl Godwin by exalting Leofric, Duke of Mercia, and Siward, Duke of
Northumberland, to an extravagant greatness. The
consequence was this: he did not humble Godwin,
but raised him potent rivals. When, therefore, this
prince died, the lawful successor to the crown, who
had nothing but right in his favor, was totally
eclipsed by the splendor of the great men who had
adorned themselves with the spoils of royalty. The
throne was now the prize of faction; and Harold, the
son of Godwin, having the strongest faction, carried
it. By this success the opposite parties were inflamed with a new occasion of rancor and animosity,
and an incurable discontent was raised in the minds
of Edwin and Morcar, the sons of Duke Leofric, who
inherited their father's power and popularity: but
this animosity operated nothing in favor of the legitimate heir, though it weakened the hands of the gov
erning prince.

The death of Harold was far from putting an end
to these evils; it rather unfolded more at large the
fatal consequences of the ill measures which had
been pursued. Edwin and Morcar set on foot once
more their practices to obtain the crown; and when
they found themselves baffled, they retired in discontent from the councils of the nation, withdrawing
thereby a very large part of its strength and authority. The council of the nation, which was formed of
the clashing factions of a few great men, (for the
rest were nothing,) divided, disheartened, weakened,
without head, without direction, dismayed by a terrible defeat, submitted, because they saw no other
course, to a conqueror whose valor they had experi-

enced, and who had hitherto behaved with great appearances of equity and moderation. As for the grandees, they were contented rather to submit to this foreign prince than to those whom they regarded as their equals and enemies.

With these causes other strong ones concurred. For near two centuries the continual and bloody wars with the Danes had exhausted the nation; the peace, which for a long time they were obliged to buy dearly, exhausted it yet more; and it had not sufficient leisure nor sufficient means of acquiring wealth to yield at this time any extraordinary resources. The new people, which after so long a struggle had mixed with the English, had not yet so thoroughly incorporated with the ancient inhabitants that a perfect union might be expected between them, or that any strong, uniform, national effort might have resulted from it. Besides, the people of England were the most backward in Europe in all improvements, whether in military or in civil life. Their towns were meanly built, and more meanly fortified; there was scarcely anything that deserved the name of a strong place in the kingdom; there was no fortress which, by retarding the progress of a conqueror, might give the people an opportunity of recalling their spirits and collecting their strength. To these we may add, that the Pope's approbation of William's pretensions gave them great weight, especially amongst the clergy, and that this disposed and reconciled to submission a people whom the circumstances we have mentioned had before driven to it.

CHAPTER VII.

OF THE LAWS AND INSTITUTIONS OF THE SAXONS.

BEFORE we begin to consider the laws and constitutions of the Saxons, let us take a view of the state of the country from whence they are derived, as it is portrayed in ancient writers. This view will be the best comment on their institutions. Let us represent to ourselves a people without learning, without arts, without industry, solely pleased and occupied with war, neglecting agriculture, abhorring cities, and seeking their livelihood only from pasturage and hunting through a boundless range of morasses and forests. Such a people must necessarily be united to each other by very feeble bonds; their ideas of government will necessarily be imperfect, their freedom and their love of freedom great. From these dispositions it must happen, of course, that the intention of investing one person or a few with the whole powers of government, and the notion of deputed authority or representation, are ideas that never could have entered their imaginations. When, therefore, amongst such a people any resolution of consequence was to be taken, there was no way of effecting it but by bringing together the whole body of the nation, that every individual might consent to the law, and each reciprocally bind the other to the observation of it. This polity, if so it may be called, subsists still in all its simplicity in Poland.

But as in such a society as we have mentioned the people cannot be classed according to any political regulations, great talents have a more ample sphere in which to exert themselves than in a close and better formed society. These talents must therefore have attracted a great share of the public veneration, and drawn a numerous train after the person distinguished by them, of those who sought his protection, or feared his power, or admired his qualifications, or wished to form themselves after his example, or, in fine, of whoever desired to partake of his importance by being mentioned along with him. These the ancient Gauls, who nearly resembled the Germans in their customs, called Ambacti; the Romans called them Comites. Over these their chief had a considerable power, and the more considerable because it depended upon influence rather than institution: influence among so free a people being the principal source of power. But this authority, great as it was, never could by its very nature be stretched to despotism; because any despotic act would have shocked the only principle by which that authority was supported, the general good opinion. On the other hand, it could not have been bounded by any positive laws, because laws can hardly subsist amongst a people who have not the use of letters. It was a species of arbitrary power, softened by the popularity from whence it arose. It came from popular opinion, and by popular opinion it was corrected.

If people so barbarous as the Germans have no laws, they have yet customs that serve in their room; and these customs operate amongst them better than laws, because they become a sort of Nature both to the governors and the governed. This circumstance in some measure removed all fear of the abuse of authority, and induced the Germans to permit their chiefs * to decide upon matters of lesser moment,

* They had no other nobility; yet several families amongst them were considered as noble.

their private differences, — for so Tacitus explains the *minores res*. These chiefs were a sort of judges, but not legislators; nor do they appear to have had a share in the superior branches of the executive part of government, — the business of peace and war, and everything of a public nature, being determined, as we have before remarked, by the whole body of the people, according to a maxim general among the Germans, that what concerned all ought to be handled by all. Thus were delineated the faint and incorrect outlines of our Constitution, which has since been so nobly fashioned and so highly finished. This fine system, says Montesquieu, was invented in the woods; but whilst it remained in the woods, and for a long time after, it was far from being a fine one, — no more, indeed, than a very imperfect attempt at government, a system for a rude and barbarous people, calculated to maintain them in their barbarity.

The ancient state of the Germans was military: so that the orders into which they were distributed, their subordination, their courts, and every part of their government, must be deduced from an attention to a military principle.

The ancient German people, as all the other Northern tribes, consisted of freemen and slaves : the freemen professed arms, the slaves cultivated the ground. But men were not allowed to profess arms at their own will, nor until they were admitted to that dignity by an established order, which at a certain age separated the boys from men. For when a young man approached to virility,* he was not yet admitted as a member of the state, which was quite military,

* Arma sumere non ante cuiquam moris, quàm civitas suffecturum probaverit. — Tacitus de Mor. Germ. 13.

until he had been invested with a spear in the public
assembly of his tribe; and then he was adjudged
proper to carry arms, and also to assist in the public deliberations, which were always held armed.*
This spear he generally received from the hand of
some old and respected chief, under whom he commonly entered himself, and was admitted among his
followers.† No man could stand out as an independent individual, but must have enlisted in one of these
military fraternities; and as soon as he had so enlisted, immediately he became bound to his leader in
the strictest dependence, which was confirmed by an
oath,‡ and to his brethren in a common vow for their
mutual support in all dangers, and for the advancement and the honor of their common chief. This
chief was styled Senior, Lord, and the like terms,
which marked out a superiority in age and merit;
the followers were called Ambacti, Comites, Leudes,
Vassals, and other terms, marking submission and
dependence. This was the very first origin of civil,
or rather, military government, amongst the ancient
people of Europe; and it arose from the connection
that necessarily was created between the person who
gave the arms, or knighted the young man, and him
that received them; which implied that they were to
be occupied in his service who originally gave them.
These principles it is necessary strictly to attend to,
because they will serve much to explain the whole

* Nihil autem neque publicæ neque privatæ rei nisi armati agunt.
— Tacitus de Mor. Germ. 13.

† Cæteri robustioribus ac jam pridem probatis aggregantur. — Id.
ibid.

‡ Illum defendere, tueri, sua quoque fortia facta gloriæ ejus as-
signare, præcipuum sacramentum est. — Id. 14.

course both of government and real property, wherever the German nations obtained a settlement: the
whole of their government depending for the most
part upon two principles in our nature, — ambition,
that makes one man desirous, at any hazard or expense, of taking the lead amongst others, — and admiration, which makes others equally desirous of following him, from the mere pleasure of admiration,
and a sort of secondary ambition, one of the most
universal passions among men. These two principles, strong, both of them, in our nature, create a
voluntary inequality and dependence. But amongst
equals in condition there could be no such bond, and
this was supplied by confederacy; and as the first of
these principles created the senior and the knight,
the second produced the *conjurati fratres*, which,
sometimes as a more extensive, sometimes as a stricter bond, are perpetually mentioned in the old laws
and histories.

The relation between the lord and the vassal produced another effect, — that the leader was obliged
to find sustenance for his followers, and to maintain
them at his table, or give them some equivalent in
order to their maintenance. It is plain from these
principles, that this service on one hand, and this obligation to support on the other, could not have originally been hereditary, but must have been entirely
in the free choice of the parties.

But it is impossible that such a polity could long
have subsisted by election alone. For, in the first
place, that natural love which every man has to his
own kindred would make the chief willing to perpetuate the power and dignity he acquired in his own
blood, — and for that purpose, even during his own

life, would raise his son, if grown up, or his collater-
als, to such a rank as they should find it only necessary to continue their possession upon his death. On
the other hand, if a follower was cut off in war, or
fell by natural course, leaving his offspring destitute,
the lord could not so far forget the services of his
vassal as not to continue his allowance to his children; and these again growing up, from reason and
gratitude, could only take their knighthood at his
hands from whom they had received their education; and thus, as it could seldom happen but that
the bond, either on the side of the lord or depend-
ant, was perpetuated, some families must have been
distinguished by a long continuance of this relation,
and have been therefore looked upon in an honorable light, from that only circumstance from whence
honor was derived in the Northern world. Thus
nobility was seen in Germany; and in the earliest
Anglo-Saxon times some families were distinguished
by the title of Ethelings, or of noble descent. But
this nobility of birth was rather a qualification for
the dignities of the state than an actual designation
to them. The Saxon ranks are chiefly designed to
ascertain the quantity of the composition for personal injuries against them.

But though this hereditary relation was created
very early, it must not be mistaken for such a regular inheritance as we see at this day: it was an
inheritance only according to the principles from
whence it was derived; by them it was modified.
It was originally a military connection; and if a
father left his son under a military age, so as that
he could neither lead nor judge his people, nor
qualify the young men who came up under him to

take arms, — in order to continue the cliental bond, and not to break up an old and strong confederacy, and thereby disperse the tribe, who should be pitched upon to head the whole, but the worthiest of blood of the deceased leader, he that ranked next to him in his life ?* And this is Tanistry, which is a succession made up of inheritance and election, a succession in which blood is inviolably regarded, so far as it was consistent with military purposes. It was thus that our kings succeeded to the throne throughout the whole time of the Anglo-Saxon empire. The first kings of the Franks succeeded in the same manner, and without all doubt the succession of all the inferior chieftains was regulated by a similar law. Very frequent examples occur in the Saxon times, where the son of the deceased king, if under age, was entirely passed over, and his uncle, or some remoter relation, raised to the crown; but there is not a single instance where the election has carried it out of the blood. So that, in truth, the controversy, which has been managed with such heat, whether in the Saxon times the crown was hereditary or elective, must be determined in some degree favorably for the litigants on either side; for it was certainly both hereditary and elective within the bounds which we have mentioned. This order prevailed in Ireland, where the Northern customs were retained some hundreds of years after the rest of Europe had in a great measure receded from them. Tanistry continued in force there until the beginning of the last century. And we have greatly to regret the narrow notions of our lawyers, who abolished the

* Deputed authority, guardianship, &c., not known to the Northern nations; they gained this idea bv intercourse with the Romans.

authority of the Brehon law, and at the same time
kept no monuments of it, — which if they had done,
there is no doubt but many things of great value
towards determining many questions relative to the
laws, antiquities, and manners of this and other countries had been preserved.   But it is clear, though it
has not been, I think, observed, that the ascending
collateral branch was much regarded amongst the
ancient Germans, and even preferred to that of the
immediate possessor, as being, in case of an accident
arriving to the chief, the presumptive heir, and him
on whom the hope of the family was fixed : and this is
upon the principles of Tanistry.   And the rule seems
to have taken such deep root as to have much influenced a considerable article of our feudal law : for,
what is very singular, and, I take it, otherwise unaccountable, a collateral warranty bound, even without
any descending assets, where the lineal did not, unless something descended ; and this subsisted invariably in the law until this century.

Thus we have seen the foundation of the Northern
government and the orders of their people, which
consisted of dependence and confederacy : that the
principal end of both was military ; that protection
and maintenance were due on the part of the chief,
obedience on that of the follower ; that the followers
should be bound to each other as well as to the chief ;
that this headship was not at first hereditary, but that
it continued in the blood by an order of its own,
called Tanistry.

All these unconnected and independent parts were
only linked together by a common council : and here
religion interposed.   Their priests, the Druids, having
a connection throughout each state, united it.   They

called the assembly of the people: and here their general resolutions were taken; and the whole might rather be called a general confederacy than a government. In no other bonds, I conceive, were they united before they quitted Germany. In this ancient state we know them from Tacitus. Then follows an immense gap, in which undoubtedly some changes were made by time; and we hear little more of them until we find them Christians, and makers of written laws.

In this interval of time the origin of kings may be traced out. When the Saxons left their own country in search of new habitations, it must be supposed that they followed their leaders, whom they so much venerated at home; but as the wars which made way for their establishment continued for a long time, military obedience made them familiar with a stricter authority. A subordination, too, became necessary among the leaders of each band of adventurers: and being habituated to yield an obedience to a single person in the field, the lustre of his command and the utility of the institution easily prevailed upon them to suffer him to form the band of their union in time of peace, under the name of King. But the leader neither knew the extent of the power he received, nor the people of that which they bestowed. Equally unresolved were they about the method of perpetuating it,—sometimes filling the vacant throne by election, without regard to, but more frequently regarding, the blood of the deceased prince; but it was late before they fell into any regular plan of succession, if ever the Anglo-Saxons attained it. Thus their polity was formed slowly; the prospect clears up by little and little; and this species of an irregular republic we see turned into a monarchy as irregular.

It is no wonder that the advocates for the several parties among us find something to favor their several notions in the Saxon government, which was never supported by any fixed or uniform principle.

To comprehend the other parts of the government of our ancestors, we must take notice of the orders into which they were classed. As well as we can judge in so obscure a matter, they were divided into nobles or gentlemen, freeholders, freemen that were not freeholders, and slaves. Of these last we have little to say, as they were nothing in the state. The nobles were called Thanes, or servants. It must be remembered that the German chiefs were raised to that honorable rank by those qualifications which drew after them a numerous train of followers and dependants.* If it was honorable to be followed by a numerous train, so it was honorable in a secondary degree to be a follower of a man of consideration; and this honor was the greater in proportion to the quality of the chief, and to the nearness of the attendance on his person. When a monarchy was formed, the splendor of the crown naturally drowned all the inferior honors; and the attendants on the person of the king were considered as the first in rank, and derived their dignity from their service. Yet as the Saxon government had still a large mixture of the popular, it was likewise requisite, in order to raise a man to the first rank of thanes, that he should have a suitable attendance and sway amongst the people. To support him in both of these, it was necessary that he should have a competent estate. Therefore in this service of the king, this attendance on himself, and this estate to support both, the dig

---

* Jud. Civ. Lund. apud Wilk. post p. 68.

nity of a thane consisted. I understand here a thane of the first order.

Every thane, in the distribution of his lands, had two objects in view: the support of his family, and the maintenance of his dignity. He therefore retained in his own hands a parcel of land near his house, which in the Saxon times was called inland, and afterwards his demesne, which served to keep up his hospitality: and this land was cultivated either by slaves, or by the poorer sort of people, who held lands of him by the performance of this service. The other portion of his estate he either gave for life or lives to his followers, men of a liberal condition, who served the greater thane, as he himself served the king. They were called Under-Thanes, or, according to the language of that time, Theoden.* They served their lord in all public business; they followed him in war; and they sought justice in his court in all their private differences. These may be considered as freeholders of the better sort, or indeed a sort of lesser gentry; therefore, as they were not the absolute dependants, but in some measure the peers of their lord, when they sued in his court, they claimed the privilege of all the German freemen, the right of judging one another: the lord's steward was only the register. This domestic court, which continued in full vigor for many ages, the Saxons called Hall-mote, from the place in which it was held; ^{Hallmote, or Court-Baron.} the Normans, who adopted it, named it a Court-Baron. This court had another department, in which the power of the lord was more absolute. From the most ancient times the German nobility

* Spelman of Feuds, ch. 5.

considered themselves as the natural judges of those who were employed in the cultivation of their lands, looking on husbandmen with contempt, and only as a parcel of the soil which they tilled: to these the Saxons commonly allotted some part of their out-lands to hold as tenants at will, and to perform very low services for them. The differences of these inferior tenants were decided in the lord's court, in which his steward sat as judge; and this manner of tenure probably gave an origin to copyholders.* Their estates were at will, but their persons were free: nor can we suppose that villains, if we consider villains as synonymous to slaves, could ever by any natural course have risen to copyholders; because the servile condition of the villain's person would always have prevented that stable tenure in the lands which the copyholders came to in very early times. The merely servile part of the nation seems never to have been known by the name of Villains or Ceorles, but by those of Bordars, Esnes, and Theowes.

As there were large tracts throughout the country not subject to the jurisdiction of any thane, the inhabitants of which were probably some remains of the ancient Britons not reduced to absolute slavery, and such Saxons as had not attached themselves to the fortunes of any leading man, it was proper to find some method of uniting and governing these detached parts of the nation, which had not been brought into order by any private dependence. To answer this end, the whole kingdom was divided into

---

* Fuerunt etiam in conquestu liberi homines, qui libere tenuerunt tenementa sua per libera servitia vel per liberas consuetudines. — For the original of copyholds, see Bracton, Lib. I. fol. 7.

Shires, these into Hundreds, and the Hundreds into Tithings.* This division was not made, as it is generally imagined, by King Alfred, though he might have introduced better regulations concerning it; it prevailed on the continent, wherever the Northern nations had obtained a settlement; and it is a species of order extremely obvious to all who use the decimal notation : when for the purposes of government they divide a county, tens and hundreds are the first modes of division which occur. The Tithing, which was the smallest of these divisions, consisted of ten heads of families, free, and of some consideration. These held a court every fortnight, which they called the Folkmote, or Leet, and there became Tithing Court. reciprocally bound to each other and to the public for their own peaceable behavior and that of their families and dependants. Every man in the kingdom, except those who belonged to the seigneurial courts we have mentioned, was obliged to enter himself into some tithing : to this he was inseparably attached ; nor could he by any means quit it without license from the head of the tithing ; because, if he was guilty of any misdemeanor, his district was obliged to produce him or pay his fine. In this man-

---

* Ibi debent populi omnes et gentes universæ singulis annis, semel in anno scilicet, convenire, scilicet in capite Kal. Maii, et se fide et sacramento non fracto ibi in unam et simul confœderare, et consolidare sicut conjurati fratres ad defendendum regnum contra alienigenas et contra inimicos, unâ cum domino suo rege, et terras et honores illius omni fidelitate cum eo servare, et quod illi ut domino suo regi intra et extra regnum universum Britanniæ fideles esse volunt. — LL. Ed. Conf. c. 35. — Of Heretoches and their election, vide Id. eodem.

Prohibitum erat etiam in eadem lege, ne quis emeret vivum animal vel pannum usatum sine plegiis et bonis testibus. — Of other particulars of buying and selling, vide Leges Ed. Conf. 38.

ner was the whole nation, as it were, held under sureties: a species of regulation undoubtedly very wise with regard to the preservation of peace and order, but equally prejudicial to all improvement in the minds or the fortunes of the people, who, fixed invariably to the spot, were depressed with all the ideas of their original littleness, and by all that envy which is sure to arise in those who see their equals attempting to mount over them. This rigid order deadened by degrees the spirit of the English, and narrowed their conceptions. Everything was new to them, and therefore everything was terrible; all activity, boldness, enterprise, and invention died away. There may be a danger in straining too strongly the bonds of government. As a life of absolute license tends to turn men into savages, the other extreme of constraint operates much in the same manner: it reduces them to the same ignorance, but leaves them nothing of the savage spirit. These regulations helped to keep the people of England the most backward in Europe; for though the division into shires and hundreds and tithings was common to them with the neighboring nations, yet the *frankpledge* seems to be a peculiarity in the English Constitution; and for good reasons they have fallen into disuse, though still some traces of them are to be found in our laws.

Hundred Court.
Ten of these tithings made an Hundred. Here in ordinary course they held a monthly court for the centenary, when all the suitors of the subordinate tithings attended. Here were determined causes concerning breaches of the peace, small debts, and such matters as rather required a speedy than a refined justice.

There was in the Saxon Constitution a great simplicity. The higher order of courts were but the
transcript of the lower, somewhat more extended
in their objects and in their power; and their power over the inferior courts proceeded only from their
being a collection of them all. The County County
or Shire Court was the great resort for jus- Court.
tice (for the four great courts of record did not then
exist). It served to unite all the inferior districts
with one another, and those with the private jurisdiction of the thanes. This court had no fixed place.
The alderman of the shire appointed it. Hither came
to account for their own conduct, and that of those
beneath them, the bailiffs of hundreds and tithings
and boroughs, with their people, — the thanes of
either rank, with their dependants, — a vast concourse of the clergy of all orders: in a word, of
all who sought or distributed justice. In this mixed
assembly the obligations contracted in the inferior
courts were renewed, a general oath of allegiance
to the king was taken, and all debates between the
several inferior coördinate jurisdictions, as well as the
causes of too much weight for them, finally determined. In this court presided (for in strict signifi-
cation he does not seem to have been a judge) an
officer of great consideration in those times, called
the Ealdorman of the Shire. With him sat Ealdorman
the bishop, to decide in whatever related to and Bishop.
the Church, and to mitigate the rigor of the law by
the interposition of equity, according to the species
of mild justice that suited the ecclesiastical character. It appears by the ancient Saxon laws, that the
bishop was the chief acting person in this court. The
reverence in which the clergy were then held, the

superior learning of the bishop, his succeeding to the power and jurisdiction of the Druid, all contributed to raise him far above the ealdorman, and to render it in reality his court. And this was probably the reason of the extreme lenity of the Saxon laws. The canons forbade the bishops to meddle in cases of blood. Amongst the ancient Gauls and Germans the Druid could alone condemn to death; so that on the introduction of Christianity there was none who could, in ordinary course, sentence a man to capital punishment: necessity alone forced it in a few cases.

Concerning the right of appointing the Alderman of the Shire there is some uncertainty. That he was anciently elected by his county is indisputable; that an alderman of the shire was appointed by the crown seems equally clear from the writings of King Alfred. A conjecture of Spelman throws some light upon this affair. He conceives that there were two aldermen with concurrent jurisdiction, one of whom was elected by the people, the other appointed by the king. This is very probable, and very correspondent to the nature of the Saxon Constitution, which was a species of democracy poised and held together by a degree of monarchical power. If the king had no officer to represent him in the county court, wherein all the ordinary business of the nation was then transacted, the state would have hardly differed from a pure democracy. Besides, as the king had in every county large landed possessions, either in his demesne, or to reward and pay his officers, he would have been in a much worse condition than any of his subjects, if he had been destitute of a magistrate to take care of his rights and to do justice to his numerous vassals. It appears, as well as we can judge in so obscure a matter, that the popular alderman was elected for a year only, and that the royal alderman held his place at the king's pleasure. This latter office, however, in process of time, was granted for life; and it grew afterwards to be hereditary in many shires.

We cannot pretend to say when the Sheriff came to be substituted in the place of the The Sheriff. Ealdorman: some authors think King Alfred the contriver of this regulation. It might have arisen from the nature of the thing itself. As several persons of consequence enough to obtain by their interest or power the place of alderman were not sufficiently qualified to perform the duty of the office, they contented themselves with the honorary part, and left the judicial province to their substitute.* The business of the robe to a rude martial people was contemptible and disgusting. The thanes, in their private jurisdictions, had delegated their power of judging to their reeves, or stewards; and the earl, or alderman, who was in the shire what the thane was in his manor, for the same reasons officiated by his deputy, the shire-reeve. This is the origin of the Sheriff's Tourn, which decided in all affairs, Sheriff's civil and criminal, of whatever importance, Tourn. and from which there lay no appeal but to the Witenagemote. Now there scarce remains the shadow of a body formerly so great: the judge being reduced almost wholly to a ministerial officer; and to

* Sheriff in the Norman times was merely the king's officer, not the earl's. The earl retained his ancient fee, without jurisdiction; the sheriff did all the business. The elective sheriff must have disappeared on the Conquest; for then all land was the king's, either immediately or mediately, and therefore his officer governed.

the court there being left nothing more than the cognizance of pleas under forty shillings, unless by a particular writ or special commission. But by what steps such a revolution came on it will be our business hereafter to inquire.

Witenage-mote.   The Witenagemote or Saxon Parliament, the supreme court, had authority over all the rest, not upon any principle of subordination, but because it was formed of all the rest. In this assembly, which was held annually, and sometimes twice a year, sat the earls and bishops and greater thanes, with the other officers of the crown.* So far as we can judge by the style of the Saxon laws, none but the thanes, or nobility, were considered as necessary constituent parts of this assembly, at least whilst it acted deliberatively. It is true that great numbers of all ranks of people attended its session, and gave by their attendance, and their approbation of what was done, a sanction to the laws; but when they consented to anything, it was rather in the way of acclamation than by the exercise of a deliberate voice, or a regular assent or negative. This may be explained by considering the analogy of the inferior assemblies. All persons, of whatever rank, attended at the county courts; but they did not go there as judges, they went to sue for justice, — to be informed of their duty, and to be bound to the performance of it. Thus all sorts of people attended at the Witenagemotes, not to make laws, but to attend at the promulgation of the laws; † as among so free

---

* How this assembly was composed, or by what right the members sat in it, I cannot by any means satisfy myself. What is here said is, I believe, nearest to the truth.

† Hence, perhaps, all men are supposed cognizant of the law.

a people every institution must have wanted much of its necessary authority, if not confirmed by the general approbation. Lambard is of opinion that in these early times the commons sat, as they do at this day, by representation from shires and boroughs; and he supports his opinion by very plausible reasons. A notion of this kind, so contrary to the simplicity of the Saxon ideas of government, and to the genius of that people, who held the arts and commerce in so much contempt, must be founded on such appearances as no other explanation can account for.

To the reign of Henry the Second, the citizens and burgesses were little removed from absolute slaves. They might be taxed individually at what sum the king thought fit to demand; or they might be discharged by offering the king a sum, from which, if he accepted it, the citizens were not at liberty to recede; and in either case the demand was exacted with severity, and even cruelty. A great difference is made between taxing them and those who cultivate lands: because, says my author, their property is easily concealed; they live penuriously, are intent by all methods to increase their substance, and their immense wealth is not easily exhausted. Such was their barbarous notion of trade and its importance. The same author, speaking of the severe taxation, and violent method of extorting it, observes that it is a very proper method, — and that it is very just that a degenerate officer, or other freeman, rejecting his condition for sordid gain, should be punished beyond the common law of freemen.

I take it that those who held by ancient demesne did not prescribe simply not to contribute to the expenses of the knight of the shire; but they pre-

scribed, as they did in all cases, upon a general principle, to pay no tax, nor to attend any duty of whatever species, because they were the king's villains.
The argument is drawn from the poverty of the boroughs, which ever since the Conquest have been of
no consideration, and yet send members to Parliament; which they could not do, but by some privileges inherent in them, on account of a practice of
the same kind in the Saxon times, when they were
of more repute. It is certain that many places now
called boroughs were formerly towns or villages in
ancient demesne of the king, and had, as such, writs
directed to them to appear in Parliament, that they
might make a free gift or benevolence, as the boroughs did; and from thence arose the custom of
summoning them. This appears by sufficient records. And it appears by records also, that it was
much at the discretion of the sheriff what boroughs
he should return; a general writ was directed to
him to return for all the boroughs in a shire; sometimes boroughs which had formerly sent members to
Parliament were quite passed over, and others, never
considered as such before, were returned. What is
called the prescription on this occasion was rather a
sort of rule to direct the sheriff in the execution of
his general power than a right inherent in any boroughs. But this was long after the time of which
we speak. In whatever manner we consider it, we
must own that this subject during the Saxon times
is extremely dark. One thing, however, is, I think,
clear from the whole tenor of their government, and
even from the tenor of the Norman Constitution
long after: that their Witenagemotes or Parliaments were unformed, and that the rights by which

the members held their seats were far from being exactly ascertained. The *Judicia Civitatis Londoniæ* afford a tolerable insight into the Saxon method of making and executing laws. First, the king called together his bishops, and such other persons *as he thought proper*. This council, or Witenagemote, having made such laws as seemed convenient, they then swore to the observance of them. The king sent a notification of these proceedings to each Burgmote, where the people of that court also swore to the observance of them, and confederated, by means of mutual strength and common charge, to prosecute delinquents against them. Nor did there at that time seem to be any other method of enforcing new laws or old. For as the very form of their government subsisted by a confederacy continually renewed, so, when a law was made, it was necessary for its execution to have again recourse to confederacy, which was the great, and I should almost say the only, principle of the Anglo-Saxon government.

What rights the king had in this assembly is a matter of equal uncertainty.* The laws generally run in his name, with the assent of his wise men, &c. But considering the low estimation of royalty in those days, this may rather be considered as the voice of the executive magistrate, of the person who compiled the law and propounded it to the Witenagemote for their consent, than of a legislator dictating from his own proper authority. For then, it seems, the law was digested by the king or his council for the assent of the general assembly. That

---

* Debet etiam rex omnia rite facere in regno, et per judicium procerum regni. — Debet . . . . justitiam per consilium procerum regni sui tenere. — Leges Ed. 17.

order is now reversed. All these things are, I think, sufficient to show of what a visionary nature those systems are which would settle the ancient Constitution in the most remote times exactly in the same form in which we enjoy it at this day, — not considering that such mighty changes in manners, during so many ages, always must produce a considerable change in laws, and in the forms as well as the powers of all governments.

We shall next consider the nature of the laws passed in these assemblies, and the judicious manner of proceeding in these several courts which we have described.

Saxon laws.

The Anglo-Saxons trusted more to the strictness of their police, and to the simple manners of their people, for the preservation of peace and order, than to accuracy or exquisite digestion of their laws, or to the severity of the punishments which they inflicted.* The laws which remain to us of that people seem almost to regard two points only: the suppressing of riots and affrays, — and the regulation of the several ranks of men, in order to adjust the fines for delinquencies according to the dignity of the person offended, or to the quantity of the offence. In all other respects their laws seem very imperfect. They often speak in the style of counsel as well as that of command. In the collection of laws attributed to Alfred we have the Decalogue

---

* The non-observance of a regulation of police was always heavily punished by barbarous nations; a slighter punishment was inflicted upon the commission of crimes. Among the Saxons most crimes were punished by fine; wandering from the highway without sounding an horn was death. So among the Druids, — to enforce exactness in time at their meetings, he that came last after the time appointed was punished with death.

transcribed, with no small part of the Levitical law; in the same code are inserted many of the Saxon institutions, though these two laws were in all respects as opposite as could possibly be imagined. These indisputable monuments of our ancient rudeness are a very sufficient confutation of the panegyrical declamations in which some persons would persuade us that the crude institutions of an unlettered people had attained an height which the united efforts of necessity, learning, inquiry, and experience can hardly reach to in many ages. We must add, that, although as one people under one head there was some resemblance in the laws and customs of our Saxon ancestors throughout the kingdom, yet there was a considerable difference, in many material points, between the customs of the several shires: nay, that in different manors subsisted a variety of laws not reconcilable with each other, some of which custom, that caused them, has abrogated; others have been overruled by laws or public judgment to the contrary; not a few subsist to this time.

The Saxon laws, imperfect and various as they were, served in some tolerable degree a people who had by their Constitution an eye on each other's concerns, and decided almost all matters of any doubt amongst them by methods which, however inadequate, were extremely simple. They judged every controversy either by the conscience of the parties, or by the country's opinion of it, or what they judged an appeal to Providence. They were unwilling to submit to the trouble of weighing contradictory testimonies; and they were destitute of those critical rules by which evidence is sifted, the true distinguished from the false, the certain from

the uncertain. Originally, therefore, the defendant
Purgation by oath. in the suit was put to his oath, and if on
oath he denied the debt or the crime with
which he was charged, he was of course acquitted.
But when the first fervors of religion began to decay,
and fraud and the temptations to fraud to increase,
they trusted no longer to the conscience of the party.
They cited him to an higher tribunal, — the immediate judgment of God. Their trials were so many
conjurations, and the magical ceremonies of barbarity
and heathenism entered into law and religion. This
supernatural method of process they called God's
By ordeal. Dome; it is generally known by the name
of *Ordeal*, which in the Saxon language signifies the Great Trial. This trial was made either by
fire or water: that by fire was principally reserved
for persons of rank; that by water decided the fate
of the vulgar; sometimes it was at the choice of the
party. A piece of iron, kept with a religious veneration in some monastery, which claimed this privilege
as an honor, was brought forth into the church upon
the day of trial; and it was there again consecrated
to this awful purpose by a form of service still extant.
A solemn mass was performed; and then the party
accused appeared, surrounded by the clergy, by his
judges, and a vast concourse of people, suspended
and anxious for the event; all that assisted purified
themselves by a fast of three days; and the accused,
who had undergone the same fast, and received the
sacrament, took the consecrated iron, of about a
pound weight, heated red, in his naked hand, and in
that manner carried it nine feet. This done, the
hand was wrapped up and sealed in the presence of
the whole assembly. Three nights being passed, the

seals were opened before all the people : if the hand
was found without any sore inflicted by the fire, the
party was cleared with universal acclamation ; if on
the contrary a raw sore appeared, the party, condemned by the judgment of Heaven, had no further
plea or appeal.   Sometimes the accused walked over
nine hot irons: sometimes boiling water was used ;
into this the man dipped his hand to the arm.   The
judgment by water was accompanied by the solemnity of the same ceremonies.   The culprit was thrown
into a pool of water, in which if he did not sink, he
was adjudged guilty, as though the element (they
said) to which they had committed the trial of his
innocency had rejected him.

Both these species of ordeal, though they equally
appealed to God, yet went on different principles.
In the fire ordeal a miracle must be wrought to acquit the party ; in the water a miracle was necessary
to convict him.   Is there any reason for this extraordinary distinction ? or must we resolve it solely into
the irregular caprices of the human mind ?   The
greatest genius which has enlightened this age seems
in this affair to have been carried by the sharpness of
his wit into a subtilty hardly to be justified by the
way of thinking of that unpolished period.   Speaking of the reasons for introducing this method of
trial, " *Qui ne voit*," says he, " *que, chez un peuple ex-
ercé à manier des armes, la peau rude et calleuse ne de-
voit pas recevoir assez l'impression du fer chaud*, ...
*pour qu'il y parût trois jours après ?   Et s'il y parois-
soit, c'étoit une marque que celui qui faisoit l'épreuve
étoit un efféminé*."   And this mark of effeminacy, he
observes, in those warlike times, supposed that the man
has resisted the principles of his education, that he is

insensible to honor, and regardless of the opinion of his country. But supposing the effect of hot iron to be so slight even on the most callous hands, of which, however, there is reason to doubt, yet we can hardly admit this reasoning, when we consider that women were subjected to this fire ordeal, and that no other women than those of condition could be subjected to it. Montesquieu answers the objection, which he foresaw would be made, by remarking, that women might have avoided this proof, if they could find a champion to combat in their favor; and he thinks a just presumption might be formed against a woman of rank who was so destitute of friends as to find no protector. It must be owned that the barbarous people all over Europe were much guided by presumptions in all their judicial proceedings; but how shall we reconcile all this with the custom of the Anglo-Saxons, among whom the ordeal was in constant use, and even for women, without the alternative of the combat, to which it appears this people were entire strangers? What presumption can arise from the event of the water ordeal, in which no callosity of hands, no bravery, no skill in arms, could be in any degree serviceable? The causes of both may with more success be sought amongst the superstitious ideas of the ancient Northern world. Amongst the Germans the administration of the law was in the hands of the priests or Druids.* And as the Druid worship paid the highest respect to the elements of

---

* The Druids judged not as magistrates, but as interpreters of the will of Heaven. "Ceterum neque animadvertere, neque vincire, neque verberare quidem, nisi sacerdotibus permissum; non quasi in pœnam, nec ducis jussu, sed velut Deo imperante," says Tacitus, de Mor. German. 7.

fire and water, it was very natural that they who
abounded with so many conjurations for the discovery of doubtful facts or future events should make
use of these elements in their divination. It may
appear the greater wonder, how the people came to
continue so long, and with such obstinacy, after the
introduction of Christianity, and in spite of the frequent injunctions of the Pope, whose authority was
then much venerated, in the use of a species of proof
the insufficiency of which a thousand examples might
have detected. But this is perhaps not so unaccountable. Persons were not put to this trial, unless
there was pretty strong evidence against them, something sufficient to form what is equivalent to a *cor-
pus delicti;* they must have been actually found
guilty by the *duodecemvirale judicium*, before they
could be subjected in any sort to the ordeal. It
was in effect showing the accused an indulgence
to give him this chance, even such a chance as it
was, of an acquittal; and it was certainly much
milder than the torture, which is used, with full
as little certainty of producing its end, among the
most civilized nations. And the ordeal without question frequently operated by the mere terror. Many
persons, from a dread of the event, chose to discover
rather than to endure the trial. Of those that did
endure it, many must certainly have been guilty.
The innocency of some who suffered could never be
known with certainty. Others by accident might
have escaped; and this apparently miraculous escape
had great weight in confirming the authority of this
trial. How long did we continue in punishing innocent people for witchcraft, though experience might,
to thinking persons, have frequently discovered the

injustice of that proceeding! whilst to the generality a thousand equivocal appearances, confessions
from fear or weakness, in fine, the torrent of popular prejudice rolled down through so many ages, conspired to support the delusion.

Compurga-
tion.   To avoid as much as possible this severe mode of trial, and at the same time
to leave no inlet for perjury, another method of clearing was devised. The party accused of any crime,
or charged in a civil complaint, appeared in court
with some of his neighbors, who were called his Compurgators; and when on oath he denied the charge,
they swore that they believed his oath to be true.*
These compurgators were at first to be three; afterwards five were required; in process of time twelve
became necessary.† As a man might be charged
by the opinion of the country, so he might also be
discharged by it: twelve men were necessary to find
him guilty, twelve might have acquitted him. If
opinion supports all government, it not only supported in the general sense, but it directed every
minute part in the Saxon polity. A man who did
not seem to have the good opinion of those among
whom he lived was judged to be guilty, or at least
capable of being guilty, of every crime. It was upon this principle that a man who could not find
the security of some tithing or friborg for his behavior,‡ he that was upon account of this universal

* Si quis emendationem oppidorum vel pontium vel profectionem
militarem detrectaverit, compenset regi cxx solidis, ... vel pur-
get se, et nominentur ei xiv, et eligantur xi. — Leges Cnuti, 62.

† Si accusatio sit, et purgatio male succedat, judicet Episcopus. —
Leges Cnuti, 53.

‡ Every man not privileged, whether he be paterfamilias, (heorth-

desertion called Friendless Man, was by our ancestors condemned to death, — a punishment which the lenity of the English laws in that time scarcely inflicted for any crime, however clearly proved: a circumstance which strongly marks the genius of the Saxon government.

On the same principle from which the trial by the oath of compurgators was derived, Trial by the Country. was derived also the Trial by the Country, which was the method of taking the sense of the neighborhood on any dubious fact. If the matter was of great importance, it was put in the full Shiremote; and if the general voice acquitted or condemned, decided for one party or the other, this was final in the cause. But then it was necessary that all should agree: for it does not appear that our ancestors, in those days, conceived how any assembly could be supposed to give an assent to a point concerning which several who composed that assembly thought differently. They had no idea that a body composed of several could act by the opinion of a small majority. But experience having shown that this method of trial was tumultuary and uncertain, they corrected it by the idea of compurgation. The party concerned was no longer put to his oath, — he simply pleaded; the compurgators swore as before in ancient times; therefore the jury were strictly from the neighborhood, and

fest,*) or pedissequa, (folghere,†) must enter into the hundred and tithing, and all above twelve to swear he will not be a thief or consenting to a thief. — Leges Cnuti, 19.

* Heorthfeste, — the same with Husfastene, i. e. the master of a family, from the Saxon, Hearthfæst, i. e. fixed to the house or hearth.

† The Folgheres, or Folgeres, were the menial servants or followers of the Husfastene, or Housekeepers. — Bracton, Lib. III., Tract. 2, cap. 10. Leges Hen. I. cap. 8.

were supposed to have a personal knowledge of the man and the fact. They were rather a sort of evidence than judges : and from hence is derived that singularity in our laws, that most of our judgments are given upon verdict, and not upon evidence, contrary to the laws of most other countries. Neither are our juries bound, except by one particular statute, and in particular cases, to observe any positive testimony, but are at liberty to judge upon presumptions. These are the first rude chalkings-out of our jurisprudence. The Saxons were extremely imperfect in their ideas of law, — the civil institutions of the Romans, who were the legislators of mankind, having never reached them. The order of our courts, the discipline of our jury, by which it is become so elaborate a contrivance, and the introduction of a sort of scientific reason in the law, have been the work of ages.

As the Saxon laws did not suffer any transaction, whether of the sale of land or goods, to pass but in the shire and before witnesses, so all controversies of them were concluded by what they called the *scyre witness.** This was tried by the oaths of the parties, by *vivâ voce* testimony, and the producing of charters and records. Then the people, laity and clergy, whether by plurality of votes or by what other means is not very certain, affirmed the testimony in favor of one of the claimants. Then the proceeding was signed, first by those who held the court, and then by the persons who affirmed the judgment, who also swore to it in the same manner.†

---

* Si quis terram defenderit testimonio provinciæ, &c. — Leges Cnuti, 76 : And sethe land gewerod hebbe be scyre gewitnesse.

† See, in Madox, the case in Bishop of Bathes Court. See also

The Saxons were extremely moderate in their punishments. Murder and treason were compounded, and a fine set for every offence. Forfeiture for felony was incurred only by those that fled. The punishment with death was very rare, — with torture unknown. In all ancient nations, the punishment of crimes was in the family injured by them, particularly in case of murder.* This brought deadly feuds amongst the people, which, in the German nations particularly, subsisted through several generations. But as a fruitless revenge could answer little purpose to the parties injured and was ruinous to the public peace, by the interposal of good offices they were prevailed upon to accept some composition in lieu of the blood of the aggressor, and peace was restored. The Saxon government did little more than act the part of arbitrator between the contending parties, exacted the payment of this composition, and reduced it to a certainty. However, the king, as the sovereign of all, and the sheriff, as the judicial officer, had their share in those fines. This unwillingness to shed blood, which the Saxon customs gave rise to, the Christian religion confirmed. Yet was it not altogether so imperfect as to have no punishment adequate to those great delinquencies

Punishments.

Brady, 272, where the witnesses on one side offer to swear, or join battle with the other.

* Parentibus occisi fiat emendatio, vel guerra eorum portetur; unde Anglicè proverbium habetur, Bige spere of side, oththe bær: id est, Eme lanceam a latere, aut fer. — Leges Ed. 12.

The fines on the town or hundred.

Parentes murdrati sex marcas haberent, rex quadraginta. [This different from the ancient usage, where the king had half.] Si parentes deessent, dominus ejus reciperet. Si dominum non haberet, felagus ejus, id est, fide cum eo ligatus. — Leges Ed. 15.

which tend entirely to overturn a state, public robbery, murder of the lord.*

Origin of suc-
cession.   As amongst the Anglo-Saxons government
depended in some measure upon land-prop-
erty, it will not be amiss to say something upon their
manner of holding and inheriting their lands. It
must not be forgot that the Germans were of Scythian original, and had preserved that way of life and
those peculiar manners which distinguished the parent nation. As the Scythians lived principally by
pasturage and hunting, from the nature of that way
of employment they were continually changing their
habitations. But even in this case some small degree
of agriculture was carried on, and therefore some sort
of division of property became necessary. This division was made among each tribe by its proper chief.

Annual
property.   But their shares were allotted to the several individuals only for a year, lest they
should come to attach themselves to any certain habitation: a settlement being wholly contrary to the
genius of the Scythian manners.

> Campestres melius Scythæ,
> Quorum plaustra vagas rite trahunt domos,
>   Vivunt, et rigidi Getæ,
> Immetata quibus jugera liberas
>   Fruges et Cererem ferunt,
> Nec cultura placet longior annuâ.

---

* Purveyance. Vide Leges Cnuti, 67.

Si quis intestatus ex hac vita decedat, sive sit per negligentiam
ejus, sive per mortem subitaneam, tunc non assumat sibi dominus
plus possessionis (æhta) ipsius quam justum armamentum; sed post
mortem possessio (æhtgescyft) ejus quam justissime distribuatur
uxori et liberis, et propinquis cognatis, cuilibet pro dignitate quæ ad
cum pertinet. — Leges Cnuti, 68.

This custom of an annual property probably continued amongst the Germans as long as they remained
in their own country ; but when their conquests carried them into other parts, another object besides the
possession of the land arose, which obliged them to
make a change in this particular. In the distribution of the conquered lands, the ancient possessors
of them became an object of consideration, and the
management of these became one of the principal
branches of their polity. It was expedient towards
holding them in perfect subjection, that they should
be habituated to obey one person, and that a kind
of cliental relation should be created between them ;
therefore the land, with the slaves, and the people in
a state next to slavery, annexed to it, was Estates for
bestowed for life in the general distribution. life.
When life-estates were once granted, it seemed a natural consequence that inheritances should Inheritance.
immediately supervene. When a durable
connection is created between a certain man and a
certain portion of land by a possession for his whole
life, and when his children have grown up and have
been supported on that land, it seems so great an
hardship to separate them, and to deprive thereby
the family of all means of subsisting, that nothing
could be more generally desired nor more reasonably
allowed than an inheritance ; and this reasonableness
was strongly enforced by the great change wrought
in their affairs when life-estates were granted. Whilst
according to the ancient custom lands were only
given for a year, there was a rotation so quick that
every family came in its turn to be easily provided for,
and had not long to wait ; but the children of a tenant for life, when they lost the benefit of their father's

possession, saw themselves as it were immured upon every side by the life-estates, and perceived no reasonable hope of a provision from any new arrangement. These inheritances began very early in England. By a law of King Alfred it appears that they were then of a very ancient establishment: and as such inheritances were intended for great stability, they fortified them by charters; and therefore they were called Book-land. This was done with regard to the possession of the better sort: the meaner, who were called *ceorles*, if they did not live in a dependence on some thane, held their small portions of land as an inheritance likewise, — not by charter, but by a sort of prescription. This was called Folk-land. These estates of inheritance, both the greater and the meaner, were not fiefs; they were to all purposes allodial, and had hardly a single property of a feud; they descended equally to all the children, males and females, according to the custom of gavelkind, a custom absolutely contrary to the genius of the feudal tenure; and whenever estates were granted in the later Saxon times by the bounty of the crown with an intent that they should be inheritable, so far were they from being granted with the complicated load of all the feudal services annexed, that in all the charters of that kind which subsist they are bestowed with a full power of alienation, *et liberi ab omni seculari gravamine.* This was the general condition of those inheritances which were derived from the right of original conquest, as well to all the soldiers as to the leader; and these estates, as it is said, were not even forfeitable, no, not for felony, as if that were in some sort the necessary consequence of an

Book-land.

Folk-land.

inheritable estate. So far were they from resembling a fief. But there were other possessions which bore a nearer resemblance to fiefs, Saxon fiefs. at least in their first feeble and infantile state of the tenure, than those inheritances which were held by an absolute right in the proprietor. The great officers who attended the court, commanded armies, or distributed justice must necessarily be paid and supported ; but in what manner could they be paid ? In money they could not, because there was very little money then in Europe, and scarce any part of that little came into the prince's coffers. The only method of paying them was by allotting lands for their subsistence whilst they remained in his service. For this reason, in the original distribution, vast tracts of land were left in the hands of the king. If any served the king in a military command, his land may be said to have been in some sort held by knight-service. If the tenant was in an office about the king's person, this gave rise to sergeantry ; the persons who cultivated his lands may be considered as holding by socage. But the long train of services that made afterwards the learning of the tenures were then not thought of, because these feuds, if we may so call them, had not then come to be inheritances, — which circumstance of inheritance gave rise to the whole feudal system. With the Anglo-Saxons the feuds continued to the last but a sort of pay or salary of office. The *trinoda necessitas*, so much spoken of, which was to attend the king in his expeditions, and to contribute to the building of bridges and repair of highways, never bound the lands by way of tenure, but as a political regulation, which equally affected every class and condition of men and every species of possession.

Gavelkind.   The manner of succeeding to lands in England at this period was, as we have observed, by Gavelkind, — an equal distribution amongst the children, males and females. The ancient Northern nations had but an imperfect notion of political power. That the possessor of the land should be the governor of it was a simple idea; and their schemes extended but little further. It was not so in the Greek and Italian commonwealths. In those the property of the land was in all respects similar to that of goods, and had nothing of jurisdiction annexed to it; the government there was a merely political institution. Amongst such a people the custom of distribution could be of no ill consequence, because it only affected property. But gavelkind amongst the Saxons was very prejudicial; for, as government was annexed to a certain possession in land, this possession, which was continually changing, kept the government in a very fluctuating state: so that their civil polity had in it an essential evil, which contributed to the sickly condition in which the Anglo-Saxon state always remained, as well as to its final dissolution.

BOOK III.

CHAPTER I.

BEFORE the period of which we are going to treat, England was little known or considered in Europe. Their situation, their domestic calamities, and their ignorance circumscribed the views and politics of the English within the bounds of their own island. But the Norman conqueror threw down all these barriers. The English laws, manners, and maxims were suddenly changed; the scene was enlarged; and the communication with the rest of Europe, being thus opened, has been preserved ever since in a continued series of wars and negotiations. That we may, therefore, enter more fully into the matters which lie before us, it is necessary that we understand the state of the neighboring continent at the time when this island first came to be interested in its affairs.

The Northern nations who had overran the Roman Empire were at first rather actuated by avarice than ambition, and were more intent upon plunder than conquest; they were carried beyond their original purposes, when they began to form regular governments, for which they had been prepared by no just ideas of legislation. For a long time, therefore, there was little of order in their affairs or foresight in their designs. The Goths, the Burgundians, the Franks, the Vandals, the Suevi, after they had prevailed over the Roman Empire, by turns prevailed over each other in continual wars, which were carried on upon no principles of a determinate policy, entered into upon motives of brutality and caprice, and ended as fortune and rude violence chanced to prevail. Tumult, anarchy, confusion, overspread the face of Europe; and an obscurity rests upon the transactions of that time which suffers us to discover nothing but its extreme barbarity.

Before this cloud could be dispersed, the Saracens, another body of barbarians from the South, animated by a fury not unlike that which gave strength to the Northern irruptions, but heightened by enthusiasm, and regulated by subordination and an uniform policy, began to carry their arms, their manners, and religion into every part of the universe. Spain was entirely overwhelmed by the torrent of their armies, Italy and the islands were harassed by their fleets, and all Europe alarmed by their vigorous and frequent enterprises. Italy, who had so long sat the mistress of the world, was by turns the slave of all nations. The possession of that fine country was hotly disputed between the Greek Emperor and the Lombards, and it suffered infinitely by that contention. Germany, the parent of so many nations, was exhausted by the swarms she had sent abroad.

However, in the midst of this chaos there were principles at work which reduced things to a certain form, and gradually unfolded a system in which the chief movers and main springs were the Papal and the Imperial powers, — the aggrandizement or diminution of which have been the drift of almost all the politics, intrigues, and wars which have employed and distracted Europe to this day.

From Rome the whole Western world had received its Christianity; she was the asylum of what learning had escaped the general desolation; and even in her ruins she preserved something of the majesty of her ancient greatness. On these accounts she had a respect and a weight which increased every day amongst a simple religious people, who looked but a little way into the consequences of their actions. The rudeness of the world was very favorable for the establishment of an empire of opinion. The moderation with which the Popes at first exerted this empire made its growth unfelt until it could no longer be opposed; and the policy of later Popes, building on the piety of the first, continually increased it: and they made use of every instrument but that of force. They employed equally the virtues and the crimes of the great; they favored the lust of kings for absolute authority, and the desire of subjects for liberty; they provoked war, and mediated peace; and took advantage of every turn in the minds of men, whether of a public or private nature, to extend their influence, and push their power from ecclesiastical to civil, from subjection to independency, from independency to empire.

France had many advantages over the other parts of Europe. The Saracens had no permanent success in that country. The same hand which expelled those invaders deposed the last of a race of heavy and degenerate princes, more like Eastern monarchs than German leaders, and who had neither the force to repel the enemies of their kingdom nor to assert their own sovereignty. This usurpation placed on

the throne princes of another character, princes who
were obliged to supply their want of title by the vig-
or of their administration. The French monarch had
need of some great and respected authority to throw
a veil over his usurpation, and to sanctify his newly acquired power by those names and appearances
which are necessary to make it respectable to the
people. On the other hand, the Pope, who hated the
Grecian Empire, and equally feared the success of
the Lombards, saw with joy this new star arise in the
North, and gave it the sanction of his authority.
Presently after he called it to his assistance. Pepin
passed the Alps, relieved the Pope, and invested him
with the dominion of a large country in the best part
of Italy.

Charlemagne pursued the course which was
marked out for him, and put an end to the Lom-
bard kingdom, weakened by the policy of his father
and the enmity of the Popes, who never willingly saw
a strong power in Italy. Then he received from the
hand of the Pope the Imperial crown, sanctified by
the authority of the Holy See, and with it the title
of Emperor of the Romans, a name venerable from
the fame of the old Empire, and which was supposed to carry great and unknown prerogatives ;
and thus the Empire rose again out of its ruins in
the West, and, what is remarkable, by means of one
of those nations which had helped to destroy it. If
we take in the conquests of Charlemagne, it was also
very near as extensive as formerly; though its constitution was altogether different, as being entirely on
the Northern model of government. From Charlemagne the Pope received in return an enlargement
and a confirmation of his new territory. Thus the

Papal and Imperial powers mutually gave birth to each other. They continued for some ages, and in some measure still continue, closely connected, with a variety of pretensions upon each other, and on the rest of Europe.

Though the Imperial power had its origin in France, it was soon divided into two branches, the Gallic and the German. The latter alone supported the title of Empire; but the power being weakened by this division, the Papal pretensions had the greater weight. The Pope, because he first revived the Imperial dignity, claimed a right of disposing of it, or at least of giving validity to the election of the Emperor. The Emperor, on the other hand, remembering the rights of those sovereigns whose title he bore, and how lately the power which insulted him with such demands had arisen from the bounty of his predecessors, claimed the same privileges in the election of a Pope. The claims of both were somewhat plausible; and they were supported, the one by force of arms, and the other by ecclesiastical influence, powers which in those days were very nearly balanced. Italy was the theatre upon which this prize was disputed. In every city the parties in favor of each of the opponents were not far from an equality in their numbers and strength. Whilst these parties disagreed in the choice of a master, by contending for a choice in their subjection they grew imperceptibly into freedom, and passed through the medium of faction and anarchy into regular commonwealths. Thus arose the republics of Venice, of Genoa, of Florence, Sienna, and Pisa, and several others. These cities, established in this freedom, turned the frugal and ingenious spirit contracted in such commu-

nities to navigation and traffic; and pursuing them
with skill and vigor, whilst commerce was neglected and despised by the rustic gentry of the martial
governments, they grew to a considerable degree of
wealth, power, and civility.

. The Danes, who in this latter time preserved the
spirit and the numbers of the ancient Gothic people,
had seated themselves in England, in the Low Countries, and in Normandy. They passed from thence to
the southern part of Europe, and in this romantic age
gave rise in Sicily and Naples to a new kingdom and
a new line of princes.

All the kingdoms on the continent of Europe were
governed nearly in the same form; from whence
arose a great similitude in the manners of their inhabitants. The feodal discipline extended itself everywhere, and influenced the conduct of the courts
and the manners of the people with its own irregular
martial spirit. Subjects, under the complicated laws
of a various and rigorous servitude, exercised all the
prerogatives of sovereign power. They distributed
justice, they made war and peace at pleasure. The
sovereign, with great pretensions, had but little power; he was only a greater lord among great lords,
who profited of the differences of his peers; therefore no steady plan could be well pursued, either in
war or peace. This day a prince seemed irresistible
at the head of his numerous vassals, because their
duty obliged them to war, and they performed this
duty with pleasure. The next day saw this formidable power vanish like a dream, because this fierce
undisciplined people had no patience, and the time of
the feudal service was contained within very narrow
limits. It was therefore easy to find a number of

persons at all times ready to follow any standard, but it was hard to complete a considerable design which required a regular and continued movement. This enterprising disposition in the gentry was very general, because they had little occupation or pleasure but in war, and the greatest rewards did then attend personal valor and prowess. All that professed arms became in some sort on an equality. A knight was the peer of a king, and men had been used to see the bravery of private persons opening a road to that dignity. The temerity of adventurers was much justified by the ill order of every state, which left it a prey to almost any who should attack it with sufficient vigor. Thus, little checked by any superior power, full of fire, impetuosity, and ignorance, they longed to signalize themselves, wherever an honorable danger called them; and wherever that invited, they did not weigh very deliberately the probability of success.

The knowledge of this general disposition in the minds of men will naturally remove a great deal of our wonder at seeing an attempt founded on such slender appearances of right, and supported by a power so little proportioned to the undertaking as that of William, so warmly embraced and so generally followed, not only by his own subjects, but by all the neighboring potentates. The Counts of Anjou, Bretagne, Ponthieu, Boulogne, and Poictou, sovereign princes, — adventurers from every quarter of France, the Netherlands, and the remotest parts of Germany, laying aside their jealousies and enmities to one another, as well as to William, ran with an inconceivable ardor into this enterprise, captivated with the splendor of the object, which obliterated all thoughts of the uncertainty of the event. William kept up this fervor by promises of large territories to all his allies and associates in the country to be reduced by their united efforts. But after all it became equally necessary to reconcile to his enterprise the three great powers of whom we have just spoken, whose disposition must have had the most influence on his affairs.

His feudal lord, the King of France, was bound by his most obvious interests to oppose the further aggrandizement of one already too potent for a vassal. But the King of France was then a minor; and Baldwin, Earl of Flanders, whose daughter William had married, was regent of the kingdom. This circumstance rendered the remonstrance of the French Council against his design of no effect: indeed, the opposition of the Council itself was faint; the idea of having a king under vassalage to their crown might have dazzled the more superficial courtiers; whilst those who thought more deeply were unwilling to discourage an enterprise which they believed would probably end in the ruin of the undertaker. The Emperor was in his minority, as well as the King of France; but by what arts the Duke prevailed upon the Imperial Council to declare in his favor, whether or no by an idea of creating a balance to the power of France, if we can imagine that any such idea then subsisted, is altogether uncertain; but it is certain that he obtained leave for the vassals of the Empire to engage in his service, and that he made use of this permission. The Pope's consent was obtained with still less difficulty. William had shown himself in many instances a friend to the Church and a favorer of the clergy. On this occasion he promised to improve those happy beginnings in proportion to the means he should acquire by the favor of the Holy See. It is said that he even proposed to hold his new kingdom as a fief from Rome. The Pope, therefore, entered heartily into his interests; he excommunicated all those that should oppose his enterprise, and sent him, as a means of insuring success, a consecrated banner.

CHAPTER II.

REIGN OF WILLIAM THE CONQUEROR.

AFTER the Battle of Hastings, the taking of Dover, the surrender of London, and the submission of the principal nobility, William had nothing left but to order in the best manner the kingdom he had so happily acquired. Soon after his coronation, fearing the sudden and ungoverned motions of so great a city, new to subjection, he left London until a strong citadel could be raised to overawe the people. This was built where the Tower of London now stands. Not content with this, he built three other strong castles in situations as advantageously chosen, at Norwich, at Winchester, and at Hereford, securing not only the heart of affairs, but binding down the extreme parts of the kingdom. And as he observed from his own experience the want of fortresses in England, he resolved fully to supply that defect, and guard the kingdom both against internal and foreign enemies. But he fortified his throne yet more strongly by the policy of good government. To London he confirmed by charter the liberties it had enjoyed under the Saxon kings, and endeavored to fix the affections of the Eng-

A. D. 1066.

lish in general by governing them with equity according to their ancient laws, and by treating them on all occasions with the most engaging deportment. He set up no pretences which arose from absolute conquest. He confirmed their estates to all those who had not appeared in arms against him, and seemed not to aim at subjecting the English to the Normans, but to unite the two nations under the wings of a common parental care. If the Normans received estates and held lucrative offices and were raised by wealthy matches in England, some of the English were enriched with lands and dignities and taken into considerable families in Normandy. But the king's principal regards were showed to those by whose bravery he had attained his greatness. To some he bestowed the forfeited estates, which were many and great, of Harold's adherents; others he satisfied from the treasures his rival had amassed; and the rest, quartered upon wealthy monasteries, relied patiently on the promises of one whose performances had hitherto gone hand in hand with his power. There was another circumstance which conduced much to the maintaining, as well as to the making, his conquest. The posterity of the Danes, who had finally reduced England under Canute the Great, were still very numerous in that kingdom, and in general not well liked by nor well affected to the old Anglo-Saxon inhabitants. William wisely took advantage of this enmity between the two sorts of inhabitants, and the alliance of blood which was between them and his subjects. In the body of laws which he published he insists strongly on this kindred, and declares that the Normans and Danes ought to be as sworn brothers against all men: a policy which probably united these people to him, or at least so confirmed the ancient jealousy which subsisted between them and the original English as to hinder any cordial union against his interests.

When the king had thus settled his acquisitions by all the methods of force and policy, he thought it expedient to visit his patrimonial territory, which, with regard to its internal state, and the jealousies which his additional greatness revived in many of the bordering princes, was critically situated. He appointed to the regency in his absence his brother Odo, an ecclesiastic, whom he had made Bishop of Bayeux, in France, and Earl of Kent, with great power and pre-eminence, in England, — a man bold, fierce, ambitious, full of craft, imperious, and without faith, but well versed in all affairs, vigilant, and courageous. To him he joined William Fitz-Osbern, his justiciary, a person of consummate prudence and great integrity. But not depending on this disposition, to secure his conquest, as well as to display its importance abroad, under a pretence of honor, he carried with him all the chiefs of the English nobility, the popular Earls Edwin and Morcar, and, what was of most importance, Edgar Atheling, the last branch of the royal stock of the Anglo-Saxon kings, and infinitely dear to all the people.

The king managed his affairs abroad with great address, and covered all his negotiations for the security of his Norman dominions under the magnificence of continual feasting and unremitted diversion, which, without an appearance of design, displayed his wealth and power, and by that means facilitated his measures. But whilst he was thus employed, his absence from England gave an opportunity to several humors to break out, which the late change had bred, but which the amazement likewise produced by that violent change, and the presence of their conqueror, wise, vigilant, and severe, had hitherto repressed. The ancient line of their kings displaced, the only thread on which it hung carried out of the kingdom and ready to be cut off by the jealousy of a merciless usurper, their liberties none by being precarious, and the daily insolencies and rapine of the Normans intolerable, — these discontents were increased by the tyranny and rapaciousness of the regent, and they were fomented from abroad by Eustace, Count of Boulogne. But the people, though ready to rise in all parts, were destitute of leaders, and the insurrections actually made were not carried on in concert, nor directed to any determinate object; so that the king, returning speedily,

A. D. 1607.

and exerting himself everywhere with great vigor, in a short time dissipated these ill-formed projects. However, so general a dislike to William's government had appeared on this occasion, that he became in his turn disgusted with his subjects, and began to change his maxims of rule to a rigor which was more conformable to his advanced age and the sternness of his natural temper. He resolved, since he could not gain the affections of his subjects, to find such matter for their hatred as might weaken them, and fortify his own authority against the enterprises which that hatred might occasion. He revived the tribute of Danegelt, so odious from its original cause and that of its revival, which he caused to be strictly levied throughout the kingdom. He erected castles at Nottingham, at Warwick, and at York, and filled them with Norman garrisons. He entered into a stricter inquisition for the discovery of the estates forfeited on his coming in; paying no regard to the privileges of the ecclesiastics, he seized upon the treasures which, as in an inviolable asylum, the unfortunate adherents to Harold had deposited in monasteries. At the same time he entered into a resolution of deposing all the English bishops, on none of whom he could rely, and filling their places with Normans. But he mitigated the rigor of these proceedings by the wise choice he made in filling the places of those whom he had deposed, and gave by that means these violent changes the air rather of reformation than oppression. He began with Stigand, Archbishop of Canterbury. A synod was called, in which, for the first time in England, the Pope's legate *a latere* is said to have presided. In this council, Stigand, for simony and for other crimes, of which it is easy to convict those who are out of favor, was solemnly degraded from his dignity. The king filled his place with Lanfranc, an Italian. By his whole conduct he appeared resolved to reduce his subjects of all orders to the most perfect obedience.

The people, loaded with new taxes, the nobility, degraded and threatened, the clergy, deprived of their immunities and influence, joined in one voice of discontent, and stimulated each other to the most desperate resolutions. The king was not unapprised of these motions, nor negligent of them. It is thought he meditated to free himself from much of his uneasiness by seizing those men on whom the nation in its distresses used to cast its eyes for relief. But whilst he digested these measures, Edgar Atheling, Edwin and Morcar, Waltheof, the son of Siward, and several others, eluded his vigilance, and escaped into Scot-

A. D. 1068.

land, where they were received with open arms by King Malcolm. The Scottish monarch on this occasion married the sister of Edgar; and this match engaged him more closely to the accomplishment of what his gratitude to the Saxon kings and the rules of good policy had before inclined him. He entered at last into the cause of his brother-in-law and the distressed English. He persuaded the King of Denmark to enter into the same measures, who agreed to invade England with a fleet of a thousand ships. Drone, an Irish king, declared in their favor, and supplied the sons of Earl Godwin with vessels and men, with which they held the English coast in continual alarms.

Whilst the forces of this powerful confederacy were collecting on all sides, and prepared to enter England, equal dangers threatened from within the kingdom. Edric the Forester, a very brave and popular Saxon, took up arms in the counties of Hereford and Salop, the country of the ancient Silures, and inhabited by the same warlike and untamable race of men. The Welsh strengthened him with their forces, and Cheshire joined in the revolt. Hereward le Wake, one of the most

A. D. 1069.

brave and indefatigable soldiers of his time, rushed with a numerous band of fugitives and outlaws from the fens of Lincoln and the Isle of Ely, from whence, protected by the situation of the place, he had for some time carried on an irregular war against the Normans. The sons of Godwin landed with a strong body in the West; the fire of rebellion ran through the kingdom; Cornwall, Devon, Dorset, at once threw off the yoke. Daily skirmishes were fought in every part of the kingdom, with various

success and with great bloodshed. The Normans
retreated to their castles, which the English had
rarely skill or patience to master; out of these they
sallied from time to time, and asserted their dominion. The conquered English for a moment resumed
their spirit; the forests and morasses, with which
this island then abounded, served them for fortifications, and their hatred to the Normans stood in
the place of discipline; each man, exasperated by
his own wrongs, avenged them in his own manner.
Everything was full of blood and violence: murders,
burnings, rapine, and confusion overspread the whole
kingdom. During these distractions, several of the
Normans quitted the country, and gave up their
possessions, which they thought not worth holding
in continual horror and danger.

In the midst of this scene of disorder, the king
alone was present to himself and to his affairs. He
first collected all the forces on whom he could depend within the kingdom, and called powerful succors from Normandy. Then he sent a strong body
to repress the commotions in the West; but he reserved the greatest force and his own presence against
the greatest danger, which menaced from the North.
The Scots had penetrated as far as Durham; they
had taken the castle, and put the garrison to the
sword. A like fate attended York from the Danes,
who had entered the Humber with a formidable
fleet. They put this city into the hands of the English malcontents, and thereby influenced all the
northern counties in their favor. William,
when he first perceived the gathering of the   A. D. 1070.
storm, endeavored, and with some success, to break
the force of the principal blow by a correspondence at

the court of Denmark ; and now he entirely blunted
the weapon by corrupting, with a considerable sum
the Danish general. It was agreed, to gratify tha
piratical nation, that they should plunder some part
of the coast, and depart without further disturbance
By this negotiation the king was enabled to march
with an undissipated force against the Scots and the
principal body of the English. Everything yielded.
The Scots retired into their own country. Some
of the most obnoxious of the English fled along
with them. One desperate party, under the brave
Waltheof, threw themselves into York, and ventured alone to resist his victorious army. William
pressed the siege with vigor, and, notwithstanding
the prudent dispositions of Waltheof, and the prodigies of valor he displayed in its defence, standing
alone in the breach, and maintaining his ground gal-
lantly and successfully, the place was at last reduced
by famine. The king left his enemies no time to
recover this disaster ; he followed his blow, and drove
all who adhered to Edgar Atheling out of all the
countries northward of the Humber. This tract he
resolved entirely to depopulate, influenced by revenge, and by distrust of the inhabitants, and partly
with a view of opposing an hideous desert of sixty
miles in extent as an impregnable barrier against
all attempts of the Scots in favor of his disaffected
subjects. The execution of this barbarous project
was attended with all the havoc and desolation that
it seemed to threaten. One hundred thousand are
said to have perished by cold, penury, and disease.
The ground lay untilled throughout that whole space
for upwards of nine years. Many of the inhabitants
both of this and all other parts of England fled into

Scotland; but they were so received by King Malcolm as to forget that they had lost their country. This wise monarch gladly seized so fair an opportunity, by the exertion of a benevolent policy, to people his dominions, and to improve his native subjects. He received the English nobility according to their rank, he promoted them to offices according to their merit, and enriched them by considerable estates from his own demesne. From these noble refugees several considerable families in Scotland are descended.

William, on the other hand, amidst all the excesses which the insolence of victory and the cruel precautions of usurped authority could make him commit, gave many striking examples of moderation and greatness of mind. He pardoned Waltheof, whose bravery he did not the less admire because it was exerted against himself. He restored him to his ancient honors and estates; and thinking his family strengthened by the acquisition of a gallant man, he bestowed upon him his niece Judith in marriage. On Edric the Forester, who lay under his sword, in the same generous manner he not only bestowed his life, but honored it with an addition of dignity.

The king, having thus, by the most politic and the most courageous measures, by art, by force, by severity, and by clemency, dispelled those clouds which had gathered from every quarter to overwhelm him, returned triumphant to Winchester, where, as if he had newly acquired the kingdom, he was crowned with great solemnity. After this he proceeded to execute the plan he had long proposed of modelling the state according to his own pleasure, and of fixing his authority upon an immovable foundation.

There were few of the English who in the late dis-

turbances had not either been active against the Normans or shown great disinclination to them. Upon
some right, or some pretence, the greatest part of
their lands were adjudged to be forfeited. William
gave these lands to Normans, to be held by the tenure of knight-service, according to the law which
modified that service in all parts of Europe. These
people he chose because he judged they must be faithful to the interest on which they depended; and this
tenure he chose because it raised an army without
expense, called it forth at the least warning, and
seemed to secure the fidelity of the vassal by the
multiplied ties of those services which were inseparably annexed to it. In the establishment of these
tenures, William only copied the practice which was
now become very general. One fault, however, he
seems to have committed in this distribution : the
immediate vassals of the crown were too few; the
tenants *in capite* at the end of this reign did not exceed seven hundred; the eyes of the subject met too
many great objects in the state besides the state
itself; and the dependence of the inferior people
was weakened by the interposal of another authority
between them and the crown, and this without being
at all serviceable to liberty. The ill consequence of
this was not so obvious whilst the dread of the English made a good correspondence between the sovereign and the great vassals absolutely necessary; but
it afterwards appeared, and in a light very offensive
to the power of our kings.

As there is nothing of more consequence in a state
than the ecclesiastical establishment, there was nothing to which this vigilant prince gave more of his attention. If he owed his own power to the influence

of the clergy, it convinced him how necessary it was to prevent that engine from being employed in its turn against himself. He observed, that, besides the influence they derived from their character, they had a vast portion of that power which always attends property. Of about sixty thousand knights' fees, which England was then judged to contain, twenty-eight thousand were in the hands of the clergy; and these they held discharged of all taxes, and free from every burden of civil or military service : a constitution undoubtedly no less prejudicial to the authority of the state than detrimental to the strength of the nation, deprived of so much revenue, so many soldiers, and of numberless exertions of art and industry, which were stifled by holding a third of the soil in dead hands out of all possibility of circulation. William in a good measure remedied these evils, but with the great offence of all the ecclesiastic orders. At the same time that he subjected the Church lands to military service, he obliged each monastery and bishopric to the support of soldiers, in proportion to the number of knights' fees that they possessed. No less jealous was he of the Papal pretensions, which, having favored so long as they served him as the instruments of his ambition, he afterwards kept within very narrow bounds. He suffered no communication with Rome but by his knowledge and approbation. He had a bold and ambitious Pope to deal with, who yet never proceeded to extremities with nor gained one advantage over William during his whole reign, — although he had by an express law reserved to himself a sort of right in approving the Pope chosen, by forbidding his subjects to yield obedience to any whose right the king had not acknowledged.

To form a just idea of the power and greatness of this king, it will be convenient to take a view of his revenue. And I the rather choose to dwell a little upon this article, as nothing extends to so many objects as the public finances, and consequently nothing puts in a clearer or more decisive light the manner of the people, and the form, as well as the powers, of government at any period.

The first part of this consisted of the demesne The lands of the crown were, even before the Conquest, very extensive. The forfeitures consequent to that great change had considerably increased them. It appears from the record of Domesday, that the king retained in his own hands no fewer than fourteen hundred manors. This alone was a royal revenue. However, great as it really was, it has been exaggerated beyond all reason. Ordericus Vitalis, a writer almost contemporary, asserts that this branch alone produced a thousand pounds a day,* — which, valuing the pound, as it was then estimated, at a real pound of silver, and then allowing for the difference in value since that time, will make near twelve millions of our money. This account, coming from such an authority, has been copied without examination by all the succeeding historians. If we were to admit the truth of it, we must entirely change our ideas concerning the quantity of money which then circulated in Europe. And it is a matter altogether monstrous and incredible in an age when there was little traffic in this nation, and the traffic of all nations circulated but little real coin, when the tenants paid the

---

* I have known, myself, great mistakes in calculation by computing, as the produce of every day in the year, that of one extraordinary day.

greatest part of their rents in kind, and when it may be greatly doubted whether there was so much current money in the nation as is said to have come into the king's coffers from this one branch of his revenue only. For it amounts to a twelfth part of all the circulating species which a trade infinitely more extensive has derived from sources infinitely more exuberant, to this wealthy nation, in this improved age. Neither must we think that the whole revenue of this prince ever rose to such a sum. The great fountain which fed his treasury must have been Danegelt, which, upon any reasonable calculation, could not possibly exceed 120,000*l*. of our money, if it ever reached that sum. William was observed to be a great hoarder, and very avaricious; his army was maintained without any expense to him, his demesne supported his household; neither his necessary nor his voluntary expenses were considerable. Yet the effects of many years' scraping and hoarding left at his death but 60,000*l*., — not the sixth part of one year's income, according to this account, of one branch of his revenue; and this was then esteemed a vast treasure. Edgar Atheling, on being reconciled to the king, was allowed a mark a day for his expenses, and he was thought to be allowed sufficiently, though he received it in some sort as an equivalent for his right to the crown. I venture on this digression, because writers in an ignorant age, making guesses at random, impose on more enlightened times, and affect by their mistakes many of our reasonings on affairs of consequence; and it is the error of all ignorant people to rate unknown times, distances, and sums very far beyond their real extent. There is even something childish and whimsical in computing this revenue, as the original author has done, at so much a day. For my part, I do not imagine it so difficult to come at a pretty accurate decision of the truth or falsehood of this story.

The above-mentioned manors are charged with rents from five to an hundred pounds each. The greatest number of those I have seen in print are under fifty; so that we may safely take that number as a just medium; and then the whole amount of the demesne rents will be 70,000*l.*, or 210,000*l.* of our money. This, though almost a fourth less than the sum stated by Vitalis, still seems a great deal too high, if we should suppose the whole sum, as that author does, to be paid in money, and that money to be reckoned by real pounds of silver. But we must observe, that, when sums of money are set down in old laws and records, the interpretation of those words, pounds and shillings, is for the most part oxen, sheep, corn, and provision. When real coin money was to be paid, it was called white money, or *argentum album*, and was only in a certain stipulated proportion to what was rendered in kind, and that proportion generally very low. This method of paying rent, though it entirely overturns the prodigious idea of that monarch's pecuniary wealth, was far from being less conducive to his greatness. It enabled him to feed a multitude of people, — one of the surest and largest sources of influence, and which always outbuys money in the traffic of affections. This revenue, which was the chief support of the dignity of our Saxon kings, was considerably increased by the revival of Danegelt, of the imposition of which we have already spoken, and which is supposed to have produced an annual income of 40,000*l.* of money, as then valued.

The next branch of the king's revenue were the feudal duties, by him first introduced into England, — namely, ward, marriage, relief, and aids. By the first, the heir of every tenant who held immediately from the crown, during his minority, was in ward for his body and his land to the king; so that he had the formation of his mind at that early and ductile age to mould to his own purposes, and the entire profits of his estate either to augment his demesne or to gratify his dependants: and as we have already seen how many and how vast estates, or rather, princely possessions, were then held immediately of the crown, we may comprehend how important an article this must have been.

Though the heir had attained his age before the death of his ancestor, yet the king intruded between him and his inheritance, and obliged him to redeem, or, as the term then was, to relieve it. The quantity of this relief was generally pretty much at the king's discretion, and often amounted to a very great sum.

But the king's demands on his rents in chief were not yet satisfied. He had a right and interest in the marriage of heirs, both males and females, virgins and widows, — and either bestowed them at pleasure on his favorites, or sold them to the best bidder. The king received for the sale of one heiress the sum of 20,000*l.*, or 60,000*l.* of our present money, — and this at a period when the chief estates were much reduced. And from hence was derived a great source of revenue, if this right were sold, — of influence and attachment, if bestowed.

Under the same head of feudal duties were the casual aids to knight his eldest son and marry his eldest daughter. These duties could be paid but once, and, though not considerable, eased him in these articles of expenses.

After the feudal duties, rather in the order than in point of value, was the profit which arose from the sale of justice. No man could then sue in the king's court by a common or public right, or without paying largely for it, — sometimes the third, and sometimes even half, the value of the estate or debt sued for. These presents were called oblations; and the records preceding Magna Charta, and for some time after, are full of them. And, as the king thought fit, this must have added greatly to his power or wealth, or indeed to both.

The fines and amercements were another branch; and this, at a time when disorders abounded, and almost every disorder was punished by a fine, was a much greater article than at first could readily be imagined, — especially when we consider that there were no limitations in this point but the king's mercy, particularly in all offences relating to the forest, which were of various kinds, and very strictly inquired into. The sale of offices was not less considerable. It appears that all offices at that time were, or might be, legally and publicly sold, — that the king had many and very rich employments in his gift, and, though it may appear strange, not inferior to, if they did not exceed, in number and consequence, those of our present establishment. At one time the great seal was sold for three thousand marks. The office of sheriff was then very lucrative: this charge was almost always sold. Sometimes a county paid a sum to the king, that he might appoint a sheriff whom they liked; sometimes they paid as largely to prevent him from appointing a

person disagreeable to them ; and thus the king
had often from the same office a double profit in
refusing one candidate and approving the other.   If
some offices were advantageous, others were burdensome ; and the king had the right, or was at least in
the unquestioned practice, of forcing his subjects to
accept these employments, or to pay for their immunity ; by which means he could either punish his
enemies or augment his wealth, as his avarice or
his resentments prevailed.

The greatest part of the cities and trading towns
were under his particular jurisdiction, and indeed in
a state not far removed from slavery.   On these he
laid a sort of imposition, at such a time and in such
a proportion as he thought fit.   This was called a
tallage.   If the towns did not forthwith pay the sum
at which they were rated, it was not unusual, for
their punishment, to double the exaction, and to
proceed in levying it by nearly the same methods
and in the same manner now used to raise a con-
tribution in an enemy's country.

But the Jews were a fund almost inexhaustible.
They were slaves to the king in the strictest sense ;
insomuch that, besides the various tallages and fines
extorted from them, none succeeded to the inheritance of his father without the king's license and an
heavy composition.   He sometimes even made over
a wealthy Jew as a provision to some of his favorites
for life.   They were almost the only persons who exercised usury, and thus drew to themselves the odium
and wealth of the whole kingdom ; but they were
only a canal, through which it passed to the royal
treasury.   And nothing could be more pleasing and
popular than such exactions : the people rejoiced,

when they saw the Jews plundered,—not considering that they were a sort of agents for the crown, who, in proportion to the heavy taxes they paid, were obliged to advance the terms and enforce with greater severity the execution of their usurious contracts. Through them almost the whole body of the nobility were in debt to the king; and when he thought proper to confiscate the effects of the Jews, the securities passed into his hands; and by this means he must have possessed one of the strongest and most terrible instruments of authority that could possibly be devised, and the best calculated to keep the people in an abject and slavish dependence.

The last general head of his revenue were the customs, prisages, and other impositions upon trade. Though the revenue arising from traffic in this rude period was much limited by the then smallness of its object, this was compensated by the weight and variety of the exactions levied by an occasional exertion of arbitrary power, or the more uniform system of hereditary tyranny. Trade was restrained, or the privilege granted, on the payment of tolls, passages, paages, pontages, and innumerable other vexatious imposts, of which only the barbarous and almost unintelligible names subsist at this day.

These were the most constant and regular branches of the revenue. But there were other ways innumerable by which money, or an equivalent in cattle, poultry, horses, hawks, and dogs, accrued to the exchequer. The king's interposition in marriages, even where there was no pretence from tenure, was frequently bought, as well as in other negotiations of less moment, for composing of quarrels, and the like; and, indeed, some appear on the records, of so

strange and even ludicrous a nature, that it would
not be excusable to mention them, if they did not
help to show from how many minute sources this
revenue was fed, and how the king's power descended to the most inconsiderable actions of private life.*
It is not easy to penetrate into the true meaning of
all these particulars, but they equally suffice to show
the character of government in those times. A prince
furnished with so many means of distressing enemies
and gratifying friends, and possessed of so ample a
revenue entirely independent of the affections of his
subjects, must have been very absolute in substance
and effect, whatever might have been the external
forms of government.

For the regulation of all these revenues, and for
determining all questions which concerned them, a
court was appointed, upon the model of a court of
the same nature, said to be of ancient use in Normandy, and called the Exchequer.

There was nothing in the government of William
conceived in a greater manner, or more to be com-
mended, than the general survey he took of his
conquest. An inquisition was made throughout
the kingdom concerning the quantity of land which
was contained in each county, — the name of the
deprived and the present proprietor, — the stock
of slaves, and cattle of every kind, which it contained. All these were registered in a book, each

* The Bishop of Winchester fined for not putting the king in
mind to give a girdle to the Countess of Albemarle. — Robertus de
Vallibus debet quinque optimos palafredos, ut rex taceret de uxore
Henrici Pinel. — The wife of Hugh de Nevil fined in two hundred
hens, that she might lie with her husband for one night; another
that he might rise from his infirmity; a third, that he might eat.

article beginning with the king's property, and proceeding downward, according to the rank of the proprietors, in an excellent order, by which might be known at one glance the true state of the royal revenues, the wealth, consequence, and natural connections of every person in the kingdom, — in order to ascertain the taxes that might be imposed, and, to serve purposes in the state as well as in civil causes, to be general and uncontrollable evidence of property. This book is called Domesday or the Judgment Book, and still remains a grand monument of the wisdom of the Conqueror, — a work in all respects useful and worthy of a better age.

The Conqueror knew very well how much discontent must have arisen from the great revolutions which his conquest produced in all men's property, and in the general tenor of the government. He, therefore, as much as possible to guard against every sudden attempt, forbade any light or fire to continue in any house after a certain bell, called curfew, had sounded. This bell rung at about eight in the evening. There was policy in this; and it served to prevent the numberless disorders which arose from the late civil commotions.

For the same purpose of strengthening his authority, he introduced the Norman law, not only in its substance, but in all its forms, and ordered that all proceedings should be had according to that law in the French language.* The change wrought by the former part of this regulation could not have been very grievous; and it was partly the necessary consequence of the establishment of the new tenures,

* For some particulars of the condition of the English of this time, vide Eadmer, p. 110.

and which wanted a new law to regulate them: in other respects the Norman institutions were not very different from the English. But to force, against nature, a new language upon a conquered people, to make them strangers in those courts of justice in which they were still to retain a considerable share, to be reminded, every time they had recourse to government for protection, of the slavery in which it held them, — this is one of those acts of superfluous tyranny from which very few conquering nations or parties have forborne, though no way necessary, but often prejudicial to their safety.

These severities, and affronts more galling than severities, drove the English to A. D. 1071. another desperate attempt, which was the last convulsive effort of their expiring freedom. Several nobles, prelates, and others, whose estates had been confiscated, or who were in daily apprehension of their confiscation, fled into the fens of Lincoln and Ely, where Hereward still maintained his ground. This unadvised step completed the ruin of the little English interest that remained. William hastened to fill up the sees of the bishops and the estates of the nobles with his Norman favorites. He pressed the fugitives with equal vivacity; and at once to cut off all the advantage they derived from their situation, he penetrated into the Isle of Ely by a wooden bridge two miles in length; and by the greatness of the design, and rapidity of the execution, as much as by the vigor of his charge, compelled them to surrender at discretion. Hereward alone escaped, who disdained to surrender, and had cut his way through his enemies, carrying his virtue and his sword, as his passports, wheresoever fortune should conduct him. He escaped happily into Scotland, where, as usual, the king was making some slow movements for the relief of the English. William lost no time to oppose him, and had passed with infinite difficulty through a desert of his own making to the frontiers of Scotland Here he found the enemy strongly intrenched. The causes of the war being in a good measure spent by William's late successes, and neither of the princes choosing to risk a battle in a country where the consequences of a defeat must be so dreadful, they agreed to an accommodation, which included a pardon for Edgar Atheling on a renunciation of his title to the crown. William on this occasion showed, as he did on all occasions, an honorable and disinterested sense of merit, by receiving Hereward to his friendship, and distinguishing him by particular favors and bounties. Malcolm, by his whole conduct, never seemed intent upon coming to extremities with William: he was satisfied with keeping this great warrior in some awe, without bringing things to a decision, that might involve his kingdom in the same calamitous fate that had oppressed England; whilst his wisdom enabled him to reap advantages from the fortunes of the conquered, in drawing so many useful people into his dominions, and from the policy of the Conqueror, in imitating those feudal regulations which he saw his neighbor force upon the English, and which appeared so well calculated for the defence of the kingdom. He compassed this the more easily, because the feudal policy, being the discipline of all the considerable states in Europe, appeared the masterpiece of government.

If men who have engaged in vast designs could ever promise themselves repose, William, after so many

victories, and so many political regulations to secure
the fruit of them, might now flatter himself with some
hope of quiet.   But disturbances were preparing for
his old age from a new quarter, from whence they
were less expected and less tolerable, — from the Normans, his companions in victory, and from his family,
which he found not less difficulty in governing than
his kingdom.   Nothing but his absence from England
was wanting to make the flame blaze out.   The num-
erless petty pretensions which the petty lords his
neighbors on the continent had on each other and
on William, together with their restless disposition
and the intrigues of the French court, kept alive a
constant dissension, which made the king's presence
on the continent frequently necessary.   The Duke of
Anjou had at this time actually invaded his
dominions.   He was obliged to pass over in-   A. D. 1073.
to Normandy with an army of fifty thousand men.
William, who had conquered England by the assistance of the princes on the continent, now turned
against them the arms of the English, who served him
with bravery and fidelity; and by their means he soon
silenced all opposition, and concluded the terms of an
advantageous peace.   In the mean time his Norman
subjects in England, inconstant, warlike, independent, fierce by nature, fiercer by their conquest, could
scarcely brook that subordination in which their safety consisted.   Upon some frivolous pretences, chiefly
personal disgusts,* a most dangerous conspiracy was
formed : the principal men among the Normans were
engaged in it; and foreign correspondence was not
wanting.   Though this conspiracy was chiefly formed

* Upon occasion of a ward refused in marriage. Wright thinks
the feudal right of marriage not then introduced.

and carried on by the Normans, they knew so well the use which William on this occasion would not fail to make of his English subjects, that they endeavored, as far as was consistent with secrecy, to engage several of that nation, and above all, the Earl Waltheof, as the first in rank and reputation among his countrymen. Waltheof, thinking it base to engage in any cause but that of his country against his benefactor, unveils the whole design to Lanfranc, who immediately took measures for securing the chief conspirators He dispatched messengers to inform the king of his danger, who returned without delay at the head of his forces, and by his presence, and his usual bold activity, dispersed at once the vapors of this conspiracy. The heads were punished. The rest, left under the shade of a dubious mercy, were awed into obedience. His glory was, however, sullied by his putting to death Waltheof, who had discovered the conspiracy ; but he thought the desire the rebels had shown of engaging him in their designs demonstrated sufficiently that Waltheof still retained a dangerous power. For as the years, so the suspicions, of this politic prince increased, — at whose time of life generosity begins to appear no more than a splendid weakness.

A.D. 1079. These troubles were hardly appeased, when others began to break forth in his own family, which neither his glory, nor the terror which held a great nation in chains, could preserve in obedience to him. To remove in some measure the jealousy of the court of France with regard to his invasion of England, he had promised upon his acquisition of that kingdom to invest his eldest son, Robert, with the Duchy of Normandy. But as his new acquisition did not seem so secure as it was great and magnificent, he was far from any thoughts of resigning his hereditary dominions, which he justly considered as a great instrument in maintaining his conquests, and a necessary retreat, if he should be deprived of them by the fortune of war. So long as the state of his affairs in England appeared unsettled, Robert acquiesced in the reasonableness of this conduct; but when he saw his father established on his throne, and found himself growing old in an inglorious subjection, he began first to murmur at the injustice of the king, soon after to cabal with the Norman barons and at the court of France, and at last openly rose in rebellion, and compelled the vassals of the Duchy to do him homage. The king was not inclined to give up to force what he had refused to reason. Unbroken with age, unwearied with so many expeditions, he passed again into Normandy, and pressed his son with the vigor of a young warrior.

This war, which was carried on without anything decisive for some time, ended by a very extraordinary and affecting incident. In one of those skirmishes which were frequent according to the irregular mode of warfare in those days, William and his son Robert, alike in a forward and adventurous courage, plunged into the thickest of the fight, and unknowingly encountered each other. But Robert, superior by fortune, or by the vigor of his youth, wounded and unhorsed the old monarch, and was just on the point of pursuing his unhappy advantage to the fatal extremity, when the well-known voice of his father at once struck his ears and suspended his arm. Blushing for his victory, and overwhelmed with the united emotions of grief, shame, and returning piety, he fell on his knees, poured out a flood of tears, and, embracing

his father, besought him for pardon. The tide of nature returning strongly on both, the father in his turn
embraced his son, and bathed him with his tears;
whilst the combatants on either side, astonished at so
unusual a spectacle, suspended the fight, applauded
this striking act of filial piety and paternal tenderness,
and pressed that it might become the prelude to a lasting peace. Peace was made, but entirely to the advantage of the father, who carried his son into England, to secure Normandy from the dangers to which
his ambition and popularity might expose that dukedom.

That William might have peace upon no part, the
Welsh and Scots took advantage of these troubles in
his family to break into England: but their expeditions were rather incursions than invasions: they
wasted the country, and then retired to secure their
plunder. But William, always troubled, always in
action, and always victorious, pursued them and com
pelled them to a peace, which was not concluded but
by compelling the King of Scotland and all the princes
of Wales to do him homage. How far this homage
extended with regard to Scotland I find it difficult to
determine.

Robert, who had no pleasure but in action, as soon
as this war was concluded, finding that he could not
regain his father's confidence, and that he had no
credit at the court of England, retired to that of
France. Edgar Atheling saw likewise that the in-
nocence of his conduct could not make amends for
the guilt of an undoubted title to the crown, and that
the Conqueror, soured by continual opposition, and
suspicious through age and the experience of mankind, regarded him with an evil eye. He therefore

αesired leave to accompany Robert out of the kingdom, and then to make a voyage to the Holy Land.
This leave was readily granted.   Edgar, having displayed great valor in useless acts of chivalry abroad,
after the Conqueror's death returned to England,
where he long lived in great tranquillity, happy in
himself, beloved by all the people, and unfeared by
those who held his sceptre, from his mild and inactive virtue.

William had been so much a stranger to
repose that it became no longer an object A. D. 1084.
desirable to him.   He revived his claim to the Vexin
Français, and some other territories on the confines
of Normandy.   This quarrel, which began between
him and the King of France on political motives, was
increased into rancor and bitterness, first, by a boy-
ish contest at chess between their children, which
was resented, more than became wise men, by the
fathers ; it was further exasperated by taunts and
mockeries yet less becoming their age and dignity,
but which infused a mortal venom into the war.
William entered first into the French territories, wantonly wasting the country, and A. D. 1087.
setting fire to the towns and villages.   He entered
Mantes, and as usual set it on fire ; but whilst he
urged his horse over the smoking ruins, and pressed
forward to further havoc, the beast, impatient of the
hot embers which burned his hoofs, plunged and
threw his rider violently on the saddle-bow.   The
rim of his belly was wounded ; and this wound, as
William was corpulent and in the decline of life,
proved fatal.   A rupture ensued, and he died at
Rouen, after showing a desire of making amends
for his cruelty by restitutions to the towns he had

destroyed, by alms and endowments, the usual fruits of a late penitence, and the acknowledgments which expiring ambition pays to virtue.

There is nothing more memorable in history than the actions, fortunes, and character of this great man, — whether we consider the grandeur of the plans he formed, the courage and wisdom with which they were executed, or the splendor of that success which, adorning his youth, continued without the smallest reverse to support his age, even to the last moments of his life. He lived above seventy years, and reigned within ten years as long as he lived, sixty over his dukedom, above twenty over England, — both of which he acquired or kept by his own magnanimity, with hardly any other title than he derived from his arms : so that he might be reputed, in all respects, as happy as the highest ambition, the most fully gratified, can make a man. The silent inward satisfactions of domestic happiness he neither had nor sought. He had a body suited to the character of his mind, erect, firm, large, and active, whilst to be active was a praise, — a countenance stern, and which became command. Magnificent in his living, reserved in his conversation, grave in his common deportment, but relaxing with a wise facetiousness, he knew how to relieve his mind and preserve his dignity : for he never forfeited by a personal acquaintance that esteem he had acquired by his great actions. Unlearned in books, he formed his understanding by the rigid discipline of a large and complicated experience. He knew men much, and therefore generally trusted them but little ; but when he knew any man to be good, he reposed in him an entire confidence, which prevented his prudence from

degenerating into a vice. He had vices in his composition, and great ones; but they were the vices of a
great mind: ambition, the malady of every extensive
genius, — and avarice, the madness of the wise: one
chiefly actuated his youth, — the other governed his
age. The vices of young and light minds, the joys
of wine and the pleasures of love, never reached his
aspiring nature. The general run of men he looked
on with contempt, and treated with cruelty when they
opposed him. Nor was the rigor of his mind to be
softened but with the appearance of extraordinary
fortitude in his enemies, which, by a sympathy con-
genial to his own virtues, always excited his admiration and insured his mercy. So that there were often
seen in this one man, at the same time, the extremes
of a savage cruelty, and a generosity that does honor
to human nature. Religion, too, seemed to have a
great influence on his mind, from policy, or from
better motives; but his religion was displayed in the
regularity with which he performed its duties, not in
the submission he showed to its ministers, which was
never more than what good government required.
Yet his choice of a counsellor and favorite was, not
according to the mode of the time, out of that order,
and a choice that does honor to his memory. This
was Lanfranc, a man of great learning for the times,
and extraordinary piety. He owed his elevation to
William; but though always inviolably faithful, he
never was the tool or flatterer of the power which
raised him; and the greater freedom he showed, the
higher he rose in the confidence of his master. By
mixing with the concerns of state he did not lose his
religion and conscience, or make them the covers or
instruments of ambition; but tempering the fierce

policy of a new power by the mild lights of religion, he became a blessing to the country in which he was promoted. The English owed to the virtue of this stranger, and the influence he had on the king, the little remains of liberty they continued to enjoy, and at last such a degree of his confidence as in some sort counterbalanced the severities of the former part of his reign.

CHAPTER III.

REIGN OF WILLIAM THE SECOND, SURNAMED RUFUS.

A. D. 1087.   WILLIAM had by his queen Matilda three sons, who survived him,—Robert, William, and Henry. Robert, though in an advanced age at his father's death, was even then more remarkable for those virtues which make us entertain hopes of a young man than for that steady prudence which is necessary when the short career we are to run will not allow us to make many mistakes. He had, indeed, a temper suitable to the genius of the time he lived in, and which therefore enabled him to make a considerable figure in the transactions which distinguished that period. He was of a sincere, open, candid nature; passionately fond of glory; ambitious, without having any determinate object in view; vehement in his pursuits, but inconstant; much in war, which he understood and loved. But guiding himself, both in war and peace, solely by the impulses of an unbounded and irregular spirit, he filled the world with an equal admiration and pity of his splendid qualities and great misfortunes. William was of a character very different. His views were short, his designs few, his genius narrow, and his manners brutal; full of craft, rapacious, without faith, without religion; but circumspect, steady, and courageous for his ends, not for glory. These qualities secured to him that fortune which the virtues of Robert deserved. Of Henry we shall speak hereafter.

We have seen the quarrels, together with the causes of them, which embroiled the Conqueror with his eldest son, Robert. Although the wound was skinned over by several temporary and palliative accommodations, it still left a soreness in the father's mind, which influenced him by his last will to cut off Robert from the inheritance of his English dominions. Those he declared he derived from his sword, and therefore he would dispose of them to that son whose dutiful behavior had made him the most worthy. To William, therefore, he left his crown; to Henry he devised his treasures: Robert possessed nothing but the Duchy, which was his birthright. William had some advantages to enforce the execution of a bequest which was not included even in any of the modes of succession which then were admitted. He was at the time of his father's death in England, and had an opportunity of seizing the vacant government, a thing of great moment in all disputed rights. He had also, by his presence, an opportunity of engaging some of the most considerable leading men in his interests. But his greatest strength was derived from the adherence to his cause of Lanfranc, a prelate of the greatest authority amongst the English as well as the Normans, both from the place he had held in the Conqueror's esteem, whose memory all men respected, and from his own great and excellent qualities. By the advice of this prelate the new monarch professed to be entirely governed. And as an earnest of his future reign, he renounced all the rigid maxims of conquest, and swore to protect the Church and the people, and to govern by St. Edward's Laws, — a promise extremely grateful and popular to all parties: for the Normans, finding the English passionately desirous of these laws, and only knowing that they were in general favorable to liberty and conducive to peace and order, became equally clamorous for their reëstablishment. By these measures, and the weakness of those which were adopted by Robert, William established himself

A. D. 1088.

on his throne, and suppressed a dangerous conspiracy formed by some Norman noblemen in the interests of his brother, although it was fomented by all the art and intrigue which his uncle Odo could put in practice, the most bold and politic man of that age.

The security he began to enjoy from this success, and the strength which government receives by merely continuing, gave room to his natural dispositions to break out in several acts of tyranny and injustice. The forest laws were executed with rigor, the old impositions revived, and new laid on. Lanfranc made representations to the king on this conduct, but they produced no other effect than the abatement of his credit, which from that moment to his death, which happened soon after, was very little in the

A. D. 1089.

government. The revenue of the vacant see was seized into the king's hands. When the Church lands were made subject to military service, they seemed to partake all the qualities of the military tenure, and to be subject to the same burdens; and as on the death of a military vassal his land was in ward-ship of the lord until the heir had attained his age, so there arose a pretence, on the vacancy of a bishopric, to suppose the land in ward with the king until the seat should be filled. This principle, once established, opened a large field for various lucrative abuses; nor could it be supposed, whilst the vacancy turned to such good account, that a necessitous or avaricious king would show any extraordinary haste to put the bishoprics and abbacies out of his power. In effect, William always kept them a long time vacant, and in the vacancy granted away much of their possessions, particularly several manors belonging to the see of Canterbury; and when he filled this see, it was only to prostitute that dignity by disposing of it to the highest bidder.

To support him in these courses he chose for his minister Ralph Flambard, a fit instrument in his designs, and possessed of such art and eloquence as to color them in a specious manner. This man inflamed all the king's passions, and encouraged him in his unjust enterprises. It is hard to say which was most unpopular, the king or his minister. But Flambard, having escaped a conspiracy against his life, and having punished the conspirators severely, struck such a general terror into the nation, that none dared to oppose him. Robert's title alone stood in the king's way, and he knew that this must be a perpetual source of disturbance to him. He resolved, therefore, to put him in peril for his own dominions. He collected a large army, and entering into Normandy, he began a war, at first with great success, on account of a difference between the Duke and his brother Henry. But their common dread of William reconciled them; and this reconciliation put them in a condition of procuring an equal peace, the chief conditions of which were, that Robert should be put in pos session of certain seigniories in England, and that each, in case of survival, should succeed to the other's dominions. William concluded this peace the more readily, because Malcolm, King of Scotland, who hung over him, was ready upon every advantage to invade his territories, and had now actually entered England with a powerful army. Robert, who courted action, without regarding what interest might have dictated, immediately on concluding the treaty entered into his brother's service in this war against the Scots; which, on the king's return, being in appearance laid asleep by an accommodation, broke out with redoubled fury the following year. The King of Scotland, provoked to this rupture by the haughtiness of William, was circumvented by the artifice and fraud of one of his ministers: under an appearance of negotiation, he was attacked and killed, together with his only son. This was a grievous wound to Scotland, in the loss of one of the wisest and bravest of her kings, and in the domestic distractions which afterwards tore that kingdom to pieces.

A. D. 1093.

No sooner was this war ended, than William, freed from an enemy which had given himself and his father so many alarms, renewed his ill treatment of his brother, and refused to abide by the terms of the late treaty. Robert, incensed at these repeated perfidies, returned to Normandy with thoughts full of revenge and war. But he found that the artifices and bribes of the King of England had corrupted the greatest part of his barons, and filled the country with faction and disloyalty. His own facility of temper had relaxed all the

A. D. 1094.

bands of government, and contributed greatly to these disorders. In this distress he was obliged to have recourse to the King of France for succor. Philip, who was then on the throne, entered into his quarrel. Nor was William, on his side, backward; though prodigal to the highest degree, the resources of his tyranny and extortion were inexhaustible. He was enabled to enter Normandy once more with a considerable army. But the opposition, too, was considerable; and the war had probably been spun out to a great length, and had drawn on very bloody consequences, if one of the most extraordinary A. D. 1096. events which are contained in the history of mankind had not suspended their arms, and drawn all inferior views, sentiments, and designs into the vortex of one grand project. This was the Crusade, which, with astonishing success, now began to be preached through all Europe. This design was then, and it continued long after, the principle which influenced the transactions of that period both at home and abroad; it will, therefore, not be foreign to our subject to trace it to its source.

As the power of the Papacy spread, the see of Rome began to be more and more an object of ambition; the most refined intrigues were put in practice to attain it; and all the princes of Europe interested themselves in the contest. The election of Pope was not regulated by those prudent dispositions which have since taken place; there were frequent pretences to controvert the validity of the election, and of course several persons at the same time laid claim to that dignity. Popes and Antipopes arose. Europe was rent asunder by these disputes, whilst some princes maintained the rights of one party, and

some defended the pretensions of the other : sometimes the prince acknowledged one Pope, whilst his
subjects adhered to his rival.   The scandals occasioned by these schisms were infinite ; and they
threatened a deadly wound to that authority whose
greatness had occasioned them.   Princes were taught
to know their own power.   That Pope who this day
was a suppliant to a monarch to be recognized by
him could with an ill grace pretend to govern him
with an high hand the next.   The lustre of the Holy
See began to be tarnished, when Urban the Second,
after a long contest of this nature, was universally
acknowledged.   That Pope, sensible by his own experience of the ill consequence of such disputes,
sought to turn the minds of the people into another
channel, and by exerting it vigorously to give a new
strength to the Papal power.   In an age so ignorant,
it was very natural that men should think a great
deal in religion depended upon the very scene where
the work of our Redemption was accomplished.   Pilgrimages to Jerusalem were therefore judged highly
meritorious, and became very frequent.   But the
country which was the object of them, as well as
several of those through which the journey lay, were
in the hands of Mahometans, who, against all the
rules of humanity and good policy, treated the Christian pilgrims with great indignity.   These, on their
return, filled the minds of their neighbors with hatred and resentment against those infidels.   Pope
Urban laid hold on this disposition, and encouraged
Peter the Hermit, a man visionary, zealous, enthusiastic, and possessed of a warm irregular eloquence
adapted to the pitch of his hearers, to preach an
expedition for the delivery of the Holy Land.

Great designs may be started and the spirit of them inspired by enthusiasts, but cool heads are required to bring them into form. The Pope, not relying solely on Peter, called a council at Clermont, where an infinite number of people of all sorts were assembled. Here he dispensed with a full hand benedictions and indulgences to all persons who should engage in the expedition; and preaching with great vehemence in a large plain, towards the end of his discourse, somebody, by design or by accident, cried out, "It is the will of God!" This voice was repeated by the next, and in a moment it circulated through this innumerable people, which rung with the acclamation of "It is the will of God! It is the will of God!"* The neighboring villages caught up those oracular words, and it is incredible with what celerity they spread everywhere around into places the most distant. This circumstance, then considered as miraculous, contributed greatly to the success of the Hermit's mission. No less did the disposition of the nobility throughout Europe, wholly actuated with devotion and chivalry, contribute to forward an enterprise so suited to the gratification of both these passions. Everything was now in motion; both sexes, and every station and age and condition of life, engaged with transport in this holy warfare.† There was even a danger that Europe would be entirely exhausted by the torrents that were rushing out to deluge Asia. These vast bodies, collected without choice, were conducted without skill or order; and they succeeded accordingly. Women and children composed no small part of those armies, which were headed by priests; and

* Maimbourg.   † Chron. Sax 204.

it is hard to say which is most lamentable, the destruction of such multitudes of men, or the frenzy which drew it upon them. But this design, after innumerable calamities, began at last to be conducted in a manner worthy of so grand and bold a project. Raimond, Count of Toulouse, Godfrey of Bouillon, and several other princes, who were great captains as well as devotees, engaged in the expedition, and with suitable effects. But none burned more to signalize his zeal and courage on this occasion than Robert, Duke of Normandy, who was fired with the thoughts of an enterprise which seemed to be made for his genius. He immediately suspended his interesting quarrel with his brother, and, instead of contesting with him the crown to which he had such fair pretensions, or the duchy of which he was in possession, he proposed to mortgage to him the latter during five years for a sum of thirteen thousand marks of gold. William, who had neither sense of religion nor thirst of glory, intrenched in his secure and narrow policy, laughed at a design that had deceived all the great minds in Europe. He extorted, as usual, this sum from his subjects, and immediately took possession of Normandy; whilst Robert, at the head of a gallant army, leaving his hereditary dominions, is gone to cut out unknown kingdoms in Asia.

Some conspiracies disturbed the course of the reign, or rather tyranny, of this prince: as plots usually do, they ended in the ruin of those who contrived them, but proved no check to the ill government of William. Some disturbances, too, he had from the incursions of the Welsh, from revolts in Normandy, and from a war, that began and ended without any·

thing memorable either in the cause or consequence, with France.

He had a dispute at home which at another time had raised great disturbances; but nothing was now considered but the expedition to the Holy Land. After the death of Lanfranc, William omitted for a long time to fill up that see, and had even alienated a considerable portion of the revenue. A fit of sickness, however, softened his mind; and the clergy, taking advantage of those happy moments, among other parts of misgovernment which they advised him to correct, particularly urged him to fill the vacant sees. He filled that of Canterbury with Anselm, Bishop of Bec, a man of great piety and learning, but inflexible and rigid in whatever related to the rights, real or supposed, of the Church. This prelate refused to accept the see of Canterbury, foreseeing the troubles that must arise from his own dispositions and those of the king; nor was he prevailed upon to accept it, but on a promise of indemnification for what the temporalities of the see had suffered. But William's sickness and pious resolutions ending together, little care was taken about the execution of this agreement. Thus began a quarrel between this rapacious king and inflexible archbishop. Soon after, Anselm declared in favor of Pope Urban, before the king had recognized him, and thus subjected himself to the law which William the Conqueror had made against accepting a Pope without his consent. The quarrel was inflamed to the highest pitch; and Anselm desiring to depart the kingdom, the king consented.

The eyes of all men being now turned towards the great transactions in the East, _{A. D. 1100.}

William, Duke of Guienne, fired by the success and glory that attended the holy adventurers, resolved to take the cross ; but his revenues were not sufficient to support the figure his rank required in this expedition.   He applied to the King of England, who, being master of the purses of his subjects, never wanted money; and he was politician enough to avail himself of the prodigal, inconsiderate zeal of the times to lay out this money to great advantage. He acted the part of usurer to the Croises; and as he had taken Normandy in mortgage from his brother Robert, having advanced the Duke of Guienne a sum on the same conditions, he was ready to confirm his bargain by taking possession, when he was killed in hunting by an accidental stroke of an arrow which pierced his heart. This accident happened in the New Forest, which his father with such infinite oppression of the people had made, and in which they both delighted extremely. In the same forest the Conqueror's eldest son, a youth of great hopes, had several years before met his death from the horns of a stag ; and these so memorable fates to the same family and in the same place easily inclined men to think this a judgment from Heaven: the people consoling themselves under their sufferings with these equivocal marks of the vengeance of Providence upon their oppressors.

We have painted this prince in the colors in which he is drawn by all the writers who lived the nearest to his time. Although the monkish historians, affected with the partiality of their character, and with the sense of recent injuries, expressed themselves with passion concerning him, we have no other guides to follow. Nothing, indeed, in his life appears to vindicate his character ; and it makes strongly for his disadvantage, that, without any great end of government, he contradicted the prejudices of the age in which he lived, the general and common foundation of honor, and thereby made himself obnoxious to that body of men who had the sole custody of fame, and could alone transmit his name with glory or disgrace to posterity.

CHAPTER IV.

REIGN OF HENRY I.

HENRY, the youngest son of the Conqueror, was hunting at the same time and in the A. D. 1100. same forest in which his brother met his fate. He was not long before he came to a resolution of seizing on the vacant crown. The order of succession had already been broken ; the absence of Duke Robert, and the concurrence of many circumstances altogether resembling those which had been so favorable to the late monarch, incited him to a similar attempt. To lose no time at a juncture when the use of a moment is often decisive, he went directly to Winchester, where the regalia and the treasures of the crown were deposited. But the governor, a man of resolution, and firmly attached to Robert, positively refused to deliver them. Henry, conscious that great enterprises are not to be conducted in a middle course, prepared to reduce him by force of arms. During this contest, the news of the king's death, and the attempts of Henry, drew great numbers of the nobility to Winchester, and with them a vast concourse of the inferior people. To the nobility he set forth his title to the crown in the most plausible manner it could bear: he alleged that he was born after his father had acquired his kingdom, and that he was therefore natural heir of the crown; but that his brother was, at best, only born to the inheritance of a dukedom. The nobility heard the claim of this prince; but they were more generally inclined to Robert, whose birthright, less questionable in itself, had been also confirmed by a solemn treaty. But whilst they retired to consult, Henry, well apprised of their dispositions, and who therefore was little inclined to wait the result of their debates, threw himself entirely upon the populace. To them he said little concerning his title, as he knew such an audience is little moved with a discussion of rights, but much with the spirit and manner in which they are claimed; for which reason he began by drawing his sword, and swearing, with a bold and determined air, to persist in his pretensions to his last breath. Then turning to the crowd, and remitting of his severity, he began to soothe them with the promises of a milder government than they had experienced either beneath his brother or his father; the Church should enjoy her immunities, the people their liberties, the nobles their pleasures; the forest laws should cease; the distinction of Englishman and Norman be heard no more. Next he expatiated on the grievances of the former reigns, and promised to redress them all. Lastly, he spoke of his brother Robert, whose dissoluteness, whose inactivity, whose unsteady temper, nay, whose very virtues, threatened nothing but ruin to any country which he should govern. The people received this popular harangue, delivered by a prince whose person was full of grace and majesty, with shouts of joy and rapture. Immediately they rush to the house where the council is held, which they surround, and with clamor and menaces demand Henry for their king. The nobility were terrified by the sedition; and remembering how little present Robert had been on a former occasion to his own interests, or to those who defended him, they joined their voice to that of the people, and Henry was proclaimed without opposition. The treasure which he seized he divided amongst those that seemed wavering in his cause; and that he might secure his new and disputed right by every method, he proceeded without delay to London to be crowned, and to sanctify by the solemnity of the unction the choice of the people. As the churchmen in those days were the arbiters of everything, and as no churchman possessed more credit than Anselm, Archbishop of Canterbury, who had been persecuted and banished by his brother, he recalled that prelate, and by every mark of confidence confirmed him in his interests. Two other steps he took, equally prudent and politic: he confirmed and enlarged the privileges of the city of London, and gave to the whole kingdom a charter of liberties, which was the first of the kind, and laid the foundation of those successive charters which at last completed the freedom of the subject. In fine, he cemented the whole fabric of his power by marrying Maud, daughter of Malcolm, King of Scotland, by the sister of Edgar Atheling, — thus to insure the affection of the English, and, as he flattered himself, to have a sure succession to his children.

The Crusade being successfully finished by the taking of Jerusalem, Robert returned into Europe. He

had acquired great reputation in that war, in which
he had no interest; his real and valuable rights he
prosecuted with languor. Yet such was the respec
paid to his title, and such the attraction of his per
sonal accomplishments, that, when he had at las
taken possession of his Norman territories

A. D. 1101.

and entered England with an army to as
sert his birthright, he found most of the Norma
barons, and many of the English, in readiness to
join him. But the diligence of Anselm, who em
ployed all his credit to keep the people firm to the
oath they had taken, prevented him from profiting
of the general inclination in his favor. His friend
began to fall off by degrees, so that he was induced
as well by the situation of his affairs as the flexibility
of his temper, to submit to a treaty on the plan of
that he had formerly entered into with his brother
Rufus.

This treaty being made, Robert returned to his
dukedom, and gave himself over to his natural indolence and dissipation. Uncured by his mis-

A. D. 1103.

fortunes of a loose generosity that flowed
indiscriminately on all, he mortgaged every branch of
his revenue, and almost his whole domain. His barons, despising his indigence, and secure in the benignity of his temper, began to assume the unhappy privilege of sovereigns. They made war on each other at
pleasure, and, pursuing their hostilities with the most
scandalous license, they reduced that fine country
to a deplorable condition. In vain did the people,
ruined by the tyranny and divisions of the great,
apply to Robert for protection: neither from his
circumstances nor his character was he able to afford them any effectual relief; whilst Henry, who

by his bribes and artifices kept alive the disorder of
which he complained and profited, formed a party in
Normandy to call him over, and to put the dukedom under his protection. Accordingly, he prepared
a considerable force for the expedition, and taxed
his own subjects, arbitrarily, and without mercy, for
the relief he pretended to afford those of his brother.
His preparations roused Robert from his indolence,
and united likewise the greater part of his barons
to his cause, unwilling to change a master whose
only fault was his indulgence of them for the severe
vigilance of Henry. The King of France espoused
the same side; and even in England some emotions
were excited in favor of the Duke by indignation for
the wrongs he had suffered and those he was going
to suffer. Henry was alarmed, but did not renounce
his design. He was to the last degree jealous of his
prerogative; but knowing what immense resources
kings may have in popularity, he called on this occasion a great council of his barons and prelates,
and there, by his arts and his eloquence, in both
which he was powerful, he persuaded the assembly
to a hearty declaration in his favor, and to a large
supply. Thus secured at home, he lost no time to
pass over to the continent, and to bring
the Norman army to a speedy engage- A. D. 1106.
ment. They fought under the walls of Tinchebrai,
where the bravery and military genius of Robert,
never more conspicuous than on that day, were
borne down by the superior fortune and numbers
of his ambitious brother. He was made prisoner;
and notwithstanding all the tender pleas of their
common blood, in spite of his virtues, and even of
his misfortunes, which pleaded so strongly for mercy,

the rigid conqueror held him in various prisons until his death, which did not happen until after a rigorous confinement of eighteen, some say twenty-seven, years. This was the end of a prince born with a thousand excellent qualities, which served no other purpose than to confirm, from the example of his misfortunes, that a facility of disposition and a weak beneficence are the greatest vices that can enter into the composition of a monarch, equally ruinous to himself and to his subjects.

A. D. 1107. The success of this battle put Henry in possession of Normandy, which he held ever after with very little disturbance. He fortified his new acquisition by demolishing the castles of those turbulent barons who had wasted and afterwards enslaved their country by their dissensions. Order and justice took place, until everything was reduced to obedience ; then a severe and regular oppression succeeded the former disorderly tyranny. In England A. D. 1108. things took the same course. The king no longer doubted his fortune, and therefore no longer respected his promises or his charter. The forests, the savage passion of the Norman princes, for which both the prince and people paid so dearly, were maintained, increased, and guarded with laws more rigorous than before. Taxes were largely and arbitrarily assessed. But all this tyranny did not weaken, though it vexed the nation, because the great men were kept in proper subjection, and justice was steadily administered.

The politics of this remarkable reign consisted of three branches : to redress the gross abuses which prevailed in the civil government and the revenue, to humble the great barons, and keep the aspiring spirit of the clergy within proper bounds. The introduction of a new law with a new people at the Conquest had unsettled everything: for whilst some adhered to the Conqueror's regulations, and others contended for those of St. Edward, neither of them were well executed or properly obeyed. The king, therefore, with the assistance of his justiciaries, compiled a new body of laws, in order to find a temper between both. The coin had been miserably debased, but it was restored by the king's vigilance, and preserved by punishments, cruel, but terrifying in their example. There was a savageness in all the judicial proceedings of those days, that gave even justice itself the complexion of tyranny: for whilst a number of men were seen in all parts of the kingdom, some castrated, some without hands, others with their feet cut off, and in various ways cruelly mangled, the view of a perpetual punishment blotted out the memory of the transient crime, and government was the more odious, which, out of a cruel and mistaken mercy, to avoid punishing with death, devised torments far more terrible than death itself.

But nothing called for redress more than the disorders in the king's own household. It was considered as an incident annexed to their tenure, that the socage vassals of the crown, and so of all the subordinate barons, should receive their lord and all his followers, and supply them in their progresses and journeys, which custom continued for some ages after in Ireland, under the name of *coshering*. But this indefinite and ill-contrived charge on the tenant was easily perverted to an instrument of much oppression by the disorders of a rude and licentious court; insomuch that the tenants, in fear for their substance,

for the honor of their women, and often for their
lives, deserted their habitations and fled into the
woods on the king's approach. No circumstance
could be more dishonorable to a prince ; but happily,
like many other great abuses, it gave rise to a great
reform, which went much further than its immediate
purposes. This disorder, which the punishment of
offenders could only palliate, was entirely taken away
by commuting personal service for a rent in money ;
which regulation, passing from the king to all the inferior lords, in a short time wrought a great change
in the state of the nation. To humble the great
men, more arbitrary methods were used. The adherence to the title of Robert was a cause, or a pretence, of depriving many of their vast possessions,
which were split or parcelled out amongst the king's
creatures, with great injustice to particulars, but in
the consequences with general and lasting benefit.
The king held his courts, according to the custom,
at Christmas and Easter, but he seldom kept both
festivals in the same place. He made continual progresses into all parts of his kingdom, and brought
the royal authority and person home to the doors
of his haughty barons, which kept them in strict
obedience during his long and severe reign.

His contests with the Church, concerning the right
of investiture, were more obstinate and more dangerous. As this is an affair that troubled all Europe
as well as England, and holds deservedly a principal
place in the story of those times, it will not be imper-
tinent to trace it up to its original. In the early
times of Christianity, when religion was only drawn
from its obscurity to be persecuted, when a bishop
was only a candidate for martyrdom, neither the pre

'erment, nor the right of bestowing it, were sought
with great ambition. Bishops were then elected, and
often against their desire, by their clergy and the
people : the subordinate ecclesiastical districts were
provided for in the same manner. After the Roman
Empire became Christian, this usage, so generally established, still maintained its ground. However, in
the principal cities, the Emperor frequently exercised
the privilege of giving a sanction to the choice, and
sometimes of appointing the bishop; though, for the
most part, the popular election still prevailed. But
when the Barbarians, after destroying the Empire,
had at length submitted their necks to the Gospel,
their kings and great men, full of zeal and gratitude
to their instructors, endowed the Church with large
territories and great privileges. In this case it was
but natural that they should be the patrons of those
dignities and nominate to that power which arose
from their own free bounty. Hence the bishoprics
in the greatest part of Europe became in effect, whatever some few might have been in appearance, merely donative. And as the bishoprics formed so many
seigniories, when the feudal establishment was completed, they partook of the feudal nature, so far as
they were subjects capable of it; homage and fealty
were required on the part of the spiritual vassal;
the king, on his part, gave the bishop the investiture,
or livery and seizin of his temporalities, by the delivery of a ring and staff. This was the original manner
of granting feudal property, and something like it is
still practised in our base-courts. Pope Adrian confirmed this privilege to Charlemagne by an express
grant. The clergy of that time, ignorant, but inquis-
itive, were very ready at finding types and mysteries

in every ceremony : they construed the staff into an emblem of the pastoral care, and the ring into a type of the bishop's allegorical marriage to his church, and therefore supposed them designed as emblems of a jurisdiction merely spiritual. The Papal pretensions increased with the general ignorance and superstition ; and the better to support these pretensions, it was necessary at once to exalt the clergy extremely, and, by breaking off all ties between them and their natural sovereigns, to attach them wholly to the Roman see. In pursuance of this project, the Pope first strictly forbade the clergy to receive investitures from laymen, or to do them homage. A council held at Rome entirely condemned this practice ; and the condemnation was the less unpopular, because the investiture gave rise to frequent and flagrant abuses, especially in England, where the sees were on this pretence with much scandal long held in the king's hands, and afterwards as scandalously and publicly sold to the highest bidder. So it had been in the last reign, and so it continued in this.

Henry, though vigorously attacked, with great resolution maintained the rights of his crown with regard to investitures, whilst he saw the Emperor, who claimed a right of investing the Pope himself, subdued by the thunder of the Vatican. His chief opposition was within his own kingdom. Anselm, Archbishop of Canterbury, a man of unblamable life, and of learning for his time, but blindly attached to the rights of the Church, real or supposed, refused to consecrate those who received investitures from the king. The parties appealed to Rome. Rome, unwilling either to recede from her pretensions or to provoke a powerful monarch, gives a dubious answer. Meanwhile the contest grows hotter. Anselm is obliged to quit the kingdom, but is still inflexible. At last, the king, who, from the delicate situation of his affairs in the beginning of his reign, had been obliged to temporize for a long time, by his usual prudent mixture of management with force obliged the Pope to a temperament which seemed extremely judicious. The king received homage and fealty from his vassal; the investiture, as it was generally understood to relate to spiritual jurisdiction, was given up, and on this equal bottom peace was established. The secret of the Pope's moderation was this: he was at that juncture close pressed by the Emperor, and it might be highly dangerous to contend with two such enemies at once; and he was much more ready to yield to Henry, who had no reciprocal demands on him, than to the Emperor, who had many and just ones, and to whom he could not yield any one point without giving up an infinite number of others very material and interesting.

As the king extricated himself happily from so great an affair, so all the other difficulties of his reign only exercised, without endangering him. The efforts of France in favor of the son of Robert were late, desultory, and therefore unsuccessful. That youth, endued with equal virtue and more prudence than his father, after exerting many useless acts of unfortunate bravery, fell in battle, and freed Henry from all disturbance on the side of France. The incursions of the Welsh in this reign only gave him an opportunity of confining that people within narrower bounds. At home he was well obeyed by his subjects; abroad he dignified his family by splendid alliances. His daughter Matilda he married to the Emperor.

But his private fortunes did not flow with so even a course as his public affairs. His only son, William, with a natural daughter, and many of the flower of the young nobility, perished at sea between Normandy and England. From that fatal accident the king was never seen to smile. He sought in vain from a second marriage to provide a male successor; but when he saw all prospect of this at an end, he called a great council of his barons and prelates. His daughter Matilda, after the decease of the Emperor, he had given in marriage to Geoffrey Plantagenet, Count of Anjou. As she was his only remaining issue, he caused her to be acknowledged as his successor by the great council; he enforced this acknowledgment by solemn oaths of fealty, — a sanction which he weakened rather than confirmed by frequent repetition: vainly imagining that on his death any ties would bind to the respect of a succession so little respected by himself, and by the violation of which he had procured his crown. Having taken these measures in favor of his daughter, he died in Normandy, but in a good old age, and in the thirty-sixth year of a prosperous reign.

A. D. 1120.

A. D. 1127.

CHAPTER V.

REIGN OF STEPHEN.

ALTHOUGH the authority of the crown had been exercised with very little restraint during the three preceding reigns, the succession to it, or even the principles of the succession, were but ill ascertained: so that a doubt might justly have arisen,

A. D. 1135.

whether the crown was not in a great measure elective.   This uncertainty exposed the nation, at the
death of every king, to all the calamities of a civil
war; but it was a circumstance favorable to the designs of Stephen, Earl of Boulogne, who was son of
Stephen, Earl of Blois, by a daughter of the Conquer-
or.   The late king had raised him to great employments, and enriched him by the grant of several
lordships.   His brother had been made Bishop of
Winchester; and by adding to it the place of his
chief justiciary, the king gave him an opportunity of
becoming one of the richest subjects in Europe, and
of extending an unlimited influence over the clergy
and the people.   Henry trusted, by the promotion of
two persons so near him in blood, and so bound by
benefits, that he had formed an impenetrable fence
about the succession; but he only inspired into Stephen the design of seizing on the crown by bringing him so near it.   The opportunity was favorable.   The king died abroad; Matilda was absent
with her husband; and the Bishop of Winchester,
by his universal credit, disposed the churchmen to
elect his brother, with the concurrence of the greatest part of the nobility, who forgot their oaths, and
vainly hoped that a bad title would necessarily produce a good government.   Stephen, in the flower
of youth, bold, active, and courageous, full of generosity and a noble affability, that seemed to reproach
the state and avarice of the preceding kings, was not
wanting to his fortune.   He seized immediately the
immense treasures of Henry, and by distributing
them with a judicious profusion removed all doubts
concerning his title to them.   He did not spare even
the royal demesne, but secured himself a vast number

of adherents by involving their guilt and interest in his own. He raised a considerable army of Flemings, in order to strengthen himself against another turn of the same instability which had raised him to the throne; and, in imitation of the measures of the late king, he concluded all by giving a charter of liberties as ample as the people at that time aspired to. This charter contained a renunciation of the forests made by his predecessor, a grant to the ecclesiastics of a jurisdiction over their own vassals, and to the people in general an immunity from unjust tallages and exactions. It is remarkable, that the oath of allegiance taken by the nobility on this occasion was conditional: it was to be observed so long as the king observed the terms of his charter, — a condition which added no real security to the rights of the subject, but which proved a fruitful source of dissension, tumult, and civil violence.

The measures which the king hitherto pursued were dictated by sound policy; but he took another step to secure his throne, which in fact took away all its security, and at the same time brought the country to extreme misery, and to the brink of utter ruin.

At the Conquest there were very few fortifications in the kingdom. William found it necessary for his security to erect several. During the struggles of the English, the Norman nobility were permitted (as in reason it could not be refused) to fortify their own houses. It was, however, still understood that no new fortress could be erected without the king's special license. These private castles began very early to embarrass the government. The royal castles were scarcely less troublesome: for, as everything was then in tenure, the governor held his place by the tenure of castle-guard; and thus, instead of a simple officer, subject to his pleasure, the king had to deal with a feudal tenant, secure against him by law, if he performed his services, and by force, if he was unwilling to perform them. Every resolution of government required a sort of civil war to put it in execution. The two last kings had taken and demolished several of these castles; but when they found the reduction of any of them difficult, their custom frequently was, to erect another close by it, tower against tower, ditch against ditch: these were called Malvoisins, from their purpose and situation. Thus, instead of removing, they in fact doubled the mischief. Stephen, perceiving the passion of the barons for these castles, among other popular acts in the beginning of his reign, gave a general license for erecting them. Then was seen to arise in every corner of the kingdom, in every petty seigniory, an inconceivable multitude of strongholds, the seats of violence, and the receptacles of murderers, felons, debasers of the coin, and all manner of desperate and abandoned villains. Eleven hundred and fifteen of these castles were built in this single reign. The barons, having thus shut out the law, made continual inroads upon each other, and spread war, rapine, burning, and desolation throughout the whole kingdom. They infested the highroads, and put a stop to all trade by plundering the merchants and travellers. Those who dwelt in the open country they forced into their castles, and after pillaging them of all their visible substance, these tyrants held them in dungeons, and tortured them with a thousand cruel inventions to extort a discovery of their hidden wealth. The lamentable representation given by history of those barbarous times justifies the

pictures in the old romances of the castles of giants
and magicians. A great part of Europe was in the
same deplorable condition. It was then that some
gallant spirits, struck with a generous indignation at
the tyranny of these miscreants, blessed solemnly by
the bishop, and followed by the praises and vows of
the people, sallied forth to vindicate the chastity of
women and to redress the wrongs of travellers and
peaceable men. The adventurous humor inspired by
the Crusade heightened and extended this spirit; and
thus the idea of knight-errantry was formed.

A. D. 1138.   Stephen felt personally these inconveniences; but because the evil was too stubborn to be redressed at once, he resolved to proceed
gradually, and to begin with the castles of the bishops, — as they evidently held them, not only against
the interests of the crown, but against the canons
of the Church. From the nobles he expected no
opposition to this design : they beheld with envy the
pride of these ecclesiastical fortresses, whose battle-
ments seemed to insult the poverty of the lay barons.
This disposition, and a want of unanimity among the
clergy themselves, enabled Stephen to succeed in his
attempt against the Bishop of Salisbury, one of the
first whom he attacked, and whose castles, from their
strength and situation, were of the greatest importance. But the affairs of this prince were so circumstanced that he could pursue no council that was not
dangerous. His breach with the clergy let in the party of his rival, Matilda. This party was supported by
Robert, Earl of Gloucester, natural son to the late king,
— a man powerful by his vast possessions, but more
formidable through his popularity, and the courage and
abilities by which he had acquired it. Several other

circumstances weakened the cause of Stephen. The charter, and the other favorable acts, the scaffolding of his ambition, when he saw the structure raised, he threw down and contemned. In order to maintain his troops, as well as to attach men to his cause, where no principle bound them, vast and continual largesses became necessary: all his legal revenue had been dissipated; and he was therefore obliged to have recourse to such methods of raising money as were evidently illegal. These causes every day gave some accession of strength to the party against him; the friends of Matilda were encouraged to appear in arms; a civil war ensued, long A. D. 1139. and bloody, prosecuted as chance or a blind rage directed, by mutual acts of cruelty and treachery, by frequent surprisals and assaults of castles, and by a number of battles and skirmishes fought to no determinate end, and in which nothing of the military art appeared, but the destruction which it caused. Various, on this occasion, were the reverses of fortune, while Stephen, though embarrassed by the weakness of his title, by the scantiness of his finances, and all the disorders which arose from both, supported his tottering throne with wonderful activity and courage; but being at length defeated and made A. D. 1141. prisoner under the walls of Lincoln, the clergy openly declare for Matilda. The city of London, though unwillingly, follows the example of the clergy. The defection from Stephen was growing universal.

But Matilda, puffed up with a greatness which as yet had no solid foundation and stood merely in personal favor, shook it in the minds of all men by assuming, together with the insolence of conquest, the haughty rigor of an established dominion. Her title appeared but too good in the resemblance she bore to the pride of the former kings. This made the first ill success in her affairs fatal. Her great support, the Earl of Gloucester, was in his turn made prisoner. In exchange for his liberty that of Stephen was procured, who renewed the war with his usual vigor. As he apprehended an attempt from Scotland in favor of Matilda, descended from the blood royal of that nation, to balance this weight, he persuaded the King of France to declare in his favor, alarmed as he was by the progress of Henry, the son of Matilda, and Geoffrey, Count of Anjou. This prince, no more than sixteen years of age, after receiving knighthood from David, King of Scotland, began to display a courage and capacity destined to the greatest things. Of a complexion which strongly inclined to pleasure, he listened to nothing but ambition; at an age which is usually given up to passion, he submitted delicacy to politics, and even in his marriage only remembered the interests of a sovereign, — for, without examining too scrupulously into her character, he married Eleanor, the heiress of Guienne, though divorced from her husband for her supposed gallantries in the Holy Land. He made use of the accession of power which he acquired by this match to assert his birthright to Normandy. This he did with great success, because he was favored by the general inclination of the people for the blood of their ancient lords. Flushed with this prosperous beginning, he aspired to greater things; he obliged the King of France to submit to a truce; and then he turned his arms to support the rights of his family in England, from whence Matilda retired, unequal to the troublesome part she had long acted. Worn out with age, and the clashing of furious factions, she shut herself up in a monastery, and left to her son the succession of a civil war. Stephen was now pressed with renewed vigor. Henry had rather the advantage in the field ; Stephen had the possession of the government. Their fortunes appearing nearly balanced, and the fuel of dissension being consumed by a continual and bloody war of thirteen years, an accommodation was proposed and accepted. Henry found it dangerous to refuse his consent, as the bishops and barons, even of his own party, dreaded the consequences, if a prince, in the prime of an ambitious youth, should establish an hereditary title by the force of foreign arms. This treaty, signed at Wallingford, left the possession A. D. 1153. of the crown for his life to Stephen, but secured the succession to Henry, whom that prince adopted. The castles erected in this reign were to be demolished ; the exorbitant grants of the royal demesne to be resumed. To the son of Stephen all his private possessions were secured.

Thus ended this tedious and ruinous civil war. Stephen survived it near two years ; and now, finding himself more secure as the lawful tenant than he had been as the usurping proprietor of the crown, he no longer governed on the maxims of necessity. He made no new attempts in favor of his family, but spent the remainder of his reign in correcting the disorders which arose from his steps in its commencement, and in healing the wounds of so long and cruel a war. Thus he left the kingdom in peace to his successor, but his character, as it is usual where party is concerned, greatly disputed. Wherever

his natural dispositions had room to exert themselves, they appeared virtuous and princely ; but
the lust to reign, which often attends great virtues,
was fatal to his, frequently hid them, and always rendered them suspected.

CHAPTER VI.

REIGN OF HENRY II.

A. D. 1154. THE death of Stephen left an undisputed
succession for the first time since the death
of Edward the Confessor.   Henry, descended equally
from the Norman Conqueror and the old English
kings, adopted by Stephen, acknowledged by the
barons, united in himself every kind of title.   It
was grown into a custom for the king to grant a
charter of liberties on his accession to the crown.
Henry also granted a charter of that kind, confirming that of his grandfather ; but as his situation was
very different from that of his predecessors, his charter was different, — reserved, short, dry, conceived in
general terms, — a gift, not a bargain.   And, indeed,
there seems to have been at that juncture but little
occasion to limit a power which seemed not more
than sufficient to correct all the evils of an unlimited
liberty.   Henry spent the beginning of his reign in
repairing the ruins of the royal authority, and in restoring to the kingdom peace and order, along with
its ancient limits ; and he may well be considered as
the restorer of the English monarchy.   Stephen had
sacrificed the demesne of the crown, and many of its
rights, to his subjects ; and the necessity of the times

obliged both that prince and the Empress Matilda to purchase, in their turns, the precarious friendship of the King of Scotland by a cession of almost all the country north of the Humber. But Henry obliged the King of Scotland to restore his acquisitions, and to renew his homage. He took the same methods with his barons. Not sparing the grants of his mother, he resumed what had been so lavishly squandered by both of the contending parties, who, to establish their claims, had given away almost everything that made them valuable. There never was a prince in Europe who better understood the advantages to be derived from its peculiar constitution, in which greater acquisitions of dominion are made by judicious marriages than by success in war: for, having added to his patrimonial territories of Anjou and Normandy the Duchy of Guienne by his own marriage, the male issue of the Dukes of Brittany failing, he took the opportunity of marriage his third son, Geoffrey, then an infant, to A. D. 1158. the heiress of that important province, an infant also; and thus uniting by so strong a link his northern to his southern dominions, he possessed in his own name, or in those of his wife and son, all that fine and extensive country that is washed by the Atlantic Ocean, from Picardy quite to the foot of the Pyrenees.

Henry, possessed of such extensive territories, and aiming at further acquisitions, saw with indignation that the sovereign authority in all of them, especially in England, had been greatly diminished. By his resumptions he had, indeed, lessened the greatness of several of the nobility. He had by force of arms reduced those who forcibly held the crown lands, and deprived them of their own estates for their

rebellion. He demolished many castles, those perpetual resources of rebellion and disorder. But the
great aim of his policy was to break the power of
the clergy, which each of his predecessors, since Edward, had alternately strove to raise and to depress,
— at first in order to gain that potent body to their
interests, and then to preserve them in subjection
to the authority which they had conferred. The
clergy had elected Stephen; they had deposed Stephen, and elected Matilda; and in the instruments
which they used on these occasions they affirmed
in themselves a general right of electing the kings
of England. Their share both in the elevation and
depression of that prince showed that they possessed
a power inconsistent with the safety and dignity
of the state. The immunities which they enjoyed
seemed no less prejudicial to the civil economy, —
and the rather, as, in the confusion of Stephen's
reign, many, to protect themselves from the prevailing violence of the time, or to sanctify their own
disorders, had taken refuge in the clerical character.
The Church was never so full of scandalous persons, who, being accountable only in the ecclesiastical
courts, where no crime is punished with death, were
guilty of every crime. A priest had about this time
committed a murder attended with very aggravat-
ing circumstances. The king, willing at once to
restore order and to depress the clergy, laid hold
of this favorable opportunity to convoke the cause to
his own court, when the atrociousness of the crime
made all men look with an evil eye upon the claim
of any privilege which might prevent the severest
justice. The nation in general seemed but little
inclined to controvert so useful a regulation with
so potent a prince.

Amidst this general acquiescence one man was found bold enough to oppose him, who for eight years together embroiled all his affairs, poisoned his satisfactions, endangered his dominions, and at length in his death triumphed over all the power and policy of this wise and potent monarch. This was Thomas à-Becket, a man memorable for the great glory and the bitter reproaches he has met with from posterity. This person was the son of a respectable citizen of London. He was bred to the study of the civil and canon law, the education then used to qualify a man for public affairs, in which he soon made a distinguished figure. By the royal favor and his own abilities, he rose, in a rapid succession through several considerable employments, from an office under the sheriff of London, to be High Chancellor of the kingdom. In this high post he showed a spirit as elevated; but it was rather a military spirit than that of the gownman, — magnificent to excess in his living and appearance, and distinguishing himself in the tournaments and other martial sports of that age with much ostentation of courage and expense. The king, who favored him greatly, and expected a suitable return, on the vacancy, destined Becket, yet a layman, to the see of Canterbury, and hoped to find in him a warm promoter of the reformation he intended. Hardly a priest, he was made the first prelate in the kingdom. But no sooner A. D. 1162. was he invested with the clerical character than the whole tenor of his conduct was seen to change all at once: of his pompous retinue a few plain servants only remained ; a monastic temperance regulated his table ; and his life, in all respects formed to the most rigid austerity, seemed to prepare him for that superiority he was resolved to assume, and the conflicts he foresaw he must undergo in this attempt.

It will not be unpleasing to pause a moment at this remarkable period, in order to view in what consisted that greatness of the clergy, which enabled them to bear so very considerable a sway in all public affairs, — what foundations supported the weight of so vast a power, — whence it had its origin, — what was the nature, and what the ground, of the immunities they claimed, — that we may the more fully enter into this important controversy, and may not judge, as some have inconsiderately done, of the affairs of those times by ideas taken from the present manners and opinions.

It is sufficiently known, that the first Christians, avoiding the Pagan tribunals, tried most even of their civil causes before the bishop, who, though he had no direct coercive power, yet, wielding the sword of excommunication, had wherewithal to enforce the execution of his judgments. Thus the bishop had a considerable sway in temporal affairs, even before he was owned by the temporal power. But the Emperors no sooner became Christian than, the idea of profaneness being removed from the secular tribunals, the causes of the Christian laity naturally passed to that resort where those of the generality had been before. But the reverence for the bishop still remained, and the remembrance of his former jurisdiction. It was not thought decent, that he, who had been a judge in his own court, should become a suitor in the court of another. The body of the clergy likewise, who were supposed to have no secular concerns for which they could litigate, and removed by their character from all suspicion of violence, were left to be tried by their own ecclesiastical superiors. This was, with a little variation, sometimes in extending, sometimes in restraining the bishops' jurisdiction, the condition of things whilst the Roman Empire subsisted. But though their immunities were great and their possessions ample, yet, living under an absolute form of government, they were powerful only by influence. No jurisdictions were annexed to their lands; they had no place in the senate; they were no order in the state.

From the settlement of the Northern nations the clergy must be considered in another light. The Barbarians gave them large landed possessions; and by giving them land, they gave them jurisdiction, which, according to their notions, was inseparable from it. They made them an order in the state; and as all the orders had their privileges, the clergy had theirs, and were no less steady to preserve and ambitious to extend them. Our ancestors, having united the Church dignities to the secular dignities of baronies, had so blended the ecclesiastical with the temporal power in the same persons that it became almost impossible to separate them. The ecclesiastical was, however, prevalent in this composition, drew to it the other, supported it, and was supported by it. But it was not the devotion only, but the necessity of the times, that raised the clergy to the excess of this greatness. The little learning which then subsisted remained wholly in their hands. Few among the laity could even read; consequently the clergy alone were proper for public affairs. They were the statesmen, they were the lawyers; from them were often taken the bailiffs of the seigneurial courts, sometimes the sheriffs of counties, and almost constantly the justiciaries of the kingdom.* The Norman kings, always jealous of their order, were always forced to employ them. In abbeys the law was studied; abbeys were the palladiums of the public liberty by the cusody of the royal charters and most of the records. Thus, necessary to the great by their knowledge, venerable to the poor by their hospitality, dreadful to all by the power of excommunication, the character of the clergy was exalted above everything in the state; and it could no more be otherwise in those days than it is possible it should be so in ours.

William the Conqueror made it one principal point of his politics to reduce the clergy; but all the steps he took in it were not equally well calculated to answer this intention. When he subjected the Church lands to military service, the clergy complained bitterly, as it lessened their revenue: but I imagine it did not lessen their power in proportion; for by this regulation they came, like other great lords, to have their military vassals, who owed them homage and fealty; and this rather increased their consideration amongst so martial a people. The kings who succeeded him, though they also aimed at reducing the ecclesiastical power, never pursued their scheme on a great or legislative principle. They seemed rather desirous of enriching themselves by the abuses in the Church than earnest to correct them. One day they plundered and the next day they founded monasteries, as their rapaciousness or their scruples chanced to predominate; so that every attempt of that kind, having rather the air of tyranny than reformation, could never be heartily approved or seconded by the body of the people.

* Seld. Tithes, p. 482.

The bishops must always be considered in the double capacity of clerks and barons. Their courts, therefore, had a double jurisdiction: over the clergy and laity of their diocese for the cognizance of crimes against ecclesiastical law, and over the vassals of their barony as lords paramount. But these two departments, so different in their nature, they frequently confounded, by making use of the spiritual weapon of excommunication to enforce the judgments of both; and this sentence, cutting off the party from the common society of mankind, lay equally heavy on all ranks: for, as it deprived the lower sort of the fellowship of their equals and the protection of their lord, so it deprived the lord of the services of his vassals, whether he or they lay under the sentence. This was one of the grievances which the king proposed to redress.

As some sanction of religion is mixed with almost every concern of civil life, and as the ecclesiastical court took cognizance of all religious matters, it drew to itself not only all questions relative to tithes and advowsons, but whatever related to marriages, wills, the estate of intestates, the breaches of oaths and contracts, — in a word, everything which did not touch life or feudal property.

The ignorance of the bailiffs in lay courts, who were only possessed of some feudal maxims and the traditions of an uncertain custom, made this recourse to the spiritual courts the more necessary, where they could judge with a little more exactness by the lights of the canon and civil laws.

This jurisdiction extended itself by connivance, by necessity, by custom, by abuse, over lay persons and affairs. But the immunity of the clergy from lay cognizances was claimed, not only as a privilege essential to the dignity of their order, supported by the canons, and countenanced by the Roman law, but as a right confirmed by all the ancient laws of England.

Christianity, coming into England out of the bosom of the Roman Empire, brought along with it all those ideas of immunity. The first trace we can find of this exemption from lay jurisdiction in England is in the laws of Ethelred; * it is more fully established in those of Canute; † but in the code of Henry I. it is twice distinctly affirmed.‡ This immunity from the secular jurisdiction, whilst it seemed to encourage acts of violence in the clergy towards others, encouraged also the violence of others against them. The murder of a clerk could not be punished at this time by death; it was against a spiritual person, an offence wholly spiritual, of which the secular courts took no sort of cognizance. In the Saxon times two circumstances made such an exemption less a cause of jealousy: the sheriff sat with the bishop, and the spiritual jurisdiction was, if not under the control, at least under the inspection of the lay officer; and then, as neither laity nor clergy were capitally punished for any offence, this privilege did not create so invidious and glaring a distinction between them. Such was the power of the clergy, and such the immunities, which the king proposed to diminish.

Becket, who had punished the ecclesiastic for his

---

* LL. Ethelred. Si presbyter homicida fieret, &c.

† LL. Cnuti, 38, De Ministro Altaris Homicida. Idem, 40, De Ordinato Capitis reo.

‡ LL. H. I. 57, De Querela Vicinorum; and 56 [66 ?]. De Ordinato qui Vitam forisfaciat, in Fœd. Alured. et Guthurn., apud Spel Concil. 376, 1st vol.; LL. Edw. et Guthurn., 3, De Correctione Ordinatorum.

crime by ecclesiastical law, refused to deliver him over
to the secular judges for further punishment, on the
principle of law, that no man ought to be twice questioned for the same offence. The king, pro- A. D. 1164.
voked at this opposition, summoned a coun-
cil of the barons and bishops at Clarendon ; and here,
amongst others of less moment, the following were
unanimously declared to be the ancient prerogatives
of the crown. And it is something remarkable, and
certainly makes much for the honor of their moderation, that the bishops and abbots who must have composed so large and weighty a part of the great council
seem not only to have made no opposition to regulations which so remarkably contracted their jurisdiction, but even seem to have forwarded them.

1st. A clerk accused of any crime shall appear in
the king's court, that it may be judged whether he
belongs to ecclesiastical or secular cognizance. If
to the former, a deputy shall go into the bishop's
court to observe the trial; if the clerk be convicted,
he shall be delivered over to the king's justiciary to
be punished.

2nd. All causes concerning presentation, all causes concerning Frankalmoign, all actions concerning
breach of faith, shall be tried in the king's court.

3rd. The king's tenant *in capite* shall not be excommunicated without the king's license.

4th. No clerk shall go out of the kingdom without
giving security that he will do nothing to the prejudice of the king or nation. And all appeals shall be
tried at home.

These are the most material of the Constitutions or
Assizes of Clarendon, famous for having been the first
legal check given to the power of the clergy in Eng-

land. To give these constitutions the greater weight, it was thought proper that they should be confirmed by a bull from the Pope. By this step the king seemed to doubt the entireness of his own authority in his dominions; and by calling in foreign aid when it served his purpose, he gave it a force and a sort of legal sanction when it came to be employed against himself. But as no negotiation had prepared the Pope in favor of laws designed in reality to abridge his own power, it was no wonder that he rejected them with indignation. Becket, who had not been prevailed on to accept them but with infinite reluctance, was no sooner apprised of the Pope's disapprobation than he openly declared his own; he did penance in the humblest manner for his former acquiescence, and resolved to make amends for it by opposing the new constitutions with the utmost zeal. In this disposition the king saw that the Archbishop might be more easily ruined than humbled, and his ruin was resolved. Immediately a number of suits, on various pretences, were commenced against him, in every one of which he was sure to be foiled; but these making no deadly blow at his fortunes, he was called to account for thirty thousand pounds which he was accused of having embezzled during his chancellorship. It was in vain that he pleaded a full acquittance from the king's son, and Richard de Lucy, the guardian and justiciary of the kingdom, on his resignation of the seals; he saw it was already determined against him. Far from yielding under these repeated blows, he raised still higher the ecclesiastical pretensions, now become necessary to his own protection. He refused to answer to the charge, and appealed to the Pope, to whom alone he seemed to acknowledge any real subjection. A great ferment ensued on this appeal. The courtiers advised that he should be thrown into prison, and that his temporalities should be seized. The bishops, willing to reduce Becket without reducing their own order, proposed to accuse him before the Pope, and to pursue him to degradation. Some of his friends pressed him to give up his cause; others urged him to resign his dignity. The king's servants threw out menaces against his life. Amidst this general confusion of passions and councils, whilst every one according to his interests expected the event with much anxiety, Becket, in the disguise of a monk, escaped out of the nation, and threw himself into the arms of the King of France.

Henry was greatly alarmed at this secession, which put the Archbishop out of his power, but left him in full possession of all his ecclesiastical weapons. An embassy was immediately dispatched to Rome, in order to accuse Becket; but as Becket pleaded the Pope's own cause before the Pope himself, he obtained an easy victory over the king's ambassadors. Henry, on the other hand, took every measure to maintain his authority: he did everything worthy of an able politician, and of a king tenacious of his just authority. He likewise took measures not only to humble Becket, but also to lower that chair whose exaltation had an ill influence on the throne: for he encouraged the Bishop of London to revive a claim to the primacy; and thus, by making the rights of the see at least dubious, he hoped to render future prelates more cautious in the exercise of them. He inhibited, under the penalty of high treason, all ecclesiastics from going out of his dominions without license, or any emissary of the Pope's or Archbishop's

from entering them with letters of excommunication
or interdict. And that he might not supply arms
against himself, the Peter-pence were collected with
the former care, but detained in the royal treasury,
that matter might be left to Rome both for hope and
fear. In the personal treatment of Becket all the
proceedings were full of anger, and by an unnecessary and unjust severity greatly discredited both the
cause and character of the king; for he stripped of
their goods and banished all the Archbishop's kindred, all who were in any sort connected with him,
without the least regard to sex, age, or condition.
In the mean time, Becket, stung with these affronts,
impatient of his banishment, and burning with all
the fury and the same zeal which had occasioned it,
continually threatened the king with the last exertions of ecclesiastical power; and all things were
thereby, and by the absence and enmity of the head
of the English Church, kept in great confusion.

During this unhappy contention several treaties
were set on foot; but the disposition of all the parties who interested themselves in this quarrel very
much protracted a determination in favor of either
side. With regard to Rome, the then Pope was Al-
exander the Third, one of the wisest prelates who
had ever governed that see, and the most zealous for
extending its authority. However, though incessant-
ly solicited by Becket to excommunicate the king and
to lay the kingdom under an interdict, he was unwilling to keep pace with the violence of that enraged
bishop. Becket's view was single; but the Pope had
many things to consider: an Antipope then subsisted, who was strongly supported by the Emperor; and
Henry had actually entered into a negotiation with

this Emperor and this pretended Pope. On the other hand, the king knew that the lower sort of people in England were generally affected to the Archbishop, and much under the influence of the clergy. He was therefore fearful to drive the Pope to extremities by wholly renouncing his authority. These dispositions in the two principal powers made way for several conferences leading to peace. But for a long time all their endeavors seemed rather to inflame than to allay the quarrel. Whilst the king, steady in asserting his rights, remembered with bitterness the Archbishop's opposition, and whilst the Archbishop maintained the claims of the Church with an haughtiness natural to him, and which was only augmented by his sufferings, the King of France appeared sometimes to forward, sometimes to perplex the negotiation : and this duplicity seemed to be dictated by the situation of his affairs. He was desirous of nourishing a quarrel which put so redoubted a vassal on the defensive ; but he was also justly fearful of driving so powerful a prince to forget that he was a vassal. All parties, however, wearied at length with a contest by which all were distracted, and which in its issue promised nothing favorable to any of them, yielded at length to an accommodation, founded rather on an oblivion and silence of past disputes than on the settlement of terms for preserving future tranquillity.

Becket returned in a sort of triumph to his see. Many of the dignified clergy, and not a few of the barons, lay under excommunication for the share they had in his persecution ; but, neither broken by adversity nor softened by good fortune, he relented nothing of his severity, but referred them all for their absolution to the Pope. Their resentments were revived with additional bitterness ; new affronts were offered to the Archbishop, which brought on new excommunications and interdicts. The contention thickened on all sides, and things seemed running precipitately to the former dangerous extremities, when the account of these contests was brought, with much aggravation against Becket, to the ears of the king, then in Normandy, who, foreseeing a new series of troubles, broke out in a violent passion of grief and anger, — "I have no friends, or I had not so long been insulted by this haughty priest !" Four knights who attended near his person, thinking that the complaints of a king are orders for revenge, and hoping a reward equal to the importance and even guilt of the service, silently departed ; and passing with great diligence into England, in a short time they arrived at Canterbury. They entered the cathedral ; they fell on the Archbishop, just on the point of celebrating divine service, and with repeated blows of their clubs they beat him to the ground, they broke his skull in pieces, and covered the altar with his blood and brains.

A. D. 1171.   The horror of this barbarous action, increased by the sacredness of the person who suffered and of the place where it was committed, diffused itself on all sides with incredible rapidity. The clergy, in whose cause he fell, equalled him to the most holy martyrs ; compassion for his fate made all men forget his faults ; and the report of frequent miracles at his tomb sanctified his cause and character, and threw a general odium on the king. What became of the murderers is uncertain : they were neither protected by the king nor punished by the laws, for the reason we have not long since mentioned

The king with infinite difficulty extricated himself from the consequences of this murder, which threatened, under the Papal banners, to arm all Europe against him; nor was he absolved, but by renouncing the most material parts of the Constitutions of Clarendon, by purging himself upon oath of the murder of Becket, by doing a very humiliating penance at his tomb to expiate the rash words which had given occasion to his death, and by engaging to furnish a large sum of money for the relief of the Holy Land, and taking the cross himself as soon as his affairs should admit it. The king probably thought his freedom from the haughtiness of Becket cheaply purchased by these condescensions: and without question, though Becket might have been justifiable, perhaps even laudable, for his steady maintenance of the privileges which his Church and his order had acquired by the care of his predecessors, and of which he by his place was the depository, yet the principles upon which he supported these privileges, subversive of all good government, his extravagant ideas of Church power, the schemes he meditated, even to his death, to extend it yet further, his violent and unreserved attachment to the Papacy, and that inflexible spirit which all his virtues rendered but the more dangerous, made his death as advantageous, at that time, as the means by which it was effected were sacrilegious and detestable.

Between the death of Becket and the king's absolution he resolved on the execution of a design by which he reduced under his dominion a country not more separated from the rest of Europe by its situation than by the laws, customs, and way of life of the inhabitants: for the people of Ireland, with no difference but that of religion, still retained the native manners of the original Celtæ. The king had meditated this design from the very beginning of his reign, and had obtained a bull from the then Pope, Adrian the Fourth, an Englishman, to authorize the attempt. He well knew, from the internal weakness and advantageous situation of this noble island, the easiness and importance of such a conquest. But at this particular time he was strongly urged to his engaging personally in the enterprise by two other powerful motives. For, first, the murder of Becket had bred very ill humors in his subjects, the chiefs of whom, always impatient of a long peace, were glad of any pretence for rebellion; it was therefore expedient, and serviceable to the crown, to find an employment abroad for this spirit, which could not exert itself without being destructive at home. And next, as he had obtained the grant of Ireland from the Pope, upon condition of subjecting it to Peter-pence, he knew that the speedy performance of this condition would greatly facilitate his recovering the good graces of the court of Rome. Before we give a short narrative of the reduction of Ireland, I propose to lay open to the reader the state of that kingdom, that we may see what grounds Henry had to hope for success in this expedition.

Ireland is about half as large as England. In the temperature of the climate there is little difference, other than that more rain falls; as the country is more mountainous, and exposed full to the westerly wind, which, blowing from the Atlantic Ocean, prevails during the greater part of the year. This moisture, as it has enriched the country with large and frequent rivers, and spread out a number of fair and

magnificent lakes beyond the proportion of other places, has on the other hand incumbered the island
with an uncommon multitude of bogs and morasses;
so that in general it is less praised for corn than pasturage, in which no soil is more rich and luxuriant.
Whilst it possesses these internal means of wealth, it
opens on all sides a great number of ports, spacious
and secure, and by their advantageous situation inviting to universal commerce. But on these ports,
better known than those of Britain in the time of the
Romans, at this time there were few towns, scarce
any fortifications, and no trade that deserves to be
mentioned.

The people of Ireland lay claim to a very extravagant antiquity, through a vanity common to all nations. The accounts which are given by their ancient chronicles of their first settlements are generally tales confuted by their own absurdity. The
settlement of the greatest consequence, the best au-
thenticated, and from which the Irish deduce the
pedigree of the best families, is derived from Spain:
it was called Clan Milea, or the descendants of Mile-
sius, and Kin Scuit, or the race of Scyths, afterwards
known by the name of Scots. The Irish historians
suppose this race descended from a person called
Gathel, a Scythian by birth, an Egyptian by education, the contemporary and friend of the prophet
Moses. But these histories, seeming clear-sighted in
the obscure affairs of so blind an antiquity, instead
of passing for treasuries of ancient facts, are regarded
by the judicious as modern fictions. In cases of this
sort rational conjectures are more to be relied on
than improbable relations. It is most probable that
Ireland was first peopled from Britain. The coasts

of these countries are in some places in sight of each other. The language, the manners, and religion of the most ancient inhabitants of both are nearly the same. The Milesian colony, whenever it arrived in Ireland, could have made no great change in the manners or language; as the ancient Spaniards were a branch of the Celtæ, as well as the old inhabitants of Ireland. The Irish language is not different from that of all other nations, as Temple and Rapin, from ignorance of it, have asserted; on the contrary, many of its words bear a remarkable resemblance not only to those of the Welsh and Armoric, but also to the Greek and Latin. Neither is the figure of the letters very different from the vulgar character, though their order is not the same with that of other nations, nor the names, which are taken from the Irish proper names of several species of trees: a circumstance which, notwithstanding their similitude to the Roman letters, argues a different original and great antiquity. The Druid discipline anciently flourished in that island. In the fourth century it fell down before the preaching of St. Patrick. Then the Christian religion was embraced and cultivated with an uncommon zeal, which displayed itself in the number and consequence of the persons who in all parts embraced the contemplative life. This mode of life, and the situation of Ireland, removed from the horror of those devastations which shook the rest of Europe, made it a refuge for learning, almost extinguished everywhere else. Science flourished in Ireland during the seventh and eighth centuries. The same cause which destroyed it in other countries also destroyed it there. The Danes, then pagans, made themselves masters of the island, after a long

and wasteful war, in which they destroyed the sciences along with the monasteries in which they were
cultivated. By as destructive a war they were at
length expelled ; but neither their ancient science
nor repose returned to the Irish, who, falling into
domestic distractions as soon as they were freed from
their foreign enemies, sunk quickly into a state of
ignorance, poverty, and barbarism, which must have
been very great, since it exceeded that of the rest
of Europe. The disorders in the Church were equal
to those in the civil economy, and furnished to the
Pope a plausible pretext for giving Henry a commission to conquer the kingdom, in order to reform it.

The Irish were divided into a number of tribes or
clans, each clan forming within itself a separate government. It was ordered by a chief, who was not
raised to that dignity either by election or by the ordinary course of descent, but as the eldest and worthiest of the blood of the deceased lord. This order
of succession, called Tanistry, was said to have been
invented in the Danish troubles, lest the tribe, during
a minority, should have been endangered for want of
a sufficient leader. It was probably much more ancient : but it was, however, attended with very great
and pernicious inconveniencies, as it was obviously an
affair of difficulty to determine who should be called
the worthiest of the blood ; and a door being always
left open for ambition, this order introduced a greater mischief than it was intended to remedy. Almost
every tribe, besides its contention with the neighboring tribes, nourished faction and discontent within itself. The chiefs we speak of were in general called
Tierna, or Lords, and those of more consideration
Riagh, or Kings. Over these were placed five kings

more eminent than the rest, answerable to the five
provinces into which the island was anciently divided.   These again were subordinate to one head, who
was called Monarch of all Ireland, raised to that power by election, or, more properly speaking, by violence.

Whilst the dignities of the state were disposed of
by a sort of election, the office of judges, who were
called Brehons, the trades of mechanics, and even
those arts which we are apt to consider as depending principally on natural genius, such as poetry and
music, were confined in succession to certain races:
the Irish imagining that greater advantages were to
be derived from an early institution, and the affection
of parents desirous of perpetuating the secrets of
their art in their families, than from the casual efforts
of particular fancy and application.   This is much in
the strain of the Eastern policy; but these and many
other of the Irish institutions, well enough calculated
to preserve good arts and useful discipline, when these
arts came to degenerate, were equally well calculated
to prevent all improvement and to perpetuate corruption, by infusing an invincible tenaciousness of ancient customs.

The people of Ireland were much more addicted to
pasturage than agriculture, not more from the quality of their soil than from a remnant of the Scythian
manners.   They had but few towns, and those not
fortified, each clan living dispersed over its own territory.   The few walled towns they had lay on the
sea-coast; they were built by the Danes, and held
after they had lost their conquests in the inland
parts: here was carried on the little foreign trade
which the island then possessed.

The Irish militia was of two kinds: one called

kerns, which were foot, slightly armed with a long knife or dagger, and almost naked ; the other, *gallog-lasses,* who were horse, poorly mounted, and generally armed only with a battle-axe. Neither horse nor foot made much use of the spear, the sword, or the bow. With indifferent arms, they had still worse discipline. In these circumstances, their natural bravery, which, though considerable, was not superior to that of their invaders, stood them in little stead.

Such was the situation of things in Ireland, when Dermot, King of Leinster, having violently carried away the wife of one of the neighboring petty sovereigns, Roderic, King of Connaught and Monarch of Ireland, joined with the injured husband to punish so flagrant an outrage, and with their united forces spoiled Dermot of his territories, and obliged him to abandon the kingdom. The fugitive prince, not unapprised of Henry's designs upon his country, threw himself at his feet, implored his protection, and promised to hold of him, as his feudatory, the sovereignty he should recover by his assistance. Henry was at this time at Guienne. Nothing could be more agreeable to him than such an incident ; but as his French dominions actually lay under an interdict, on account of his quarrel with Becket, and all his affairs, both at home and abroad, were in a troubled and dubious situation, it was not prudent to remove his person, nor venture any considerable body of his forces on a distant enterprise. Yet not willing to lose so favorable an opportunity, he warmly recommended the cause of Dermot to his regency in England, permitting and encouraging all persons to arm in his favor : a permission, in this age of enterprise, greedily accepted by many; but the person who

A. D. 1167.

brought the most assistance to it, and indeed gave
a form and spirit to the whole design, was Richard,
Earl of Strigul, commonly known by the name of
Strongbow. Dermot, to confirm in his interest this
potent and warlike peer, promised him his daughter
in marriage, with the reversion of his crown.

The beginnings of so great an enterprise were
formed with a very slender force. Not four hundred
men landed near Wexford: they took the
town by storm. When reinforced, they did
not exceed twelve hundred; but, being joined with
three thousand men by Dermot, with an incredible
rapidity of success they reduced Waterford, Dublin,
Limerick, the only considerable cities in Ireland. By
the novelty of their arms they had obtained some
striking advantages in their first engagements; and
by these advantages they attained a superiority of
opinion over the Irish, which every success increased.
Before the effect of this first impression had time to
wear off, Henry, having settled his affairs
abroad, entered the harbor of Cork with a
fleet of four hundred sail, at once to secure the conquest, and the allegiance of the conquerors. The fame
of so great a force arriving under a prince dreaded
by all Europe very soon disposed all the petty princes,
with their King Roderic, to submit and do homage
to Henry. They had not been able to resist the arms
of his vassals, and they hoped better treatment from
submitting to the ambition of a great king, who left
them everything but the honor of their independency, than from the avarice of adventurers, from which
nothing was secure. The bishops and the body of
the clergy greatly contributed to this submission,
from respect to the Pope, and the horror of their

A. D. 1169.

A. D. 1171.

late defeats, which they began to regard as judgments. A national council was held at Cashel for
bringing the Church of Ireland to a perfect conformity in rites and discipline to that of England. It is
not to be thought that in this council the temporal
interests of England were entirely forgotten. Many
of the English were established in their particular
conquests under the tenure of knights' service, now
first introduced into Ireland: a tenure which, if it
has not proved the best calculated to secure the obedience of the vassal to the sovereign, has never failed
in any instance of preserving a vanquished people
in obedience to the conquerors. The English lords
built strong castles on their demesnes; they put
themselves at the head of the tribes whose chiefs
they had slain; they assumed the Irish garb and
manners; and thus, partly by force, partly by policy, the first English families took a firm root in Ireland. It was, indeed, long before they were able entirely to subdue the island to the laws of England;
but the continual efforts of the Irish for more than
four hundred years proved insufficient to dislodge
them.

Whilst Henry was extending his conquests to the
western limits of the known world, the whole fabric
of his power was privately sapped and undermined,
and ready to overwhelm him with the ruins, in the
very moment when he seemed to be arrived at the
highest and most permanent point of grandeur and
glory. His excessive power, his continual accessions
to it, and an ambition which by words and actions
declared that the whole world was not sufficient for
a great man, struck a just terror into all the potentates near him: he was, indeed, arrived at that pitch

of greatness, that the means of his ruin could only
be found in his own family. A numerous offspring,
which is generally considered as the best defence of
the throne, and the support as well as ornament of
declining royalty, proved on this occasion the principal part of the danger. Henry had in his lawful bed,
besides daughters, four sons, Henry, Richard, Geoffrey, and John, all growing up with great hopes from
their early courage and love of glory. No father was
ever more delighted with these hopes, nor more tender and indulgent to his children. A custom had
long prevailed in France for the reigning king to
crown his eldest son in his lifetime. By this policy,
in turbulent times, and whilst the principles of succession were unsettled, he secured the crown to his
posterity. Henry gladly imitated a policy enforced
no less by paternal affection than its utility to public
peace. He had, during his troubles with Becket,
crowned his son Henry, then no more than sixteen
years old. But the young king, even on the day
of his coronation, discovered an haughtiness which
threatened not to content itself with the share of authority to which the inexperience of his youth and
the nature of a provisional crown confined him. The
name of a king continually reminded him that he
only possessed the name. The King of France,
whose daughter he had espoused, fomented a discontent which grew with his years. Geoffrey, who
had married the heiress of Bretagne, on the death
of her father claimed to no purpose the entire sovereignty of his wife's inheritance, which Henry, under a pretence of guardianship to a son of full age,
still retained in his hands. Richard had not the same
plausible pretences, but he had yet greater ambition.

He contended for the Duchy of Guienne before his mother's death, which alone could give him the color of a title to it. The queen, his mother, hurried on by her own unquiet spirit, or, as some think, stimulated by jealousy, encouraged their rebellion against her husband. The King of France, who moved all the other engines, engaged the King of Scotland, the Earl of Flanders, then a powerful prince, the Earl of Blois, and the Earl of Boulogne in the conspiracy. The barons in Bretagne, in Guienne, and even in England, were ready to take up arms in the same cause; whether it was that they perceived the uniform plan the king had pursued in order to their reduction, or were solely instigated by the natural fierceness and levity of their minds, fond of every dangerous novelty. The historians of that time seldom afford us a tolerable insight into the causes of the transactions they relate; but whatever were the causes of so extraordinary a conspiracy, it was not discovered until the moment it was ready for execution. The first token of it appeared in the young king's demand to have either England or Normandy given up to him. The refusal of this demand served as a signal to all parties to put themselves in motion. The younger Henry fled into France; Louis entered Normandy with a vast army; the barons of Bretagne under Geoffrey, and those of Guienne under Richard, rose in arms; the King of Scotland pierced into England; and the Earl of Leicester, at the head of fourteen thousand Flemings, landed in Suffolk.

It was on this trying occasion that Henry displayed a greatness independent of all fortune. For, beset by all the neighboring powers, opposed by his own children, betrayed by his wife, abandoned by one part of his subjects, uncertain of the rest, every part of his state rotten and suspicious, his magnanimity grew beneath the danger; and when all the ordinary resources failed, he found superior resources in his own courage, wisdom, and activity. There were at that time dispersed over Europe bodies of mercenary troops, called Brabançons, composed of fugitives from different nations, men who were detached from any country, and who, by making war a perpetual trade, and passing from service to service, had acquired an experience and military knowledge uncommon in those days. Henry took twenty thousand of these mercenaries into his service, and, as he paid them punctually, and kept them always in action, they served him with fidelity. The Papal authority, so often subservient, so often prejudicial to his designs, he called to his assistance in a cause which did not misbecome it, — the cause of a father attacked by his children. This took off the ill impression left by Becket's death, and kept the bishops firm in their allegiance. Having taken his measures with judgment, he pursued the war in Normandy with vigor. In this war his mercenaries had a great and visible advantage over the feudal armies of France: the latter, not so useful while they remained in the field, entered it late in the summer, and commonly left it in forty days. The King of France was forced to raise the siege of Verneuil, to evacuate Normandy, and agree to a truce. Then, at the head of his victorious Brabançons, Henry marched into Brittany with an incredible expedition. The rebellious army, astonished as much by the celerity of his march as the fury of his attack, was totally routed. The principal towns and castles were reduced soon

A. D. 1173.

after. The custody of the conquered country being lodged in faithful hands, he flew to the relief of England. There his natural son Geoffrey, Bishop elect of Ely, faithful during the rebellion of all his legitimate offspring, steadily maintained his cause, though with forces much inferior to his zeal. The king, before he entered into action, thought it expedient to perform his expiation at the tomb of Becket. Hardly had he finished this ceremony, when A.D. 1174. the news arrived that the Scotch army was totally defeated, and their king made prisoner. This victory was universally attributed to the prayers of Becket; and whilst it established the credit of the new saint, it established Henry in the minds of his people: they no longer looked upon their king as an object of the Divine vengeance, but as a penitent reconciled to Heaven, and under the special protection of the martyr he had made. The Flemish army, after several severe checks, capitulated to evacuate the kingdom. The rebellious barons submitted soon after. All was quiet in England; but the King of France renewed hostilities in Normandy, and laid siege to Rouen. Henry recruited his army with a body of auxiliary Welsh, arrived at Rouen with his usual expedition, raised the siege, and drove the King of France quite out of Normandy. It was then that he agreed to an accommodation, and in the terms of peace, which he dictated in the midst of victory to his sons, his subjects, and his enemies, there was seen on one hand the tenderness of a father, and on the other the moderation of a wise man, not insensible of the mutability of fortune.

The war which threatened his ruin being so happily ended, the greatness of the danger served only to enhance his glory; whilst he saw the King of France humbled, the Flemings defeated, the King of Scotland a prisoner, and his sons and subjects reduced to the bounds of their duty. He employed this interval of peace to secure its continuance, and to prevent a return of the like evils; for which reason he made many reforms in the laws and polity of his dominions. He instituted itinerant justices, to weaken the power of the great barons, and even of the sheriffs, who were hardly more obedient, — an institution which, with great public advantages, has remained to our times. In the spirit of the same policy he armed the whole body of the people : the English commonalty had been in a manner disarmed ever since the Conquest. In this regulation we may probably trace the origin of the militia, which, being under the orders of the crown rather in a political than a feudal respect, were judged more to be relied on than the soldiers of tenure, to whose pride and power they might prove a sort of counterpoise. Amidst these changes the affairs of the clergy remained untouched. The king had experienced how dangerous it was to attempt removing foundations so deeply laid both in strength and opinion. He therefore wisely aimed at acquiring the favor of that body, and turning to his own advantage a power he should in vain attempt to overthrow, but which he might set up against another power, which it was equally his interest to reduce.

Though these measures were taken with the greatest judgment, and seemed to promise a peaceful evening to his reign, the seeds of rebellion remained still at home, and the dispositions that nourished them were rather increased abroad. The parental author

A.D. 1176.

ity, respectable at all times, ought to have the greatest force in times when the manners are rude and
the laws imperfect. At that time Europe had not
emerged out of barbarism, yet this great natural bond
of society was extremely weak. The number of foi
eign obligations and duties almost dissolved the family obligations. From the moment a young man was
knighted, so far as related to his father, he became
absolute master of his own conduct; but he contracted at the same time a sort of filial relation with the
person who had knighted him. These various principles of duty distracted one another. The custom
which then prevailed, of bestowing lands and jurisdictions, under the name of Appanages, to the sons
of kings and the greater nobility, gave them a power
which was frequently employed against the giver;
and the military and licentious manners of the age
almost destroyed every trace of every kind of regular
authority. In the East, where the rivalship of brothers is so dangerous, such is the force of paternal power amongst a rude people, we scarce ever hear of a
son in arms against his father. In Europe, for several ages, it was very common. It was Henry's great
misfortune to suffer in a particular manner from this
disorder.

Philip succeeded Louis, King of France.
He followed closely the plan of his prede- A. D. 1180.
cessor, to reduce the great vassals, and the King of
England, who was the greatest of them; but he followed it with far more skill and vigor, though he
made use of the same instruments in the work. He
revived the spirit of rebellion in the princes, Henry's
sons. These young princes were never in harmony
with each other but in a confederacy against their

father, and the father had no recourse but in the melancholy safety derived from the disunion of his children. This he thought it expedient to increase; but such policy, when discovered, has always a dangerous effect. The sons, having just quarrelled enough to give room for an explanation of each other's designs, and to display those of their father, enter into a new conspiracy. In the midst of these motions the young king dies, and showed at his death such signs of a sincere repentance as served to revive the old king's tenderness, and to take away all comfort for his loss. The death of his third son, Geoffrey, followed close upon the heels of this funeral. He died at Paris, whither he had gone to concert measures against his father. Richard and John remained. Richard, fiery, restless, ambitious, openly took up arms, and pursued the war with implacable rancor, and such success as drove the king, in the decline of his life, to a dishonorable treaty; nor was he then content, but excited new troubles. John was his youngest and favorite child; in him he reposed all his hopes, and consoled himself for the undutifulness of his other sons; but after concluding the treaty with the King of France and Richard, he found too soon that John had been as deep as any in the conspiracy. This was his last wound: afflicted by his children in their deaths and harassed in their lives, mortified as a father and a king, worn down with cares and sorrows more than with years, he died, cursing his fortune, his children, and the hour of his birth. When he perceived that death approached him, by his own desire he was carried into a church and laid at the altar's foot. Hardly had he expired, when he was

A. D. 1183.

A. D. 1186.

A. D. 1189.

stripped, then forsaken by his attendants, and left a long time a naked and unheeded body in an empty church : affording a just consolation for the obscurity of a mean fortune, and an instructive lesson how little an outward greatness and enjoyments foreign to the mind contribute towards a solid felicity, in the example of one who was the greatest of kings and the unhappiest of mankind.

CHAPTER VII.

REIGN OF RICHARD I.

WHILST Henry lived, the King of France had always an effectual means of breaking his power by the divisions in his family. But now Rich- Richard I. ard succeeded to all the power of his father, A. D. 1189. with an equal ambition to extend it, with a temper infinitely more fiery and impetuous, and free from every impediment of internal dissension. These circumstances filled the mind of Philip with great and just uneasiness. There was no security but in finding exercise for the enterprising genius of the young king at a distance from home. The new Crusade afforded an advantageous opportunity. A little before his father's death, Richard had taken the cross in conjunction with the King of France. So precipitate were the fears of that monarch, that Richard was hardly crowned when ambassadors were dispatched to England to remind him of his obligation, and to pique his pride by acquainting him that their master was even then in readiness to fulfil his part of their common vow. An enterprise of this sort was extremely agreeable to the genius of Richard, where religion sanctified the thirst of military glory, and where the glory itself seemed but the more desirable by being unconnected with interest. He immediately accepted the proposal, and resolved to insure the success as well as the lustre of his expedition by the magnificence of his preparations. Not content with the immense treasures amassed by his father, he drew in vast sums by the sale of almost all the demesnes of the crown, and of every office under it, not excepting those of the highest trust. The clergy, whose wealth and policy enabled them to take advantage of the necessity and weakness of the Croises, were generally the purchasers of both. To secure his dominions in his absence, he made an alliance with the princes of Wales, and with the King of Scotland. To the latter he released, for a sum of money, the homage which had been extorted by his father.

His brother John gave him most uneasiness; but finding it unworthy, or impracticable, to use the severer methods of jealous policy, he resolved to secure his fidelity by loading him with benefits. He bestowed on him six earldoms, and gave him in marriage the Lady Avisa, sole heiress of the great house of Gloucester; but as he gave him no share in the regency, he increased his power, and left him discontented in a kingdom committed to the care of new men, who had merited their places by their money.

It will be proper to take a view of the condition of the Holy Land at the time when this third Crusade was set on foot to repair the faults committed in the two former. The conquests of the Croises, extending over Palestine and a part of Syria, had been erected into a sovereignty under the name

of the Kingdom of Jerusalem. This kingdom, ill-
ordered within, surrounded on all sides by powerful
enemies, subsisted by a strength not its own for
near ninety years. But dissensions arising about
the succession to the crown, between Guy of Lusig-
nan and Raymond, Earl of Tripoli, Guy, either because he thought the assistance of the European
princes too distant, or that he feared their decision,
called in the aid of Saladin, Sultan of Egypt. This
able prince immediately entered Palestine. As the
whole strength of the Christians in Palestine depended upon foreign succor, he first made himself
master of the maritime towns, and then Jerusalem
fell an easy prey to his arms; whilst the competitors
contended with the utmost violence for a kingdom
which no longer existed for either of them. All Europe was alarmed at this revolution. The banished
Patriarch of Jerusalem filled every place with the
distresses of the Eastern Christians. The Pope ordered a solemn fast to be forever kept for this loss,
and then, exerting all his influence, excited a new
Crusade, in which vast numbers engaged with an
ardor unabated by their former misfortunes; but
wanting a proper subordination rather than a sufficient force, they made but a slow progress, A. D. 1190.
when Richard and Philip, at the head of
more than one hundred thousand chosen men, the
one from Marseilles, the other from Genoa, set sail
to their assistance.

In his voyage to the Holy Land accident presented
Richard with an unexpected conquest. A   A. D. 1191.
vessel of his fleet was driven by a storm
to take shelter in the Isle of Cyprus. That island
was governed by a prince named Isaac, of the im-

perial family of the Comneni, who not only refused
all relief to the sufferers, but plundered them of
the little remains of their substance. Richard, re-
senting this inhospitable treatment, aggravated by
the insolence of the tyrant, turned his force upon
Cyprus, vanquished Isaac in the field, took the capital city, and was solemnly crowned king of that
island. But deeming it as glorious to give as to
acquire a crown, he soon after resigned it to Lusi
gnan, to satisfy him for his claim on Jerusalem; in
whose descendants it continued for several generations, until, passing by marriage into the family of
Cornaro, a Venetian nobleman, it was acquired to
that state, the only state in Europe which had any
real benefit by all the blood and treasure lavished
in the Holy War.

Richard arrived in Palestine some time after the
King of France. His arrival gave new vigor to the
operations of the Croises. He reduced Acre to surrender at discretion, which had been in vain besieged
for two years, and in the siege of which an infinite
number of Christians had perished; and so much
did he distinguish himself on this and on all occasions, that the whole expedition seemed to rest on his
single valor. The King of France, seeing him fully
engaged, had all that he desired. The climate was
disagreeable to his constitution, and the war, in
which he acted but a second part, to his pride.
He therefore hastened home to execute his projects against Richard, amusing him with oaths made
to be violated, — leaving, indeed, a part of his forces under the Duke of Burgundy, but with private
orders to give him underhand all possible obstruc-
tion. Notwithstanding the desertion of his ally,

Richard continued the war with uncommon alac·
rity. With very unequal numbers he engaged and
defeated the whole army of Saladin, and slew forty
thousand of his best troops. He obliged him to
evacuate all the towns on the sea-coast, and spread
the renown and terror of his arms over all Asia. A
thousand great exploits did not, however, enable him
to extend his conquests to the inland country. Jealousy, envy, cabals, and a total want of discipline
reigned in the army of the Croises. The climate,
and their intemperance more than the climate, wasted
them with a swift decay. The vow which brought
them to the Holy Land was generally for a limited
time, at the conclusion of which they were always
impatient to depart. Their armies broke up at the
most critical conjunctures, — as it was not the necessity of the service, but the extent of their vows,
which held them together. As soon, therefore, as
they had habituated themselves to the country, and
attained some experience, they were gone; and new
men supplied their places, to acquire experience by
the same misfortunes, and to lose the benefit of it by
the same inconstancy. Thus the war could never be
carried on with steadiness and uniformity. On the
other side, Saladin continually repaired his losses;
his resources were at hand; and this great captain
very judiciously kept possession of that mountainous
country which, formed by a perpetual ridge of Liba-
nus, in a manner walls in the sea-coast of Palestine.
There he hung, like a continual tempest, ready to
burst over the Christian army. On his rear was the
strong city of Jerusalem, which secured a communication with the countries of Chaldea and Mesopo-
tamia, from whence he was well supplied with every-

thing. If the Christians attempted to improve their successes by penetrating to Jerusalem, they had a city powerfully garrisoned in their front, a country wasted and destitute of forage to act in, and Saladin with a vast army on their rear advantageously posted to cut off their convoys and reinforcements.

Richard was laboring to get over these disadvantages, when he was informed by repeated expresses of the disorder of his affairs in Europe, — disorders which arose from the ill dispositions he had made at his departure. The heads of his regency had abused their power; they quarrelled with each other, and the nobility with them. A sort of a civil war had arisen, in which they were deposed. Prince John was the main spring of these dissensions; he engaged in a close communication of councils with the King of France, who had seized upon several places in Normandy. It was with regret that Richard found himself obliged to leave a theatre on which he had planned such an illustrious scene of action. A constant emulation in courtesy and politeness, as well as in military exploits, had been kept up between him and Saladin. He now concluded a truce with that generous enemy, and on his departure sent a messenger to assure him that on its expiration he would not fail to be again in Palestine. Saladin replied, that, if he must lose his kingdom, he would choose to lose it to the King of England. Thus Richard
A. 192
returned, leaving Jerusalem in the hands of the Saracens; and this end had an enterprise in which two of the most powerful monarchs in Europe were personally engaged, an army of upwards of one hundred thousand men employed, and to furnish which the whole Christian world had been vexed and

exhausted. It is a melancholy reflection, that the spirit of great designs can seldom be inspired, but where the reason of mankind is so uncultivated that they can be turned to little advantage.

With this war ended the fortune of Richard, who found the Saracens less dangerous than his Christian allies. It is not well known what motive induced him to land at Aquileia, at the bottom of the Gulf of Venice, in order to take his route by Germany; but he pursued his journey through the territories of the Duke of Austria, whom he had personally affronted at the siege of Acre. And now, neither keeping himself out of the power of that prince, nor rousing his generosity by seeming to confide in it, he attempted to get through his dominions in disguise. Sovereigns do not easily assume the private character; their pride seldom suffers their disguise to be complete: besides, Richard had made himself but too well known. The Duke, transported with the opportunity of base revenge, discovered him, seized him, and threw him into prison; from whence he was only released to be thrown into another. The Emperor claimed him, and, without regarding in this unfortunate captive the common dig- A. D. 1193. nity of sovereigns, or his great actions in the common cause of Europe, treated him with yet greater cruelty. To give a color of justice to his violence, he proposed to accuse Richard at the Diet of the Empire upon certain articles relative to his conduct in the Holy Land.

The news of the king's captivity caused the greatest consternation in all his good subjects; but it revived the hopes and machinations of Prince John, who bound himself by closer ties than ever to the

King of France, seized upon some strongholds in England, and, industriously spreading a report of his brother's death, publicly laid claim to the crown as lawful successor. All his endeavors, however, served only to excite the indignation of the people, and to attach them the more firmly to their unfortunate prince. Eleanor, the queen dowager, as good a mother as she had been a bad wife, acted with the utmost vigor and prudence to retain them in their duty, and omitted no means to procure the liberty of her son. The nation seconded her with a zeal, in their circumstances, uncommon. No tyrant ever imposed so severe a tax upon his people as the affection of the people of England, already exhausted, levied upon themselves. The most favored religious orders were charged on this occasion. The Church plate was sold. The ornaments of the most holy relics were not spared. And, indeed, nothing serves more to demonstrate the poverty of the kingdom, reduced by internal dissensions and remote wars, at that time, than the extreme difficulty of collecting the king's ransom, which amounted to no more than one hundred thousand marks of silver, Cologne weight. For raising this sum, the first taxation, the most heavy and general that was ever known in England, proved altogether insufficient. Another taxation was set on foot. It was levied with the same rigor as the former, and still fell short. Ambassadors were sent into Germany with all that could be raised, and with hostages for the payment of whatever remained. The king met these ambassadors as he was carried in chains to plead his cause before the Diet of the Empire. The ambassadors burst into tears at this affecting sight, and wept aloud; but Richard, though touched no

less with the affectionate loyalty of his subjects than
with his own fallen condition, preserved his dignity
entire in his misfortunes, and with a cheerful air inquired of the state of his dominions, the behavior of
the King of Scotland, and the fidelity of his brother,
the Count John. At the Diet, no longer protected
by the character of a sovereign, he was supported by
his personal abilities. He had a ready wit and great
natural eloquence; and his high reputation and the
weight of his cause pleading for him more strongly,
the Diet at last interested itself in his favor, and prevailed on the Emperor to accept an excessive ransom
for dismissing a prisoner whom he detained without
the least color of justice. Philip moved heaven and
earth to prevent his enlargement: he negotiated, he
promised, he flattered, he threatened, he outbid his
extravagant ransom. The Emperor, in his own nature more inclined to the bribe, which tempted him
to be base, hesitated a long time between these offers.
But as the payment of the ransom was more certain
than Philip's promises, and as the instances of the
Diet, and the menaces of the Pope, who protected
Richard, as a prince serving under the Cross, were of
more immediate consequence than his threats, Richard was at length released; and though it is said the
Emperor endeavored to seize him again, to extort an
other ransom, he escaped safely into England.

Richard, on his coming to England, found
all things in the utmost confusion; but be- A. D. 1194.
fore he attempted to apply a remedy to so obstinate
a disease, in order to wipe off any degrading ideas
which might have arisen from his imprisonment, he
caused himself to be new crowned. Then holding
his Court of Great Council at Southampton, he made

some useful regulations in the distribution of justice. He called some great offenders to a strict account. Count John deserved no favor, and he lay entirely at the king's mercy, who, by an unparalleled generosity, pardoned him his multiplied offences, only depriving him of the power of which he had made so bad a use. Generosity did not oblige him to forget the hostilities of the King of France. But to prosecute the war money was wanting, which new taxes and new devices supplied with difficulty and with dishonor. All the mean oppressions of a necessitous government were exercised on this occasion. All the grants which were made on the king's departure to the Holy Land were revoked, on the weak pretence that the purchasers had sufficient recompense whilst they held them. Necessity seemed to justify this, as well as many other measures that were equally violent. The whole revenue of the crown had been dissipated; means to support its dignity must be found; and these means were the least unpopular, as most men saw with pleasure the wants of government fall upon those who had started into a sudden greatness by taking advantage of those wants.

Richard renewed the war with Philip, which continued, though frequently interrupted by truces, for about five years. In this war Richard signalized himself by that irresistible courage which on all occasions gave him a superiority over the King of France. But his revenues were exhausted; a great scarcity reigned both in France and England; and the irregular manner of carrying on war in those days prevented a clear decision in favor of either party. Richard had still an eye on the Holy Land, which he considered as the only province worthy of

his arms; and this continually diverted his thoughts
from the steady prosecution of the war in France.
The Crusade, like a superior orb, moved along with
all the particular systems of politics of that time,
and suspended, accelerated, or put back all operations on motives foreign to the things themselves.
In this war it must be remarked that Richard made
a considerable use of the mercenaries who had been
so serviceable to Henry the Second; and the King
of France, perceiving how much his father, Louis,
had suffered by a want of that advantage, kept on
foot a standing army in constant pay, which none
of his predecessors had done before him, and which
afterwards for a long time very unaccountably fell
into disuse in both kingdoms.

Whilst this war was carried on by intervals and
starts, it came to the ears of Richard that a nobleman of Limoges had found on his lands a considerable hidden treasure.   The king, necessitous and
rapacious to the last degree, and stimulated by the
exaggeration and marvellous circumstances which
always attend the report of such discoveries, immediately sent to demand the treasure, under pretence
of the rights of seigniory.   The Limosin, either because he had really discovered nothing or that he
was unwilling to part with so valuable an acquisition, refused to comply with the king's demand, and
fortified his castle.   Enraged at the disappointment,
Richard relinquished the important affairs in which
he was engaged, and laid siege to this castle with all
the eagerness of a man who has his heart set upon a
trifle.   In this siege he received a wound from an
arrow, and it proved mortal; but in the last, as in all
the other acts of his life, something truly noble shone

out amidst the rash and irregular motions of his mind. The castle was taken before he died. The man from whom Richard had received the wound was brought before him. Being asked why he levelled his arrow at the king, he answered, with an undaunted countenance, " that the king with his own hand had slain his two brothers ; that he thanked God who gave him an opportunity to revenge their deaths even with the certainty of his own." Richard, more touched with the magnanimity of the man than offended at the injury he had received or the boldness of the answer, ordered that his life should be spared. He appointed his brother John to the succession ; and with these acts ended a life and reign distinguished by a great variety of fortunes in different parts of the world, and crowned with great military glory, but without any accession of power to himself, or prosperity to his people, whom he entirely neglected, and reduced, by his imprudence and misfortunes, to no small indigence and distress.

A. D. 1199.

In many respects, a striking parallel presents itself between this ancient King of England and Charles the Twelfth, of Sweden. They were both inordinately desirous of war, and rather generals than kings. Both were rather fond of glory than ambitious of empire. Both of them made and deposed sovereigns. They both carried on their wars at a distance from home. They were both made prisoners by a friend and ally. They were both reduced by an adversary inferior in war, but above them in the arts of rule. After spending their lives in remote adventures, each perished at last near home in enterprises not suited to the splendor of their former exploits. Both died childless. And both, by

the neglect of their affairs and the severity of their
government, gave their subjects provocation and encouragement to revive their freedom. In all these
respects the two characters were alike; but Richard
fell as much short of the Swedish hero in temperance, chastity, and equality of mind as he exceeded
him in wit and eloquence. Some of his sayings are
the most spirited that we find in that time; and some
of his verses remain, which in a barbarous age might
have passed for poetry.

CHAPTER VIII.

REIGN OF JOHN.

WE are now arrived at one of the most
memorable periods in the English story,
whether we consider the astonishing revolutions
which were then wrought, the calamities in which
both the prince and people were involved, or the
happy consequences which, arising from the midst
of those calamities, have constituted the glory and
prosperity of England for so many years. We shall
see a throne founded in arms, and augmented by
the successive policy of five able princes, at once
shaken to its foundations: first made tributary by
the arts of a foreign power; then limited, and almost overturned, by the violence of its subjects.
We shall see a king, to reduce his people to obedience, draw into his territories a tumultuary foreign
army, and destroy his country instead of establishing
his government. We shall behold the people, grown
desperate, call in another foreign army, with a foreign

A. D. 1199.

prince at its head, and throw away that liberty which they had sacrificed everything to preserve. We shall see the arms of this prince successful against an established king in the vigor of his years, ebbing in the full tide of their prosperity, and yielding to an infant: after this, peace and order and liberty restored, the foreign force and foreign title purged off, and all things settled as happily as beyond all hope.

Richard dying without lawful issue, the succession to his dominions again became dubious. They consisted of various territories, governed by various rules of descent, and all of them uncertain. There were two competitors: the first was Prince John, youngest son of Henry the Second; the other was Arthur, son of Constance of Bretagne, by Geoffrey, the third son of that monarch. If the right of consanguinity were only considered, the title of John to the whole succession had been indubitable. If the right of representation had then prevailed, which now universally prevails, Arthur, as standing in the place of his father, Geoffrey, had a solid claim. About Brittany there was no dispute. Anjou, Poitou, Touraine, and Guienne declared in favor of Arthur, on the principle of representation. Normandy was entirely for John. In England the point of law had never been entirely settled, but it seemed rather inclined to the side of con sanguinity. Therefore in England, where this point was dubious at best, the claim of Arthur, an infant and a stranger, had little force against the pretensions of John, declared heir by the will of the late king, supported by his armies, possessed of his treasures, and at the head of a powerful party. He secured in his interests Hubert, Archbishop of Canterbury, and Glanville, the chief justiciary, and by them the body of the ecclesiastics and the law. It is remarkable, also, that he paid court to the cities and boroughs, which is the first instance of that policy : but several of these communities now happily began to emerge from their slavery, and, taking advantage of the necessities and confusion of the late reign, increased in wealth and consequence, and had then first attained a free and regular form of administration. The towns new to power declared heartily in favor of a prince who was willing to allow that their declaration could confer a right. The nobility, who saw themselves beset by the Church, the law, and the burghers, had taken no measures, nor even a resolution, and therefore had nothing left but to concur in acknowledging the title of John, whom they knew and hated. But though they were not able to exclude him from the succession, they had strength enough to oblige him to a solemn promise of restoring those liberties and franchises which they had always claimed without having ever enjoyed or even perfectly understood. The clergy also took advantage of the badness of his title to establish one altogether as ill founded. Hubert, Archbishop of Canterbury, in the speech which he delivered at the king's coronation, publicly affirmed that the crown of England was of right elective. He drew his examples in support of this doctrine, not from the histories of the ancient Saxon kings, although a species of election within a certain family had then frequently prevailed, but from the history of the first kings of the Jews : without doubt in order to revive those pretensions which the clergy first set up in the election of Stephen, and which they had since been obliged to conceal, but had not entirely forgotten.

John accepted a sovereignty weakened in the very act by which he acquired it; but he submitted to the times. He came to the throne at the age of thirty-two. He had entered early into business, and had been often involved in difficult and arduous enterprises, in which he experienced a variety of men and fortunes. His father, whilst he was very young, had sent him into Ireland, which kingdom was destined for his portion, in order to habituate that people to their future sovereign, and to give the young prince an opportunity of conciliating the favor of his new subjects. But he gave on this occasion no good omens of capacity for government. Full of the insolent levity of a young man of high rank without education, and surrounded with others equally unpractised, he insulted the Irish chiefs, and, ridiculing their uncouth garb and manners, he raised such a disaffection to the English government, and so much opposition to it, as all the wisdom of his father's best officers and counsellors was hardly able to overcome. In the decline of his father's life he joined in the rebellion of his brothers, with so much more guilt as with more ingratitude and hypocrisy. During the reign of Richard he was the perpetual author of seditions and tumults ; and yet was pardoned, and even favored by that prince to his death, when he very unaccountably appointed him heir to all his dominions.

It was of the utmost moment to John, who had no solid title, to conciliate the favor of all the world. Yet one of his first steps, whilst his power still remained dubious and unsettled, was, on pretence of consanguinity, to divorce his wife Avisa, with whom he had lived many years, and to marry Isabella of Angoulême, a woman of extraordinary beauty, but

who had been betrothed to Hugh, Count of Marche:
thus disgusting at once the powerful friends of his
divorced wife, and those of the Earl of Marche, whom
he had so sensibly wronged.

The King of France, Philip Augustus, saw with
pleasure these proceedings of John, as he had before
rejoiced at the dispute about the succession. He had
been always employed, and sometimes with success,
to reduce the English power through the reigns of
one very able and one very warlike prince. He had
greater advantages in this conjuncture, and a prince
of quite another character now to contend with. He
was therefore not long without choosing his part;
and whilst he secretly encouraged the Count of
Marche, already stimulated by his private wrongs, he
openly supported the claim of Arthur to the Duchies
of Anjou and Touraine. It was the character of this
prince readily to lay aside and as readily to reassume
his enterprises, as his affairs demanded. He saw
that he had declared himself too rashly, and that he
was in danger of being assaulted upon every side.
He saw it was necessary to break an alliance, which
the nice circumstances and timid character of John
would enable him to do. In fact, John was at this
time united in a close alliance with the Emperor and
the Earl of Flanders; and these princes were engaged in a war with France. He had then a most
favorable opportunity to establish all his claims, and
at the same time to put the King of France out of a
condition to question them ever after. But A.D. 1200.
he suffered himself to be overreached by
the artifices of Philip: he consented to a treaty of
peace, by which he received an empty acknowledgment of his right to the disputed territories, and in

return for which acknowledgment he renounced his alliance with the Emperor. By this act he at once strengthened his enemy, gave up his ally, and lowered his character with his subjects and with all the world.

A. D. 1201. This treaty was hardly signed, when the ill consequences of his conduct became evident. The Earl of Marche and Arthur immediately renewed their claims and hostilities under the protection of the King of France, who made a strong diversion by invading Normandy. At the commencement of these motions, John, by virtue of a prerogative hitherto undisputed, summoned his English barons to attend him into France; but instead of a compliance with his orders, he was surprised with a solemn demand of their ancient liberties. It is astonishing that the barons should at that time have ventured on a resolution of such dangerous importance, as they had provided no sort of means to support them. But the history of those times furnishes many instances of the like want of design in the most momentous affairs, and shows that it is in vain to look for political causes for the actions of men, who were most commonly directed by a brute caprice, and were for the greater part destitute of any fixed principles of obedience or resistance. The king, sensible of the weakness of his barons, fell upon some of their castles with such timely vigor, and treated those whom he had reduced with so much severity, that the rest immediately and abjectly submitted. He levied a severe tax upon their fiefs; and thinking himself more strengthened by this treasure than the forced service of his barons, he excused the personal attendance of most of them, and, passing into Normandy, he raised an army there. He found that his enemies had united their forces, and invested the castle of Mirebeau, a place of impor- tance, in which his mother, from whom he derived his right to Guienne, was besieged. He flew to the relief of this place with the spirit of a greater char- acter, and the success was answerable. The Breton and Poitevin army was defeated, his mother was freed, and the young Duke of Brittany and his sis- ter were made prisoners. The latter he sent into England, to be confined in the castle of Bristol; the former he carried with him to Rouen. The good fortune of John now seemed to be at its highest point; but it was exalted on a precipice; and this great victory proved the occasion of all the evils which afflicted his life.

John was not of a character to resist the tempta- tion of having the life of his rival in his hands. All historians are as fully agreed that he murdered his nephew as they differ in the means by which he accomplished that crime. But the report was soon spread abroad, variously heightened in the circum- stances by the obscurity of the fact, which left all men at liberty to imagine and invent, and excited all those sentiments of pity and indignation which a very young prince of great hopes, cruelly murdered by his uncle, naturally inspire. Philip had never missed an occasion of endeavoring to ruin the King of England: and having now acquired an opportu- nity of accomplishing that by justice which he had in vain sought by ambition, he filled every place with complaints of the cruelty of John, whom, as a vassal to the crown of France, the king accused of the mur- der of another vassal, and summoned him to Paris to

be tried by his peers. It was by no means consistent
either with the dignity or safety of John to appear to
this summons. He had the argument of kings to
justify what he had done. But as in all great crimes
there is something of a latent weakness, and in a vicious caution something material is ever neglected,
John, satisfied with removing his rival, took no
thought about his enemy; but whilst he saw himself sentenced for non-appearance in the
Court of Peers, whilst he saw the King of
France entering Normandy with a vast army in consequence of this sentence, and place after place, castle after castle, falling before him, he passed his time
at Rouen in the profoundest tranquillity, indulging
himself in indolent amusements, and satisfied with
vain threatenings and boasts, which only added
greater shame to his inactivity. The English barons who had attended him in this expedition, disaffected from the beginning, and now wearied with
being so long witnesses to the ignominy of their
sovereign, retired to their own country, and there
spread the report of his unaccountable sloth and
cowardice. John quickly followed them; and returning into his kingdom, polluted with the charge
of so heavy a crime, and disgraced by so many follies, instead of aiming by popular acts to reëstablish
his character, he exacted a seventh of their movables
from the barons, on pretence that they had deserted
his service. He laid the same imposition on the clergy, without giving himself the trouble of seeking for
a pretext. He made no proper use of these great
supplies, but saw the great city of Rouen, always
faithful to its sovereigns, and now exerting the most
strenuous efforts in his favor, obliged at length to

A. D. 1203.

surrender, without the least attempt to relieve it. Thus the whole Duchy of Normandy, originally acquired by the valor of his ancestors, and the source from which the greatness of his family had been derived, after being supported against all shocks for three hundred years, was torn forever from the stock of Rollo, and reunited to the crown of France. Immediately all the rest of the provinces which he held on the continent, except a part of Guienne, despairing of his protection, and abhorring his government, threw themselves into the hands of Philip.

Meanwhile the king by his personal vices completed the odium which he had acquired by the impotent violence of his government. Uxorious and yet dissolute in his manners, he made no scruple frequently to violate the wives and daughters of his nobility, that rock on which tyranny has so often split. Other acts of irregular power, in their greatest excesses, still retain the characters of sovereign authority; but here the vices of the prince intrude into the families of the subject, and, whilst they aggravate the oppression, lower the character of the oppressor.

In the disposition which all these causes had concurred universally to diffuse, the slightest motion in his kingdom threatened the most dangerous consequences. Those things which in quiet times would have only raised a slight controversy, now, when the minds of men were exasperated and inflamed, were capable of affording matter to the greatest revolutions. The affairs of the Church, the winds which mostly governed the fluctuating people, were to be regarded with the utmost attention. Above all, the person who filled the see of Canterbury, which stood on a level with the throne itself, was a matter of the last importance. Just at this critical time died Hubert, archbishop of that see, a man who had a large share in procuring the crown for John, and in weakening its authority by his acts at the ceremony of the coronation, as well as by his subsequent conduct. Immediately on the death of this prelate, a cabal of obscure monks, of the Abbey of St. Augustin, assemble by night, and first binding themselves by a solemn oath not to divulge their proceedings, until they should be confirmed by the Pope, they elect one Reginald, their sub-prior, Archbishop of Canterbury. The person elected immediately crossed the seas; but his vanity soon discovered the secret of his greatness. The king received the news of this transaction with surprise and indignation. Provoked at such a contempt of his authority, he fell severely on the monastery, no less surprised than himself at the clandestine proceeding of some of its members. But the sounder part pacified him in some measure by their submission. They elected a person recommended by the king, and sent fourteen of the most respectable of their body to Rome, to pray that the former proceedings should be annulled, and the later and more regular confirmed. To this matter of contention another was added. A dispute had long subsisted between the suffragan bishops of the province of Canterbury and the monks of the Abbey of St. Austin, each claiming a right to elect the metropolitan. This dispute was now revived, and pursued with much vigor. The pretensions of the three contending parties were laid before the Pope, to whom such disputes were highly pleasing, as he knew that all claimants willingly conspire to flatter and aggrandize that authority from which they expect a confirmation

of their own. The first election he nulled, because
its irregularity was glaring. The right of the bishops was entirely rejected: the Pope looked with an
evil eye upon those whose authority he was every day
usurping. The second election was set aside, as made
at the king's instance: this was enough to make it
very irregular. The canon law had now grown up
to its full strength. The enlargement of the prerogative of the Pope was the great object of this jurisprudence, — a prerogative which, founded on fictitious
monuments, that are forged in an ignorant age, easily admitted by a credulous people, and afterwards
confirmed and enlarged by these admissions, not satisfied with the supremacy, encroached on every minute part of Church government, and had almost
annihilated the episcopal jurisdiction throughout Europe. Some canons had given the metropolitan a
power of nominating a bishop, when the circumstances of the election were palpably irregular; and
as it does not appear that there was any other judge
of the irregularity than the metropolitan himself, the
election below in effect became nugatory. The Pope,
taking the irregularity in this case for granted, in virtue of this canon, and by his plenitude of power, ordered the deputies of Canterbury to proceed to a new
election. At the same time he recommended to their
choice Stephen Langton, their countryman, — a person already distinguished for his learning, of irre-
proachable morals, and free from every canonical impediment. This authoritative request the monks had
not the courage to oppose in the Pope's presence and
in his own city. They murmured, and submitted.

In England this proceeding was not so easily rati-
fied. John drove the monks of Canterbury from

their monastery, and, having seized upon their revenues, threatened the effects of the same indignation against all those who seemed inclined to acquiesce in the proceedings of Rome. But Rome
had not made so bold a step with intention to recede. On the king's positive refusal to admit Langton, and the expulsion of the monks of Canterbury,
England was laid under an interdict. Then
A. D. 1208. divine service at once ceased throughout the
kingdom; the churches were shut; the sacraments
were suspended; the dead were buried without hon
or, in highways and ditches, and the living deprived
of all spiritual comfort. On the other hand, the king
let loose his indignation against the ecclesiastics, —
seizing their goods, throwing many into prison, and
permitting or encouraging all sorts of violence against
them. The kingdom was thrown into the most terrible confusion; whilst the people, uncertain of the
object or measure of their allegiance, and distracted
with opposite principles of duty, saw themselves deprived of their religious rites by the ministers of
religion, and their king, furious with wrongs not
caused by them, falling indiscriminately on the innocent and the guilty: for John, instead of soothing
his people in this their common calamity, sought to
terrify them into obedience. In a progress which he
made into the North, he threw down the inclosures
of his forests, to let loose the wild beasts upon their
lands; and as he saw the Papal proceedings increase
with his opposition, he thought it necessary to strength-
en himself by new devices. He extorted hostages and
a new oath of fidelity from his barons. He raised a
great army, to divert the thoughts of his subjects
from brooding too much on their distracted condi-

tion. This army he transported into Ireland; and as it happened to his father in a similar dispute with the Pope, whilst he was dubious of his hereditary kingdom, he subdued Ireland. At this time he is said to have established the English laws in that kingdom, and to have appointed itinerant justices.

At length the sentence of excommunication was fulminated against the king. In the same year the same sentence was pronounced upon the Emperor Otho; and this daring Pope was not afraid at once to drive to extremities the two greatest princes in Europe. And truly, nothing is more remarkable than the uniform steadiness of the court of Rome in the pursuits of her ambitious projects. For, knowing that pretensions which stand merely in opinion cannot bear to be questioned in any part, though she had hitherto seen the interdict produce but little effect, and perceived that the excommunication itself could draw scarce one poor bigot from the king's service, yet she receded not the least point from the utmost of her demand. She broke off an accommodation just on the point of being concluded, because the king refused to repair the losses which the clergy had suffered, though he agreed to everything else, and even submitted to receive the archbishop, who, being obtruded on him, had in reality been set over him. But the Pope, bold as politic, determined to render him perfectly submissive, and to this purpose brought out the last arms of the ecclesiastic stores, which were reserved for the most extreme occasions. Having first released the English subjects from their oath of allegiance, by an unheard-of presumption, he formally deposed John from his throne and dignity; he invited the King of France to take possession of the forfeited crown ; he called forth all persons from all parts of Europe to assist in this expedition, by the pardons and privileges of those who fought for the Holy Land.

This proceeding did not astonish the world. The King of France, having driven John from all he held on the continent, gladly saw religion itself invite him to further conquests. He summoned all his vassals, under the penalty of felony, and the opprobrious name of *culvertage*,* (a name of all things dreaded by both nations,) to attend in this expedition ; and such force had this threat, and the hope of plunder in England, that a very great army was in a short time assembled. A fleet also rendezvoused in the mouth of the Seine, by the writers of these times said to consist of seventeen hundred sail. On this occasion John roused all his powers. He called upon all his people who by the duty of their tenure or allegiance were obliged to defend their lord and king, and in his writs stimulated them by the same threats of *culvertage* which had been employed against him. They operated powerfully in his favor. His fleet in number exceeded the vast navy of France ; his army was in everything but heartiness to the cause equal, and, extending along the coast of Kent, expected the descent of the French forces.

A. D. 1213.

Whilst these two mighty armies overspread the opposite coasts, and the sea was covered with their fleets, and the decision of so vast an event was hourly expected, various thoughts arose in the minds of those who moved the springs of these affairs. John, at the

---

* A word of uncertain derivation, but which signifies some scandalous species of cowardice.

Lead of one of the finest armies in the world, trembled inwardly, when he reflected how little he possessed or merited their confidence. Wounded by the consciousness of his crimes, excommunicated by the Pope, hated by his subjects, in danger of being at once abandoned by heaven and earth, he was filled with the most fearful anxiety. The legates of the Pope had hitherto seen everything succeed to their wish. But having made use of an instrument too great for them to wield, they apprehended, that, when it had overthrown their adversary, it might recoil upon the court of Rome itself; that to add England to the rest of Philip's great possessions was not the way to make him humble; and that in ruining John to aggrandize that monarch, they should set up a powerful enemy in the place of a submissive vassal.

They had done enough to give them a superiority in any negotiation, and they privately sent an embassy to the King of England. Finding him very tractable, they hasted to complete the treaty. The Pope's legate, Pandulph, was intrusted with this affair. He knew the nature of men to be such that they seldom engage willingly, if the whole of an hardship be shown them at first, but that, having advanced a certain length, their former concessions are an argument with them to advance further, and to give all because they have already given a great deal. Therefore he began with exacting an oath from the king, by which, without showing the extent of his design, he engaged him to everything he could ask. John swore to submit to the legate in all things relating to his excommunication. And first he was obliged to accept Langton as archbishop; then to restore the monks of Canterbury, and other deprived ecclesiastics, and to

make them a full indemnification for all their losses.
And now, by these concessions, all things seemed to
be perfectly settled. The cause of the quarrel was
entirely removed. But when the king expected for
so perfect a submission a full absolution, the legate
began a labored harangue on his rebellion, his tyran
ny, and the innumerable sins he had committed, and
in conclusion declared that there was no way left to
appease God and the Church but to resign his crown
to the Holy See, from whose hands he should receive
it purified from all pollutions, and hold it for the future by homage and an annual tribute.

John was struck motionless at a demand so extravagant and unexpected. He knew not on which side
to turn. If he cast his eyes toward the coast of
France, he there saw his enemy Philip, who considered him as a criminal as well as an enemy, and who
aimed not only at his crown, but his life, at the head
of an innumerable multitude of fierce people, ready
to rush in upon him. If he looked at his own army,
he saw nothing there but coldness, disaffection, uncertainty, distrust, and a strength in which he knew
not whether he ought most to confide or fear. On
the other hand, the Papal thunders, from the wounds
of which he was still sore, were levelled full at his
head. He could not look steadily at these complicated difficulties: and truly it is hard to say what
choice he had, if any choice were left to kings in what
concerns the independence of their crown. Surrounded, therefore, with these difficulties, and that all
his late humiliations might not be rendered as ineffectual as they were ignominious, he took the last
step, and in the presence of a numerous assembly of
his peers and prelates, who turned their eyes from

this mortifying sight, formally resigned his crown to the Pope's legate, to whom at the same time he did homage and paid the first fruits of his tribute. Nothing could be added to the humiliation of the king upon this occasion, but the insolence of the legate, who spurned the treasure with his foot, and let the crown remain a long time on the ground, before he restored it to the degraded owner.

In this proceeding the motives of the king may be easily discovered; but how the barons of the kingdom, who were deeply concerned, suffered without any protestation the independency of the crown to be thus forfeited is mentioned by no historian of that time. In civil tumults it is astonishing how little regard is paid by all parties to the honor or safety of their country. The king's friends were probably induced to acquiesce by the same motives that had influenced the king. His enemies, who were the most numerous, perhaps saw his abasement with pleasure, as they knew this action might be one day employed against him with effect. To the bigots it was enough that it aggrandized the Pope. It is perhaps worthy of observation that the conduct of Pandulph towards King John bore a very great affinity to that of the Roman consuls to the people of Carthage in the last Punic War, — drawing them from concession to concession, and carefully concealing their design, until they made it impossible for the Carthaginians to resist. Such a strong resemblance did the same ambition produce in such distant times; and it is far from the sole instance in which we may trace a similarity between the spirit and conduct of the former and latter Rome in their common design on the liberties of mankind.

The legates, having thus triumphed over the king, passed back into France, but without relaxing the interdict or excommunication, which they still left hanging over him, lest he should be tempted to throw off the chains of his new subjection. Arriving in France, they delivered their orders to Philip with as much haughtiness as they had done to John. They told him that the end of the war was answered in the humiliation of the King of England, who had been rendered a dutiful son of the Church, — and that, if the King of France should, after this notice, proceed to further hostilities, he had to apprehend the same sentence which had humbled his adversary. Philip, who had not raised so great an army with a view of reforming the manners of King John, would have slighted these threats, had he not found that they were seconded by the ill dispositions of a part of his own army. The Earl of Flanders, always disaffected to his cause, was glad of this opportunity to oppose him, and, only following him through fear, withdrew his forces, and now openly opposed him. Philip turned his arms against his revolted vassal. The cause of John was revived by this dissension, and his courage seemed rekindled. Making one effort of a vigorous mind, he brought his fleet to an action with the French navy, which he entirely destroyed on the coast of Flanders, and thus freed himself from the terror of an invasion. But when he intended to embark and improve his success, the barons refused to follow him. They alleged that he was still excommunicated, and that they would not follow a lord under the censures of the Church. This demonstrated to the king the necessity of a speedy absolution ; and he received it this year from the hands of Cardinal Langton.

That archbishop no sooner came into the kingdom than he discovered designs very different from those which the Pope had raised him to promote. He formed schemes of a very deep and extensive nature, and became the first mover in all the affairs which distinguish the remainder of this reign. In the oath which he administered to John on his absolution, he did not confine himself solely to the ecclesiastical grievances, but made him swear to amend his civil government, to raise no tax without the consent of the Great Council, and to punish no man but by the judgment of his court. In these terms we may see the Great Charter traced in miniature. A new scene of contention was opened; new pretensions were started; a new scheme was displayed. One dispute was hardly closed, when he was involved in another; and this unfortunate king soon discovered that to renounce his dignity was not the way to secure his repose. For, being cleared of the excommunication, he resolved to pursue the war in France, in which he was not without a prospect of success; but the barons refused upon new pretences, and not a man would serve. The king, incensed to find himself equally opposed in his lawful and unlawful commands, prepared to avenge himself in his accustomed manner, and to reduce the barons to obedience by carrying war into their estates. But he found by this experiment that his power was at an end. The Archbishop followed him, confronted him with the liberties of his people, reminded him of his late oath, and threatened to excommunicate every person who should obey him in his illegal proceedings. The king, first provoked, afterwards terrified at this resolution, forbore to prosecute the recusants.

The English barons had privileges, which they knew to have been violated ; they had always kept up the memory of the ancient Saxon liberty ; and if they were the conquerors of Britain, they did not think that their own servitude was the just fruit of their victory. They had, however, but an indistinct view of the object at which they aimed; they rather felt their wrongs than understood the cause of them ; and having no head nor council, they were more in a condition of distressing their king and disgracing their country by their disobedience than of applying any effectual remedy to their grievances. Langton saw these dispositions, and these wants. He had conceived a settled plan for reducing the king, and all his actions tended to carry it into execution. This prelate, under pretence of holding an ecclesiastical synod, drew together privately some of the principal barons to the Church of St. Paul in London. There, having expatiated on the miseries which the kingdom suffered, and having explained at the same time the liberties to which it was entitled, he produced the famous charter of Henry the First, long concealed, and of which, with infinite difficulty, he had procured an authentic copy. This he held up to the barons as the standard about which they were to unite. These were the liberties which their ancestors had received by the free concession of a former king, and these the rights which their virtue was to force from the present, if (which God forbid !) they should find it necessary to have recourse to such extremities. The barons, transported to find an authentic instrument to justify their discontent and to explain and sanction their pretensions, covered the Archbishop with praises, readily confeder-

ated to support their demands, and, binding themselves by every obligation of human and religious
faith to vigor, unanimity, and secrecy, they depart to
confederate others in their design.

This plot was in the hands of too many to be perfectly concealed; and John saw, without knowing
how to ward it off, a more dangerous blow levelled
at his authority than any of the former. He had no
resources within his kingdom, where all ranks and
orders were united against him by one common
hatred. Foreign alliance he had none, among temporal powers. He endeavored, therefore, if possible,
to draw some benefit from the misfortune of his new
circumstances: he threw himself upon the protection
of the Papal power, which he had so long and with
such reason opposed. The Pope readily received him
into his protection, but took this occasion to make
him purchase it by another and more formal resignation of his crown. His present necessities and his
habits of humiliation made this second degradation
easy to the king. But Langton, who no longer acted
in subservience to the Pope, from whom he had now
nothing further to expect, and who had put himself
at the head of the patrons of civil liberty, loudly ex-
claimed at this indignity, protested against the resignation, and laid his protestation on the altar.

This was more disagreeable to the barons than the
first resignation, as they were sensible that he now
degraded himself only to humble his subjects. They
were, however, once more patient witnesses to that
ignominious act, — and were so much overawed by
the Pope, or had brought their design to so little
maturity, that the king, in spite of it, still found
means and authority to raise an army, with which he

A. D. 1214. made a final effort to recover some part of his dominions in France. The juncture was altogether favorable to his design. Philip had all his attention abundantly employed in another quarter, against the terrible attacks of the Emperor Otho in a confederacy with the Earl of Flanders. John, strengthened by this diversion, carried on the war in Poitou for some time with good appearances. The Battle of Bouvines, which was fought this year, put an end to all these hopes. In this battle, the Imperial army, consisting of one hundred and fifty thousand men, were defeated by a third of their number of French forces. The Emperor himself, with difficulty escaping from the field, survived but a short time a battle which entirely broke his strength. So signal a success established the grandeur of France upon immovable foundations. Philip rose continually in reputation and power, whilst John continually declined in both; and as the King of France was now ready to employ against him all his forces, so lately victorious, he sued, by the mediation of the Pope's legate, for a truce, which was granted to him for five years. Such truces stood in the place of regular treaties of peace, which were not often made at that time.

The barons of England had made use of the king's absence to bring their confederacy to form; and now, seeing him return with so little credit, his allies discomfited, and no hope of a party among his subjects, they appeared in a body before him at London. All in complete armor, and in the guise of defiance, they presented a petition, very humble in the language, but excessive in the substance, in which they declared their liberties, and prayed that

A. D. 1215.

they might be formally allowed and established by
the royal authority. The king resolved not to submit to their demands ; but being at present in no
condition to resist, he required time to consider of so
important an affair. The time which was granted to
the king to deliberate he employed in finding means
to avoid a compliance. He took the cross, by which
he hoped to render his person sacred ; he obliged the
people to renew their oath of fealty ; and, lastly, he
had recourse to the Pope. Fortified by all the devices which could be used to supply the place of a
real strength, he ventured, when the barons renewed
their demands, to give them a positive refusal ; he
swore by the feet of God (his usual oath) that he
would never grant them such liberties as must make
a slave of himself.

The barons, on this answer, immediately fly to
arms: they rise in every part ; they form an army,
and appoint a leader ; and as they knew that no design can involve all sorts of people or inspire them
with extraordinary resolution, unless it be animated
with religion, they call their leader the Marshal of
the Army of God and Holy Church. The king was
wholly unprovided against so general a defection.
The city of London, the possession of which has
generally proved a decisive advantage in the English civil wars, was betrayed to the barons. He
might rather be said to be imprisoned than defended in the Tower of London, to which close
siege was laid ; whilst the marshal of the barons'
army, exercising the prerogatives of royalty, issued
writs to summon all the lords to join the army of liberty, threatening equally all those who should adhere
to the king and those who betrayed an indifference to

the cause by their neutrality. John, deserted by all, had no resource but in temporizing and submission. Without questioning in any part the terms of a treaty which he intended to observe in none, he agreed to everything the barons thought fit to ask, hoping that the exorbitancy of their demands would justify in the eyes of the world the breach of his promises. The instruments by which the barons secured their liberties were drawn up in form of charters, and in the manner by which grants had been usually made to monasteries, with a preamble signifying that it was done for the benefit of the king's soul and those of his ancestors. For the place of solemnizing this remarkable act they chose a large field, overlooked by Windsor, called Running-mede, which, in our present tongue, signifies the Meadow of Council, — a place long consecrated by public opinion, as that wherein the quarrels and wars which arose in the English nation, when divided into kingdoms or factions, had been terminated from the remotest times. Here it was that King John, on the 15th day of June, in the year of our Lord 1215, signed those two memorable instruments which first disarmed the crown of its unlimited prerogatives, and laid the foundation of English liberty. One was called the Great Charter; the other, the Charter of the Forest. If we look back to the state of the nation at that time, we shall the better comprehend the spirit and necessity of these grants.

Besides the ecclesiastical jurisprudence, at that time, two systems of laws, very different from each other in their object, their reason, and their authority, regulated the interior of the kingdom: the Forest Law, and the Common Law. After the Northern nations had settled here, and in other parts of Europe, hunting, which had formerly been the chief means of their subsistence, still continued their favorite diversion. Great tracts of each country, wasted by the wars in which it was conquered, were set apart for this kind of sport, and guarded in a state of desolation by strict laws and severe penalties. When such waste lands were in the hands of subjects, they were called Chases; when in the power of the sovereign, they were denominated Forests. These forests lay properly within the jurisdiction of no hundred, county, or bishopric; and therefore, being out both of the Common and the Spiritual Law, they were governed by a law of their own, which was such as the king by his private will thought proper to impose. There were reckoned in England no less than sixty-eight royal forests, some of them of vast extent. In these great tracts were many scattered inhabitants; and several persons had property of woodland, and other soil, inclosed within their bounds. Here the king had separate courts and particular justiciaries; a complete jurisprudence, with all its ceremonies and terms of art, was formed; and it appears that these laws were better digested and more carefully enforced than those which belonged to civil government. They had, indeed, all the qualities of the worst of laws. Their professed object was to keep a great part of the nation desolate. They hindered communication and destroyed industry. They had a trivial object, and most severe sanctions; for, as they belonged immediately to the king's personal pleasures, by the lax interpretation of treason in those days, all considerable offences against the Forest Law, such as killing the beasts of game, were considered as high treason, and punished, as high treason then was, by truncation of limbs and loss of eyes and testicles. Hence arose a thousand abuses, vexatious suits, and pretences for imposition upon all those who lived in or near these places. The deer were suffered to run loose upon their lands; and many oppressions were used with relation to the claim of commonage which the people had in most of the forests. The Norman kings were not the first makers of the Forest Law; it subsisted under the Saxon and Danish kings. Canute the Great composed a body of those laws, which still remains. But under the Norman kings they were enforced with greater rigor, as the whole tenor of the Norman government was more rigorous. Besides, new forests were frequently made, by which private property was outraged in a grievous manner. Nothing, perhaps, shows more clearly how little men are able to depart from the common course of affairs than that the Norman kings, princes of great capacity, and extremely desirous of absolute power, did not think of peopling these forests, places under their own uncontrolled dominion, and which might have served as so many garrisons dispersed throughout the country. The Charter of the Forests had for its object the disafforesting several of those tracts, the prevention of future afforestings, the mitigation and ascertainment of the punishments for breaches of the Forest Law.

The Common Law, as it then prevailed in England, was in a great measure composed of some remnants of the old Saxon customs, joined to the feudal institutions brought in at the Norman Conquest. And it is here to be observed, that the constitutions of Magna Charta are by no means a renewal of the Laws of St. Edward,. or the ancient Saxon laws, as our historians and law-writers generally, though very groundlessly, assert. They bear no resemblance in any particular to the Laws of St. Edward, or to any other collection of these ancient institutions. Indeed, how should they? The object of Magna Charta is the correction of the feudal policy, which was first introduced, at least in any regular form, at the Conquest, and did not subsist before it. It may be further observed, that in the preamble to the Great Charter it is stipulated that the barons shall *hold* the liberties there granted *to them and their heirs, from the king and his heirs;* which shows that the doctrine of an·unalienable tenure was always uppermost in their minds. Their idea even of liberty was not (if I may use the expression) perfectly free; and they did not claim to possess their privileges upon any natural principle or independent bottom, but just as they held their lands from the king. This is worthy of observation.

By the Feudal Law, all landed property is, by a feigned conclusion, supposed to be derived, and therefore to be mediately or immediately held, from the crown. If some estates were so derived, others were certainly procured by the same original title of conquest by which the crown itself was acquired, and the derivation from the king could in reason only be considered as a fiction of law. But its consequent rights being once supposed, many real charges and burdens grew from a fiction made only for the preservation of subordination; and in consequence of this, a great power was exercised over the persons and estates of the tenants. The fines on the succession to an estate, called in the feudal language *reliefs*, were not fixed to any certainty, and were therefore frequently made so excessive that they might rather be considered as redemptions or new purchases than acknowledgments of superiority and tenure. With respect to that most important article of marriage, there was, in the very nature of the feudal holding, a great restraint laid upon it. It was of importance to the lord that the person who received the feud should be submissive to him; he had, therefore, a right to interfere in the marriage of the heiress who inherited the feud. This right was carried further than the necessity required: the male heir himself was obliged to marry according to the choice of his lord; and even widows, who had made one sacrifice to the feudal tyranny, were neither suffered to continue in the widowed state nor to choose for themselves the partners of their second bed. In fact, marriage was publicly set up to sale. The ancient records of the Exchequer afford many instances where some women purchased by heavy fines the privilege of a single life, some the free choice of an husband, others the liberty of rejecting some person particularly disagreeable. And what may appear extraordinary, there are not wanting examples where a woman has fined in a considerable sum, that she might not be compelled to marry a certain man; the suitor, on the other hand, has outbid her, and solely by offering more for the marriage than the heiress could to prevent it, he carried his point directly and avowedly against her inclinations. Now, as the king claimed no right over his immediate tenants that they did not exercise in the same or in a more oppressive manner over their vassals, it is hard to conceive a more general and cruel grievance than this shameful market, which so universally outraged the most sacred relations among mankind. But the tyranny over women was not over with the marriage. As the king seized into his hands the estate of every deceased tenant in order to secure his relief, the widow was driven often by an heavy composition to purchase the admission to her dower, into which it should seem she could not enter without the king's consent.

All these were marks of a real and grievous servitude. The Great Charter was made, not to destroy the root, but to cut short the overgrown branches of the feudal service: first, in moderating and in reducing to a certainty the reliefs which the king's tenants paid on succeeding to their estate according to their rank; and, secondly, in taking off some of the burdens which had been laid on marriage, whether compulsory or restrictive, and thereby preventing that shameful market which had been made in the persons of heirs, and the most sacred things amongst mankind.

There were other provisions made in the Great Charter that went deeper than the feudal tenure, and affected the whole body of the civil government. A great part of the king's revenue then consisted in the fines and amercements which were imposed in his courts. A fine was paid there for liberty to commence or to conclude a suit. The punishment of offences by fine was discretionary; and this discretionary power had been very much abused. But by Magna Charta things were so ordered, that a delinquent might be punished, but not ruined, by a fine or amercement; because the degree of his offence, and the rank he held, were to be taken into consideration. His freehold, his merchandise, and

those instruments by which he obtained his livelihood were made sacred from such impositions.

A more grand reform was made with regard to
the administration of justice. The kings in those
days seldom resided long in one place, and their
courts followed their persons. This erratic justice
must have been productive of infinite inconvenience
to the litigants. It was now provided that civil
suits, called *Common Pleas*, should be fixed to some
certain place. Thus one branch of jurisdiction was
separated from the king's court, and detached from
his person. They had not yet come to that maturity of jurisprudence as to think this might be
made to extend to criminal law also, and that the
latter was an object of still greater importance. But
even the former may be considered as a great revolution. A tribunal, a creature of mere law, independent of personal power, was established; and this
separation of a king's authority from his person was
a matter of vast consequence towards introducing
ideas of freedom, and confirming the sacredness and
majesty of laws.

But the grand article, and that which cemented
all the parts of the fabric of liberty, was this, —
that "no freeman shall be taken, or imprisoned, or
disseized, or outlawed, or banished, or in any wise
destroyed, but by judgment of his peers."

There is another article of nearly as much consequence as the former, considering the state of the
nation at that time, by which it is provided that the
barons shall grant to their tenants the same liberties
which they had stipulated for themselves. This prevented the kingdom from degenerating into the worst
imaginable government, a feudal aristocracy. The

English barons were not in the condition of those great princes who had made the French monarchy so low in the preceding century, or like those who reduced the Imperial power to a name. They had been brought to moderate bounds by the policy of the first and second Henrys, and were not in a condition to set up for petty sovereigns by an usurpation equally detrimental to the crown and the people. They were able to act only in confederacy; and this common cause made it necessary to consult the common good, and to study popularity by the equity of their proceedings. This was a very happy circumstance to the growing liberty.

These concessions were so just and reasonable, that, if we except the force, no prince could think himself wronged in making them. But to secure the observance of these articles, regulations were made, which, whilst they were regarded, scarcely left a shadow of regal power. And the barons could think of no measures for securing their freedom, but such as were inconsistent with monarchy. A council of twenty-five barons was to be chosen by their own body, without any concurrence of the king, in order to hear and determine upon all complaints concerning the breach of the charter; and as these charters extended to almost every part of government, a tribunal of his enemies was set up who might pass judgment on all his actions. And that force might not be wanting to execute the judgments of this new tribunal, the king agreed to issue his own writs to all persons, to oblige them to take an oath of obedience to the twenty-five barons, who were empowered to distress him by seizure of his lands and castles, and by every possible method, until the grievance

complained of was redressed according to their pleasure: his own person and his family were alone exempted from violence.

By these last concessions, it must be confessed, he
was effectually dethroned, and with all the circumstances of indignity which could be imagined. He
had refused to govern as a lawful prince, and he
saw himself deprived of even his legal authority.
He became of no sort of consequence in his kingdom; he was held in universal contempt and de-
rision; he fell into a profound melancholy. It was
in vain that he had recourse to the Pope, whose
power he had found sufficient to reduce, but not
to support him. The censures of the Holy See,
which had been fulminated at his desire, were little
regarded by the barons, or even by the clergy, supported in this resistance by the firmness of their
archbishop, who acted with great vigor in the cause
of the barons, and even delivered into their hands
the fortress of Rochester, one of the most important
places in the kingdom. After much meditation the
king at last resolved upon a measure of the most extreme kind, extorted by shame, revenge, and despair,
but, considering the disposition of the time, much
the most effectual that could be chosen. He dispatched emissaries into France, into the Low Countries and Germany, to raise men for his service. He
had recourse to the same measures to bring his kingdom to obedience which his predecessor, William, had
used to conquer it. He promised to the adventurers
in his quarrel the lands of the rebellious barons, and
it is said even empowered his agents to make charters of the estates of several particulars. The ut
most success attended these negotiations in an age

when Europe abounded with a warlike and poor nobility, with younger brothers, for whom there was
no provision in regular armies, who seldom entered
into the Church, and never applied themselves to
commerce, and when every considerable family was
surrounded by an innumerable multitude of retain-
ers and dependants, idle, and greedy of war and pil-
lage. The Crusade had universally diffused a spirit
of adventure; and if any adventure had the Pope's
approbation, it was sure to have a number of followers.

John waited the effect of his measures. He kept
up no longer the solemn mockery of a court, in
which a degraded king must always have been the
lowest object. He retired to the Isle of Wight: his
only companions were sailors and fishermen, among
whom he became extremely popular. Never was he
more to be dreaded than in this sullen retreat, whilst
the barons amused themselves by idle jests and vain
conjectures on his conduct. Such was the strange
want of foresight in that barbarous age, and such
the total neglect of design in their affairs, that the
barons, when they had got the charter, which was
weakened even by the force by which it was obtained
and the great power which it granted, set no watch
upon the king, seemed to have no intelligence of
the great and open machinations which were carrying on against them, and had made no sort of dispositions for their defence. They spent their time
in tournaments and bear-baitings, and other diver-
sions suited to the fierce rusticity of their manners.
At length the storm broke forth, and found them utterly unprovided. The Papal excommunication, the
indignation of their prince, and a vast army of law-

less and bold adventurers were poured down at once upon their heads. Such numbers were engaged in this enterprise that forty thousand are said to have perished at sea. Yet a number still remained sufficient to compose two great armies, one of which, with the enraged king at its head, ravaged without mercy the North of England, whilst the other turned all the West to a like scene of blood and desolation. The memory of Stephen's wars was renewed, with every image of horror, misery, and crime. The barons, dispersed and trembling in their castles, waited who should fall the next victim. They had no army able to keep the field. The Archbishop, on whom they had great reliance, was suspended from his functions. There was no hope even from submission: the king could not fulfil his engagements to his foreign troops at a cheaper rate than the utter ruin of his barons.

In these circumstances of despair they resolved to have recourse to Philip, the ancient enemy of their country. Throwing off all allegiance to John, they agreed to accept Louis, the son of that monarch, as their king. Philip had once more an opportunity of bringing the crown of England into his family, and he readily embraced it. He immediately sent his son into England with seven hundred ships, and slighted the menaces and excommunications of the Pope, to attain the same object for which he had formerly armed to support and execute them. The affairs of the barons assumed quite a new face by this reinforcement, and their rise was as sudden and striking as their fall. The foreign army of King John, without discipline, pay, or order, ruined and wasted in the midst of its successes, was

A. D. 1216.

little able to oppose the natural force of the country, called forth and recruited by so considerable a
succor. Besides, the French troops who served under John, and made a great part of his army, immediately went over to the enemy, unwilling to serve
against their sovereign in a cause which now began
to look desperate. The son of the King of France
was acknowledged in London, and received the homage of all ranks of men. John, thus deserted, had
no other ally than the Pope, who indeed served him
to the utmost of his power, but with arms to which
the circumstances of the time alone can give any
force. He excommunicated Louis and his adherents;
he laid England under an interdict; he threatened
the King of France himself with the same sentence:
but Philip continued firm, and the interdict had little effect in England. Cardinal Langton, by his remarkable address, by his interest in the Sacred College, and his prudent submissions, had been restored
to the exercise of his office; but, steady to the cause
he had first espoused, he made use of the recovery
of his authority to carry on his old designs against
the king and the Pope. He celebrated divine service in spite of the interdict, and by his influence
and example taught others to despise it. The king,
thus deserted, and now only solicitous for his personal safety, rambled, or rather fled, from place to
place, at the head of a small party. He was in great
danger in passing a marsh in Norfolk, in which he
lost the greatest part of his baggage, and his most
valuable effects. With difficulty he escaped to the
monastery of Swineshead, where, violently agitated
by grief and disappointments, his late fatigue and
the use of an improper diet threw him into a fever,

of which he died in a few days at Newark, not without suspicion of poison, after a reign, or rather a
struggle to reign, for eighteen years, the most turbulent and calamitous both to king and people of
any that are recorded in the English history.

It may not be improper to pause here for a few
moments, and to consider a little more minutely the
causes which had produced the grand revolution
in favor of liberty by which this reign was distinguished, and to draw all the circumstances which
led to this remarkable event into a single point of
view. Since the death of Edward the Confessor only
two princes succeeded to the crown upon undisputed titles. William the Conqueror established his by
force of arms. His successors were obliged to court
the people by yielding many of the possessions and
many of the prerogatives of the crown ; but they
supported a dubious title by a vigorous administration, and recovered by their policy, in the course of
their reign, what the necessity of their affairs obliged
them to relinquish for the establishment of their power. Thus was the nation kept continually fluctuating between freedom and servitude. But the principles of freedom were predominant, though the thing
itself was not yet fully formed. The continual struggle of the clergy for the ecclesiastical liberties laid
open at the same time the natural claims of the people ; and the clergy were obliged to show some respect for those claims, in order to add strength to
their own party. The concessions which Henry the
Second made to the ecclesiastics on the death of
Becket, which were afterwards confirmed by Richard
the First, gave a grievous blow to the authority of
the crown ; as thereby an order of so much power

and influence triumphed over it in many essential points. The latter of these princes brought it very low by the whole tenor of his conduct. Always abroad, the royal authority was felt in its full vigor, without being supported by the dignity or softened by the graciousness of the royal presence. Always in war, he considered his dominions only as a resource for his armies. The demesnes of the crown were squandered. Every office in the state was made vile by being sold. Excessive grants, followed by violent and arbitrary resumptions, tore to pieces the whole contexture of the government. The civil tumults which arose in that king's absence showed that the king's lieutenants at least might be disobeyed with impunity. Then came John to the crown. The arbitrary taxes which he imposed very early in his reign, which offended even more by the improper use made of them than their irregularity, irritated the people extremely, and joined with all the preceding causes to make his government contemptible. Henry the Second, during his contests with the Church, had the address to preserve the barons in his interests. Afterwards, when the barons had joined in the rebellion of his children, this wise prince found means to secure the bishops and ecclesiastics. But John drew upon himself at once the hatred of all orders of his subjects. His struggle with the Pope weakened him; his submission to the Pope weakened him yet more. The loss of his foreign territories, besides what he lost along with them in reputation, made him entirely dependent upon England: whereas his predecessors made one part of their territories subservient to the preservation of their authority in another, where it was en-

dangered. Add to all these causes the personal character of the king, in which there was nothing uniform
or sincere, and which introduced the like unsteadi-
ness into all his government. He was indolent, yet
restless, in his disposition; fond of working by violent methods, without any vigor; boastful, but continually betraying his fears; showing on all occasions such a desire of peace as hindered him from
ever enjoying it. Having no spirit of order, he never looked forward, — content by any temporary expedient to extricate himself from a present difficulty.
Rash, arrogant, perfidious, irreligious, unquiet, he
made a tolerable head of a party, but a bad king, and
had talents fit to disturb another's government, not
to support his own.

A most striking contrast presents itself between
the conduct and fortune of John and his adversary
Philip. Philip came to the crown when many of the
provinces of France, by being in the hands of too
powerful vassals, were in a manner dismembered
from the kingdom; the royal authority was very low
in what remained. He reunited to the crown a country as valuable as what belonged to it before; he reduced his subjects of all orders to a stricter obedience than they had given to his predecessors; he
withstood the Papal usurpation, and yet used it as an
instrument in his designs: whilst John, who inherited a great territory and an entire prerogative, by his
vices and weakness gave up his independency to the
Pope, his prerogative to his subjects, and a large part
of his dominions to the King of France.

CHAPTER IX.

FRAGMENT. — AN ESSAY TOWARDS AN HISTORY OF THE LAWS OF ENGLAND.

THERE is scarce any object of curiosity more rational than the origin, the progress, and the various revolutions of human laws. Political and military relations are for the greater part accounts of the ambition and violence of mankind: this is an history of their justice. And surely there cannot be a more pleasing speculation than to trace the advances of men in an attempt to imitate the Supreme Ruler in one of the most glorious of His attributes, and to attend them in the exercise of a prerogative which it is wonderful to find intrusted to the management of so weak a being. In such an inquiry we shall, indeed, frequently see great instances of this frailty; but at the same time we shall behold such noble efforts of wisdom and equity as seem fully to justify the reasonableness of that extraordinary disposition by which men, in one form or other, have been always put under the dominion of creatures like themselves. For what can be more instructive than to search out the first obscure and scanty fountains of that jurisprudence which now waters and enriches whole nations with so abundant and copious a flood, — to observe the first principles of RIGHT springing up, involved in superstition and polluted with violence, until by length of time and favorable circumstances it has worked itself into clearness: the laws sometimes lost and trodden down in the confusion of wars and tumults, and sometimes overruled by the hand of power; then, victorious over tyranny, growing stronger, clearer, and more decisive by the violence they had suffered; enriched even by those foreign conquests which threatened their entire destruction; softened and mellowed by peace and religion; improved and exalted by commerce, by social intercourse, and that great opener of the mind, ingenuous science?

These certainly were great encouragements to the study of historical jurisprudence, particularly of our own. Nor was there a want of materials or help for such an undertaking. Yet we have had few attempts in that province. Lord Chief Justice Hale's History of the Common Law is, I think, the only one, good or bad, which we have. But with all the deference justly due to so great a name, we may venture to assert that this performance, though not without merit, is wholly unworthy of the high reputation of its author. The sources of our English law are not well, nor indeed fairly, laid open; the ancient judicial proceedings are touched in a very slight and transient manner; and the great changes and remarkable revolutions in the law, together with their causes, down to his time, are scarcely mentioned.

Of this defect I think there were two principal causes. The first, a persuasion, hardly to be eradicated from the minds of our lawyers, that the English law has continued very much in the same state from an antiquity to which they will allow hardly any sort of bounds. The second is, that it was formed and grew up among ourselves; that it is in every respect peculiar to this island; and that, if the Roman or any foreign laws attempted to intrude into its composition, it has always had vigor enough to shake them off, and return to the purity of its primitive constitution.

These opinions are flattering to national vanity and
professional narrowness; and though they involved
those that supported them in the most glaring contradictions, and some absurdities even too ridiculous to
mention, we have always been, and in a great measure still are, extremely tenacious of them. If these
principles are admitted, the history of the law must
in a great measure be deemed superfluous. For to
what purpose is a history of a law of which it is
impossible to trace the beginning, and which during
its continuance has admitted no essential changes?
Or why should we search foreign laws or histories for
explanation or ornament of that which is wholly our
own, and by which we are effectually distinguished
from all other countries? Thus the law has been
confined and drawn up into a narrow and inglorious
study, and that which should be the leading science
in every well-ordered commonwealth remained in all
the barbarism of the rudest times, whilst every other
advanced by rapid steps to the highest improvement
both in solidity and elegance; insomuch that the
study of our jurisprudence presented to liberal and
well-educated minds, even in the best authors, hardly
anything but barbarous terms, ill explained, a coarse,
but not a plain expression, an indigested method, and
a species of reasoning the very refuse of the schools,
which deduced the spirit of the law, not from original
justice or legal conformity, but from causes foreign
to it and altogether whimsical. Young men were
sent away with an incurable, and, if we regard the
manner of handling rather than the substance, a very
well-founded disgust. The famous antiquary, Spelman, though no man was better formed for the most
laborious pursuits, in the beginning deserted the study

of the law in despair, though he returned to it again when a more confirmed age and a strong desire of knowledge enabled him to wrestle with every difficulty.

The opinions which have drawn the law into such narrowness, as they are weakly founded, so they are very easily refuted. With regard to that species of eternity which they attribute to the English law, to say nothing of the manifest contradictions in which those involve themselves who praise it for the frequent improvements it has received, and at the same time value it for having remained without any change in all the revolutions of government, it is obvious, on the very first view of the Saxon laws, that we have entirely altered the whole frame of our jurisprudence since the Conquest. Hardly can we find in these old collections a single title which is law at this day; and one may venture to assert, without much hazard, that, if there were at present a nation governed by the Saxon laws, we should find it difficult to point out another so entirely different from everything we now see established in England.

This is a truth which requires less sagacity than candor to discover. The spirit of party, which has misled us in so many other particulars, has tended greatly to perplex us in this matter. For as the advocates for prerogative would, by a very absurd consequence drawn from the Norman Conquest, have made all our national rights and liberties to have arisen from the grants, and therefore to be revocable at the will of the sovereign, so, on the other hand, those who maintained the cause of liberty did not support it upon more solid principles. They would hear of no beginning to any of our privileges,

orders, or laws, and, in order to gain them a reverence, would prove that they were as old as the nation; and to support that opinion, they put to the
torture all the ancient monuments. Others, pushing
things further, have offered a still greater violence to
them. N. Bacon, in order to establish his republican system, has so distorted all the evidence he has
produced, concealed so many things of consequence,
and thrown such false colors upon the whole argument, that I know no book so likely to mislead the
reader in our antiquities, if yet it retains any authority. In reality, that ancient Constitution and those
Saxon laws make little or nothing for any of our
modern parties, and, when fairly laid open, will be
found to compose such a system as none, I believe,
would think it either practicable or desirable to establish. I am sensible that nothing has been a larger
theme of panegyric with all our writers on politics
and history than the Anglo-Saxon government; and
it is impossible not to conceive an high opinion of its
laws, if we rather consider what is said of them than
what they visibly are. These monuments of our pris-
tine rudeness still subsist; and they stand· out of
themselves indisputable evidence to confute the popular declamations of those writers who would persuade us that the crude institutions of an unlettered
people had reached a perfection which the united
efforts of inquiry, experience, learning, and necessity
have not been able to attain in many ages.

But the truth is, the present system of our laws,
like our language and our learning, is a very mixed
and heterogeneous mass: in some respects our own ;
in more borrowed from the policy of foreign nations,
and compounded, altered, and variously modified, ac-

cording to the various necessities which the manners, the religion, and the commerce of the people have at different times imposed. It is our business, in some measure, to follow and point out these changes and improvements : a task we undertake, not from any ability for the greatness of such a work, but purely to give some short and plain account of these matters to the very ignorant.

The Law of the Romans seems utterly to have expired in this island together with their empire, and that, too, before the Saxon establishment. The Anglo-Saxons came into England as conquerors. They brought their own customs with them, and doubtless did not take laws from, but imposed theirs upon, the people they had vanquished. These customs of the conquering nation were without question the same, for the greater part, they had observed before their migration from Germany. The best image we have of them is to be found in Tacitus. But there is reason to believe that some changes were made suitable to the circumstances of their new settlement, and to the change their constitution must have undergone by adopting a kingly government, not indeed with unlimited sway, but certainly with greater powers than their leaders possessed whilst they continued in Germany. However, we know very little of what was done in these respects until their conversion to Christianity, a revolution which made still more essential changes in their manners and government. For immediately after the conversion of Ethelbert, King of Kent, the missionaries, who had introduced the use of letters, and came from Rome full of the ideas of the Roman civil establishment, must have observed the gross defect arising from a want of written and permanent laws. The king,* from their report of the Roman method, and in imitation of it, first digested the most material customs of this kingdom into writing, without having adopted any-thing from the Roman law, and only adding some regulations for the support and encouragement of the new religion. These laws still exist, and strongly mark the extreme simplicity of manners and pover-ty of conception of the legislators. They are writ-ten in the English of that time; and, indeed, all the laws of the Anglo-Saxons continued in that language down to the Norman Conquest. This was different from the method of the other Northern nations, who made use only of the Latin language in all their codes. And I take the difference to have arisen from this. At the time when the Visigoths, the Lom-bards, the Franks, and the other Northern nations on the continent compiled their laws, the provincial Romans were very numerous amongst them, or, in-deed, composed the body of the people. The Latin language was yet far from extinguished; so that, as the greatest part of those who could write were Ro-mans, they found it difficult to adapt their characters to these rough Northern tongues, and therefore chose to write in Latin, which, though not the language of the legislator, could not be very incommodious, as they could never fail of interpreters; and for this reason, not only their laws, but all their ordinary transactions, were written in that language. But in England, the Roman name and language having en-tirely vanished in the seventh century, the mission-ary monks were obliged to contend with the diffi-

* Decreta illi judiciorum juxta exempla Romanorum cum con-silio sapientium constituit. — Beda, Eccl. Hist. Lib. II. c. 5.

culty, and to adapt foreign characters to the English language; else none but a very few could possibly have drawn any advantage from the things they meant to record. And to this it was owing that many, even the ecclesiastical constitutions, and not a few of the ordinary evidences of the land, were written in the language of the country.

This example of written laws being given by Ethelbert, it was followed by his successors, Edric and Lothaire. The next legislator amongst the English was Ina, King of the West Saxons, a prince famous in his time for his wisdom and his piety. His laws, as well as those of the above-mentioned princes, still subsist. But we must always remember that very few of these laws contained any new regulation, but were rather designed to affirm their ancient customs, and to preserve and fix them; and accordingly they are all extremely rude and imperfect. We read of a collection of laws by Offa, King of the Mercians; but they have been long since lost.

The Anglo-Saxon laws, by universal consent of all writers, owe more to the care and sagacity of Alfred than of any of the ancient kings. In the midst of a cruel war, of which he did not see the beginning nor live to see the end, he did more for the establishment of order and justice than any other prince has been known to do in the profoundest peace. Many of the institutions attributed to him undoubtedly were not of his establishment: this shall be shown, when we come to treat more minutely of the institutions. But it is clear that he raised, as it were, from the ashes, and put new life and vigor into the whole body of the law, almost lost and forgotten in the ravages of the Danish war; so that, having revived, and in all likelihood improved, several ancient national regulations, he has passed for their author, with a reputation perhaps more just than if he had invented them. In the prologue which he wrote to his own code, he informs us that he collected there whatever appeared to him most valuable in the laws of Ina and Offa and others of his progenitors, omitting what he thought wrong in itself or not adapted to the time; and he seems to have done this with no small judgment.

The princes who succeeded him, having by his labors enjoyed more repose, turned their minds to the improvement of the law; and there are few of them who have not left us some collection more or less complete.

When the Danes had established their empire, they showed themselves no less solicitous than the English to collect and enforce the laws: seeming desirous to repair all the injuries they had formerly committed against them. The code of Canute the Great is one of the most moderate, equitable, and full, of any of the old collections. There was no material change, if any at all, made in their general system by the Danish conquest. They were of the original country of the Saxons, and could not have differed from them in the groundwork of their policy. It appears by the league between Alfred and Guthrum, that the Danes took their laws from the English, and accepted them as a favor. They were more newly come out of the Northern barbarism, and wanted the regulations necessary to a civil society. But under Canute the English law received considerable improvement. Many of the old English customs, which, as that monarch justly observes, were truly odious,

were abrogated; and, indeed, that code is the last
we have that belongs to the period before the Conquest. That monument called the Laws of Edward
the Confessor is certainly of a much later date; and
what is extraordinary, though the historians after the
Conquest continually speak of the Laws of King Edward, it does not appear that he ever made a collection, or that any such laws existed at that time. It
appears by the preface to the Laws of St. Edward,
that these written constitutions were continually falling into disuse. Although these laws had undoubtedly their authority, it was, notwithstanding, by traditionary customs that the people were for the most
part governed, which, as they varied somewhat in
different provinces, were distinguished accordingly by
the names of the West Saxon, the Mercian, and the
Danish Law; but this produced no very remarkable
inconvenience, as those customs seemed to differ from
each other, and from the written laws, rather in the
quantity and nature of their pecuniary mulcts than
in anything essential.

If we take a review of these ancient constitutions,
we shall observe that their sanctions are mostly confined to the following objects.

1st. The preservation of the peace. This is one
of the largest titles; and it shows the ancient Saxons
to have been a people extremely prone to quarrelling
and violence. In some cases the law ventures only
to put this disposition under regulations: * prescrib-
ing that no man shall fight with another until he has
first called him to justice in a legal way; and then
lays down the terms under which he may proceed to
hostilities. The other less premeditated quarrels, in

* Leg. Ælfred. 38, De Pugna.

meetings for drinking or business, were considered as more or less heinous, according to the rank of the person in whose house the dispute happened, or, to speak the language of that time, whose peace they had violated.

2d. In proportioning the pecuniary mulcts imposed by them for all, even the highest crimes, according to the dignity of the person injured, and to the quantity of the offence. For this purpose they classed the people with great regularity and exactness, both in the ecclesiastic and the secular lines, adjusting with great care the ecclesiastical to the secular dignities; and they not only estimated each man's life according to his quality, but they set a value upon every limb and member, down even to teeth, hair, and nails; and these are the particulars in which their laws are most accurate and best defined.

3d. In settling the rules and ceremonies of their oaths, their purgations, and the whole order and process of their superstitious justice : for by these methods they seem to have decided all controversies.

4th. In regulating the several fraternities of Frankpledges, by which all the people were naturally bound to their good behavior to one another and to their superiors; in all which they were excessively strict, in order to supply by the severity of this police the extreme laxity and imperfection of their laws, and the weak and precarious authority of their kings and magistrates.

These, with some regulations for payment of tithes and Church dues, and for the discovery and pursuit of stealers of cattle, comprise almost all the titles deserving notice in the Saxon laws. In those laws

there are frequently to be observed particular institutions, well and prudently framed ; but there is no
appearance of a regular, consistent, and stable jurisprudence. However, it is pleasing to observe something of equity and distinction gradually insinuating
itself into these unformed materials, and some transient flashes of light striking across the gloom which
prepared for the full day that shone out afterwards.
The clergy, who kept up a constant communication
with Rome, and were in effect the Saxon legislators,
could not avoid gathering some informations from a
law which never was perfectly extinguished in that
part of the world. Accordingly we find one of its
principles had strayed hither so early as the time of
Edric and Lothaire.* There are two maxims † of
civil law in their proper terms in the code of Canute
the Great, who made and authorized that collection
after his pilgrimage to Rome ; and at this time, it is
remarkable, we find the institutions of other nations
imitated. In the same collection there is an express
reference to the laws of the Werini. From hence it
is plain that the resemblance between the polity of
the several Northern nations did not only arise from
their common original, but also from their adopting,
in some cases, the constitutions of those amongst
them who were most remarkable for their wisdom.

In this state the law continued until the Norman
Conquest. But we see that even before that period
the English law began to be improved by taking in
foreign learning; we see the canons of several councils mixed indiscriminately with the civil constitu-

* Justum est ut proles matrem sequatur. — Edric and Lothaire.

† Negatio potior est affirmatione. Possessio proprior est habenti
quam deinceps repetenti. — L. Cnut.

tions; and, indeed, the greatest part of the reasoning and equity to be found in them seems to be
derived from that source.

Hitherto we have observed the progress of the Saxon laws, which, conformably to their manners, were
rude and simple, — agreeably to their confined situation, very narrow, — and though in some degree, yet
not very considerably, improved by foreign communication. However, we can plainly discern its three
capital sources. First, the ancient traditionary customs of the North, which, coming upon this and the
other civilized parts of Europe with the impetuosity
of a conquest, bore down all the ancient establishments, and, by being suited to the genius of the people, formed, as it were, the great body and main
stream of the Saxon laws. The second source was
the canons of the Church. As yet, indeed, they
were not reduced into system and a regular form of
jurisprudence; but they were the law of the clergy,
and consequently influenced considerably a people
over whom that order had an almost unbounded
authority. They corrected, mitigated, and enriched
those rough Northern institutions; and the clergy
having once bent the stubborn necks of that people to
the yoke of religion, they were the more easily susceptible of other changes introduced under the same
sanction. These formed the third source, — namely,
some parts of the Roman civil law, and the customs
of other German nations. But this source appears
to have been much the smallest of the three, and was
yet inconsiderable.

The Norman Conquest is the great era of our laws.
At this time the English jurisprudence, which had
hitherto continued a poor stream, fed from some few,

and those scanty sources, was all at once, as from a
mighty flood, replenished with a vast body of foreign
learning, by which, indeed, it might be said rather to
have been increased than much improved: for this
foreign law, being imposed, not adopted, for a long
time bore strong appearances of that violence by
which it had been first introduced. All our monuments bear a strong evidence to this change. New
courts of justice, new names and powers of officers,
in a word, a new tenure of land as well as new possessors of it, took place. Even the language of public proceedings was in a great measure changed.

END OF VOL. VII.